Consuming the Carib

How are the sensual and aesthetic pleasures of Caribbean tourism linked to the region's violent histories of invasion, slavery and economic exploitation? Is ethical consumption possible in a world of extreme inequalities between rich and poor nations?

In this unique and surprising re-assessment of the making of the modern Atlantic world Mimi Sheller reveals how everyday patterns of consumption have shaped the Caribbean passage from slave societies to service economies.

Tracking the transatlantic circulation of people, commodities, images and ideas, each chapter reveals unexpected links such as those between eighteenth-century botany and modern pharmaceutical giants, between the enslaved workers on sugar plantations and 'postcolonial' sex workers, and between the first boycotts of slave-grown sugar and the contemporary fair trade movement.

Consuming the Caribbean will entice anyone who has dreamed of a tropical beach holiday, swilled a rum punch while listening to reggae music, or wondered where their bananas came from. Discover how consumers in the United States and Europe have participated in the creation of distorted fantasy islands of leisure and holiday romance, while the people of the Caribbean have struggled to produce their own freedom against all the odds.

Mimi Sheller is Lecturer in Sociology at Lancaster University.

International Library of Sociology
Founded by Karl Mannheim
Editor: John Urry
Lancaster University

Consuming the Caribbean

From Arawaks to Zombies

Mimi Sheller

Routledge
Taylor & Francis Group

LONDON AND NEW YORK

First published 2003
by Routledge
2 Park Square, Milton Park, Abingdon, Oxon OX14 4RN

Simultaneously published in the USA and Canada
by Routledge
270 Madison Avenue, New York, NY 10016

Reprinted 2004 (twice)

Routledge is an imprint of the Taylor & Francis Group

Typeset in Baskerville by RefineCatch Limited, Bungay, Suffolk
Printed and bound in Great Britain by MPG Books Ltd, Bodmin

British Library Cataloguing in Publication Data
A catalogue record for this book is available from the British Library

Library of Congress Cataloging in Publication Data
Sheller, Mimi.
   Consuming the Caribbean: from Arawaks to Zombies/Mimi Sheller.
      p. cm. – (International library of sociology)
Includes bibliographical references and index.
   1. Caribbean Area–Commerce–Moral and ethical aspects. 2.
Exports–Caribbean Area. 3. Consumption (Economics)–Moral and ethical
aspects. 4. Exploitation. I. Title. II. Series.

   HF3312 .S54 2003
   339. 4'7'09729–dc21   2002014810

   ISBN 0–415–25759–X (hbk)
   ISBN 0–415–25760–3 (pbk)

Contents

Illustrations

Plates

Map

Acknowledgements

Research for this project has been generously supported by the British Academy, the Arts and Humanities Research Board, and the Faculty of Social Sciences at Lancaster University. Their support enabled me to travel to many archives and conferences, in England, the United States, and the Caribbean, which has made this work possible. For access to their collections and for help from their librarians and staff I would like to thank the Schomburg Center for Research in Black Culture, New York Public Library, and the Library Company of Philadelphia. In England, I am thankful for the use of the British Library, the Bristol Central Library, the Liverpool City Library, the Birmingham Central Library, the Wellcome Library for the History and Understanding of Medicine, and the Britain Yearly Meeting's Library at Friends House in London.

I would first and foremost like to thank my friends and colleagues here at Lancaster who have supported and encouraged this project in so many ways, helping me to refine my arguments and realise new ways of looking at this work. Though I take full responsibility for the outcome, I can say that it would not have been the same without their input. I want to thank most especially Sara Ahmed and Jackie Stacey, whose detailed comments on the full text helped me to create an incredibly fruitful dialogue between their work and my own. And thanks to John Urry not only for supporting this project from its inception, but also for mentoring the extension of my work into new areas. Thanks also to Claudia Castañeda, Ann Cronin, Anne-Marie Fortier, Sarah Franklin, Timothy Hickman, Hilary Hinds, John Law, Maureen McNeil, Paolo Palladino, Jules Pidduck, Steve Pumfrey, Celia Roberts, Andrew Sayer, Andrew Stafford, Lucy Suchman, Shirley Tate, Imogen Tyler, and Michael Winstanley. Many thanks as well to Pennie Drinkall, Claire O'Donnell, Karen Gammon, Catherine Gorton, and Joann Bowker for helping me manage day-to-day teaching and administration while trying to write this book.

I would also like to thank my friends and colleagues in the Society for Caribbean Studies, who have also been very supportive of my work over many years. Thanks especially to Sandra Courtman, Gad Heuman, David Howard, Cecily Jones, David Lambert, Diana Paton, and Mary Turner. Many other colleagues in Britain, the US, and the Caribbean have shared their ideas with me, inspired me, or supported the writing of this book in other ways. I would like to personally thank Janet Abu-Lughod, Charles Arthur, Edward Baugh, Hilary Beckles, Ian Cook, J. Michael Dash, Mustafa Emirbayer, Michel DeGraff, Peter Hulme, Antonio Lauria, Daniel Miller, Shalini Puri, Patricia Saunders, Joel Stillerman, Gina Ulysse, and Kevin Yelvington.

Several academic audiences have given me valuable feedback on this work while it was in progress. Parts of Chapter 1 were presented to the Department of Sociology, Reading University (December 2001), and to the Workshop on Ethnographies of 'The Centre', sponsored by the Centre for Science Studies at Lancaster University (September 2001). Parts of Chapter 2 were presented to the Social and Cultural History Seminar, Lancaster University (November 2001), and to the Society for Caribbean Studies Annual Conference, University of Nottingham (July 2001). An earlier version of Chapter 3 was presented to the Institute for Commonwealth Studies Caribbean Seminar Series, London (May 2001), and to the Institute for Cultural Research Seminar Series, Lancaster University (May 2001). An early version of Chapter 4 was presented to the Caribbean Research Seminar in the North, at our first meeting at Lancaster University (January 2001). And, finally, parts of Chapter 6 were presented to the (Re)thinking Caribbean Culture Conference, University of the West Indies, Cave Hill, Barbados (June 2001). Thanks to everyone at these events who asked questions, contributed comments, or gave support for my work.

For permission to reproduce visual images I would like to thank Bristol Central Library, the British Library, the Library Company of Philadelphia, Liverpool City Library, the Pierpont Morgan Library, the Schomburg Center for Research in Black Culture, and the artist Lucian Freud. And many thanks to Mari Shullaw, James McNally, Nicole Krull and the rest of the production team at Routledge, who have seen through the editing of my manuscript with great efficiency. Special thanks also to Susan Forsyth for her excellent indexing.

In regard to the style of referencing used here, I have found it more convenient for the reader to see all of the historical sources used in each chapter in one place. So I have adopted a hybrid referencing system, using notes with full references for all primary sources, which are separated in the bibliography at the end of the text. Otherwise, all secondary sources cited use the Harvard system of parenthetical references, and these works can be found in the section of secondary sources in the bibliography.

In regard to American and British spellings, I have used British spellings throughout for my own writing, but many of the quotations contain American spellings, which I have retained. However, where I have picked up theoretical terms with a transatlantic provenance, such as 'creolization', 'tropicalization', and 'globalization', I have used the prevailing American spelling. These eccentricities reflect the location of this work as a transatlantic and interdisciplinary project, which must travel between worlds, as well as my own sense of home being spread across these distant places.

Finally, but most importantly, I want to thank my family for supporting me through many years of studying the Caribbean, and for always being enthusiastic about the research I was embarking upon. My father has been an ardent advocate of my work, and an eagle-eyed proofreader, while my mother, as ever, has provided political inspiration. And the greatest thanks especially to Simon who has been by my side and in my thoughts during much of the time I have spent working on this project, and who shared my anticipation of finishing it as we awaited the birth of our baby. I want to dedicate this book to Alexandra Liberty, who shared in its gestation – from the crashing waves at Bathsheba on the Atlantic coast of Barbados, to the green hills of the Northwest of England, and a warm transatlantic welcome into her extended family in Philadelphia.

Lancaster, England
December 2002

Introduction

Although the Caribbean lies at the heart of the western hemisphere and was historically pivotal in the rise of Europe to world predominance, it has nevertheless been spatially and temporally eviscerated from the imaginary geographies of 'Western modernity'. The imagined community of the West has no space for the islands that were its origin, the horizon of its self-perception, the source of its wealth. Unmoved by the warm Caribbean waters that course through its Gulf Stream, the 'North Atlantic' community of nations turns a cold shoulder to its neighbours to the south. As C.L.R. James once put it, the Caribbean is 'in but not of the West' (cited in S. Hall 1996: 246). Displaced from the main narratives of modernity, the shores that Columbus first stumbled upon now appear only in tourist brochures, or in occasional disaster tales involving hurricanes, boat-people, drug barons, dictators, or revolutions. Despite its indisputable narrative position at the origin of the plot of Western modernity, history has been edited and the Caribbean left on the cutting-room floor. Having washed its hands of history, the North can now present itself as the hero in the piece, graciously donating democratic tutelage, economic aid, foreign investment, military advisers, and police support to the Caribbean region.

The exclusion of the Caribbean from the imagined time-space of Western modernity occurs not only within popular culture and the media, but also within academic discourse. How has this physical incorporation but symbolic exclusion of the Caribbean from 'the West' made certain ideas of Western modernity viable? What kinds of global relations have allowed for this hiatus, this forgetting, this break between Western modernity and the Caribbean? Can we re-think the history of modernity in a way that recognises this double gesture of Caribbean colonisation and expulsion, incorporation and erasure? And how can heretofore marginal colonial histories be reintegrated into foundational studies of 'the West', rather than envisioned as perpetually outside its borders?

There has been a serious failing amongst scholars of 'modernity', 'late modernity', and 'postmodernity' to recognise the connections between 'the centre' (whether defined as Europe, the US, the West, the North, the metropolis, etc.) and other parts of the world which have been constructed as 'peripheral' (Miller 1994). Since its origins in the nineteenth century social theory has continually used non-Western places as counterfoils for Western modernity, 'backwards' places against which processes of modern urbanisation, industrialisation, dem-ocratisation, rationalisation, individualisation, and so on could be gauged. Max Weber's comparative sociology, for example, rested on a fundamental contrast between the 'dynamic' rational West and the 'absences' of conditions for modern-isation in the 'stationary' irrational Orient; Marx and Engels's notion of the 'Asiatic mode of production' contrasted 'the socio-economic stagnation of the Orient with the revolutionary character of capitalist society' (Turner 1994: 39–41). As Anne McClintock argues in regard to nineteenth-century colonial tropes, 'In the mapping of progress, images of "archaic" time – that is non-European time – were systematically evoked to identify what was historically new about industrial modernity' (McClintock 1995: 40). Entire continents, like Africa, were envisioned as 'anachronistic space . . . a land perpetually out of time in modernity, marooned and historically abandoned' (ibid.: 41).

Yet even today this style of argument remains ingrained within social theory. Within the discipline of sociology, in particular, accounts of modernity proceed as if the so-called 'developing world' or Third World can simply be bracketed off from the central concerns, models, and theories of the contemporary condition (e.g. Giddens 1990, 1991; Beck 1992; Bauman 2000). While some admit that their work focuses only on the 'North Atlantic rim' (Urry 2000), others incorporate Orientalist imagery of peripheral dwellers and places into contemporary theory in highly problematic ways (e.g. Deleuze and Guattari 1992; cf. Kaplan 1996). Anthony Giddens, for example, states that,

> I use the term 'modernity' in a very general sense, to refer to the institutions and modes of behaviour established first of all in post-Feudal Europe, but which in the twentieth century increasingly have become world-historical in their impact. 'Modernity' can be understood as roughly equivalent to 'the industrial world'.
>
> (Giddens 1991: 14–15)

Thus even a social theorist who claims to be sensitive to time-space geographies turns a claim about historical temporality into a spatial distinction. What is it, then, that separates the 'industrial world' from what he refers to as 'developing societies' and 'people living in more traditional settings, outside the most strongly "developed" portions of the world' (ibid.: 22)? Are these people not also living lives in 'modernity', lives enabled and constrained by the same processes that have made the West 'modern'?

Countering these trends, postcolonial theorists have tried to recast the heroic narrative of Western modernity, including prevalent accounts of the origins of cherished 'modern' values such as freedom, emancipation, and democracy. Draw-ing especially on the work of Frantz Fanon, postcolonial theorists have explored the violent embrace of the coloniser and the colonised. 'The whole point of Fanon's work,' insists Edward Said, 'is to force the European metropolis to think its history *together with* the history of the colonies awakening from the cruel stupor and absurd immobility of imperial dominion' (Said 1989: 223; Schwarz 1996:

13). This has involved a critical re-thinking not only of the narrative plot and temporality of history, but also of the material and conceptual 'border zones' between home and colony, citizen and alien, West and East, First World and Third World. Recent interrogations of colonial and postcolonial processes of historical relation call into question any easy conceptual separation of the metropolitan 'core' and the colonial 'periphery', which have always been deeply 'interpellated' (Bhabha 1994; Gilroy 1993; S. Hall 1996; Lavie and Swedenburg 1996; Mercer 1994). From a Caribbean perspective, a long vein of counter-history has debunked the myth of emancipation as a progressive project that originated in European humanism without reference to the ideologies and political projects of those who were enslaved by European 'democratic' states (James [1938] 1989; Patterson 1991; cf. Sheller 2000). History itself is becoming a hybrid production, in which the supposedly impermeable borders of each national history no longer hold water and colonial histories always seep through, attached to the bodies and commodities that circulate through imperial systems (Burton 1997; McClintock 1995).

The anachronistic spaces and evicted peripheries of contemporary social theory are also apparent in the social imaginary of wider cultural contexts such as the media and popular culture. Most Europeans and North Americans lack an informed context in which to make sense of their connections to the Caribbean, both in the past and today. In England, for example, civic institutions like maritime museums struggle to incorporate the story of the slave trade and colonial slavery into their celebratory displays on maritime trade. Many resort to a spatial quarantine of exhibits on slavery in special galleries apart from the main exhibit (Lancaster) or in the basement (Liverpool), if it is recognised at all (London lacks a museum dedicated to slavery).[1] In the United States dedicated activists have founded a wide range of local sites that commemorate aspects of slavery and emancipation, but remarkably there is as yet no national museum to commemorate slavery or emancipation (Oostindie 2001).[2] The crucial ties of the United States to the transatlantic and Caribbean world are also seldom visible. Given these everyday erasures and amnesia, this 'silencing of the past' (Trouillot 1995) both in academia and in educational institutions such as museums, it comes as no surprise that it remains incomprehensible to most people why Caribbean history might matter to them.[3]

Countering these trends, this book aims to demonstrate how contemporary consumer cultures are directly connected not only to the wealth generated by slavery, but also to the contemporary inequalities between the 'underdeveloped' Caribbean and the 'modern West'. *Consuming the Caribbean* explores the myriad ways in which Western European and North American publics have unceasingly consumed the natural environment, commodities, human bodies, and cultures of the Caribbean over the past five hundred years. The overall aim of this historical sociology of the *longue durée* is to identify persistent continuities – as well as crucial fields of resistance and unintended consequences – in the complex flows of material, cultural, and ethical relations between producer, consumer, and consumed in the transatlantic world. The mobile flows of consumption under investigation here include: edible plants (sugar cane, bananas, tropical fruits); stimulants (coffee, tobacco, rum, cannabis); human bodies (slaves, indentured labourers, contemporary 'service workers'); cultural products (texts, images, music); knowledge collection (studies of botany, ethnology, linguistics); and entire 'natures' and landscapes consumed as tropical paradise. In actually tracing the direct and indirect linkages between people in the 'overdeveloped' world and the 'people without history' (Wolf 1982) in the 'underdeveloped' world, we can begin to see how these linkages are premised on everyday practices of consumption in the consumer societies of the North.

Inasmuch as we are all directly implicated in perpetuating asymmetrical relations with distant others, recognising the continuity in modes of consumption of the Caribbean from the era of slavery until today has important implications for the current global debate over an apology and reparations for slavery. The European nations involved in the slave trade agreed at the United Nations World Conference on Racism, held in Durban, South Africa in September 2001, to make some sort of apology for slavery, but they have avoided the calls for some form of material reparation. The overall thrust of my work is to support the claim for reparations (cf. Higman 1999: 227–37). The nations involved in the slave trade and enslavement of millions of Africans hold not only a moral responsibility for the past benefits they gained from that system, but also an ethical obligation towards those who have suffered from the legacy of the institutionalised inequalities of slave systems. In systematically forgetting slavery and failing to recognise its legacies in our midst, all of us who live in post-slavery societies today are implicated in silencing the past and distorting the present.[4]

Slavery, however, is not only an economic relation; it is also a cultural, symbolic, spiritual, bodily and affective relation, thus its legacies are manifold. Economic reparation in and of itself will not be sufficient redress if we are unable to recognise the ongoing inequality of multifaceted relations of power within the Atlantic world. Another aim of this book, then, is to bring together within one analytic framework an analysis of both economic relations and symbolic relations of consumption, which together constitute transatlantic consumer cultures. By interrogating the 'biographies of products' (Beck 2000: 146) and the 'career[s] of objects' (Lury 1997: 77) – as well as texts and images – that have travelled the Atlantic world, I hope to show how ordinary practices of consumption implicate some (northern) regions of the world in the material impoverishment of (tropical) others, and in forms of symbolic violence and cultural appropriation. My account highlights the histories of 'consumer movements' in the sense of both ethical social movements and the literal mobility of consuming publics.

How do forms of mobility, stabilisation, and consumption combine to locate the Caribbean as a place apart from the West? The ties that bind the Caribbean to other places, I argue, are premised on everyday practices of consumption that occur through economies of movement, touch, and taste in overlapping fields of economic consumption, political consumption, and cultural consumption. In recognising such circuits of consumption it becomes evident how various mobilities are crucial not only to the formation of world systems of trade and production, but also to the constitution of world systems of consumption. In following the tracks of mobility and consumption, however, we must also attend to the things and people that are kept in place in order to enable the mobility of others (Ahmed 2000; Ahmed *et al.* forthcoming; Cresswell 2001). How, for example, did the enslavement of human beings fix them in chains in order that they could be moved, and then hold them in place as coerced labourers even after 'emancipation'? How did European proximity to slaves and consumption of slave produce lead to certain kinds of physical or emotional attachments? In what ways did Europeans *dwell with* slavery? How was Europe transformed by its traffic with the Caribbean?[5]

The movements of objects and people into and out of the Caribbean, and the efforts by travellers and tourists in particular to move through the Caribbean, to 'fix' images of the Caribbean, and to capture or collect objects from the Caribbean will be crucial in the account that follows. In tracing movements of many kinds into and out of the Caribbean this book will contribute to a more complicated history and theory of 'travel', linking together the colonial and the postcolonial, the scientific and the aesthetic, the material and the symbolic. In broadening the concept of travel to include many kinds of mobility, one can begin to draw links between seemingly disparate patterns of colonisation, forced transportation, commodity trade, consumption, migration, tourism, and representation. I am interested, therefore, both in the 'biographies of objects' which track different forms of material mobility, and in the biographies of people who move (or who cannot move), which indicate forms of human and cultural mobility.

First, though, what do I mean by the Caribbean? It is often defined as the island groupings of the Greater Antilles, Lesser Antilles, and the Bahamas, plus certain coastal zones of South and Central America sharing a cultural and historical relation to the island plantation societies (e.g. Suriname, Guyana, Belize) (see Map). Instead of a geographical or cultural-historical definition, however, I want to follow the lead of Sarah Franklin, Celia Lury, and Jackie Stacey in their study of *Global Nature, Global Culture* (2000), and think of the Caribbean as an effect, a fantasy, a set of practices, and a context (theoretical terms which they use to describe 'global nature'). This is not to suggest that the Caribbean is 'illusory, immaterial, or a matter of ideas and imagination alone – far from it' (2000: 5). In so far as the Caribbean is both denaturalised and renaturalised as 'natural paradise', it defies separation into the real versus the imagined; what we think of as material or actual is always already formed by the spectacular and the virtual (ibid.: 224). As Polly Pattullo describes the tourist resort image of the Caribbean,

> It is the fortune, and the misfortune, of the Caribbean to conjure up the idea of 'heaven on earth' or 'a little bit of paradise' in the collective European imagination ... the region, whatever the brutality of its history, kept its reputation as a Garden of Eden before the Fall. The idea of a tropical island was a further seductive image: small, a 'jewel' in a necklace chain, far from

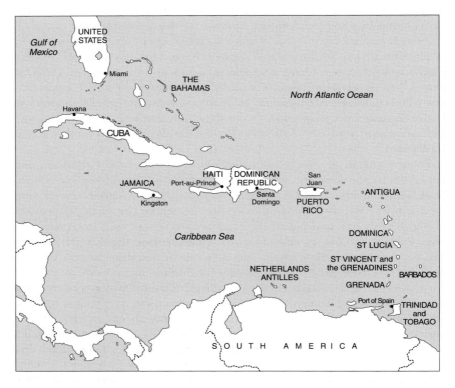

Map 0.1 Map of the Caribbean.

centres of industry and pollution, a simple place, straight out of Robinson Crusoe. Not only the place, but the people too, are required to conform to the stereotype.

(Pattullo 1996: 142)

In its seductive appeal, the Caribbean is both real and imaginary. The imagining of the Caribbean is, as Appadurai puts it, 'an organised field of "social practices", a form of work . . . and a form of negotiation between sites of agency' (Appadurai 1996 cited in Franklin *et al.* 2000: 224). This work of imagination has powerfully shaped transatlantic cultures over the past five hundred years, and has shaped the Caribbean in a high-stakes game of making and remaking of places, cultures, bodies, and natures. The chapters that follow can be understood as dealing with different 'sites of agency' through which multiplex material and symbolic social practices and fantasies of proximity and distance together constitute an organised field whose effect is what we call 'the Caribbean'.

This illusory yet materialised Caribbean exists at the crossroads of multifaceted networks of mobility, formed by the material and symbolic travels of both people and things, and by those people and things which do not move. The very idea of this region as a single place, its naming, and its contemporary material existence are constituted by mobilities of many different kinds: flows of people, commodities, texts, images, capital, and knowledge. In some periods or contexts it has been imagined as a single place, in others it is more commonly divided into various colonial zones or national entities. I will not offer a comparative history of the differences between colonies, nations, or regions within the Caribbean, a complex task which others have undertaken (e.g. Knight 1990; Stinchcombe 1996). Rather, in the chapters that follow I will consider how a general imaginary of the Caribbean totality has been invented and mobilised. To historians I must apologise for sacrificing some of the specificity of time, place, and context; however, the payoff is a wider appreciation of an ongoing process connecting places and cultures across contexts and eras. The linkage of the Caribbean into some kinds of global 'scapes' (Urry 2000; Appadurai 1996) and its crucial de-linkage from others depends, I suggest, on a global economy of mobilisation and immobilisation of commodities, people, and cultures tied together through relations of consumption. I emphasise in each chapter that the linkages, ties, and attachments between different sites of agency are as significant as the mobilities and flows through which the Caribbean is produced.

In considering the sites of agency within the Caribbean, it is crucial to note that recent research and writing on the Caribbean emphasises resistance to colonialism (and more recently neo-imperialism and globalization) and the creative agency of people who are not simply victims of history, but survivors. Recent scholarship has re-shaped understandings of the powerful forces of slave rebellion and resistance (Price 1973; Genovese 1979; Heuman 1986; Fick 1990); women's resistance (Bush 1990; Beckles 1989a, 1999); post-emancipation popular politics (Heuman 1994; Helg 1995; Sheller 2000); and the making of freedom itself (Holt 1992; Cooper *et al.* 2000). Some would even go so far as to say that it is damaging to continue to repeat the story of colonial domination since it was always riddled with weak points, contradictions, and openings for the supposedly colonised and enslaved to seize control. Nevertheless, I still want to insist that the emotive and figurative moorings of the colonial relations that shaped economic, cultural, material, and human exchanges between the North Atlantic region and the Caribbean in previous centuries continue to inform that relation today. Until we have more fully described the parameters of this unequal relationship we will not be in a position to address the contemporary inequalities of power between these world regions and the people who inhabit them. Any effort to embark upon a cultural project of re-imagining the agency of the Caribbean subaltern cannot avoid the weight of mythic accumulation that figures such as the Maroon, the 'slave rebel', or the revolutionary always reiterate (cf. Spivak 1999). In that sense, rather than calling for a heroic Caribbean agent of self-emancipation to appear on the stage of history, I am instead calling upon those living in contemporary post-slavery societies (which I recognise as my own authorial location) to take responsibility for their own practices of consumption.

In linking together the practices of seventeenth-century exploration, eighteenth-century scientific collection, nineteenth-century travel writing, and twentieth-century cultural representation and 'area studies', this book demonstrates how the Caribbean became an object of study produced in Northern academic centres and an object of desire in popular cultures of consumption. Inasmuch as a place called 'the Caribbean' was (and is) a projection of Euro-American fantasies and desires, my direct object of study is not the people and cultures of the region. Each Caribbean society has its own rich history, literature, language, music, art, cuisine, and quite different political and economic situations. Yet they have been collapsed into a single entity, and my concern here is to better understand what something called the Caribbean has come *to mean* and *to do* for people from Western Europe and North America. In sum, this study is best understood as an analysis of the 'invention' of the idea of the Caribbean in Euro-American culture; but it is deeply rooted in an appreciation of the powerful effects of the material relations of consumption which link together places, people, plants, things, capital, texts, and images.

Part I of this book, 'Natural and material mobilities', concentrates on charting the ways in which inanimate objects from the Caribbean were animated within networks of colonial (and postcolonial) power and knowledge. In Chapter 1 a theoretical framework is established for the analysis of mobilities/immobilities and I track some of the exemplary forms of mobility that have shaped the Atlantic world from the seventeenth century until today. In Chapter 2 I focus on the consumption of Caribbean nature and landscapes in three different periods of colonial and postcolonial capitalism, each with distinctive visual regimes and iconic imagery. Then, following a critical review of some of the recent literature on the birth of European consumer cultures, I focus in Chapter 3 on the consumption of edibles, articles of pleasure, and plantation commodities, from the first pineapple to the latest fair trade banana. The emphasis in this first half of the book is on the mobilities and stabilisations of material objects such as plants, natural products, agricultural commodities, written texts, and visual images of landscapes. In tracing these diverse mobilities I begin to develop an approach to an 'ethics of consumption' in which the connections between producer, consumer, and consumed are put into play with and against each other. Although I cannot do full justice to the meaning of 'ethics', I take it to suggest an 'intimate responsibility for the other' (Ahmed 2000: 137). I understand my own work, the work of this book, to be implicated in articulating an ethics of responsibility of Northern consumer societies towards the Caribbean, however problematic such a responsibility remains.[6]

In Part II, 'Bodies and cultural hybridities', I return to the arrival of Columbus in the New World, and use this encounter to launch an exploration of the mobility of bodies, representations of bodies, and the diseases that ravage bodies. Reading travel narratives and tourist literature, while addressing questions of racialisation, hybridisation, and creolization, the emphasis in this half of the book is on the mobilities and stabilisations of peoples, images, discourses, and cultures. The book concludes with a close reading of discourses of creolization within global culture, and a self-reflexive analysis of the production of academic knowledge about the Caribbean from particular locations and within the context of particular theoretical itineraries. The structure of this account, then, is not chronological, but thematic, looking to the past but always pressing towards the present. This requires a method of juxtaposing historical moments, and often making great temporal leaps from one period to another. The logic of these leaps is to disrupt linear narratives of 'progressive' modernisation and to demonstrate persistent and durable inequalities. The reader will also have to bear with being moved backwards and forwards in time as each chapter encapsulates a different version of the same history (see the Appendix for a chronological overview of Caribbean relations with Europe and the United States). Disorienting though this may be, I hope it will be productive of an ethical regrounding for understanding how each of us living in today's post-slavery Atlantic world is implicated in the Caribbean in many different ways, and how the Caribbean is intimately connected not only to all of our pasts, but also to our futures.

Part I

Natural and material mobilities

1 The binding mobilities of consumption

The Caribbean has been repeatedly imagined and narrated as a tropical paradise in which the land, plants, resources, bodies, and cultures of its inhabitants are open to be invaded, occupied, bought, moved, used, viewed, and consumed in various ways. It is represented as a perpetual Garden of Eden in which visitors can indulge all their desires and find a haven for relaxation, rejuvenation, and sensuous abandon. Nevertheless, some of the deepest ethical dilemmas associated with capitalist modernity occurred in relation to the transatlantic commerce in slaves and in products produced by people enslaved in the Caribbean, and these debates involved an anxious introspection about the limits of human desires and pleasures. With the abolitionist boycotts of slave-grown sugar and the emergence of forms of ethical consumption in the eighteenth and nineteenth centuries, movements for consumer responsibility and accountability began to acknowledge the power of consumption to drive the global economy – and to bring misery to people in distant locales. Today the ethics of consumption are again becoming a major issue for social movements and protest groups, who are refocusing attention on the conditions under which consumer goods are being produced in far-away places, including the Caribbean (Enloe 1989; Deere *et al.* 1990; Klein 2000).

This book aims to lever the study of Western consumer culture back onto the tracks of slavery and tropical colonialism that sped it towards modernity, and to show how these relations of consumption continue to inform the inequalities of the Atlantic world today. At what point do transatlantic consuming publics take responsibility for the effects of their consuming practices – including forms of cultural consumption – on distant others? And how exactly have the imaginative and material structures that span the Atlantic–Caribbean world enabled these unequal transformations of one person's sweat and blood into another's sugar, one person's provision ground into another's playground, to continue uninterrupted for five centuries? In order to answer these questions I first want to take seriously the 'investment' of European and North American consumer societies in cultures of slavery, both in financial terms and in more personal embodied relations. Many have said that slavery was a long time ago, dusty history that no longer matters today. In order to understand the deep and ongoing connection between the contemporary Western world and the slave past it is necessary first to recognise the ways in which the circum-Atlantic and Caribbean regions have been linked together both in the past and in the present. Despite the significant shifts in patterns of world trade and regimes of consumption over the past five hundred years of transatlantic history, there are nevertheless significant continuities that remain unexplained, and often ignored.

The relation between Euro-American consumers and the Caribbean did not take place only through importing slave-produced commodities or benefiting from wealth made on the slave plantations. It is not only things or commodities that are consumed, but also entire natures, landscapes, cultures, visual representations, and even human bodies. That is to say, there are crucial forms of consumption 'at a distance' which also must be considered. During the period of colonial expansion there was an intensification of consumption within Europe and North America enabled by the wealth generated by the system of slavery. But there was also an attendant extension and proliferation of forms of consumption as Caribbean landscapes, flora and fauna, bodies and labour, images and cultural objects were all being consumed along with particular goods. It is not only 'goods' which circulated in the transatlantic world economy, but also people, texts, images, desires, and attachments.

To bring into focus the full range of consumption linkages between 'advanced' consumer societies and the post-slavery societies of the Caribbean, it is necessary to foreground the forms of mobility which connect here and there, then and now. The thematic content of this book is balanced between the history of literal practices of consumption and incorporation, and the use of figurative metaphors of cannibalism and zombification as forms of symbolic consumption. Playing on the interlocking meanings of 'Carib' and 'cannibal' ever since Columbus's confused arrival in the New World (see Hulme 1986; Barker *et al.* 1998) a typology of forms of material and symbolic consumption can be proposed. These include ingestion, invasion, incorporation, infection, appropriation, sacrifice, and exhibition, as well as various processes of possessing, destroying, using up, and wasting away. Thus I take consumption in the broadest sense, and use it as a way of understanding a broad set of relations that are at once economic, political, cultural, social, and emotional. By connecting each contemporary mode of consumption of the Caribbean with a long genealogy of progenitors, and by locating the points of friction and resistance in the flows of people, goods, and cultures, this account aims to trouble 'innocent' indulgence in the pleasures of thoughtless consumption.

The key gain from highlighting consuming practices as embodied material relations within mobile contexts is that it enables a position of individual and collective ethical responsibility to be framed as an intervention in the flows of capitalism. Consumers are responsible for a kind of agency, which should not be displaced to the level of the 'world system' as a whole as if individual choices and actions did not matter. To lay the groundwork for this exploration of transatlantic consumer culture, in this chapter I will explore the multiple meanings of consumption in relation to processes and practices of mobility and immobility. I begin with an exemplary case study of the early eighteenth-century scientist Sir Hans Sloane, whose life encapsulates many of the themes of this book. I explore the ways in which Sloane transmuted his ties to Jamaica not only into the making of his personal fortune and reputation as a scientist, but also into a physical collection that became the origin of the British Museum and a key centre of botanical knowledge and medical research. My aim is to show how the movement of objects and capital, bodies and body parts, information and texts, cultures and knowledges jointly operate in one historical instance, and to suggest that this mobilisation of plants, knowledge, and capital from colonial Jamaica continues to have effects in the world today. In the second half of the chapter I will broaden this analysis of what I call 'the binding mobilities of consumption' to encompass the flows of things, people, and culture in and around the contemporary trans-atlantic world, showing how previous patterns of exploitation continue to inform unequal relations of consumption.

Mobile making of Western knowledge centres

If, following Roland Robertson, one agrees that globalization is a cultural process which involves 'the compression of the world and the intensification of con-sciousness of the world as a whole' (Robertson 1992: 4), then the Caribbean played a crucial part in this compression and intensification of global conscious-ness. The discovery of the Caribbean islands and the continental Americas pro-duced the first physical confirmation that the world could be circumnavigated. The rapid incorporation of these 'Cannibal Isles' into an emergent Atlantic-wide, and soon global, system of trade massively expanded Europe's global reach and initiated the processes of 'time-space compression' (Harvey 1989) that still define (post)modernity. The new knowledge 'discovered' in these circumscribed island-worlds contributed to a dawning consciousness of the totality (and fragility) of nature in European science (Grove 1995), evident in the projects to collect, classify, and order everything. Through the prism of the life of one Englishman, Sir Hans Sloane (1660–1752), who was deeply involved in these discoveries, we can begin to trace in miniature some of the contours of the story to be told in this book. It goes well beyond the history of the 'triangular trade' in order to make visible other kinds of transatlantic flows – flows of natural substances, scientific knowledge, bio-power, real estate, and cultural capital – not only in the eighteenth century but having a lasting impact on our contemporary world.

Sloane was one of the foremost scientists and medical doctors of his day. He was doctor to the royal family, benefactor of the Chelsea Physic Garden, and one of the most prolific collectors of books, plants, and material objects of his age. He was elected a fellow of the Royal Society, foreign member of the Royal Academy of Sciences at Paris in 1708, President of the College of Physicians (1719–33), and President of the Royal Society (1727–40). His collections formed the core of a museum collection and library, which on his death became the foundation of the British Museum, at a cost to the public of twenty thousand pounds. His other claim to fame is that he introduced to Britain the first recipe for milk chocolate, which he had observed being used in Jamaica. Yet biographies of Sloane, histories of the Chelsea Physic Garden, and nostalgic reproductions of 'Sir Hans Sloane

Chocolate' sold at the garden today are largely silent on the 'creole' connections linking together the origins of his wealth, the foundation of his scientific reputation, and the material corpus of his collections. Sloane's relevance for this book is the central role played by his connections to Jamaica, and the extent to which the mobilisation of material things, information, and wealth from Jamaica underpinned his life's work. His story is representative of the general silencing of slavery and distanciation of the Caribbean, which are the context for the powerful concentration of knowledge, financial capital, and cultural capital that we know as London.

In 1687, the 27-year-old Sloane became the personal physician to Christopher Monck, the Second Duke of Albemarle, and accompanied him to Jamaica, where he was taking up the post of Governor. Having trained in natural history at some of the foremost botanical gardens and medical schools in Europe, Sloane took the opportunity to begin a comprehensive collection on the natural history of Jamaica. His method was,

> to search the several Places I could think afforded Natural Productions, and immediately described them in a Journal, measuring their several Parts by my Thumb, which, with a little allowance, I reckoned an Inch. . . . After I had gather'd and describ'd the Plants, I dried as fair Samples of them as I could, to bring over with me. When I met with Fruits that could not be dried or kept, I employ'd the Reverend Mr. Moore, one of the best designers I could meet with there, to take the Figures of them, as also of the Fishes, Birds, Insects, etc. in Crayons. . . . When I returned into England, I brought with me about 800 Plants, most whereof were New.[1]

Sloane remained in Jamaica for fifteen months and in 1696 published a systemic index on Jamaican plants, known as the *Catalogus Plantarum*. On his return to England he not only made his collection available for inspection by other learned men, but also had the plants brought to gardens, such as Sir Arthur Rawdon's garden in Moyra, Ireland, to be grown 'to perfection'. As Bruno Latour has argued, 'The history of science is in large part the history of the mobilisation of anything that can be made to move and shipped back home[;] . . . expeditions, collections, probes, observatories and enquiries are only some of the many ways that allow a centre to act at a distance' (Latour 1987: 225, 227).

Building on the impetus of other naturalists/collectors of the seventeenth century, Sloane collected 'Nature' on his travels and brought it back to Britain to be displayed as a curiosity, studied as natural history, and planted for research into its potentially useful medicinal properties. Less often noted are the human body parts, which also found their way into Sloane's collection. As Michael Day notes, 'His propensity for collecting human material began early in his career and he brought back a number of specimens of this kind from his travels in the West Indies'. This included items catalogued as the 'foetus of a negro' and the 'skin of the hand of a black' (Day 1994: 69, 71).[2] The classification of plants has been closely tied to the classification of humans into supposed 'races', and Sloane's work suggests an early interest in this field which would be more fully developed a century later. It is significant, though, that the West Indies offered an early field for collection of both plant and human 'materia' (as I shall discuss in Chapter 5, the Caribbean continues to be used in distinctive ways for medical research, human testing, and pharmaceutical product development).

By his scientific method of careful observation, collection, and exhaustive recording, Sloane furthered the incorporation of the New World into the material networks of European knowledge-production. His mobilisation of nature also involved what Latour refers to as the enhancement of the 'stability' and 'combinability' of the accumulated elements (Latour 1987: 227–8), through the practices of naming, ordering, cataloguing, and publishing. In 1707 he finally published his most famous work, *A Voyage to the Islands of Medera* [sic], *Barbados, Nieves, St. Christophers and Jamaica, with the Natural History of the herbs and trees, four-footed beasts, fishes, birds, insects, reptiles, etc. of the last of those islands.* In addition to a brief history and geography of the island of Jamaica, Volume One of this encyclopaedic work contains 156 drawings, mostly of plants, with some maps and depictions of farming methods; Volume Two, not published until 1725, covers trees, insects, sea creatures, birds, and other animals. His work was said to be 'productive of much benefit to science, by exciting an emulation, both in Britain and on the continent',[3] and many of the plants were propagated at gardens throughout Europe with some coming to be 'used in Medicines every day'.[4] Thus there was a close link between learning about the unknown natural products of Jamaica, collecting '*materia medica*' there, and using these substances in the medical treatment of European bodies, who ingested the substances that were thereby brought to the knowledge of European medicine. In fact in collecting plants, Sloane and other European collectors depended on the local knowledge of both aboriginal peoples and African slaves who passed on information on the specific medical uses of exotic plants unknown to Europeans.

Sloane was not only engaged in 'pure science', however, but was also a pragmatic entrepreneur interested in making new and wondrous substances available to European populations. He first observed a mixture of processed cocoa, milk and sugar being fed to sickly children in Jamaica (Minter 2000: 13), most likely slaves. He saw that this had potential to be marketed in Britain, and he brought back the recipe. He is said to have 'made a considerable amount of money from the promotion of "Sir Hans Milk Chocolate", recommended by eminent physicians as a drink "For its lightness on the Stomach and its Great use in all Consumption Cases"' (MacGregor 1994: 15; Minter 2000: 13). Banking on his reputation as a fashionable society doctor, his milk chocolate was extremely successful and the recipe was eventually purchased by the Cadbury brothers in 1849, to become the chocolate that we all know and love today.[5] Furthermore, 'on returning from Jamaica he is said to have invested "the greatest part of the Fortune he acquired there" in the bark [used in making quinine], so acquiring a valuable stock of medicine which he actively promoted by prescription (for a range of complaints beyond those hitherto treated in this way) and by writing about it in *Philosophical Transactions*'. Quinine is mainly used in the prevention and treatment of malaria, and its preparation and use for this purpose was learned from indigenous civilisations in Peru.[6] Sloane was instrumental in promoting its use in Protestant Northern Europe, where its efficacy had been doubted due to Jesuit control of its distribution. Quinine would go on to be crucial not only for enabling Europeans to survive settlement in the malarial tropics, but also aiding in the huge population movements of indentured labourers around the colonial world in the late nineteenth and early twentieth centuries (Hobhouse 1986).

Beyond Jamaica's use for natural history and medical research, it also provided other resources for the production of Sloane's fame and reputation:

> [In London] on 11 May 1695 he married Elizabeth, daughter and co-heir of John Langley, a London alderman, and widow of Fulk Rose, formerly of Jamaica. The marriage was an advantageous one for Sloane, since his wife inherited not only her father's estate but also one third of the income from her former husband's properties in Jamaica. The newly-married couple set up house in what is now 3 Bloomsbury Place, then at the centre of a fashionable residential area. There Sloane established his immensely successful practice, his patients including many of the most prestigious figures of the day.
> (MacGregor 1994: 13)

Fulk Rose was one of the original British colonists of Jamaica, and owned 3,000 acres there on his death in 1694. Each of Sloane's biographers delicately states that these estates 'yielded' or 'brought an income' of four thousand pounds (MacGregor 1994: 37 fn. 42; Minter 2000: 13). They never mention that this income was directly produced through slave labour producing sugar on huge plantations with all of their attendant coercion, rape, and mortality of slaves. In 1709, Sloane sold his wife's several plantations in Jamaica, which facilitated his purchase in 1712 of the Chelsea manor, which included the freehold of the Chelsea Physic Garden, whose perpetual lease to the Society of Apothecaries he guaranteed.[7]

The Chelsea Physic Garden (founded in 1673), was already one of the best botanical collections in Europe, but Sloane immensely extended it and made arrangements for plant specimens to be delivered annually to the Royal Society for research purposes. It was under Sloane's patronage that the Garden grew to become one of the foremost in Europe. European '*hortus botanicus*' date back to those founded in the city-states of Northern Italy in the mid-sixteenth century (Pisa, 1543; Padua and Florence, 1545), which were derived from Middle Eastern models. They then spread to schools of medicine in Bologna, Leiden, Amsterdam, Montpellier, Oxford and Edinburgh, as well as being developed by the Dutch at Cape Town by the 1670s and the French in Mauritius in the 1760s (Grove 1995). Chelsea established a crucial seed exchange with the Leiden botanic garden as early as 1683, but its networks of exchange and study were extended during the Sloane years. Numerous eighteenth-century botanical illustrators such as Jacobus von Huysum and Elizabeth Blackwell (author of *The Curious Herbal*) based their drawings of tropical plants on the Chelsea Physic collection.

Sloane acquired further material from the tropical world for his collection from William Courten (1642–1702), Leonard Plukenet (1642–1706), James Petiver (*c.*1663–1718), Christopher Merrett (1614–95), and many other plant collectors. James Reed brought plants back from Barbados, and James Harlow contributed further specimens from the West Indies in 1692 (MacGregor 1994: 23–4). Sloane's 'herbarium' was crucial to the work of the great botanist Carolus Linnaeus, who visited the Chelsea Physic Garden in the 1730s and incorporated Sloane's catalogue of Jamaican plants into his work, which remains the basis of botanical classification today. As John Cannon observes,

> It would be difficult to overstate the significance of the Sloane herbarium for the history of plant classification, as it represents by far the largest extant collection of plant specimens from the pre-Linnaean era. It is, indeed, almost certainly, the largest collection that was ever assembled during this early period. . . . Nearly all modern plant nomenclature (some lower plant groups excepted) stems from the publication in 1753 by Linnaeus of *Species Plantarum*. . . . There remain, however, a number of species which were known to him only from descriptions, with or without illustrations, in the published work of other authors: in these circumstances, modern practitioners can only regard the earlier description, accompanied perhaps by an illustration, as the 'type' of the Linnaean species. . . . It is in this context that the importance of the Sloane herbarium for modern systematists actually lies. . . . The Sloane botanical legacy is not merely a musty pile of old dried plants of purely antiquarian interest: it represents one of the ultimate reference sources for the nomenclature of plants, upon which modern electronic data banks for the transmission of information on resources of vital importance to man ultimately depend.
>
> (Cannon 1994: 136)

Sloane's plant collection has thus taken on a kind of virtual existence in these data banks, which preserve the original 'types' on which the future of life itself 'ultimately' depends. It is an early example of what Franklin, Lury and Stacey refer to as the 'cultured up' production of nature (cf. Franklin *et al.* 2000). While not wishing to exaggerate the ongoing significance of Sloane's collection, it is safe to say that it was a major resource for the development of European botany, medicine, and pharmacology, which remains activated to this day in the Chelsea Physic Garden.

Sloane's work fits into an entire web of knowledge that stretched around the world through a mobilisation, stabilisation, and combination of people, animal and plant materials, and information. Knowledge of New World environments was systematised through encyclopaedic scientific texts that named and ordered the flora and fauna, along with botanical collections in which specimens were brought back and cultivated in hothouses in Europe. 'Natural products' of the Caribbean were crucial to the developing fields of natural history, botany, medicine, and horticulture. Sloane's account of the 'natural productions' of Jamaica became a fundamental sourcebook for later medical botanical texts, which were the basis of European medical and apothecary training. In the 1810 and 1822 editions of the most important *Medical Botany* texts, for example, we find the following West Indian plants, some described with specific reference to Sloane's collection: *Guaiacum Officinale* (used in the treatment of syphilis); *Haematoxylon Campechianum* (logwood); *Quassia Simaruba* (bitter damson) and *Quassia Excelsa*; *Canella Alba* (wild cinnamon); *Myrtus Pimenta* (Allspice); *Cissampelus Pareira*; and *Geoffroya Inermis* (bastard cabbage tree).[8] It was at Chelsea that the first heated glasshouses in England were built, and Sloane's protégé Philip Miller (head of Chelsea Physic Garden, 1722–71) contributed to 'the doubling of the number of species in cultivation in Britain between 1731 and 1768' (Minter 2000: 27), including pawpaws, melons, and pineapples.

The Chelsea Physic Garden continued to be used for botanical and medical research into the modern era, and has had world-wide influence according to its recent curator Sue Minter. Some of the achievements associated with work carried out at the Garden include the introduction of the West Indian cotton species (*Gossypium hirsutum*) into Georgia, a colony founded in 1732 with Sloane's 'zealous' promotion (Minter 2000: 37; Chalmers 1816: 68). This improved strain led to a take-off in the American cotton industry in the nineteenth century, which gave slavery a new lease of life in the US South, feeding the booming textile mills of Lancashire and driving the Indian textile industry out of business (Inikori 1992).[9] Other practical developments and great achievements of the Garden include:

- the invention of 'Wardian Cases', small sealed greenhouses, which made possible the introduction of countless tropical plants to European gardens and the commercial transfer of plants from one tropical colony to another (Hobhouse 1986: 21), along with early experimentation in double glazing;
- the transplantation of tea plants from Shanghai to the Indian Himalayas in the late nineteenth century, which became the basis for the British Indian tea industry;
- the transportation of Brazilian rubber via Kew and Ceylon to Malaya, which remains central to the global rubber industry.

These global movements of plants and the development of technologies for their movement, propagation, and cultivation, as the Garden's promotional literature asserts, 'transformed the agricultural pattern of whole countries' (ibid.: 11–12). What effects such transformations had on the labouring populations who were themselves moved around to service these new industries remains invisible. It is the world-wide connections of the Garden to widely distributed locales, and the channelling of materials and knowledge made via its central nodal position, which enabled it to capitalise on the powers of mobilisation to become a 'global' centre of botanical and medical knowledge.

The Garden also claims great contributions to the field of medicine, including 'the identification of the plant which now cures nine out of ten children of their leukaemia' (Minter 2000: xii). Miller identified, cultivated, and distributed the

Madagascar periwinkle, a crucial source for alkaloids used in the treatment of cancer and one of the major species used in biochemical research today. More recently, major medical research bodies such as the Chester Beatty Research Institute and Glaxo Group Research have also used the Garden, according to Minter. Today, Glaxo Research and Development carry out random screening of plants in the Garden to try to identify new pharmacologically active compounds, though this is still complemented by ethnobotanic studies tracing 'the oral traditions of people who have used plants over the centuries'.[10] Such pharmaceutical research (or what some have more challengingly termed 'biopiracy') depends on the movement of investigators, plants, knowledge, information, research technologies, and capital investments, yet becomes operational (patented and marketed) only once it has been tested on far less mobile human populations. Large-scale research populations have tended to be found amongst the immobile labour pool of Third World countries, whose bodies-fixed-in-place enable the benefits of medicine to be mobilised for the wealthy and mobile population of the North (see Chapter 5 below on medical research carried out in Haiti).

The outcome of these many mobilities and immobilities are etched onto the map of London. Sloane's property holdings in the Knightsbridge area, bequeathed via his daughter Elizabeth to her male heirs, leave their trace in his and his son-in-law's family names on the modern map of London. Sloane Square, Sloane Street, Hans Street, Hans Place, Hans Road, Hans Crescent (the home of Harrod's), and Cadogan Square, Cadogan Street, Cadogan Gardens – all the places frequented by today's 'Sloane Rangers'. When we unravel this map of a small corner of London its dense knot of financial, cultural, and symbolic capital unfolds into a series of larger maps tracing various journeys. Far away are the slaves who were involuntarily transported from Africa to Jamaica to grow the sugar and coffee that enriched Fulk Rose. Then the voyage of a Governor of Jamaica, accompanied by Sloane, and the shipment back to England of the boxes filled with the plants, animals, and body parts collected in Jamaica. Just as crucial are the trip of Rose's widow Elizabeth back to England where she considerably enlarged her husband's estate (perhaps she was accompanied by one of her domestic slaves from Jamaica?). Then came the visits of innumerable European men of letters to see the collection at Chelsea; and the dispersal of the Garden's seeds and plants to sites around the world. While the early Caribbean collections play much less of a role in the Garden today, Sloane's original herbarium sheets remain housed in the Natural History Museum in Knightsbridge.

The story of Sloane and the Chelsea Physic Garden is indicative of the extended circuits of human, floral, faunal, capital, visual, and informational movements that constituted (and constitute) the transatlantic world. His legacy is not simply about the forgotten historical origins of transatlantic cultures of consumption, but is also about wider aspects of the present world. From the sweet taste of milk chocolate to contemporary systems of plant classification, medical botany, and life-saving pharmaceutical research, Sloane's achievements can all be traced back to Jamaican origins, though this is seldom acknowledged. Part of my argument in this book is that the accumulation of contemporary 'Western' scientific knowledge, cultural innovation, and capital continues to be made viable by far-reaching global circuits of knowledge-production premised on the consumption of the landscapes, plants, foods, bodies, and cultures of the Caribbean and other 'non-Western' places. As each of the following chapters will illustrate, these modes of consumption encompass not only flows of material things and human bodies, but also of symbolic representations, knowledge, and images. In the remainder of this chapter I will first briefly introduce some of the key relations of consumption that continue to construct the Caribbean as an 'outside' which perpetually serves as one of the constitutive grounds for Western modernity. I then conclude with a consideration of some of the ways in which mobility and immobility are co-constitutive, as certain kinds of mobility require binding others in place. Indeed the very claim to the high-velocity mobility of global modernity is only enabled by the lack of mobility on the not-quite-modern 'margins' of the West.

Binding mobilities of consumption

Western (or Northern) consumption of the Caribbean began with European 'discovery' of the New World, which was predicated on the search for a route to the spice trade of the Far East. Christopher Columbus, who will figure again in subsequent chapters, and other explorers came to the Caribbean prepared to take whatever they could: food, timber, slaves, gold, information, and 'virgin' land for new plantations. They also unleashed deadly new pathogens and feral animals, which together decimated the native populations. From this initial set of moves the history of the Atlantic world unfolds as a series of comings and goings constituted by a set of mobilities of people, objects, capital, and information. Since then, the interplay of changing possibilities for consumption and social struggles over mobility and immobility have shaped Northern Atlantic relations with (and re-inventions of) the Caribbean over roughly four phases:

1   Sixteenth to seventeenth centuries: period of 'discovery', piracy, and 'bachelor' plantation, in which European migrants took land, collected plants, and depicted a 'New World' of fruitful plenty, while Native inhabitants were dispossessed, enslaved, infected, and killed. Associated with 'mercantilism' as a specific early form of capitalism.
2   Eighteenth to mid-nineteenth centuries: exponential growth of the system of slavery in which Europeans consumed enslaved human bodies in the coerced production of both plantation commodities (for overseas consumption) and domestic and sexual services (for local consumption), while fighting wars of occupation. Associated with 'colonialism', as a specific form of capitalist articulation with the periphery.
3   Mid-nineteenth to mid-twentieth centuries: colonial/industrial system of 'free labour' and capitalist plantation commodity consumption in which workers began to migrate in search of wages and metropolitan dwellers began to travel in search of exotic pleasures, while the United States exer-

cised increasing military occupation in the region. Usually associated with the period of 'empire' and 'imperialism'.

4   Late twentieth century to today: 'postindustrial' and 'postcolonial' service consumption in which fragments of industrial processes ('off-shore' export zones) occur in the Caribbean alongside new forms of service work (including high-tech and financial services as well as tourism). Cultural commodification is linked to the explosion of tourism in the region, growth in the 'world music' industry, and new forms of informational capitalism. Period of 'post-fordism' within capitalism.

Rather than giving a chronological account of these different phases, however, the chapters of this book are organised thematically in order to show some of the continuities in the formation of consuming publics and modes of consumption right across all of these periods. As in the story of Sloane's life and achievements, we can follow the footprints of history from a sixteenth-century propagandist promoting the delights of the New World to a twentieth-century travel writer describing the delights of the latest tourist resort. From reading seventeenth-century descriptions of the first glorious taste of a pineapple, we can slide effortlessly up to contemporary debates about fair trade in tropical produce. And from the diseased and dying bodies of indigenous people and slaves we can follow a clear path to the impoverished bodies of workers in the new global economy. Before taking these journeys, I want to give an overview of some of the multiple and intersecting modes of consumption that will be the concern of this account.

The well-known outlines of the 'triangular trade', which linked Europe, Africa, the West Indies, and North America in overlapping circuits of import and export, suggest the most obvious meaning of 'consumption' in its economic sense. The flows traversing this world system of trade are sometimes reduced to simple lists of commodities: manufactured goods from Europe (glass beads, metal wares, guns and gunpowder, textiles, hats, shoes, etc.); slaves from Africa (as if people could be simply reduced to 'goods'); plantation produce and natural products from the West Indies (sugar, coffee, cocoa, ginger, indigo, tropical hardwoods, etc.) and North America (cotton, tobacco, salted cod fish, timber, hides, fur, etc.). As Barbara Solow describes this system of trade,

> What moved in the Atlantic in these centuries [sixteenth to nineteenth] was predominantly slaves, the output of slaves, the input to slave societies, and the goods and services purchased with the earnings on slave products . . . [Slavery] affected not only the countries of the slaves' origins and destinations, but, equally, those countries that invested in, supplied, or consumed the products of the slave economies. . . . In a reciprocal relationship, European demand for colonial goods, matched by a supply of slave labor to produce those goods, encouraged European development in the colonial period.
>
> (Solow 1991: 1–2)

The making of the modern world by this circuit of movement of people, goods, ships, and information is indisputable, and I shall discuss some of its direct impacts in Part I. But in what sense should this past set of relationships continue to be relevant today?

As much as the abolition of slavery was an important moment of transformation of these world-making relations between mobile colonists, enslaved people, and commodity trade, it did not end the continuing importance of economic relations that fixed Caribbean societies in a subordinate position to the European market. Even in a world without slavery the mobile capital of 'free trade' helped to hold in place and constrain the lives of 'freed labourers' long after their emancipation from slavery. The costly indemnification imposed on the revolutionary state of Haiti in 1825 for having had the nerve to appropriate the human 'property' of French slave owners allowed the great powers of the time to isolate the indebted 'black republic' and to blithely continue profiting from slavery (Sheller 1999, 2000). The twenty-million-pound compensation paid to British slave owners in 1838 legally preserved their property rights in people and dismissed any claims that the emancipated may have had for their own compensation for years of toil and suffering. And the failure of the United States to pay any compensation to slaves after the civil war in 1865 (the fabled forty acres and a mule that many felt was their due) continues to fuel debates over reparative justice today.

So material relations of consumption continue to be shaped by these contours of inequality. Yet it was not only the commerce in slaves and material goods produced by slaves that moved through this system. However much we understand the facts and figures of the triangular trade, they fail to convey fully the depth and quality of the relation between the North Atlantic world and the Caribbean. Commodities are the most obvious things circulating in any system of global trade, but I will also be considering other kinds of mobile objects ranging from ships and books to plants, drugs, and pictures. The key commodities whose circulation I will consider include not only the main Caribbean agricultural products (especially sugar, coffee, and tropical fruits), but also plant products such as wood and pharmaceuticals, medical products such as blood plasma and research populations, and cultural products such as music, literature, and theory. The mobilities of consumption are not only material, but also cultural and discursive.

As the story of Sloane suggests, informational mobility is a key form of consumption. Throughout this book I shall be reading 'texts' and 'images' which were reproduced by hand, mechanically, or later electronically, and thereby entered into circuits of exchange, display, and collection. An important early element in the emergence of consumer societies was the circulation of printed visual images. As Chandra Mukerji argues regarding the expanding market for pictorial prints in sixteenth-century Europe,

> Prints helped in the geographic spread of consumerism by carrying designs for artifacts over broad areas, shaping international patterns of taste. Of course, trade was the underlying cause of this internationalism; it permitted the movements of artisans, artifacts, patrons, and raw materials that inte-

grated consumers from different regions into a pan-European culture. But prints had a special role in this cultural integration, in part because they were easy to transport and in part because they had become easy to read.

(Mukerji 1983: 66)

Illustrated books about the Caribbean joined this flow of prints around the elite consumer markets of Europe, which would later become the basis for a more popular print culture. Indeed, the representation of the wonders of the 'New World' was probably a major impetus to the expansion of the print trade.

The printing of geographical information such as maps was also tightly linked to the expansion of the Atlantic world system in the sixteenth century. It was only as Portugal and Spain lost their monopoly on transatlantic trade that geographical information began to be printed in larger quantities, *circa* 1550 according to Mukerji (1983: 85). It was this informational flow and the new material culture it supported, she argues, that in part facilitated the shift to a new world-economy centred on North Atlantic trade with the Caribbean. Indeed some of the most important geographical books to be published in this period were Peter Martyr's 1505 *Libretto* which described Columbus's voyages to the West Indies, and Vespucci's *Mundus Novus* from around the same time (ibid.: 101). If the West Indies first entered European elite cultural circles through maps and voyagers' accounts, it was soon thereafter incorporated into a material flow of natural substances and printed visual images, which I explore further in Chapter 2. By the seventeenth century printed representations of 'the text of nature' (such as Sloane's publications) tied together the scientific networks of Europe; printed texts presented 'a reality grounded in the material world and cultural materialism of the period, in the increased production of many artifacts, including books' (ibid.: 164). These enculturations of the new 'facts' of the fascinating islands of the Caribbean required a kind of re-scaling of the world, as European intellectuals sought to digest novel, curious, and disturbing information about the New World. In recontextualising that which was strange and unbelievable they were also performing and enabling new material relations between distant places and people. They were bringing the New World into being rather than simply 'discovering' it.

Such projects of representation extended in different ways from the discovery of the New World (Greenblatt 1991), through the height of British imperialism (Richards 1993), and into the US imperial projects of the late nineteenth and early twentieth centuries (Salvatore 1996, 1998). Building on Stephen Greenblatt's notion of colonialism and empire-building as a 'representational machine', Ricardo Salvatore argues that

the construction of 'South America' [and, we can add, the Caribbean] as a territory for the projection of US capital, expertise, dreams, and power required the channelling of massive energies into the production of images and texts. . . . [Following Greenblatt] a representational machine is a set of mechanisms, processes, and apparatuses that produce and circulate representations constitutive of cultural difference. . . . The region became visible and apprehensible to North America only through concrete representational practices and devices (e.g. travel narratives, geographic handbooks, photograph albums, and ethnographic exhibits). These representational practices constituted the stuff of empire as much as the activities of North Americans in the economic, military, or diplomatic fields.

(Salvatore 1998: 71–3)

This culturally rich understanding of imperial encounters informs the approach taken in this book, wherein I will also focus on the production and circulation of textual and visual representations of the Caribbean as crucial parts of the colonising project. Although these representational practices and technologies have changed over time (see for example my discussion of changing visions of Caribbean nature in Chapter 2), they nevertheless remain subtly embedded in contemporary images and understandings of the Caribbean. As Salvatore suggests, empire is constituted 'as a chain of nodes or points of textual/image production . . . as an extended flow of information, visual images, arguments, and meanings going from South to North; as a process of accumulation of symbolic capital through multiple technologies of seeing, narrating, and displaying' (ibid.: 74). This flow and accumulation of symbolic capital continues to delimit the cultural production of 'The Caribbean' in the nodal points of metropolitan power today.

The literature of travel and exploration became a major segment in the circulation of information on and representations of the Caribbean. Thus, the archive of travel writing is a crucial source for this study. From the emergence of a modern reading public that consumed fictional tales and factual 'knowledge' about the Caribbean, there began a demand for 'true' accounts. This intersected with the production of 'expert' knowledge in the policy debates surrounding the abolition of slavery in the late eighteenth to early nineteenth century. The creation of transatlantic academic consuming publics vastly expanded in the discourse of the world anti-slavery movement in the nineteenth century, in which the Caribbean became an object of learned study, and an 'area' produced in the process of knowledge proliferation. The anti-slavery movement's keen interest in 'authentic' accounts of slavery by former slaves resulted in a plethora of published slave narratives as well as actual lecture tours and self-displays by freed slaves, both male and female (Midgley 1992; Fisch 2000). These performances of authenticity bolstered a system of knowledge-production, which has been rediscovered as an object of academic study and theorisation, for example in Caribbean literary studies and the associated interest in slave narratives (Davis and Gates 1985; Gates 1987).

Thus it is crucial to attend to the ways in which Caribbean cultural forms travel and the ways in which academic 'knowledge' of the Caribbean is produced and circulates. From the early days of collecting plants, to the first-hand accounts from travellers, to more recent area studies, 'experts' have attempted to collect, classify, and explain 'the Caribbean'. Insofar as Caribbean writers, artists, and intellectuals have fought to define their own societies and cultures, they have had to struggle against this tide of textual precedents. These are themes I return to in Chapter 6, where I consider the consumption of Caribbean literature and theory in metropolitan academia, as well as the positioning of this book itself in the skeins of power-knowledge that enwrap the Caribbean. In the remainder of this chapter, however, I want to turn to the ways in which bodies move in and out of these material and cultural circuits of things in motion. How are some bodies immobilised by the very processes that produce the mobility of other bodies, commodities, and knowledges?

Bodily (im)mobilities

Greater attention to bodies and their (im)mobilities can help to show the inter-twining of circuits of production and consumption with processes of gendering, racialisation, and domination. I will be especially concerned with the movement and stabilisation of bodies and the mobilisation of visual representations of bodies in the second part of this book. Entire global systems are configured by relations of risk and desire that depend on the proximate and distant relation between bodies in movement through both domesticated and exoticised regions. In travelling to the Caribbean with a pre-formed imaginative attachment to 'natural paradise', for example, Northern consumers are able to experience their proximity to Caribbean people as pleasurable even when it manifestly involves relations of subordination, degradation, or violation. And conversely, when Caribbean commodities are consumed in the North they are experienced as 'getting closer to' or 'touching' the essence of the Caribbean (hooks 1992; Cook and Crang 1996), even when they manifestly involve limitations on the mobility of the very people who have produced those commodities. Bodily (im)mobilities, therefore, are a crucial nexus of the systems of transatlantic exchange that depend on embodied relations of distance, proximity, and co-presence at different moments in the processes of production and consumption.

Modes of consumption can shift on three important dimensions in which embodied relations play a central part. First, the degree of commodification of the body itself (legality of slavery, indenture, prostitution and sex work, and var-ieties of personal service) determines who can and cannot move, or in what ways their movements may be controlled. Second, the means of global circulation of commodities, people, information, and images (technologies of transportation, information access, and time-space distanciation) impacts on the reach and inten-sity of certain kinds of access. And, finally, the proximity or 'co-presence' of consuming and consumed bodies at the site of consumption (depending on the triple circulation of producers, consumers, and commodities themselves) shapes the kinds of relations that may occur at different sites of agency. Some of the human mobilities that have shaped the Caribbean over the past five centuries include:

- migrations of various indigenous peoples (Arawak/Taino and Carib) into the Caribbean and their displacement by European warfare and disease;

- journeys of European explorers, planters, colonial settlers, governors, missionaries and travellers into and around the region;
- expulsion of Jews from Spain and Portugal in 1493, which brought some of them to the Caribbean in the earliest wave of European migrants;
- enslavement and forced transportation of people from many regions of Africa, with up to ten million captives making the Atlantic crossing in slave ships;
- migration of indentured contract labourers from India, China, and other imperial outposts to the Caribbean;
- movement of workers within and beyond the Caribbean in search of employment, and associated journeys of family reunification or return;
- trade diasporas of Levantine (especially Lebanese) and Chinese origin;
- incursions by North American travellers, tourists, soldiers, sailors, 'advisors' and expatriates, who often occupy, requisition, or purchase entire islands;
- flights of refugees, asylum applicants and so-called 'boat-people' seeking an escape from political terror, poverty, and the effects of underdevelopment.

From this list we can note first that human migrations are often defined as either 'voluntary' or coerced, though the actual choices of individuals may be far less clear-cut. The most extreme example of coerced mobility is the capture of humans, the process of enslavement, and the shipment of a 'human cargo' from one part of the world to another. The outcome of such enslavement generally rests on a denial of mobility at the site of slavery. Voluntary mobility, in contrast, is the choice of mobility available to the planter, the colonist, the missionary or the tourist. Yet we can also envision forms of semi-coerced or semi-voluntary mobility in relation to wives and children obligated to move with male household heads, as well as indentured labourers, refugees, asylum-seekers, exiles, and those caught up in some forms of international prostitution. The binding and transportation of people in chains as slaves, the limitations on mobility imposed by contracts of indenture, the locking up of 'runaways' and 'vagabonds', the requirements of permits and licences to engage in market trading, or the requirement of passports and visas in order to cross borders, are all different forms in which freedom of movement is blocked or limited. As I shall discuss in subsequent chapters, in each case it is the circumstance of the possibilities of travel (for some) which itself necessarily produces the techniques of limiting mobility (for others).

Second, human mobility can be understood as either permanent or temporary. The slave's passage (from Africa to the Americas in this case) was usually (though not always) permanent, while the planter's sojourn was often temporary, unless by choice the planter becomes a settler. The exile's migration to a new country is often permanent, while the tourist's visit is temporary. In between the permanent and the fleeting we might find temporary refugees, contracted agricultural workers, missionaries, asylum seekers, and those 'transnationals' who move back and forth between a 'home' country and a 'diaspora' community. Focusing on these diverse human mobilities can help to highlight the linkages between different parts of the world. Increasingly there are forms of 'transmigration' which blur the boundary between point of origin and point of departure, such as the Haitian notion of the diaspora as the 'Tenth Department' of the country. Through the migration of Haitian, Jamaican, Cuban, Dominican, Puerto Rican, and other Caribbean people into 'global cities' like New York and London, or not-so-global cities like Miami and Toronto, many parts of the metropolitan North are now said to be not only multicultural, but 'Caribbeanized'. Caribbean migration processes have to some extent offered the paradigmatic case of transnationalism (Sutton and Chaney 1987; Basch *et al.* 1994), as I shall discuss in Chapter 5. Thus the Caribbean has been used to demonstrate the solubility of national boundaries in the era of 'globalization'.[11]

While the movements of information, people, and material things are all crucial to this account, this is neither a history of ideas, nor a history of migration, nor a history of world trade *per se*. Rather, my key concern is with how flows of people, substances, and information are linked together in relations of coupling and decoupling, stickiness and fluidity, by which attachments and proximities are formed, and distancing or differentiation achieved. Although there has recently been an upsurge of interest in theories of mobility and 'nomadism', there has also been a more measured concern with the relations between mobility and dwelling, travel and attachment, fluidity and fixity.[12] As Kaplan (1996) argues, many theorists of mobility fail to distinguish between forms of elite and subaltern mobility, for example by appropriating the imagery of 'nomadism' to describe a universal postmodern subjectivity. In contrast, I insist that how and why different agents move (and how they then become located in a world system) is crucial. As Tim Cresswell puts it, 'The question of how mobilities get produced – both materially and in terms of "ideas" of mobility – means asking: Who moves? How do they move? How do particular forms of mobility become meaningful? What other movements are enabled or constrained in this process? Who benefits from this movement?' (Cresswell 2001: 25; and cf. Wrigley and Revill 2000).

Many analysts now recognise the ways in which mobility is embedded in systematically asymmetrical power relations involving a politics of lived forms of mobility and immobility in which these two terms are always already implicated in each other (Ahmed *et al.* forthcoming). In enacting all of the bodily mobilities described above, the social construction of the 'right' to mobility is crucial. As Robert Young argues in a critique of Deleuze and Guattari's notion of nomadism, paying attention to 'enforced dislocations of the peoples of the South' can help to remind us that 'colonialism operated through a forced symbiosis between territorialization as, quite literally, plantation, and the demands for labour which involved the commodification of bodies and their exchange through international trade' (Young 1995: 173). The current political debates and vehement reactions generated by the movement of asylum seekers and refugees in Europe and the United States attest to the emotionally charged situations of immobility and boundary-fixing generated by border controls, visas, and the internment of 'aliens'. Rather than a celebration of the postmodern 'nomad', then, theorists of mobility are asking who or what is able to travel a supposedly 'borderless world', and who or what is kept in place (Graham and Marvin 2001).

The key circuits of global mobility include not only the peopling of the Americas, but also the migration of Caribbean people in and around the region and beyond (Puri forthcoming). Understanding the full complexity of these flows requires attention to who or what stayed put, and to how certain mobilities have been constrained.[13] One of my key arguments, following some of the work of Sara Ahmed, is that with the mobility of some, comes the production of the immobility of others; and furthermore that the very enabling of certain kinds of mobility requires certain kinds of barriers (Ahmed 2000, 2001). In the United States foreign policy is often driven by political arguments concerning the 'flood' of immigrants that will be released from the Caribbean if conditions there become unstable, while in Britain the Jamaican 'Yardie' has become a byword for violent gun crime. These discourses reflect efforts to reinforce boundaries of belonging and difference, and helped to justify policies such as the rounding up of Haitian refugees into the US military installation at Guantánamo Bay in Cuba. Such exclusions of categories of people from the otherwise easy flows of transnational tourism and elite nomadism are often linked to discourses of disease, whether the myth of Haitians as AIDS-carriers (Farmer 1992) or more subtle notions of cultural contagion and 'infectious rhythm' (Browning 1998).

In the tourism economy in particular there are highly structured inequalities of mobility and fixity. As Gavan Titley has argued,

> Tourism depends on the circulation of a desired image of the Caribbean as untouched yet within reach; the [all-inclusive] resort, the ultimate fragmentation of the environment, allows for the untouched to be curated and fortified. . . . Any random contact, or open ensemble, admits the risk that consumer satisfaction may be confronted by uncertainty. . . . Once again, the situation is paradoxical in that it is only through the erection of barriers that the world can be offered as being without frontiers for those privileged enough to undertake the journey.
>
> (Titley 2000: 82)

Thus the ability of the tourist to enjoy moving within and through the Caribbean requires limits to be placed on the mobility of 'local' people, who are barred access to resort areas except in so far as they perform service work. The apparent freedom of movement and boundless travel in a 'world without frontiers' is produced by the techniques of binding people, places, and meanings in place. The 'untouched' Caribbean of tourist fantasy must be held in place behind walls, gates, and service smiles in order to afford the tourist the experience of getting close to it. While some people are thus fixed in place, countries such as the UK willingly recruit highly trained doctors, nurses, and teachers from its former colonial territories in the West Indies, contributing to a drain of human resources from the Caribbean and a limited welcome afforded to certain kinds of migrants.

There is clearly an interrelation between the mobilities of people and objects, and the ways in which 'dwelling-in-travel' and 'travel-in-dwelling' are achieved. As Celia Lury highlights in her discussion of tourism and the objects of travel, the boundedness of culture in objects is secured by particular modes of travelling and dwelling. . . . [It] is not simply objects-in-motion but also objects-that-stay-still that help make up tourism. It is further suggested that looking at the career or biography of objects, as they move or stay still, will add to what we can say about the lives of people that travel (and then go home), that is, tourists.

(Lury 1997: 76–7)

Thus we must look at travel and dwelling together, and at people-in-motion and people-who-stay-still, since it is all of these together which secure the boundaries of culture, the boundaries that enable tourism (or other forms of cultural 'contact') to occur. It is precisely such relations that I will be exploring in subsequent chapters.

Global fluidities of consumption and production

Having considered the mobilities of consumption and the (im)mobilities of people, in concluding this chapter I want to turn to one example of the immersion of a small Caribbean state into a global economy that is described as increasingly 'fluid' or 'liquid' (Urry 2000; Bauman 2000). The discourse of globalization has proven very attractive to Caribbean governments as they try to gain a foothold in the 'new information economy'. Business conferences in the region sport names like 'The Global New Economy: Opportunities for Caribbean Business Development' and 'Globalisation: Are We Ready?'[14] Here I want to consider how Barbados in particular has positioned itself (and been positioned) in relation to the discourses and practices of globalization. In a promotion printed by the Barbados Ministry of International Trade and Business in 1998, an image of the globe is shown with an out-of-scale island of Barbados filling up the entire Atlantic. The effect of this re-scaling is the complete erasure of Africa from this globe, as Barbados appears to sit just south of the Mediterranean. The rest of the Caribbean is also placed out of the picture, to give Barbados centre-stage on the 'global icon' of the blue planet (cf. Franklin *et al.* 2000).

The visual displacement and forgetting of not only Africa, but also Barbados's generally poorer neighbours is matched by the erasure of the colonial past and the silencing of workers in the 'new global economy' – out of sight, out of mind. The text states that in the 'information-driven economy . . . the entire planet becomes a "level playing field" with tremendous opportunities for *all* countries, large or small.' Presumably influenced by David Harvey's notion of time-space compression (Harvey 1989), they assert optimistically that 'The world is getting smaller . . . But Barbados is growing'.[15] Just as the story of Sloane and the Chelsea Physic Garden suggested an erasure of Caribbean connections, so too does Barbados's effort to reconstitute itself as a centre of the information economy depend on its ability to silence the colonial past and disavow its Caribbean connections. Like Sloane's Jamaica, Barbados is mobilised in relation to the 'centre' of the information economy, stabilised as a node in the global information network, and recombined with the 'global' to afford greater power to that centre. Yet this comforting image for Euro-American investors sits awkwardly with the cut-throat economic reality of the effects of 'free trade' on most Caribbean economies. The Barbados government is engaging in what Klak and Myers describe as 'illusions of scientific grandeur' in its efforts to target and woo foreign 'investors associated with "high technology" industries: computers, electronics, information processing, and telecommunications' (Klak and Myers 1998: 98).

Barbados initially succeeded in this strategy in the early 1980s, becoming 'by far the largest per capita industrial exporter in the Caribbean, with electronics and garments contributing the most' (ibid.: 99–100). However, by 1983 its relatively higher wage rates led US-based corporations, such as INTEL, to pull out and seek cheaper labour in places like the Dominican Republic. Investors' guidebooks to the Caribbean develop promotional 'mediascapes' by which 'governments are selling their countries and people [just] as private-sector marketing departments . . . sell consumer commodities'. They compete with each other to promote 'profits in paradise' based on 'a blissful and laid-back tropical setting with easygoing workers who are willing to work for little' (ibid.: 95, 97). If wages do become too high, companies can simply pull out and move to greener pastures where extremely low wages, lack of worker protections, and tax holidays attract them to 'offshore' export-processing zones. These 'zones' become a kind of limbo in which 'flexible' workers do not really make anything, but simply move products along the 'global assembly line' (Barry *et al.* 1984; Klein 2000). In the Montego Bay Free Trade Zone in Jamaica, for example, the high-tech connectivity of the 'Digiport' (a 'back office enclave' serving metropolitan information processing industries) is enabled by dedicated high-speed satellite telecommunications, yet workers in the 1990s were paid US$0.34 per hour (Skinner 1998; Graham and Marvin 2001: 356–7). It is the strict limitations on labour mobility, especially from the Caribbean to the United States or Europe, that keeps in place these low-wage workers to service foreign investors.

In contrast to the restrictions on labour mobility, the Caribbean has become a leader in the free-booting flight of capital across international borders. Money itself is a crucial liquid asset which has been subject to wrangling over the ease of its illegal movement into and out of weakly regulated banking sectors in the Caribbean. As Appadurai notes, there are 'increasingly complex relationships among money flows, political possibilities, and the availability of both un- and highly-skilled labor . . . even an elementary model of global political economy must take into account the deeply disjunctive relationships among human movement, technological flows, and financial transfers' (Appadurai 1996: 34–5). The movement of money is ironically one of the few sectors in which small Caribbean states have a comparative advantage. Several UK dependencies or former colonies are well-known tax havens whose unregulated banking greases the wheels of global financial velocity: Anguilla, Belize, Bermuda, the British Virgin Islands, the Cayman Islands, the Turks and Caicos, and Grenada. The current crackdown on the funding of terrorist networks suggests that these banking zones that facilitate money laundering will soon be more tightly integrated into global 'financescapes'. 'Liquid modernity' (Bauman 2000) requires complex checks and barriers to enable or constrain particular kinds of flows. As in the days of piracy and 'freebooting', the Caribbean has come to be associated with interruptions of the 'normal' flows of capital, as well as with forms of smuggling and drug-running which subvert (yet support) the formal regulated economy.[16]

These mobilisations of island-images, capital investment, commodity production, and informational economies are closely linked to control over the movements of people. Trade liberalisation has been directly linked to rises in the cost of living, decline in local industries, especially food production, a fall in standards of health and welfare, and increased emigration from the Caribbean. Thus the economic policies that support the flow of cheap consumer goods into the North have brought with them an undertow of displaced people. As Deere *et al.* (1990) point out, the policies of the Caribbean Basin Initiative, the International Monetary Fund, the World Bank and the US Agency for International Development in the 1980s,

> reinforced traditional patterns of subordination in the relationship of Caribbean economies to metropolitan centers. Specifically, in the reliance on external markets, in the primacy of export production over production for local or regional markets, and in the preeminence given to the attraction of foreign capital, current development strategies advocated by Washington . . . reinforce highly open and vulnerable economies at the expense of the welfare of Caribbean populations.
>
> (Deere *et al.* 1990: 7–8)

More recent changes in the relation between Europe and the Caribbean, driven by the rulings of the World Trade Organisation (which I will discuss in more detail in Chapter 3), have made Caribbean economies even more vulnerable and 'open'. The resulting 'economic migrants' and 'boat-people' are turned away at the US border, while increasing numbers of tourists and boat people of a more desirable kind (travelling by cruise ship and yacht) pour into Caribbean 'resorts' or buy their own 'piece of paradise'.

At the Port St. Charles 'exclusive residential community' in Barbados, for example, yachts can now pull up and moor directly outside their villas, in a gated community with its own customs and passport control facilities. It is promoted not only as 'a lucrative investment vehicle', but also as offering investors 'the less tangible but rewarding gains of pleasure and satisfaction' of 'spending vacations in their new home' and 'knowing that they own property in a beautiful country'.[17] Growth in capital is tied to moving between one's home and a home away from home, and both depend on owning a little piece of 'paradise' in which the presence and proximity of the Bajan population is carefully managed.[18] 'Exclusive' ownership is not only about owning a piece of land, but is also expressed through owning shares of time. So-called 'private residence resorts' like The Crane, in Barbados, allow 'the purchase of some of the luxury villas for only the amount of time required, while retaining the important attributes of ownership in perpetuity backed by a deed to the property'. A one-bedroom, two-bath residence of 1,120 square feet goes for US$8,750 per week, while a 1,784 square foot two-bedroom villa with private pool starts at US$13,570 per week. Even more deluxe options are available from US$21,710 per week.[19] Investors are assured, however, that their assets will increase in value. This is in a country where the average wage rate for semi-skilled workers is approximately US$2 per hour (which is relatively high among independent Caribbean countries) (Klak and Myers 1998: 99).

Despite these stark political and economic realities recent studies of Caribbean modernity and the region's insertion into the global economy nevertheless highlight the degree to which Caribbean societies have grasped the nettle of global capitalism and the 'information economy'. Rather than dwelling on the violence of the colonial past or postcolonial dependency, they highlight the Caribbean's vanguard role in the making of global modernity. Carla Freeman, for example, shows how women working in the informatics industry in Barbados are not simply exploited 'pink-collar' workers in the 'electronic sweatshop'. 'Within the broad sweep of capitalist globalization, and the expansion of the global assembly line into new realms of work,' she argues, 'local culture and notions of identity enact themselves in significant ways, reshaping the very contours of multinational industries and therefore, even in a small way, of global capitalism itself' (Freeman 2000: 63). Daniel Miller and Don Slater take this argument a step further in their ethnography of internet-use in Trinidad, which 'is not a case-study of localization or the appropriation of a global form by local cultural concerns. It is not about domesticating a technology. On the contrary, it is largely about how Trinidadians put themselves into this global arena and become part of the force that constitutes it' (Miller and Slater 2000: 7). The technologies of the global (and of modernity), in other words, are Caribbean as much as they are anything else, and it would be a mistake to see the small island-states of the Caribbean solely as victims of some outside force called 'globalization'.

Even if the people of the Caribbean are being held in place and relegated to the immobile labour pool of 'the South', Caribbean people, culture, and ideas continue to leach across the border and cannot be kept out.[20] International laws pertaining to enslavement, migration, trade liberalisation, monetary movements, and intellectual property rights have always impinged on relations of consumption, and continue to do so. At the very time that there is a growing anxiety over stopping illegal entry of human bodies at the borders of Western consumer societies, the borders of 'non-Western' countries are being forced to open to the legal entry of objects of free trade. Crucial political battles with global consequences have been waged over tariffs and free movement of commodities, such as sugar, rum, and bananas, as well as intellectual property such as music and ethnobotanical knowledge. The movements of goods and ideas are tightly connected with the movements of people and their attachments. Decisions made about economies of production, consumption, and trade have deep implications for economies of culture, emotion, and identity.

In briefly introducing the mobilities of consumption which link the Caribbean with 'the West' I have begun to demonstrate how such mobilities figure in the accumulation of financial and cultural capital, and the making of spaces of modernity in 'the West' (always problematically imagined as separate from the Caribbean). By tracing the continuities in this process from the late seventeenth century until today my aim has been to show how contemporary cultures of mobile consumption are still embedded in earlier patterns of material, human, informational, and cultural movement between the North Atlantic and the Caribbean. In the next chapter I will tell this story again, in a different way, by returning to the first moments of European entrancement with the natural wonders of the Caribbean, and tracking this relation of consumption into the everyday form of tourist imagery and fantasy island that surrounds us today.

2 Iconic islands

Nature, landscape, and the tropical
tourist gaze

The familiar sun-sea-and-sand imagery used in Caribbean tourism promotion
may seem like an endlessly repeated cliché that hardly requires any further analysis. Used to promote everything from package holidays and cruises to time-shares
and villa purchases all over the world, a more generic, global, and empty signifier
of 'the tropical island' could hardly be imagined. Alongside it a slightly different
variation draws on an ecotourism imagery of 'unspoilt' primal rainforests, waterfalls, and lush greenery in those parts of the Caribbean that still have some forest
cover (e.g. Dominica, Tobago, St. Lucia, or parts of the Greater Antilles and
Trinidad). Rather than reading these stereotypes as meaningless clichés that circulate in a global market for tropical island tourism, I want to explore specifically
how these iconic images arose, for what purposes, and with what effects. Both
kinds of imagery (palm-fringed beach and verdant forest) pick up on longstanding
visual and literary themes in Western culture based on the idea of tropical islands
as microcosms of earthly Paradise.

This chapter is concerned with consumption of the ecological environment of
the Caribbean in the widest sense and its reinvention as a 'nature' and 'landscape'
for Northern Atlantic inhabitants' pleasure and use. It could be argued that there is
no 'primal nature' in the Caribbean both because so much of it has been constructed by human intervention and because every aspect of it is dosed with a heavy
infusion of symbolic meaning and cultural allusions. Here I will consider how
Europeans moved through the Caribbean, introduced exotic species, removed
seeds, fruits, and timber, and represented Caribbean plants and landscapes verbally
and visually. Any effort to find an 'original' Caribbean immediately comes up
against the cultural remaking of its human, floral, and faunal populations (Crosby
1972). Introduced plants include many mainstays, e.g. coffee, sugar cane, bananas,
and citrus trees from the Middle East; yams and ackee trees from Africa; potatoes,
maize, and chilli peppers from the Americas; mangoes, rice, and hemp (marijuana)
from Asia; and the famous breadfruit trees brought back from Tahiti by Captain
Bligh in 1793. Introduced animals include cattle, sheep, goats, horses, cats, dogs,
rats, mongoose, farmed shrimp, and many more. People, of course, have come
from almost every part of the world. Networks of transportation infrastructure,
capital investment, and scientific work enabled these various movements of people,
animals, and plants: the contemporary Caribbean is an assemblage.

Although 'the modern traveller still perceives the landscape as bearing the imprint of bounteous serendipity', David Watts argues, 'the senses deceive' because the Caribbean has suffered major species loss and habitat degradation, including unabated faunal destruction over the last century (Watts 1990: 3, 40). As Stuart McCook points out in a study of agriculture in the Spanish Caribbean, the expansion of export crops grown on single cash-crop plantations, such as sugar, bananas, coffee, and cacao, 'unintentionally created an environment ideal for the spread of disease and pests. Global crop epidemics became commonplace as the development of steamships and railroads accelerated the spread of pathogens and pests' (McCook 2002: 21). The mobility of planters and plant varieties, and of scientists and knowledge about tropical agriculture, were thus tightly wedded to the mobility of plant diseases and vectors of agricultural catastrophe. How is it that the massive introduction of alien species, forest clearance, stripping of plant cover, soil erosion, and reef destruction in the Caribbean remain invisible in the global tourist economy where the Caribbean is packaged and sold as 'pristine' beaches and verdant rainforest? I suggest that contemporary views of tropical island landscapes are highly over-determined by the long history of literary and visual representations of the tropical island as Paradise. As Richard Grove has argued, 'the commercial and utilitarian purposes of European expansion produced a situation in which the tropical environment was increasingly utilised as the symbolic location for the idealised landscapes and aspirations of the Western imagination' (Grove 1995: 3). The island imagination today draws on these earlier precedents, and makes certain kinds of movement through the Caribbean viable. The Caribbean island is one of the first 'global icons' (cf. Franklin *et al.* 2000) to encapsulate modernity, enfolding within itself a deep history of relations of consumption, luxury, and privilege for some. Rather than calling for a recovery of an authentic Caribbean or attempting to reconstruct the indigenous or Afro-Caribbean view of the natural world (which could again be recuperated into the colonial picturesque), I will instead track how the idea of 'the Caribbean' was constructed in the European imaginary, and how this work of imagination then came to inform travel there.

There are striking continuities in representations of the Caribbean, as well as some major shifts in the European relation to tropical nature and landscapes. My focus here is the points of contact between mobile material and cultural networks, which set off flows of people and things across the Atlantic world, yet also conjoin to lock certain things in place: colonies, slaves, landed property, service workers, tourist resorts. Varied genres of representation of nature, I argue, are inseparable from changing modes of economic enterprise and consumer envelopment in the tropics. Thus Euro-American relations to Caribbean 'natural' landscapes are a crucial starting-point for understanding the social relations of power that inform their relationship to Caribbean people. I have identified three major ways of seeing or portraying the Caribbean within Northern Atlantic representational practices,[1] each of which can be roughly aligned with one of the key periods of European and later US economic relations to the region. The first arose in what I termed the period of 'discovery', piracy, and 'bachelor plantations', and concerns the 'productions of nature' as living substances with particular kinds of utilitarian value. From the original European 'discovery' of a botanical cornucopia in the tropics (heavily indebted to indigenous knowledge) to its collection, ordering, and study, botanical collection and pharmaceutical testing of tropical flora have re-shaped Europe's relation to 'nature', scientific knowledge, and conservation. The work of Sir Hans Sloane, discussed in Chapter 1, is characteristic of this approach to New World nature in the sixteenth to seventeenth centuries.

Second, I turn to the eighteenth-century 'scenic economy' in which tropical landscapes came to be viewed through a painterly aesthetic constructed around comparative evaluations of cultivated land versus wild vistas. Associated with the period of ascendance of the colonial sugar plantation system, this form of visual consumption often utilised a 'rhetoric of presence' (Pratt 1992) which offered an implicit ideological legitimisation of slavery. The visual practices that organised such views, it must be said, were not specific to the Caribbean, but can be found operating in other parts of the colonial world as well. While each visual regime may be associated with a particular era of Caribbean history, I would not insist that it occurred as such only then and there. Through the circulation of books, prints, and libraries earlier modes of seeing always resurface and leave cues in later texts. Thus my method is to collect representative examples for purposes of illustration and argument, rather than to be comprehensive.

And third, in the nineteenth century there was a renewed emphasis on 'wild' nature and the bodily experience of immersion in it. This Romantic vision of untamed tropical nature, which arose especially in the period following the abolition of slavery, was constructed around experiences of moving through Caribbean landscapes and of experiencing bodily what was already known imaginatively through literature and art. In this revival of earlier discourses of the natural productivity of the tropical island paradise, a new United States imperialism was justified as the best use of 'virgin' natural resources, which local people were thought to be incapable of capitalising on. Contemporary tourism emerged out of this romantic imperialism, though keeping remnants of the earlier representational practices as well. Each of these imaginaries and its associated images, I argue, leaves traces that continue to inform the iconicity of the Caribbean today. The Caribbean is consumed both in travelling representations (texts, images, signs) that bring the Caribbean to the consumer, and by travelling consumers who organise their experience and perceptions of the Caribbean through existing visual regimes.

Productions of nature: trade in botanical knowledge

European consumption of the Caribbean began with 'discovery', exploration, and biological devastation of the land, plants, animals, and native populations of the Caribbean from 1492 onwards. This included the incorporation of new lands into growing empires often through enslavement of the inhabitants found there;

provisioning of ships and new settlements with food, shelter, and drink; and the release of omnivorous alien species, from swine and feral cattle to bacterial and viral pathogens. 'The history of European horticulture in the Americas,' notes Alfred Crosby Jr, 'begins with the second voyage of Columbus [in 1493], when he returned to [Hispaniola] with seventeen ships, 1,200 men, and seeds and cuttings for planting of wheat, chickpeas, melons, onions, radishes, salad greens, grape vines, sugar cane, and fruit stones for the founding of orchards' (Crosby 1972: 67). Unfortunately for these colonists, neither wheat to make bread, nor grape vines to make wine, nor olive trees to make oil (the three staples of the Mediterranean diet), would flourish in the hot, wet lowlands of the West Indies. They had more success, however, in the release of domesticated animals, which by 1518 were proliferating across the Greater Antilles. Livestock were also dropped on smaller outlying islands as an emergency supply. Without predators or keepers, the numbers of these feral animals 'burgeoned so rapidly, in fact, that doubtlessly they had much to do with the extinction of certain plants, animals, and even Indians themselves, whose gardens they encroached upon' (ibid.: 75). The introduction of European diseases contributed even more to the decimation of the indigenous population, which I return to in Chapter 5.

The major hurdle facing all European projects of exploration and colonisation in the sixteenth century was the problem of survival once having arrived on the distant shores of the New World. Crucial to survival on these initial voyages was the opportunity to learn from the indigenous inhabitants found in these new lands about how to cultivate edible plants, how to hunt, and how to prepare food and shelter from what nature had to offer. As David Watts suggests, Europeans only survived in the West Indies in so far as they adapted Indian techniques and lifestyles, such as ring-barking as a method of land clearance, *conuco* agriculture based on manioc and sweet potatoes, Indian-style huts and hammocks, and canoes for transportation (Watts 1990: 174). While European mytho-history emphasises the goodwill and generosity of the 'Indians', enslavement was the most likely means of knowledge transfer for those who survived the epidemics of smallpox. European explorers in the Caribbean were therefore extremely interested in recording the forms and uses of the plants they found in use by the Arawaks or Taino, before they all died off. These could then be made available in Europe to other potential explorers and colonists, giving them handbooks for survival in these unknown wilds. Catalogues of plants were carefully drawn, along with instructions on their cultivation and uses, such as those found in the late sixteenth-century 'Drake Manuscript' or *Histoire Naturelle des Indes: Les Arbres, Plantes, Fruits, Animaux, Coquillages, Reptiles, Insectes, Oiseaux, etc, qui se trouvent dans les Indes.*[2]

Francis Drake first sailed to the New World with John Hawkins on slaving voyages in 1567–8, and returned on several other journeys. Both men were instrumental in advancing English interests in the Caribbean, at the expense of Spain. It was Hawkins who first brought sugar from Saint Domingue back to England, while Drake went on to circumnavigate the world in 1577–80, thus becoming a popular hero in England.[3] Drake's voyage 'became especially important in stimulating the entry of images of tropical nature into popular culture in England, particularly in the cheaper street literature' such as P. Brooksby's *The Voyages and Travels of that Renowned Captain Sir Francis Drake* (1683) (Grove 1995: 39). The 'Drake Manuscript' was written in French by an anonymous member of Drake's party, who painted close to two hundred watercolour images of West Indian plants and animals, and scenes of the lives of Indian, European, and African inhabitants of the Spanish territories in the New World. Here a catalogue of 'useful' plants are depicted in isolation from their natural setting, against a blank background, and accompanied by notes on their indigenous use and cultivation. A palm tree, for example, is depicted along with an accompanying text, which describes how the indigenous people made a palm wine, tasting like sherry (Plate 2.1). The separation of the tree from its surroundings serves to emphasise its form, leaf structure and unusual bark, perhaps to aid in identification. In addition to the form of the plant, it also crucially depicts how the plant was cultivated by clearing surrounding trees, and building a fire around the base to keep out 'poisonous beasts' while the palm juice is tapped into a bowl made from a gourd.

The palm would go on to become a key symbolic icon representing the entire Caribbean region. Its immediate significance can be seen in this well-known and much-reproduced seventeenth-century account of the Buccaneers, referring here to the island of Hispaniola:

> There are an abundance of Palm Trees found here, some of which are two hundred foot high, having no branches but what are upon the very top; every month one of these branches falleth off, and at the same time another sprouteth out; the leaves of this tree are seven or eight foot in length, and three or four in breadth, with which they cover their houses instead of Tyles: Also they make buckets of them to carry their Water in. The body of the Tree is so big, that two men can scarcely grasp it in the middle; yet the heart of it is so soft, that if two or three inches be pared off its outside, the rest may be sliced like new Cheese. The Inhabitants have a way of extracting an excellent Drink from this Tree; for gouging it a little above the Root, they [fr]om thence distill a sort of Liquour which in short time by fermentation becometh as strong as the richest Wine.[4]

Not only is the size of the tree staggering in terms of height, breadth, and gigantic foliage, but it also serves diverse needs as vessel, shelter, and wine. Here again we see the novelty of the tree to Europeans, who were especially attracted by the production of palm wine, since alcoholic beverages were in short supply on long sea voyages.[5] The images in the Drake Manuscript and early travel accounts fit more into the category of instruction manual or colonist's guide. Their concerns are with the ways in which people (both native and European) can make use of the plants depicted, rather than with how nature looks (as in later romantic scenic genres) or how plants can be ordered (as in later more purely botanical records).

Plate 2.1 Representing the uses of 'nature' in the contact zone.
'Palme' from The Drake Manuscript *Histoire Naturelle des Indes*. Credit: The Pierpont Morgan Library, New York. MA 3900, f.33. Photography: David A. Loggie.

Such early European views of Caribbean islands presented a fascination with a particular type of tropical landscape and particular kinds of 'natural' and 'cultivated' scenery, especially the edible kind. The Drake Manuscript's series of forty-three images of human activity depict indigenous practices such as fishing, trapping parrots and rabbits, cooking, washing and swimming, making flour, gardening, harvesting, treating wounds, hunting wild boar, spinning cotton, and net-making. The author concludes that 'They are so skilled that one could not show them any work which they could not do'. This remarkable document attests to the sophistication of the culture the Europeans found in the New World, and the extent to which they learned to survive by adapting indigenous technologies and knowledges. Even today we live in the linguistic and material penumbra of this 'contact zone' (Pratt 1992), whether firing up the 'barbecue', lounging in a 'hammock', paddling a 'canoe', lighting up a smoke of 'tobacco', or sipping 'cocoa'.[6]

But early accounts of the Caribbean are not simply utilitarian; they are also informed by an imagery of tropical fecundity and excessive fruitfulness, which conjured up utopian fantasies of sustenance without labour, even though this was manifestly at odds with the difficult experience of survival. As Grove and others have convincingly shown, such accounts draw on a range of precedents such as the biblical Garden of Eden, the classical garden of the Hesperides, and the Renaissance botanical garden, which was itself derived from Middle Eastern models. Columbus may even have believed that the Garden of Eden actually existed in the extreme Orient, but like the ancient Greek Elysium was reached by sailing West; that would explain why he took Luis de Torres, a scholar of Hebrew, Arabic, and Chaldaic with him (Prest 1981: 31). Herman Pleij has also pointed to the influence of the medieval fantasy of the perfect life existing in the 'Land of Cockaigne', where food was endlessly abundant and no labour was needed in its preparation. In one of Columbus's letters he describes the New World as 'a veritable Cockaigne' because of the abundance of food (Pleij 2001). The dream of Cockaigne was associated with other visions of life's pleasures, including abundant alcohol, easily available sex, and even immortality. All of these fantastical precedents fed into the early accounts of the New World, yet lived in tension with the clearly present danger of starvation without indigenous help or enslavement.

Such idyllic images of the West Indies also served in the propaganda campaign by which colonial adventurers sought financial backing and royal patronage for their schemes, as well as potential settlers and indentured servants to join their enterprise. Thus in one early seventeenth-century report on the wondrous edible plants of Barbados we meet with familiar tropes of a prelapsarian nature:

> A tree like a Pine, beareth a fruit so great as a Muske Melon, which hath alwayes ripe fruit, flowers or greene fruit, which will refresh two or three men, and very comfortable; Plum trees many, the fruit great and yellow, which but strained into water in foure and twenty houres will be very goode drinke; wilde figge trees there are many . . . all things we there plant doe grow exceedingly, so well as Tobacco; the corne, pease, and beanes, cut but away

the stalkes, young sprigs will grow, and so bear fruit for many yeeres together, without any more planting.[7]

Much like the Drake Manuscript, this text mixes together descriptions of plants with instructions on how to cultivate and prepare them. Coming from a land of four seasons, Europeans had never seen plants that flowered and fruited throughout the year, carrying green fruit, ripe fruit, and flowers all at the same time. As Grove notes of such writing, in discovering the tropical island 'Paradise had become a realisable geographical reality' (Grove 1995: 51); it was the Garden of Eden before the fall of Man.

It has been further suggested by early modern historians that the discovery of the 'New World' contributed to an epistemic shift in European visual representations of the natural world. During the Renaissance natural images had served an 'emblematic' function in which images of plants or animals condensed a complex web of allegorical, mythical, and epigrammatic meanings (Ashworth 1990). From about 1650 onwards, claims Ashworth (following Michel Foucault's argument in *The Order of Things* that the publication of Joannes Jonston's *Natural History* was a crucial turning-point), a modern discourse developed in which plants and animals were represented simply as what they were, rather than what they stood for. One explanation for this representational shift is that with the discovery of a new terrain and new natures, novel plants and animals entered European consciousness bereft of any accrued meanings. In the texts of the New World natural histories by writers like Charles L'Ecluse, Jan de Laet, Juan Nieremberg, and Georg Markgraf, nature was bare and for the first time unadorned with superfluous meaning:

> Their impact derived from one simple fact. The animals of the new world had no known similitudes. Anteaters and sloths do not appear in Erasmus or Alciati or Piero Valeniano; they are missing from the writings of antiquity. They came to the Old World naked, without emblematic significance . . . [Naturalists] were forced to limit their descriptions to discussions of appearance, habitat, food and whatever tales could be assembled from native populations.
>
> (Ashworth 1990: 318)

For the first time knowledge of the natural world could be – had to be – codified into 'natural facts' absent of myth, fable, or allegorical resonance. While Ashworth himself adds other explanations to this account, we can nevertheless agree that the discovery of the West Indies was crucial to a shift in European attitudes towards the natural world and its 'products'. The early modern period thus has its origins in this transatlantic context.

Europeans found tropical products from the Caribbean increasingly useful for a wide range of areas such as food, medicine, carpentry, and manufacturing processes in the seventeenth and eighteenth centuries. In this sense the tropics were consumed not only by those who voyaged there to see the landscape and taste its fruits, but also by the general populations who consumed the products that flowed back across the Atlantic. Tropical hardwoods and dyewoods were especially valued, including the West Indian Cedar (*Cedrela mexicana*) used for building and furniture making; the locust (*Hymenaea courbaril*) for large beams; the extremely hard ironwood (*Bunchosia nitida*) for fencing and mill rollers; and the dyewoods fustic (*Chlorophora tinctoria*) and *lignum vitae* (*Guaiacum officinale*) (Watts 1990: 155). The latter was not only initially believed to cure syphilis (especially used in conjunction with treatment by mercury), but also contained essential oils which preserved the wood from drying out and made it ideal for the making of marine navigational instruments. Clocks made from *lignum vitae* by John Harrison in the eighteenth century allowed the first measurement of longitude, which had revolutionary effects on European seafaring.

The French writer Père Charlevoix reported on the crucial medicinal and other uses of some of the plants exported from Jamaica in the mid-eighteenth century:

> The natural produce of Jamaica, besides sugar, cacao, and ginger, are principally pimento, or, as it is called, allspice, or Jamaica pepper . . . it is milder than other spices, and is judged to be inferior to none of them for the service which it does to cold, watery and languid stomachs . . . Besides this they have the wild cinnamon tree, whose bark is so serviceable in medicine; the manchineel, a most beautiful tree to the eye, with the fairest apple in the world, and when cut down affording a very fine ornamental wood for the joiners. . . . Here is the mahogany, in such general use with our cabinet makers; the cabbage tree, a tall plant famous for a substance, looking and tasting like cabbage, growing on the very top, and no less remarkable for the extreme hardness of its wood, which when dry is incorruptible, and hardly yields to any tool; the palma, from which is drawn a great deal of oil, much esteemed by the negroes both in food and medicine; the white wood, which never breeds the worm in ships; the soap tree, whose berries answer all purposes of washing; the mangrove and olive bark, useful to tanners; the fustic and redwood to the dyers, and lately the logwood; and their forests supply the apothecary with guaiacum, sarsaparilla, china, caffia, and tamarinds; they have aloes too; . . . The indigo plant was formerly much cultivated; the cotton tree is still so, and they send home more of its wool than all the rest of our islands together.[8]

Charlevoix's report suggests a combined interest in spices, medicines, foods, ornamental woods, and various useful plant products, reflecting the diverse ends of European exploitation of tropical nature. The tropical forests provided a wide range of materials that were incorporated into European material culture both in the Tropics and at home, enabling innumerable new commercial and domestic products from a very early date. Lists such as these were themselves part of a new genre of imperialism. Laura Brown identifies such extensive lists of 'natural products' in early eighteenth-century travel narratives with a 'rhetoric of acquisition', in which 'the mere act of proliferative listing . . . and the sense of an incalculable quantity express the period's fascination with imperialist acquisition' (Brown 1993: 43; Wheeler 1999: 18).

If the period of plantation development transformed the 'native' environments and sustainable agricultural practices that Columbus and other chroniclers had seen in the fifteenth and sixteenth centuries, European environments and attitudes toward nature were also transformed in the process of consuming other places. Most importantly, as Grove has meticulously argued, the European experience in the tropics led to the 'attachment of a new kind of social significance to nature':

> The available evidence shows that the seeds of modern conservationism developed as an integral part of the European encounter with the tropics and with local classifications and interpretations of the natural world and its symbolism. As colonial expansion proceeded, the environmental experiences of Europeans and indigenous peoples living at the colonial periphery played a steadily more dominant and dynamic part in the construction of new European evaluations of nature and in the growing awareness of the destructive impact of European economic activity on the peoples and environments of the newly 'discovered' and colonised lands.
>
> (Grove 1995: 24, 2–3)

As early as the seventeenth century the first inklings of the fragility of ecological environments and the recognition of human impacts on nature were already apparent, and the island-worlds of the Caribbean came to represent the limits of global nature. The Caribbean was crucial in this regard inasmuch as 'the full impact of the new urban market' demanding sugar, coffee, and tobacco, was 'imposed on the fragile environments of the smaller tropical islands' (ibid.: 63). By the 1660s Barbados was already suffering from deforestation, soil erosion, landslides, and loss of fertility. Wood had to be imported from Tobago and as early as the 1760s the British implemented efforts at forest conservation on the recently ceded island of St. Kitts.[9] As John Urry (1995) argues, economic exploitation, scientific investigation, visual consumption, and conservation all constitute different forms of appropriating the physical world, thus each can be construed as a way of 'consuming places'.

The awareness of European ecological impact on the Tropics, combined with a growing appreciation of 'the value of indigenous and local medico-botanical knowledge' (Grove 1995: 94), not only produced a conservationist attitude among some colonial authorities, but it also led to new attitudes towards nature in Europe. As Chandra Mukerji has shown, there was in seventeenth-century France, 'tremendous growth in the variety of vegetation (made possible in part through the design of special buildings and techniques devoted to the propagation and cultivation of rare plants and animals). . . . [C]ollecting a wide range of exotic plants in gardens of the seventeenth century was part of a larger cultural and economic shift' (Mukerji 1994: 441). Exotic plants moved from specialist botanical and medical gardens into the kitchen and pleasure gardens of great houses. Nobility sent gardeners on trading voyages to 'survey the decorative or edible plants from other cultures and collect the best of them'; and in 1672, 'Colbert wrote to the director of the West India Company asking for his people to bring back unusual fruits and flowers for the royal gardens.' Thus, she argues, 'The resulting gardens can be seen as living maps, marking the capacity of the French state to control territory and manipulate the natural resources within it; in this way they mapped the political agenda of the state. They also traced the international reach of the trading system that revolved around the state' (ibid.: 442–3). Not only were new plants introduced into Europe, then, but entirely new conceptions of landscape and territory were also developed out of the taxonomic and spatial ordering of these new materials. The formal collection of exotic plants, and their careful organisation into parterres and bordered beds informed the way in which travellers approached the tropical landscape, as a terrain from which material could be collected and knowledge gathered and systematised.

In Britain, which moved to the forefront of European 'consumer culture' in the eighteenth century, but was slower to appreciate its impact on colonial environments, landscapes and the organisation of gardens took a different form. In contrast to the boundaries and territorial impositions of the French formal garden, Mukerji suggests that English gardens (such as those designed by Capability Brown) were arranged to open up views to wider landscapes and painterly scenes, which created a sense of limitless landholding and blurred the boundaries between the cultivated and the natural (cf. Bermingham 1986).[10] In the following section we see how this view of landscape informed a new relation to Caribbean landscapes in the eighteenth century. Following the Gulf Stream north, we can also see how the 'fruits of empire' planted their seed in new environments, urban architectures, and rural landscapes in Britain. Glasshouses and tropical vegetation swept through landscape design, while major ports involved in the West Indies trade consumed its profits and goods in the Georgian building boom. Planters came back to assert their wealth in ostentatious displays of new country estates that rivalled those of the old landed aristocracy. If the appreciation of Caribbean landscapes began from a pursuit of survival, medicine, and natural science, the flow of tropical flora, fauna, and forms of cultivation across the Atlantic soon fed into a new 'scenic economy'. I refer to these ways of representing and viewing 'scenery' as an economy because they involved modes of accumulation, exchange, and consumption through which landscape was fetishised and turned into a commodity.

Scenic economies: the plantation as cultivated garden city

The tropical island has played a crucial part in the history of European literature, philosophy, and arts. Richard Grove traces the interest in tropical islands as Edens or Utopias back to Bishop Francis Godwin's *The Man in the Moone* (1638), which was set on the Atlantic island of St. Helena. William Dampier's *A New Voyage Round the World* was also influential, as were the true stories of the survival of Alexander Selkirk, who was shipwrecked on Juan Fernandez Island for over four years. The physical setting of Daniel Defoe's *Robinson Crusoe* (1719) is thought to have been modelled on the Caribbean island of Tobago as described in John Poyntz's *The Present Prospect of the Famous and Fertile Islands of Tobago* (1683), and it led to a cult of 'robinsonnades' throughout Europe (Grove 1995: 225–9). Also crucial, of course, was William Shakespeare's last play, *The Tempest*, with its vaguely Caribbean setting, which fed into what Roland Greene describes as an 'island logic' in European thought (Greene 2000: 140; cf. Hulme and Sherman 2000). All of these works knitted together to make the tropical island into a kind of 'global' icon (Franklin *et al.* 2000), inasmuch as the island logic condensed all of the material and fantastical processes of production and consumption of new worlds into a single bounded space, a microcosm of God's work. In attempting to experience, see, touch, smell, taste and represent these iconic island-worlds, new forms of sensing nature and a new relation to landscape developed in Europe.

If many early texts concerning tropical islands were instrumental and practical catalogues of useful plants, animals, and 'natural products', a second major trope in European writing on the region was the envisioning of landscape as scenery. The viewer's relation to this scenery, however, changed over time, with an early emotive tie to cultivated scenes later replaced by an affective response to 'wild' and sublime landscapes, which 'moved' the viewer through the very experience of moving through the land. Here I want to trace how the eighteenth century's rationalist representations of Caribbean nature as triumphs of cultivation shifted to an increasingly emotive and romantic stylisation of nature in the late eighteenth to early nineteenth centuries. Such shifts in perception and representation of landscapes have been explored more widely in relation to travellers in Central and South America (Manthorne 1989; Greenblatt 1991; Poole 1998). Deborah Poole, for example, suggests a relation between different representational technologies (oil painting, lithography, daguerrotype, *carte de visite*, stereoscope, studio photography, the Kodak camera) and multiple 'visual regimes coexisting in time and space' which together produced 'the imperial gaze' and its 'imperial subjects' (Poole 1998: 132). Following from this, I will not try to impose a rigid periodisation of the shift from one visual regime to another, but will simply indicate the different possibilities that were predominantly drawn on in particular periods and contexts. Each visual regime, however, continues to echo through the centuries, and more than one can often be found operating in any single text.

Sir Richard Dutton said of Barbados in 1681, that the dense population and intensive cultivation made it 'one great City adorned with gardens and a most delightful place' (Dunn 1972: 28). In contrast, in Edward Ward's *A Trip to Jamaica* (1698), he was most struck by the lack of cultivation in the island, which was by no means an earthly paradise, but 'the Dunghill of the Universe, the Refuse of the whole Creation, the Clippings of the Elements, a shapeless pile of Rubbish confus'ly jumbl'd into an Emblem of the *Chaos*, neglected by Omnipotence when form'd the World into its admirable Order' (Walcott 2000: 57). Clearly in this period 'wild nature' had no appeal to European eyes, which desired to see nature shaped, ordered, and presented. This required the exercise of certain kinds of power, which European colonisers thought the indigenous peoples were incapable of.

Throughout most of the eighteenth century the predominant theme in descriptions of the Caribbean remains the beauty of cultivated areas set within the tropical landscape. Uncultivated land could be declared '*terra nullis*' and legitimately seized. The French writer Père Charlevoix, for example, indicates this appreciation of cultivated landscape as a sign of civilised control in Barbados in the mid-eighteenth century:

> The country of Barbados has a most beautiful appearance, swelling here and there into gentle hills; shining by the cultivation of every part, by the verdure of the sugar canes, the bloom and fragrance of the number of orange, lemon, lime and citron trees, the guavas, papas, aloes, and a vast multitude of other elegant and useful plants, that rise intermixed with the houses of the gentlemen which are sown thickly on every part of the island. Even the negro huts, tho' mean, contribute to the beauty of the country; for they shade them with plantain trees, which give their villages the appearance of so many beautiful groves.[11]

Here we see the 'useful plants' still recognised, but notable for their elegance and appearance in making up a complete scene, rather than simply being noted for their use or taste. Also notable is Charlevoix's failure to see the ecological degradation that had already taken place on Barbados by this time, denuding it of forest cover. The mixture of architectural views, a god-like perspective over every part of the island at once, and idyllic groves with quaint workers was familiar in the European tradition of landscape painting and classical allegory.

Eighteenth-century depictions of the Caribbean often give a celebratory overview of a plantation, showing not only its main crops, but also the 'negro huts' and provision grounds to one side, and the mountains or hills rising in the background. Many contain labelled areas with a list of the various features, buildings, and planted areas, and highly romantic imagery of happy peasant-like workers (Plate 2.2). While a single useful plant might appear in the foreground, a theatrical sense of the overall scene predominates. So common were these images that most visitors to the West Indies came with preconceived images of the landscape, based on books they had read and paintings or engravings they had seen. Many seemed to carry an image of the Caribbean from their reading in their youth.

Daniel McKinnen, for example, cites the writings of Richard Ligon and Père Labat on Barbados, before describing his own impressions in 1804:

> At a distance the land appeared extremely bare; but as we approached it more nearly the rich and curious tropical productions captivated our eyes. On the hills the stately cabbage-trees, and on the beach the cocoanuts spreading their feathered branches, afforded a picture of which I had not formed too lively a conception from the representation of others, and to which the painter only can do adequate justice. . . . [In the Negro villages the] paths

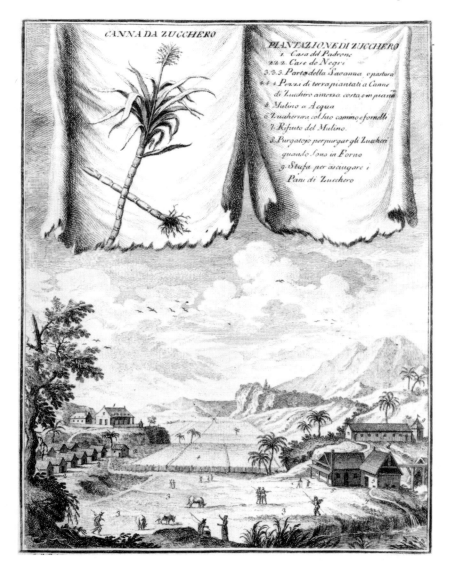

Plate 2.2 Staging the sugary scene of mastery.
Canna de Zucchero, *Il Gazzetteire Americano*, Vol. 2 (Loverno, 1763). Reproduced courtesy of the British Library.

and by-lanes in which their huts are intermingled with plantains, oranges, and jessemines, and the occasional papaw, cocoa-nut, and tamarind-trees that overshadowed this odoriferous and rural scene, formed a picture enchanting by its novelty, which seemed to realize the youthful visions of imagination.[12]

It is through the eyes of painters and 'youthful visions' from illustrated books that McKinnen gazes upon the Bajan landscape. 'Guided by the representations of others', his writing style also cribs from those same books, with their lists of fruit trees and narrator moving through the landscape. He sees before him a picture, which is not so much an experience of novelty as a realisation of childhood enchantment, the very emotional investments that had already brought him to travel to this far-away place. As Gregory argues, such 'travel-scripting' is guided by previous texts, which 'produces a serialized space of constructed visibility that allows and sometimes even requires specific objects to be seen in specific ways by a specific audience. . . . [T]hey all carry within them traces of the physical move-ment of embodied subjects through material landscapes' (Gregory 1999: 116–17). As a viewer like McKinnen traverses the Caribbean landscape he constructs its visibility along specific lines, composing plants, people, and buildings into a preconceived ordered scene.

Viewing the Barbados scenery with an eye trained in viewing landscape paint-ings, McKinnen seeks appropriate vantage points from which he can describe the landscape as if it were already a picture:

> Along the shore to the north of Bridge Town I found the road extremely picturesque. It leads through a long avenue of shady cocoa-nut trees, over-arched by their palmated and spacious leaves, and fenced on each side by prickly pears, or the blades of aloes. In occasional openings, or through the stems of the trees, you behold the masters' dwelling-houses with the negro-huts adjoining; and over a rich vale, abounding with cotton shrubs and maize, the hills at a small distance spotted with wind-mills, sugar-works, and a few lofty cabbage-trees, or cocoa-nuts. At times the road approaches the sea and leads along the beach. . . . It then winds into the plantations, where the cultivated parterres of cotton and tropical plants are often relieved by groups of cocoa-nuts and plantains, the leaves of which, in the form of squares or quadrangular figures, have a singular effect in the landscape.[13]

Rather than the author appearing as a moving agent in this excerpt, it is the road that is given agency: it 'leads' through, 'approaches', 'winds into'. He moves as if in a dream, the scene changing before him as if it were a panorama or diorama. Furthermore, rather than an 'I' beholding the scene, the text interpellates the reader, 'you behold', linked significantly to the moment of mentioning mastery and dwelling. As Mary Louise Pratt suggests in her study of imperial travel writ-ing, relations of such writers to the landscape are expressed through the relation of a viewer to a painting. Gazing through his 'imperial eyes', such landscapes are aesthetically imbued, attributed with a density of meaning, and fixed by the mastery of the seer over the seen. Such a 'monarch-of-all-I-survey scene', Pratt argues, 'involve[s] particularly explicit interaction between esthetics and ideology, in what one might call a rhetoric of presence' (Pratt 1992: 204–5). Through the rhetoric of presence the scene is not only recorded, but also ordered and made present to the reader who also masters it.

Again, though, the trees and vistas in this image serve to frame the man-made elements of cultivated ground, windmills, sugar-works, and 'negro huts'. In describing Antigua McKinnen not only highlights his preference for cultivated scenery, which informed many European views of the Caribbean in this period, but also comments *negatively* upon the scenes of untouched woods and mountains, 'unrelieved' by human intervention, in other less developed colonies. Again it is the 'garden-like' imagery, and the romantic domesticity of the 'negro huts', which draw 'the eye':

> the eye traverses a view of one of the fairest and best cultivated tracts of country in the windward islands. It is highly pleasing to a person who has recently come from the woods and mountains of the more southern colonies, to behold so extensive a scene of cleared land. . . . Nothing appears more completely like a garden than the sugar plantation under good cultivation. . . . The green fields of cane . . . were intermixed with provision grounds of yams and eddoes, or the dark and regular parterres of holed land prepared for the reception of the succeeding year's plant-canes. A large windmill on each estate; the planter's dwelling-house and sugar-works, with the negro huts, in their beautiful groves of oranges, plantains, and cocoanut trees, completed a landscape that continually recurred in passing over the island.[14]

McKinnen returns again and again to this point of view as he moves through various places. In contrast to this scene of cultivation in Antigua was the more intimidating scenery of Jamaica, where cultivated country could be left behind. Here he finds scenes of cane cultivation 'vivid' and 'romantic', while finding woods and mountains 'desert', 'wild' and 'bleak'.

> The prospect before me affording nothing for the most part but a scene of wild woods and bleak uninhabited mountains, I turned towards the south, and beheld Kingston in a most majestic and expanded view below me. A beautiful enclosed plain, enlivened by cultivation, occupied the intermediate and spacious landscape; beyond it appeared the ocean, glistening to an immeasurable extent, while the brown inaccessible mountains darkened the fore ground of the picture.[15]

Yet what is it that enlivens the scene of cultivation? Implicit in this description is the idea that cultivation of the 'West Indies' is owed to the European introduction of slavery. Ignoring the ugliness of the slave labour that went into making these 'beautiful' scenes of well-cultivated land becomes a justification for slavery. The perception of slaves' villages as in some sense scenic adds to the implicit anti-abolitionist message, while any idea of the abolition of slavery would threaten to return such lovely scenes of cultivation to 'waste' or what in Jamaica was called 'ruinate'. Many travellers echoed this emotive and implicitly ideological vision of landscape shaped by cultivation, formed into groves and domestic enclaves set amongst natural splendour. Captain J.E. Alexander described the landscape of coffee plantations around Georgetown in Granada, on the eve of emancipation in 1833, as if it were the kind of map found in eighteenth-century engravings of well-ordered slave plantations:

> From the parterre before this charming dwelling a beautiful map was spread out before us. A succession of hill and dale descended to the sea-shore; there were cultivated fields bright with the sugar-cane; verdant slopes studded with orange trees, with fruit yellow and golden, like that of the Hesperides, whilst bananas, shaddocks, guava, and mangoe trees were equally abundant. White houses were to be seen here and there among the woodland scenery, and in the far distance were the sails of the coasting vessels.[16]

Here again a kind of rhetoric of presence informs a mastery of the landscape, with the coasting vessels hinting at the circuits of trade which maintain the productive capacity of the land of slavery. Contrast this reference to the Hesperides to Thomas Carlyle's vitriolic attack on Haiti: 'Let him [the black West Indian] by his ugliness, idleness, rebellion, banish all white men from the West Indies and make it all one Haiti, – with little or no sugar growing, black Peter exterminating black Paul, and where a garden of the Hesperides might be, nothing but a tropical dog-kennel and pestiferous jungle' (Carlyle 1850, cited in C. Hall 1992: 272). Here the rhetoric of presence is made explicitly into a rhetoric of white presence in the Caribbean, bolstered by the vehemently anti-Haitian Africanist rhetoric of the European imperial project in the Caribbean (Sheller 2000). Ending slavery would lead, these writers imply, to a ruined wilderness.

In sum, I have argued in this section that an earlier instrumental interest in the natural products of the Caribbean and their uses (which drew heavily on indigenous knowledge and practices) shifted, in the eighteenth century, to a scenic appreciation of landscapes as allegorical representations of cultivation and human progress. In both cases ways of seeing the island landscape involved movement through it and the recording of images which served as iconic representations of Europe's relation to the Caribbean and of an entirely new sense of global nature. In the age of 'discovery', interest in the New World was largely acquisitive and depictions conveyed the utility of specific plants and information on how to cultivate and use them. Images of nature began to function in a new way, bereft of symbolic encrustation and inserted into an economy of acquisition. By the eighteenth century there was a greater sense of the social uses of landscape, the power and mastery encoded in certain kinds of land use, and an emotional investment in the constructive project of harnessing land to generate capital. Viewers became more educated in a painterly aesthetic, which drew on existing notions of the picturesque. The perspectives of both McKinnen and Alexander suggest they were composing the scenery of the Caribbean from the kinds of subject positions which Gregory refers to as 'viewing platforms' and 'vantage points' (Gregory 1999), as safe locations from which pre-scripted 'sights' can be taken in. As I shall discuss further in Chapter 4, such views drew on the traditions of Orientalist imagery of exotic lands of great wealth and cultivation, highlighting human control and the 'civilising' hand.

With the rise of Romanticism in the late eighteenth century, however, European feeling for certain kinds of landscape would begin to turn towards a taste for places that appeared to be wild, untamed, and untouched by man. A visualisation of primitivism and primal nature would increasingly characterise textual constructions of the Caribbean, though this was by no means unique to the Caribbean. Duncan and Gregory suggest that,

> Romanticism marked a post-Enlightenment remapping of the space of representation: it dethroned the sovereignty of Reason and glorified unconstrained impulse, individual expression and the creative spirit. It celebrated what Cardinal (1997) calls the 'agitation of personal perception' over objective observation . . . Central to romantic travel was a passion for the wildness of nature, cultural difference, and the desire to be immersed in local colour.
>
> (Duncan and Gregory 1999: 6)

This aesthetic is linked to the rise of the 'sublime' in nature, and the desire to travel to places such as the 'wilderness' of North America or the Lake District in England (Macnaghten and Urry 1998). While Colin Campbell (1987) has shown how the affective self-indulgence and hedonism at play in modern consumerism arose out of currents within European Protestantism, its origins have also been linked to the encounter of Europeans with colonial 'contact zones' (Pratt 1992; Thomas 2000). While it was the rise of this Romantic aesthetic that enabled European travellers to see the wild uncultivated side of the Caribbean in a positive light, the converse could also be argued: that it was the European encounter with the Tropics that fed into the development of the Romantic aesthetic. As I shall show in the following section, this new mode of moving through and envisioning Caribbean landscapes led away from the slave plantation as a picturesque scene, especially given the emerging abolitionist critique of slavery. However, it also revived a pre-Enlightenment discourse of primitive nature and natural resource use, which justified new modes of European and North American intervention in the Caribbean.

Entering paradise: adventure books, military ventures, and Caribbean cruising

If the early modern era denaturalised the Caribbean landscape by appropriating it and turning it into collected and ordered botanical knowledge, the Enlightenment era produced a 'cultured up' nature (Franklin *et al.* 2000) in which the Caribbean was civilised, planted like a garden, and turned into a scene of progress. In the Romantic era, though, much of the Caribbean was again 'renaturalised' as virgin wilds, to become a 'second nature' seemingly 'untouched' by man. In contrast to the eighteenth-century depictions of the most desirable parts of the

Caribbean as the highly cultivated landscape of plantations, in the nineteenth century another image began to reassert itself, one that re-valorised the desert isle vision of *Robinson Crusoe*. An emerging artistic appreciation of the sublime allowed for a reinvention of tropical nature in a more romantic genre, particularly in post-emancipation contexts. As early as the late eighteenth century landscape artists such as George Robertson began to paint a sublime vision of Caribbean nature, which was spread throughout Europe by the famous German naturalist Alexander von Humboldt (Poupeye 1998: 33–5; Pratt 1992). While scenes of cultivation still remained, this view of the tropical landscape became increasingly noticeable in popular travel literature, and with it new ways of moving through that landscape took hold.

French Romantic writers such as Chateaubriand and Rousseau were also influential. For example, writing in 1843, Granier de Cassagnac described the natural scenery of Guadeloupe in terms of how much it would impress 'the European':

> It is impossible to explain to those who have not experienced this American nature, at once so vigorous and so gentle, its innumerable and nameless beauties. The most charming little nooks and mysterious pleasure grounds, which art has designed in France, do not equal the most wild corner of these coffee plantations. . . . The European eye, habituated to the easy floral aspect of Normandy woods, or to the rustic byways of Gasconny, stops fascinated by the cyclopean aspect of this nature, which exaggerates all proportions; and it is with a kind of stupor and humility that one contemplates the colossal ferns, which the farmers do not cut, and which form one of the most precious resources of tropical timber.[17]

This imagery of colossal and impenetrable tropical forests dwarfs the scale of human intervention in the Caribbean, as if plantations had hardly made an ecological impact, and again it is the disembodied 'European eye' which 'sees' this scene, rather than a particular person. Cassagnac's work, like others, was also a defence of slavery and a critique of the use made of natural productivity by supposedly improvident free people of colour, both in Guadeloupe and in Haiti. As he concludes, following a long attack on the permanent primitivism of Africans, 'Despite everything that ignorant philanthropists may pretend, the servitude of Africans in the Antilles, far from brutalising them, elevates and ennobles them more than I could ever say' (ibid.: 240). Thus romantic stylisation of landscapes was closely tied to moral judgements and the drawing of racial boundaries.

Indeed an increasingly 'naturalised' and primordial view of Caribbean nature began to emerge in the mid-nineteenth century, with the emphasis on its wilder, primitive aspects. The English novelist Charles Kingsley popularised this style of romantic tropical scenery in books such as *At Last: A Christmas in the West Indies* (1871). Here mechanically reproduced engraved images such as 'A Tropic Beach' (Plate 2.3), and 'The High Woods' (Plate 2.4) codified a genre of tropical drawing

Plate 2.3 Tropical Edenism as 'renaturalisation'.
'A Tropic Beach' from Charles Kingsley, *At Last: A Christmas in the West Indies* (London, Macmillan & Co., 1873). Reproduced courtesy of the British Library.

Plate 2.4 Armchair adventure.
'The High Woods' from Charles Kingsley, *At Last: A Christmas in the West Indies* (London, Macmillan & Co., 1873). Reproduced courtesy of the British Library.

of remote places thick with trees and festooned with epiphytes, lianas, palms, and ferns. In the play of light and dark, foreground and distance, each of the images contains a small human figure, usually engaged in an adventure activity such as stalking or fishing, and often a wild animal such as the tortoise in the beach image, and the monkey in the forest image. The text describes the author's arrival in each of these romantic places:

> The cliffs, some thirty feet high where we stood, rose to some hundred at the mouth, in intense black and copper and olive shadows, with one bright green tree in front of the cave's mouth, on which, it seemed, the sun had never shone; while a thousand feet overhead were glimpses of the wooded mountain-tops, with tender slanting lights, for the sun was growing low, through blue-gray mist on copse and lawn high above. A huge dark-headed Balata, like a storm-torn Scotch pine, crowned the left-hand cliff; two or three young Fan-palms, just ready to topple headlong, the right-one; and beyond all, through the great gateway gleamed, as elsewhere, the foam-flecked hazy blue of the Caribbean Sea.[18]

The author here becomes an action-hero who translates the Caribbean in terms of the reader's known world (copse, lawn, Scotch pine) as he moves through scenes that come out of his experience of earlier literature of exploration and travel. Kingsley took inspiration from the early naturalist writers on the Caribbean, and imaginatively conveyed himself and his readers back to the age of 'discovery':

> It was easy, in presence of such scenery, to conceive the exaltation which possessed the souls of the first discoverers of the West Indies. What wonder if they seemed to themselves to have burst into Fairy-land – to be at such a soil, such vegetation, such fruits, what luxury must not have seemed possible to the dwellers along those shores?[19]

The 'armchair tourist' is thus invited to join in entering paradise, reinvented through his illustrations reproduced in popular publications like the *London Illustrated News*.

In contrast to McKinnen's feelings of monotony when viewing (or moving through) uncultivated land and wild woods, here such scenes become the attraction of romantic escape and adventure travel. The late nineteenth century saw a revival of piratical tales and 'Boys own' style adventure stories. *Robinson Crusoe* was reprinted in numerous illustrated versions, and the tale of survival on a desert isle took hold on the tropical imagination, replacing the eighteenth-century vision of cultivation. Contrary to the vast efforts that went into making these Caribbean landscapes hospitable to man, now they were again envisioned as natural Edens. While some celebrated the potential for escape from industrial civilisation, many more saw it as a descent into barbarism. The post-emancipation decline of plant-ations in the old colonies was coded as the fall of civilisation and regression into barbarism through the racist visions of lazy 'darkies' and unmanaged nature crowding in on once cultivated and productive colonies. Thus the imagery of sublime primitive nature, and accounts of European adventure in the island wilds, served as pleas for renewed European intervention in its economically and socially decayed colonies.

Such imagery was especially compelling for the new imperial interests of the United States, which was becoming increasingly powerful in the region, which it would soon claim as its 'backyard'. Echoing Carlyle, William Agnew Paton argued in 1888 for a US occupation of Haiti, to save it from African barbarism:

> It would be well for the Haytians – it would be their chance of redemption –
> well for the bodies and the souls of them, if some strong foreign power, or a
> committee of powers (if I may use the term), would take the island under its
> protection, and, in a spirit of enlightenment, regulate, or insist upon the
> Haytians themselves regulating, their affairs in accordance with the laws of
> Christianity and humanity. The presence of a fleet in their harbors, a few
> soldiers, a constabulary stationed in a few central positions, would encourage
> the few brave hearts that do not even yet despair of their republic to make an
> effort to check the Africanizing of the island . . . Then would begin a new era;
> from that day the regeneration of *le pays de barbares* would be assured.[20]

Though travelling as a simple tourist, Paton's grasp slips easily from viewing 'wild' landscapes to advocating seizing an entire country. It was the decay of the sugar plantations, the wildness of the mountains, and the tales of voodoo and cannibalism that informed North American views of Haiti. Echoing the earlier eighteenth-century visions of cultivation as a kind of mastery, this imperial gaze became wedded to pre-Enlightenment discourses about the 'natural fertility' of tropical lands, and produced a narrative of the need for Euro-American capability to make more productive use of this Eden. As Paton said of Dominica: 'Food is abundant, living is cheap, the island is not overcrowded; therefore the darkies have an easy time, as no one needs go hungry at any time of the year – no one, at least, who will walk into the woods, where are wild fruits and vegetables to be had at no more trouble to the would-be eater than to put forth his hand and pluck.'[21] As Hulme notes, however, 'Paton never set foot on Dominica . . . his boat merely anchored in the roadstead off Roseau while it took on passengers and mail' (Hulme 2000: 29). Paton, like so many other travel writers, visits an invented Caribbean and invents a visited Caribbean.

Pulaski Hyatt, the United States Consul in Cuba, also adopted the image of natural fertility in order to call for Cuba to be 'seized by an intelligent hand', e.g. the hand of the United States occupation of 1898, the year in which he wrote:

> On account of her wonderful garden, fruit, and agricultural resources – impos-
> sible of appreciation unless seen – which to the visitor from the unwilling soil
> and freezing winters of the North seem like a rapturous dream, Cuba has been
> proudly styled 'The Pearl of the Antilles.' Only the most positive indolence and

shiftlessness, and the long-applied withering hand of an oppressive government, have prevented Cuba from being, because of these resources alone, one
of the most, if not the most, prolific and profitable spots in the worlds . . . no
opportunity is more promising than this, if seized by an intelligent hand.

The 'North' is here posed as a place of intelligence, from which industrious
Americans can more effectively take hold of the 'prolific' and 'profitable' nature
of a dream-like Cuba. His entire book was written as a guide to prospective North
American entrepreneurs who might wish to exploit the 'resources and opportunities' of Cuba, the seizure of which is justified by its 'shiftless' and 'indolent'
inhabitants. He went on to list the many areas of agriculture and forestry in which
Cuba could surpass even California:

> Fruits yield with prodigal profuseness. Southern California, indeed, is far
> outclassed by Cuba, with its bananas, pineapples, oranges, mangoes, figs,
> lemons, limes, citrons, zapotas, pomegranates, dates, soursaps, sapodillas,
> guava, aguacate pears, mammees, custard and rose apples; its cocoanuts,
> almonds, and filberts, and innumerable other fruits and nuts. . . . The forests
> of Cuba abound in numberless hard, rare, and dye woods of the finest grain
> and colors, both somber and brilliant, suitable for practical and ornamental
> purposes, including mahogany, sabicu, rosewood, redwood, logwood, fustic,
> majagua, bamboo, and ebony. There is an abundance of lignum-vitae, so
> much sought after in the manufacture of block-sheaves, and of heavy balls
> used in bowling alleys, and of lancewood – exported for carriage shafts,
> surveyors' instruments and the like. Cedar, used for the inside of drawers and
> wardrobes, and for cigar boxes, and the tamarind, whose wood, bark, leaves,
> and flowers have an economic value, abound.[22]

Revamping Charlevoix's eighteenth-century rhetoric of acquisition, the island is
once again detailed as an economic opportunity for investors, with many new uses
for tropical hardwoods. Nature appears as prodigal, and every part of its plants
can be turned to some use. The Cubans themselves are described as incapable of
exploiting these opportunities. Hyatt concludes that 'We need to annex Cuba,
because of the great impetus it would give to all kinds of industries and business
among us. Without capital, the impoverished island will very slowly recover. After
annexation, American capital would flow there. This would mean greater wealth
for our countrymen made by them in that land.' Here the link between nature,
capital, and human mobility are clear, as the move of the US into the Caribbean
requires both human and financial capital to take hold of its 'prodigal' nature.

Charles Morris's 'handbook' to Cuba, Puerto Rico, Hawaii, and the Philippine
Islands, published in 1899, similarly described for US audiences 'our island
empire':

> In gaining these tropical islands, the United States has entered into a new and
> important business and political relation with the nations of the world.

Widely separated as they are, they possess a remarkable similarity in production. . . . By their acquisition, this country adds widely to the scope of its vegetable productions, gaining a leading place among the sugar and tobacco producers of the world, and a very prominent one among the producers of coffee and various other food substances. Its commerce with these countries bids fair to gain a great development, and their productiveness to be enormously enhanced under the stimulus of American capital and enterprise.[23]

Again we see the idea that American seizure can be justified because of the 'stimulus' it will bring to industry; Caribbean lands are in effect feminised as passive nature awaiting insemination by manly North American enterprise. Yet alongside all these gains to be made, there were also certain burdens: 'We have primitive populations to civilize, indolent populations to stimulate, hostile populations to pacify, ignorant populations to educate, oppressed populations to lift into manhood and teach the principles of liberty and the art of self-government.' Here again, the incapacity of the tropical island-dwellers to take their own economy and government in hand calls for and justifies paternalistic US intervention. Morris concludes that North Americans should rise to this challenge, for, with 'skill, energy, and enterprise, such as may be applied to this rich land in the near future under American influence, its productive powers can be greatly increased, and it may be made one of the garden spots of the earth'.[24] Earthly paradise would be restored with American ingenuity, and Caribbean populations raised to 'manhood'.[25]

As a 'denatured' nature that has been 'renaturalised' for purposes of commodification and consumption (Franklin *et al.* 2000), the Caribbean must constantly be reassembled as a primeval, untouched site of luxuriant profusion. This 'natural' assemblage is then used as the lure for economic 'development', military adventures, and tourist fantasies. Following in the footsteps of the explorers, the planters, and the armed forces, the tropical 'holiday in the sun' became a safe new means of consuming the Caribbean environment. While tourists had long visited the Caribbean, new networks of tourism developed in the late nineteenth century, as fast steam-shipping lines originally developed for the fruit trade significantly cut journey times (see Chapter 3 on the development of the banana industry). The traditional inns and guesthouses of the main towns, with their bawdy reputation (many famed as brothels), were now joined by more 'respectable' large hotels built especially for the new tourist trade, such as the Myrtle Bank Hotel in Jamaica. The Caribbean voyage was promoted as picturesque, healthful, and an escape from winter weather in the North. The ships would usually spend less than a day in port, but arrangements could be made to spend a few days in one island, and then rejoin the cruise.

Now the literature of descriptive travel was joined by a new genre, which was written specifically by tourists for the tourist market (rather than by someone framed as an explorer, adventurer, or naturalist). While occasionally dipping into history or social commentary, such works were generally aimed at describing the experience of Caribbean travel in and of itself, with no wider intellectual motive

and no explicit political purpose. Yet such 'innocent' writings are deeply implicated in what might be called a politics of the picturesque, by which the framing
of scenery became an exercise of colonial domination over Caribbean people,
informed by literary precedents. Books like Kingsley's were extremely influential
in framing how tourists conceived of, perceived, and experienced the Caribbean.
The English tourist Sady Brassey, for example, wrote of her visit to a house in
Trinidad as being:

> exactly what I had always imagined the residence of a West Indian planter to
> be like. I felt, as I sat in the cool shady room, and looked at the gay vista of
> flowers, fruit and foliage that was visible through every opening, as though I
> must be living among the scenes of one of the story-books which I had read
> so often, or that I was absolutely realising one of the many visions of
> childhood.[26]

Brassey's view of tropical nature is somewhat unusual for being composed from a
domestic interior, suggesting a female subjectivity oriented toward a more still
relation to space. Nevertheless, it still draws on childhood precedents to compose
the scene, and references the West Indian planter's mastery of the land.

More typical is a moving masculine viewer like Paton, whose views of Haiti and
Dominica I have already noted. He too drew on stereotypical visions of the
picturesque in his 1888 account of a 'Voyage in the Caribbees', travelling by
steamer from New York for a winter cruise through the Lesser Antilles. Arriving in
Antigua, Paton rode through the island to see the scenery:

> At intervals along the road we passed darkies of every age, of both sexes, on
> their way to or from town, carrying baskets of fruits and vegetables; we heard
> some of them singing, but as we approached they stepped aside to make way
> for us, and watched us in silence, always ready and delighted to return our
> greetings. Close to some of the negro shanties were little gardens planted
> with potatoes, yams, pea-bushes, arrowroot, and the like. These picturesque
> hovels, in appearance little better then New England chicken-houses . . . have
> no chimneys, for all cooking is done in the open air, over charcoal fires.[27]

As in earlier travel literature the scenery is narrated in terms of the author's
movement through it, viewing the local dwellings as picturesque even though their
poverty is made apparent. His terminology reflects the everyday racism of the
northern United States, while his idea of going 'down the islands' and viewing
the friendly 'darkies' suggests a sense of proprietorship and being at home as he
moves through this landscape. His condescending and intrusive 'tourist gaze'
(Urry 1991) turns local life into part of the tourist experience, and I shall pursue
further in Part II the modes of objectification (and hence consumption) of human
bodies in such writing.

The key point I want to emphasise for now is the way in which moving through
the islands and viewing 'the scenery' was not simply about a relation to the

landscape, but also was about a relationship to Caribbean people. As James Duncan argues, the picturesque 'is not simply a way of seeing, it is simultaneously a way of doing, a way of world-making' (Duncan 1999: 153). Whether in British India or the British West Indies, the same formulas applied: 'occasionally the native is summoned to appear before the reader. But the native is certainly not summoned in order to speak . . . but rather to be seen, to stand in for the Orient [or in our case the Caribbean], which is to say to add to the picturesqueness of the scene' (ibid.: 157). Tourists enjoyed privileges of moving through the islands both by land and by sea, gaining a kind of overview (or 'viewing platform') that allowed them to construct 'local' people as rooted to the place, unchanging scenery as 'natural' as tropical nature itself was made to appear. While my focus here is on the late nineteenth and early twentieth century, I would suggest that such relations of asymmetrical gazing continue to inform relations between tourists and Caribbean inhabitants. The picturesque vision of the Caribbean continues to be a form of world-making which allows tourists to move through the Caribbean, and to see Caribbean people simply as scenery.

Through visions of the picturesque, travellers constructed and put into practice a relation of colonial domination. In 1889, Owen T. Bulkeley wrote a 'guide for settlers in the British West Indies and tourists' companion'. His aim was to encourage renewed English settlement, investment, and tourism in the region, where 'a new and enchanting field is opened out by a tour up or down these islands, as good hotels and boarding-houses may be found in most of them, and others are springing up'.[28] Promoting sports activities like fishing and hunting, and the beautiful scenery illustrated by engravings copied from Kingsley's novels, he had this to say about arrival in Barbados:

> We are moreover instantly besieged by a fleet of craft of all descriptions, manned by shouting, swearing, and apparently pugilistic darkies. The din is indescribable. As we look over the steamer's side and watch the swarms there, waiting permission to storm the deck in quest of passengers and their impedimenta, we must think of the time when the grandparents or parents were slaves, and then we shall cease to wonder that – having been so suddenly freed from the white man's thrall, some fifty-six years ago, without due prep-aration for their after duties as co-citizens with their former oppressors – they and theirs should still retain their coarse manners and expressions; yet the ameliorating influences of education have already worked wonders, and much is expected from the rising generation.[29]

Although these 'coarse' scenes might detract from the tourist's pleasure and expectations of a desert isle, Bulkeley soon finds enjoyment in the throngs. It 'is a favourite amusement', he writes, 'to throw from the verandah copper and even silver coins to be scrambled for by the darkies below; old and young, men, women, and even children, doing everything they can to induce one to throw a coin into their hats, hands, or aprons, many a handsome dish of fruit coming to grief in the struggle for money'. The local people were so many servants, clowns, and workers for the intending colonist. As he pointed out to prospective settlers in Tobago, they could find 'cheap and good land. Indentured coolies may be had for the asking; so that intending colonists may reckon on cheap and effective labour.'[30]

Charles Stoddard, editor of the *New York Observer*, also enjoyed his Caribbean cruise in 1895. He too describes 'naked, dark-skinned youths . . . begging to dive for silver coins', and later enjoys 'the fun of seeing a mob of negro men and women scramble after dinner in the street for bits of silver which were lavishly scattered among them like corn among a flock of chickens'.[31] Influenced by Kingsley, he is impressed by the beauty of Dominica, where 'language utterly fails to describe the richness and beauty and variety of trees and shrubs and flowers and greens and colors in nature, which ravished our eyes. Odors, delicious and sensuous, filled the air, and the place seemed in all respects a woodland paradise.'[32] Yet the people within these landscapes are constantly reduced to animals or servants. He describes St. Vincentians as 'not idle, dissipated, or wicked, but only lacking in ambition. Like most of the negroes in the islands, they prefer to be governed rather than to govern . . . it seems to be almost impossible to apply the notions of civilization to them.'[33] Thus the natural landscape and the primitive people again seem to define a Caribbean picturesque which is ripe for American intervention.

Such accounts not only seem to have contributed to the desire of more British and American tourists to visit the West Indies, but also constructed the terms on which such visits would be conducted. Around the turn of the century companies such as the Royal Mail Steam Packet Company began to promote tours. Their 1901 guide listed a selection of six different itineraries, leaving from Southampton between 11 December and 19 February 1901. The Atlantic crossing took twelve days, and the ship spent two weeks in the islands, delivering and picking up mail. The guide promoted the 'opportunities for landing and sight-seeing at the various Islands', including such activities as driving up to the Morne in St. Lucia, a ride up a valley in Dominica, boating excursions, picnics, good sea bathing in St. Thomas, and a visit to the Botanic Gardens in Grenada. A longer stay in Trinidad allowed time 'to visit the Maracas Falls, Blue Basin, Coolie Village, and Botanic Gardens (where a Band plays in the afternoon)'.[34] Rides, excursions, and movement through each island are crucial to the touring experience. And, the chance to see 'Coolies' is promoted as part of the interesting scenery as much as seeing various landscapes.

Such encounters were pre-scripted by existing accounts and expectations. E.A. Hastings Jay wrote of his 'Four Months Cruising in the West Indies' in 1900 in terms of the scenery's relation to earlier literary representations of the tropics:

> Here, for the first time, was the tropical beach! How often, from childhood, I had tried to picture it from Kingsley's vivid descriptions or the histories of the early explorers. There were the cocoa-nut palms, with clusters of green cocoa-nuts growing all along the sea-line out of the soft white sand, with beautiful rainbow colours in the water as it moved lazily backwards and forwards, glittering in the brilliant sunlight.[35]

For such travellers the entire archive of travel writing that we have considered thus far informed their experience of the Caribbean. Even as they engaged in the lived experience of the tropics they always constructed it in relation to the vivid Caribbean in their imaginations. Again he quotes Kingsley:

> I looked out and was astonished to see the dark mountains of St Vincent looming up before me . . . and looking very grand and mysterious in the grey dawn. As the daylight increased, one could see that every peak was clothed to its very summit with thick forest. The colouring was exquisite, the rising sun just illuminating the forests with a soft glow. Before us was a lovely crescent-shaped bay . . . But the forests! As I gazed upon them I felt that here, indeed, were the tropics in all their splendour. My whole soul seemed to form the words 'At Last!' as I felt, like Kingsley, a deep sense of thankfulness that it had fallen to my lot to see them.[36]

These literary and visual representations of the Caribbean deeply informed Euro-American emotional engagement with the Caribbean, which was already mapped in their 'unconscious' before ever setting foot there.

Kingsley's imagery also influenced Susan de Forest Day, another visitor from New York, who had similar motives of rediscovering a childhood fantasy, though sometimes reality did not live up to expectations:

> We were going to the West Indies, for that best of all reasons, simply because we wanted to. We longed to see the palm trees and sugar cane, to eat the luscious fruits and to float over summer seas, basking in the warm tropical sun, while the trade wind softly fanned our brows . . . Without any real reason we at first find St. Thomas a trifle disappointing . . . Perhaps those bare, barren, rugged mountains, whose counterparts we had seen time and again in our own everyday America, did not come up to the ideal we had formed of the wealth and luxuriance of tropical vegetation – an ideal almost unconsciously derived from the old geographies of our childish days in which the picture of a dense jungle, with serpents gracefully festooned from tree to tree and a monkey in one corner, always was the symbol of the torrid zone.[37]

Having come in search of clichés, and wanting to immerse her body in the feel of the Tropics, Day is thrown out of her reverie by the particularity of St. Thomas as a quite 'untropical' place. While tourists on cruises generally noted the name of each place at which they stopped, they also blurred together an overall impression of 'the' Caribbean as a singular entity. It is the editing out of things that do not fit which enables this fantasy 'torrid zone' to be unceasingly packaged and sold for Northern consumers.

New guidebooks written to cater to the tourist market also capitalised on the classic literary images. James Johnston wrote one of the early guidebooks promoting Jamaica to the British and North American tourist market as 'the New Riviera' and touting its benefits as a health resort:

now the mere mention of the island's name conjures up the vision of a blue sky over a blue sea, in which is set a beautiful island of luxurious vegetation and lovely scenery; fragrant with the odour of spices and flowers, with an atmosphere refreshed by invigorating sea breezes. . . . Here is a veritable Mecca for the invalid, for what pilgrimage could hold out a greater reward than restored health?[38]

Promoting the Imperial Direct Mail Steam Service, and the famous hotels at Myrtle Bank and Constant Spring, advertisements in this book depict tourist activities such as shopping for 'Coolie jewellery . . . Indian draperies . . . Chinese curios . . . Obeah heads . . . Curios, seeds and beans' as well as postcards, photographs, and views of the island. The items for sale suggest that Caribbean culture had to be created and displayed so that it could be packaged and consumed by tourists.

As Peter Hulme (2000) argues in relation to Dominica, a series of European and US visitors to the island's Carib reserve in the late nineteenth and early twentieth century wrote narratives of travel, encounter, observation, and fantasy in which they invented the Caribs as a dying race, a remnant of colonial conquest. The US journalist Stephen Bonsal, for example, whom Hulme describes as one of the first visitors identifiable as 'a tourist in the modern sense', determined upon visiting the Caribs by night in order to see them in their wild majesty, unsullied by the modern world. After a six-hour journey across the island (probably in 1907), Bonsal and his tourist companions 'remain hidden in the shrubbery, like twitchers, waiting for the Caribs to bestir themselves' at dawn (Hulme 2000: 93). The 'guiding view' informing Bonsal's romantic and aesthetic gaze, argues Hulme, is found in his quotation from the historian Brooks Adams's *The New Empire* (1902): 'the Caribbean archipelago must either be absorbed by the economic system of the United States or lapse into barbarism.'[39] As I have suggested above, and shall argue further in Chapter 4, Anglo-American visitors continually constructed the Caribbean through a trope of barbarism, which allowed them to glide easily from viewing the tropical landscape as romantically wild to interpreting its inhabitants as primitive 'racial types'. Support for military conquest thus went hand in hand with romantic tourism and its characteristic constructions of racial boundaries, condensing around certain ideas of immersion in a 'wild nature' re-created in the 'renaturalised' paradise of the Caribbean.

Conclusion

In this chapter I have argued that the Caribbean is an invented landscape that has been both denaturalised and renaturalised, in transatlantic processes of consumption that knit together the viewing of landscapes and social relations of power between people. From the collection of botanical knowledge in the sixteenth and seventeenth centuries, to the rhetoric of presence in the rational views of the eighteenth century, and finally the romantic imperialism of the late nineteenth century, nature has been made to do different kinds of imaginary work. Each period has produced a different kind of iconicity. The first depended on the isolation of particular useful plants from their surroundings and their imbuing with indigenous knowledge that could be appropriated in Europe. These lists, catalogues, and encyclopaedias of botanical knowledge allowed Europeans to imagine for the first time the finitude of the world, the complexity, variety, but also knowable limits of nature on this fragile planet.[40] The second visual regime depended on the iconicity of the god's-eye view of a scenic panorama, placing the viewer in a position of mastery. This scene operated as an allegory of colonial progress and productivity through the harnessing of nature for the production of wealth. The third shift in iconicity, finally, turned to the dense tropical foliage and the deserted beach as symbols of a renaturalised Caribbean that could become a new backdrop for adventure and romance. Such a reinvention of nature, however, requires either a vigilant removal of 'local' people from the staging of nature, or their scenic incorporation into the natural paradigm, a theme I shall return to in Chapter 4.

The Caribbean became not only 'paintable' but also 'Kodakable', just as Gregory argues the sites/sights of ancient Egypt were photographically organised (Gregory 1999: 145). This is especially notable in Alfred Leader's *Through Jamaica with a Kodak* (1907), where the camera even appears on the book's cover, looming over the landscape like an alien landing craft (see Plate 2.5). In the foreground we see giant foliage, suggestive of an exotic locale and a wild shoreline, and on the horizon the Blue Mountains looming mysteriously; in between intervenes not only the technology of the Kodak camera, but also the cruising steamer that will bring tourists to these 'inaccessible' islands. The Caribbean characteristically becomes somewhere to move 'through' in order to take away images and experiences.

In so far as Caribbean nature has been reinvented in a number of guises, its transformation is symbolically encompassed in the shifting cultural meanings of the palm tree. The history of visual and written representations of the palm tree in European encounters with the Caribbean is significant because, as we have already seen, the palm deeply informed initial European impressions of the region's unusual flora, becoming crucial to the depiction of the islands' natural scenery. In the early modern period they were new and useful plants, to be incorporated into European understanding, collected and studied. In the scenic economy of the Enlightenment era, royal palms were often planted to mark out the boundaries of plantations, scrawling property claims across the sky. Yet the palm also served as a major symbol of African-Caribbean liberty. At the time of the French Revolution the palm took the place in the Caribbean of the French Liberty Tree in republican iconography and symbolism. It was used most prominently on the National Seal of Haiti, appearing on the Haitian flag and currency, but it also occurs as a marker of emancipation in Jamaica and other islands (Sheller 2000). Yet these revolutionary meanings of the palm (and any earlier indigenous meaning they may have had) have been usurped by more anodyne tourist imagery.[41]

From nineteenth-century romantic prints to twentieth-century tourist brochures, the palm is ubiquitous and carries the weight of meanings that condense

Plate 2.5 Kodakable Caribbean.
Cover image from Alfred Leader, *Through Jamaica With a Kodak* (Bristol, John Wright & Co., 1907). Reproduced courtesy of Bristol Central Library.

around the term 'tropical'. In the nineteenth century the palm was corralled into Victorian 'palm-houses', and domesticated as a garden feature; today there is a growing trade in hardy palms that have been bred for the Northern gardening industry, to add drama, architectural shapes, and an exotic warmth to temperate gardens. The image of the palm sums up the Caribbean tropics so effectively that it has been turned into a brand icon and marketing logo on a wide range of products and businesses associated with the Caribbean, from Island Records to the Island Trading Company. Released from the utilitarian purposes it may have suggested to writers in the seventeenth century, and from the landscapes of power it may have suggested to writers in the eighteenth century, it has become a symbol of leisure, relaxation, and carefree living. The iconicity of the Caribbean has thus been reduced from the powerful impact it had both as an entirely new world that transformed European relations to nature, and as a materialisation of the power of European capitalism to transform the world. Now it seems only to beckon a hedonistic tourism, an easygoing escape from the world, perhaps a seductive immersion in bodily pleasures.

Plants and tropical greenery still serve as powerful symbols of the imagined nature of the Caribbean, the 'Eden' that is imagined before European intrusion. Tobago, for example, lays claim to 'the oldest forest reserve in the Western hemisphere' (founded in 1763), and is promoted as a place where you can 'see the islands as Columbus first saw them'. Dominica, too, is described as 'still the primitive garden that Columbus first sighted in 1493. An area of tropical rainforests, flowers of incredible beauty and animals that exist nowhere else in the world.'[42] The island promotes its unspoiled rainforests, fresh water lake, and the twin Trafalgar waterfalls as a prime ecotourism destination. Yet this image of the 'Nature Island' is often at odds with the development of larger markets such as the cruise ship sector (Wiley 1998), not to mention the development of hydropower projects using the same natural resources. While the hotel industry requires an endless supply of 'pristine' beaches, 'untouched' coves, and 'emerald' pools, many islands struggle with the water and sewage demands of the hotel industry, and sewage is returned to the same sea in which guests swim. Although many coral reefs have been severely degraded in the Caribbean (Spalding *et al.* 2001), they have simply been replaced with man-made reefs and the popularity of diving trips continues to grow unabated. In every case 'nature' is being made to work overtime as eco-ideal, as natural 'resource', and as the ground for economic development.

It hardly needs pointing out that the same old myths of the Caribbean resort are resold *ad nauseam* today. With the development of the package holiday and the cruise ship industry it became increasingly easy for tourists to get to the Caribbean and experience its charms in a pre-packaged, easily-digestible form. Such tourism depends heavily on the branding and marketing of Paradise, to such an extent that the myths have seeped into everyday perceptions and understandings. In a British Airways magazine, for example, a report on the building of a new four-lane highway across the entire north coast of Jamaica states, with not a hint of irony, that it is ok, 'because you can't really do long-term environmental damage to Jamaica. The island is so abundantly tropical it's virtually vandal-proof. People have tried to deforest it, but the trees just grew back. The ground is so fertile that even the fence posts that the Koreans [who are building the road] banged into the earth to mark off the new road have sprouted branches.'[43] Nature here becomes a kind of self-generating power that can be endlessly consumed and can withstand all that human consumption can impose upon it. Calling up the 'bounteous serendipity' of the earliest European encounters with the iconic islands of the West Indies, the north coast road becomes the 'road to a new Eden'.

Describing nature as an autopoetic or self-generating life form removes the need for any kind of consumer guilt or anxiety. Such carefree guiltlessness is often transferred to the tourist relationship with local people. The same writer, in a somewhat confused metaphor, concludes that in Jamaica 'you'll be in the nearest thing we have on earth to the Garden of Eden, and to make it even better, it's after Eve tempted Adam with the apple'. Thus the new Eden is a perpetual garden in which sexuality can run rampant; rather than being expelled from the garden, humanity can indulge all the temptations of fertile nature and fertile sex, without guilt. Vandal-proof nature serves as a transparent metonym for sexual access to the 'natives' without consequence; the laws of nature and of morality have both apparently been temporarily suspended in this fantasy Jamaica, more vested in Hedonism than in Edenism.

The vision of the Caribbean as a second Eden remains evocative, even when facing up to the ugly histories of slavery and colonialism. As Derek Walcott puts it,

> an old map of the islands does not look like a cartography of imagined paradises, but like what they were in historical reality: a succession of crusted scabs with the curve of the archipelago a still-healing welt. No metaphor is too ugly for the hatred and cruelty the West Indies endured; yet their light is paradisal, their harbors and shielding hills, their flowering trees and windy savannas Edenic. . . . No historical collection acknowledges the fact that the beauty of the Caribbean islands could have helped the slave survive, whenever these intervals, like the light through rain clouds over a sea of sugar cane, or shadows moving over the Jamaican mountains, fell, and, in their serenity, exacted some strength, because what is surely another beauty is the strength, the endurance of the survivor.[44]

His return to an Edenic vision and poetic effort to reclaim the beauty of the Caribbean for those who survived its brutal history suggests that even at the limits of history, at the threshold of the postcolonial, there is still no escape from the cultural assemblage of Caribbean nature. But there is a kind of re-claiming of place and a raw resistance to consumption. However invented Caribbean nature may be, it has material effects and emotional affects, real consequences of consumption, which move people along different itineraries and different kinds of journeys.

If the texts considered in this chapter have predominantly emphasised the visual consumption of Caribbean landscapes and nature, in the following chapter

I counter this ocular bias with a wider sensuous engagement of the smell, taste, and bodily sensations of the transatlantic encounter. I focus on the mobilities of people and substances, which brought Europeans into risky proximity with the temptations of the New World Eden, and brought the natural products of the Caribbean flowing into European consumer societies. The full effect of the Caribbean on Europe cannot be gauged without delving into the ways in which something of it got into European and North American bodies and cultures, tunnelling into their most intimate interior realms. In following the products of transatlantic commodity culture into European public and private spaces it would be tempting to suggest that the Caribbean somehow exceeded the acquisitive grasp of European culture, and consumed consumer cultures from within. Certainly the excess of consumption was of concern to European commentators, who saw in it a slippery slope to moral corruption. But I will argue instead that the very idea of the excessiveness of Caribbean nature and its limitless consumption is a key part of a normalisation of the relation of (neo)colonial domination.

3 Tasting the Tropics

From sweet tooth to banana wars

One of the greatest stimuli to the consumption of the Caribbean has been the voracious pursuit of food, drink, and stimulants. This chapter explores the relation between consumer, producer, and the fruits of labour that flow between them within a transatlantic economy in which a Northern taste for tropical produce was created and incited. My aim is to show how interventions by 'consuming publics' in the provisioning networks of particular edible products such as sugar, coffee, or tropical fruit rest on a moral deployment of the body of the ethical consumer, from anti-slavery ethics to fair trade ethics today.[1] These ethical interventions in global trade are achieved by the framing of moral economies of the sensuous body in which the ethical consumer is produced via a direct identification with the suffering body of the labouring producer, whose blood, sweat, and tears are imagined as literally infusing the commodity. Ethical consumer movements ranging from the sugar boycotts of the anti-slavery movement in the eighteenth century to current debates over global trade liberalisation have attempted to bring these two bodies into closer proximity, even solidarity, by reflecting on how they directly touch each other through the commodity. In detailing some specific cases of the alignment of Northern consumers with Caribbean producers, I explore both the transformational potential and limitations of such strategies, and the ways in which our bodies remain ethically implicated in the contest between free trade and fair trade.

Over the past decade historical work on consumption and consumer societies has been transformed by what Jean-Christophe Agnew calls a 'backdating' of the birth of European consumer culture to the early modern period (Agnew 1994: 23). Some key examples of this change in historical perspectives on consumer culture appear in the landmark collection edited by John Brewer and Roy Porter, *Consumption and the World of Goods* (1994). Consumer culture now applies to everything from fifteenth-century Italy and sixteenth-century Holland to eighteenth-century England and twentieth-century America. Furthermore, these analyses of consumer society 'shift the lens of economic history from the study of industrial production and the proletarianization of labor to the study of private demand and the marketing of goods' (Bermingham 1995: 3). Instead of production and industrialisation, consumers have come to take centre stage, bringing with them complex drives of pleasure and desire, and hybrid economies of symbolic and material circulation. This shift parallels the cultural turn in history, and the growing interest in material culture and visual culture.

Given that the early modern consumer cultures discussed in this historiography are all thoroughly grounded in wealth produced by the slave trade and slave plantations, one would be remiss not to ask how slavery fits into this new history of 'material things'. Surprisingly, though, there is little or no mention of slavery or the slave trade in the Brewer and Porter volume (apart from a brief aside in John Wills Jr's essay on the consumption of Asian goods in Europe). Thus Simon Schama contributes an essay on 'the empire of things' in Dutch still-life painting, without referring to the origin of those things in Dutch colonial commerce, in particular the pre-eminent role of the Dutch in the slave trade in the sixteenth century. Chandra Mukerji describes how seventeenth-century French formal gardening was 'deeply entwined in an economic internationalism and cultural cosmopolitanism' based on the collection of exotic plants, yet again has nothing to say about the colonial world from which these 'exotic' plants originated. Agnew jumps awkwardly from a discussion of early modern Europe to the twentieth-century United States, leaving a yawning historical chasm in between, a massive rift in the study of consumer culture sitting squarely over the fault-line of slavery.[2] While there is slightly more attention to empire in the subsequent volume edited by Anne Bermingham and Brewer (1995), the slavery-based transatlantic economy that was driving the growth in consumption remains largely peripheral to the study of 'image, object, and text' in the European consumption of culture.

Through the work of Mukerji, Schama, Colin Campbell, and others, the modern capitalist consumer emerges as a complex bundle of impulses towards spending and saving, acquisitiveness and asceticism, gratification and deferment. Puritanism and hedonism occur as a central contradiction within capitalist modernity, which comes to be objectified within material culture (Miller 1997). These contradictions within consumer society, I argue, were closely related to concerns over the domestic and personal effects of the moral corruption of empire, associated both with its exotic luxuries and with the system of slavery itself. This chapter ranges over a wide historical terrain, from the sixteenth century until today, across Europe and the Americas, but in each case I am concerned with the ethical contradictions surrounding taste, food, and eating. That is to say, an ethics by which food mediates an intimate relationship toward others, as it passes from producer's hand to consumer's mouth and comes to be recognised as a specifically embodied relationship between bodies 'here' and bodies 'there' (cf. Ahmed 2000). How did edible substances come to objectify the contradictions of the system of slavery? How could simple products like sugar come to materially and sensuously link the suffering bodies of producers with the satiated bodies of consumers? Can eating and drinking 'bring home' the contradictions of empire?

I begin with the emergence of a European 'taste for the Tropics', as seen in travel narratives from the era of 'discovery' and exploration in which novel foods and their alluring tastes were recorded and described with vibrant sensuous intensity. In returning to these original moments of tasting the Tropics, it becomes clear that contemporary debates over the ethics of global food markets are not new, but have deep roots in the European encounter with tropical worlds. Drawing on Schama's perceptive reading of seventeenth-century Dutch still-life painting, I will examine how the luxury of consuming tropical fruits initially figured in Dutch anxieties over colonial wealth. In the fluctuating relation between consumption and constraint, gluttony and guilt, Northern consumers have long anguished over their consumption of the Caribbean. Through various phases of the formation of Atlantic markets and cultures of consumption, this initial set of dilemmas concerning bodily indulgence and moral decay, consumer luxury and producer exploitation, natural acquisitiveness and moral restraint, have repeatedly resurfaced.

Then I turn to the heyday of West Indian sugar plantations (and the slave trade that fed them) and the emergence of the sugar–tea–coffee complex in Europe. Here I focus on the tensions between acquisitive capitalism and ethical restraint in eighteenth-century Britain in particular. The consumption of slave-produced commodities had a major impact on patterns of sociability, commerce, urbanity, and private and public life in Britain. Drawing on the work of Sidney Mintz, I track the history of Europe's 'sweet tooth' and its relation to the formation of consuming publics. The anti-slavery movement latched onto the explosion in consumption of tropical plantation commodities as a way to personalise responsibility for the enslavement of other human beings. They used sugar, in particular, as an inroad into people's hearts and into the 'privacy' of their homes, where much consumption took place.[3] Moral blame for slavery could be pinned on anyone and everyone who consumed its products. Quaker anti-slavery activists especially targeted women, who bought the products of slavery, which were depicted as soaked in African blood. I focus on the boycotts of slave-grown sugar begun in the 1790s, rekindled in the 1820s, and taken to new lengths with the Free Produce Movement of the 1850s. I argue that this is an early example of 'ethical trade', which has close parallels with contemporary fair trade and social justice movements.

In the final section I concentrate on the development of the nineteenth-century fruit trade, and especially the rise of a mass market for bananas. I will consider especially how the global flow of bananas led to the recent 'banana wars' between the European Union and the United States, which has resulted in the promotion of 'ethical bananas' by British supermarkets. In each case, I argue, Northern Atlantic patterns of consumption raise questions about the relation between foods and morality, luxuriant indulgence and an ethics of restraint, free trade and fair trade. Global trade policies today, governed by the World Trade Organisation (WTO) and multilateral agreements such as the Cotonou Convention, remain inseparable from ethical questions: what should we eat, from where, produced by whom, under what conditions? There is a wider literature on 'food systems', 'provisioning networks', and 'uneven agrarian restructuring' which I will be unable to address fully here.[4] Instead, I continue to ask how an imagined yet materialised Caribbean becomes an effect, a fantasy, a set of practices, and a context for the emergence of Western modernity.

A taste for the Tropics: consumer society and the 'embarrassment' of slavery

In the earliest accounts of the West Indies it is notable that the indulgence of the sense of tasting was crucial for Europeans who entered this 'New World' of wondrous fruits and surprising sweetness. In the late fifteenth century, as noted in Chapter 2, there was already a close association in European thought between tropical islands and ancient imagery of paradisal gardens, whether Hesperidean or Edenic (Thomas 1983; Mukerji 1994; Grove 1995). The traveller's initial taste of unusual tropical fruits and belief in the 'natural' ease of their profuse growth became central to the imagery of the West Indies and helped to lure capital investment and colonists. Yet entering this foretold tropical paradise was highly risky, and the tasting of its forbidden fruit was already biblically coded through a moral discourse about corruption and mortality, sin and redemption. Reaping the sweetness of the Tropics also involved European consumers in particularly morbid relations to the bodies of other humans – Amerindians, Africans, and later Asians – whose labouring bodies produced the comestible commodities of world trade. Images of their diseased, whipped, scarred, and mutilated bodies came to figure in European moral economies of consumption, along with imagery of the 'tropicalization' and degeneracy of the European body in the Tropics. Thus debates over the moral economy of consumption were from the beginning framed in relation to a geography of bodily health, in which flesh and blood were literally consumed by morbidity and mortality.

Some of the earliest flows of botanical substances from tropical islands back into European markets were the highly valuable plant products known as 'spices', many of which were used as medicines. The category of spice included East Indian items such as pepper, nutmeg, cloves, and cinnamon, as well as West Indian products such as allspice, cocoa, and sugar. Timothy Morton has recently examined the discursive field, which he refers to as 'the poetics of spice', in which the flow of luxury trade goods across global markets incited both acquisitive commercial capitalism and moral critiques of its luxury, excess, and over-consumption (Morton 2000a). Wolfgang Schivelbusch (1992) also examines the history of a whole range of substances, which in German are called *Genussmittel*, a category denoting 'articles of pleasure' which are eaten, drunk, or inhaled including spices and condiments as well as stimulants, intoxicants, and narcotics such as tobacco, coffee, tea, alcohol, and opium. The emergence of European capitalism via the Eastern spice trade and then its replacement by the Atlantic sugar trade revolved around the ingestion of these 'dangerous substances' (Cronin forthcoming). Articles of pleasure like tobacco and sweetened coffee had powerful physiological effects on the individual body, and troubling moral implications for the social body. In contrast to the food and drinks that are consumed as necessities and form the basis of domestic agricultural markets, these pleasurable luxury items have long been linked to global markets and to debates over their moral effects (Sombart 1967; Sekora 1977; Berry 1994).

Through enslavement of others, unlimited coercive power over bodies, and the ingestion of articles of pleasure, Europeans were acutely aware that they risked physical and moral corruption. The Dutch dominated the sixteenth- and seventeenth-century slave trade and pioneered the creation of a global trade empire stitched together by the flow of commodities and wealth from colonial peripheries back to the metropolitan core. 'During the first half of the sixteenth century,' according to Schama, the city of Antwerp 'was the site not only of a spectacular accumulation of wealth but an equally extraordinary extension of knowledge of the natural world, collected on an appropriately imperial scale.' Taking over from the fifteenth-century Florentines, the Dutch became world leaders in navigation, trade, and commerce. 'Great cosmographies and *mappae mundi*; collections of flora and fauna; entomological and botanical texts; as well as of Oriental ceramics and textiles and paintings, all came to Antwerp in a burst of cultural acquisitiveness' (Schama 1994: 485). The profusion of objects of empire and their visual representation, according to Schama, came to reflect the central moral contradictions of an emerging capitalist modernity.

In the great national museums of Europe and North America we can see the remnants of this consumer culture in its exquisitely gleaming still-life paintings. Here, perishable exotic fruits from the Americas and Africa are broken open next to delicate shells and corals from the Indies, luxuriant Turkish and Persian textiles, fine Chinese and Japanese ceramics, unfinished meat and goblets spilling wine. Schama focuses our attention on a dilemma in the interpretation of these depictions of the things caught up in the net of Dutch navigation. Roland Barthes' 1953 essay 'Le monde-objet' ('The empire of things') strongly influenced interpretations of these paintings as showing a moral vacancy based on the entrepreneurial marriage of the 'domestic empire of things' and the global empire of commerce. For Barthes, these paintings were an 'exercise of power' in which 'art [was] mobilized to service the appropriation of matter'. His analysis suggested that 'Dutch culture, peculiarly egregious, naïvely vulgar in this respect, essentially consisted of what could be classified, inventoried, priced, owned and displayed. . . . The paintings that showed off this booty acted, then, as a form of augmented, or doubly-declared proprietorship, signifying the possession, not just of the expensive painting, but the class of objects itemized' (Schama 1994: 478).[5] The Dutch still-life paintings of 'the edible made visible' and the noble portraiture showing African servants alongside other valued luxuries were for Barthes a straightforward 'celebration of private property'.

However, for Schama, this reduces the 'deliberately unstable relation' which he sees in these paintings between the naturalistic and the symbolic. Rather than stating the supremacy of the material world, he argues, these paintings play upon antiphonal themes of luxury and decadence, the worldly and the eternal, materiality and spirituality, concreteness and insubstantiality. Rather than revelling in empty materialism, 'this particular commercial culture seems almost excessively anxious about both the propriety and durability of wealth. . . . Death is present at the feast' (ibid.: 482). Consumer culture thus opens up a field of ambivalence, in which the perishability of the material world undermines the pleasures of consumption. Schama's more subtle reading of the symbolism of these paintings, and more widely of 'The Embarrassment of Riches' in Dutch culture, has been influential in establishing the significance of the 'perennial combat between acquisitiveness and asceticism' in driving capitalism (Schama 1987: 338). If consumers recognise that demand drives the 'empire of things', a glimmer of moral accountability and social responsibility enters into their relation to those things. However, Schama's focus on the spiritual dilemmas of the consuming body stays within the realm of metropolitan culture, ignoring its connections to the colonial world. It is about the morality of consumption, rather than the ethics of consumer culture. Thus like other analyses of European consumer culture his also deflects attention from the enslaved bodies producing the empire of things, and thus also from the consumer's potential accountability for their enslavement. It is precisely such a recognition which was muted in the Netherlands (Drescher 1994), but which informed the much stronger British anti-slavery movement and in particular the boycotts of slave-grown produce.

Surely it is obvious that the 'embarrassment of riches' in sixteenth-century Netherlands, seventeenth- to eighteenth-century France, and eighteenth-century Britain are each linked to the 'embarrassment' of slavery? How did the triangular trade between Europe, Africa, and the Americas come to be treated as so taken for granted that it could go without saying in the study of consumer culture? Part of this blindness toward the relation between slavery and consumer culture can be attributed to cultural history's post-Marxist move away from production-oriented economic histories and labour-oriented social histories towards a concern with material things and symbolic meanings. Much of the academic literature on slavery concerns debates over modes of production and the relation of enslaved plantation labour to free wage labour. Questions of consumption only seem to arise where the commodities, material things, or goods produced by slavery are followed back to the 'domestic' scene of consumption. Thus sugar, coffee, and tobacco appear in the debates over European consumer society (e.g. Mintz 1985), but slavery itself (and the people producing these commodities) is set aside in these discussions. The historiography of slavery remains a separate sub-field from the study of 'consumer societies', while the latter oddly appear to occur without reference to the rest of the world, which thus becomes coded as non-modern and non-capitalist.

The moral dilemmas of consumption do not exist in a metropolitan vacuum, but open out into ethical dilemmas concerning Europe's relation to the world and to the people whose labour was producing the empire of things. In relation to the Caribbean, food consumption became a particularly powerful point of ethical critique both because it so intimately entered the body of the consumer, and because it so violently impinged upon the bodies of the plantation labourers enslaved to feed the consumer markets. In so far as people's bodies were implicated in consumption, anti-slavery could be framed in a way that made consumers more aware of and sensitive to their mediated yet direct relation to the enslaved bodies of suffering others. This became especially apparent due to the massive impact of tropical commodities on European diet, especially in Britain, which took over from the Netherlands as the major maritime power of the Atlantic world in the seventeenth century. In order to track the emergence of this ethical dilemma in European consumer culture, I want to take a step back from the 'high art' which concerns Schama, and begin from the far more mundane realms of popular travel writing and visual images of the Caribbean. Here we can begin to see how the tasting of exotic foods was not simply a concern of a wealthy capitalist elite, but pervaded every aspect of the movement of people and things around the Atlantic world. Travel writing depicts not only the novel articles of pleasure which fed European consumers (the world of empire flowing into Europe), but also is concerned with the everyday practices of consumption on which colonists depended for survival (the flow of Europeans into the world). In the latter case the material link between 'here and there' becomes even more clear because the tension between indulgence and restraint is located not in the symbolic realm of asceticism and spiritual redemption, but in the profane realm of the body and its potential degeneracy.

We can begin by following the routes of Caribbean produce as it made its way into European bodies and culture. Early European accounts of the New World show that they looked upon tropical landscapes first in terms of what was edible in them, and then in terms of how they could be exploited for further trade, whether in timber, metals and minerals, 'useful' plants, or humans to enslave. Columbus's journals set the pattern for this kind of promotional literature, which was developed in England in the sixteenth century by a series of propagandists for colonisation, such as Sir Humphrey Gilbert, Sir Walter Raleigh, and Richard Hakluyt. The pages of these early Caribbean travel narratives are filled with endless catalogues of fish, fowl, beast, fruits, and vegetables, and accounts of how the native Carib and Arawak peoples fished, trapped, hunted, planted, harvested, and prepared these exotic foods. The sixteenth-century Drake Manuscript, for example, introduced in Chapter 2, offered a horticultural and medical guide for prospective colonists. It depicts not only new species of plants and animals unknown to Europeans, but also indigenous methods of planting, cultivation, hunting, fishing, and food preparation (one image shows probably the earliest known European depiction of an Amerindian barbecue, accompanied with grilling instructions for meat and fish!).

Contrary to the assumption that it was only the pursuit of gold and other precious metals that drove European exploration, it was as much the desire to acquire new edible, pleasurable, and pharmaceutical substances, *things that had direct and powerful effects on the bodies of those empowered to consume them.* The most significant item of New World trade in this period was tobacco, a new and wondrous plant for Europeans. An image labelled 'Petun' in the Drake Manuscript, for example, depicts a tobacco plant and records underneath:

A special herb which the Indians use for food as well as an extremely beneficial medicine; when they are sick, they breathe in the smoke by mouth with
a straw; soon the ill humour escapes by vomiting. They often pulverize it and,
putting it in their noses, it distills several drops of water from the brain to
discharge it. It also is found very useful for toothache; laying its leaves on the

teeth, the pain disappears; it is also beneficial for alleviating eye problems and, for this, it is advisable to take the herb and steep it in water about half of a quarter of an hour and then wash one's eyes and one will experience its benefits.[6]

As in the image of the Palme (Plate 2.1) discussed above, this and other illustrations in the manuscript indicate how much Europeans depended on their indigenous 'hosts' for survival and how they sought out useful natural substances to bring back to Europe. Indigenous medical practices rather than appearing strange seem to be utterly convincing to this observer, being more advanced than those known in Europe at the time. They were learning the medicinal uses of a plant which would overwhelm European culture and health in the following centuries, and feed into a new discourse of 'addiction' which epitomises the ongoing dilemmas of indulgence and restraint (Cronin forthcoming). What is notable here is how plants and bodies were being brought into proximity in new ways, which emerged out of the material and physical mobilities of the transatlantic world.[7]

Food itself, even of the most mundane kinds, remained central to all early accounts of the New World, in part because readers knew of the difficulties of survival on 'desert isles', a favourite topic of popular literature such as pirate stories, or Defoe's *Robinson Crusoe*. Caribbean promotional literature depicts both an abundance of staples and an enticing array of new and tempting tastes. Seventeenth-century British accounts are particularly extravagant in describing foods, as in the new plantation of St. Christopher (St. Kitts) where not only are there 'cattell, goats, and hogges' available, but also iguanas, land crabs, and more to grace the table:

> Tortasses . . . Prawnes . . . divers sorts of good Sea fowle . . . Cassado . . . Potatos, Cabbages, and Radish plenty. Mayes [maize] like the Virginia wheat; we have Pine-apples, neere so bigge as an Hartichocke, but the most daintiest taste of any fruit. Plantains, an excellent and most increasing fruit; Apples, Prickell Peares, and Pease, but differing all from ours. There is Pepper . . . Sugar canes not tame, four or five foot high. . . . Gourds, Muske Melons, Water Melons, Lettice, Parsly . . . a very good fruit we call Pengromes; [and] a Pap-paw is as great as an apple, coloured like an Orange, and very good to eat.[8]

Faced with far more meagre pickings in his cold home, and far more hard labour to scrape a living from the land, the seventeenth-century Englishman hearing such an account must have felt pangs of hunger and envious longing. Yet in the early settlement period European bodies in the Caribbean teetered precipitously between fantasies of luxurious indulgence and fears of desert-isle famine, or worse, cannibalism. Was the tropical table enough to tempt him to venture investing not just capital, but even his own and his family's bodily health, in turning a profit in the West Indies?

Europeans learned how to grow many Caribbean edibles from the indigenous people they enslaved, borrowing their names and modes of preparing food and drink. Struggling to survive in thickly wooded Barbados in the late 1640s, Richard Ligon noted that 'after many tryalls, and as often failings, I learnt the secret [of making cassava flour] of an Indian woman, who shew'd me the right way of it'. Other indigenous recipes he observed included a fermented drink made from potatoes, called 'Mobbie', one from chewed cassava root, called 'Perino', and another from plantains. Indeed, Ligon reports that indigenous women were 'fetcht from other Countries' specifically to make cassava bread and Mobbie, while men were made to fish, both occupations requiring particular skills the Europeans did not possess.[9] Ligon then takes the reader on a culinary adventure through flesh, fish, fowl, and fruits. As Kim Hall perceptively argues, Ligon's *True and Exact History of Barbados* 'has more in common with the domestic manual than the travel guide. A great deal of Ligon's text is devoted to food. . . . He masters the landscape of Barbados by drawing on the familiarizing powers of the cookbook; by making everything "food", he presents the landscape as already tamed and cultivated' (K. Hall 1996: 180, 182–3).[10] In making the strange familiar through the device of a domestic cookbook, Ligon entices settlers to join in the 'domestication' of Barbados. Once basic survival was secured, the colonists began to cultivate and trade tobacco, indigo, cotton, fustick wood, and ginger. Then they invited ships, as Ligon puts it, 'to come and visit them, bringing for exchange, such commodities as they wanted, working Tools, Iron, Steel, Cloaths, Shirts, and Drawers, Hose and Shoes, Hats, and more Hands. So that beginning to taste the sweet of this Trade, they set themselves hard to work, and lived in much better condition.'[11] As Hall suggests, the 'sweet of this Trade' in Ligon's account stands in for the consumption of sweet confections in the seventeenth-century banquet, thus implying that the luxuries of the table could be found by venturing to enter the new plantations.

However it was only with the arrival of the sugar plantation system that Caribbean colonists truly tasted the 'sweet of Trade'. Dutch merchants from Brazil introduced sugar cultivation techniques into Barbados in 1641, along with capital and techniques for slave-management; by 1650 it was already profitable; by 1676 'the trade so increased as to be capable of employing 400 vessels, averaging 150 tons burden'.[12] Thus Barbados led the way in what would become the pattern for British West Indian colonial development (Dunn 1972; Beckles 1989b). England's mercantile fleet increased its tonnage by around 150 per cent in the second half of the seventeenth century. The colonial need for manufactured goods stimulated early forms of European industrialisation, especially rural industries in the hinterlands of the major ports, helping to produce the population growth that would send more colonists to the Americas. By the 1690s English re-export of colonial commodities to the European market had grown to 30 per cent of all exports (McFarlane 1994: 116–18). The growth of trade also stimulated new patterns of consumption in early eighteenth-century Britain and North America, which some have described as a 'consumer revolution' (Shammas 1990). As the profitable 'sugar frontier' spread, Europeans went on to ingest vast quantities of slave-produced commodities including sugar, coffee, rum, tobacco, cocoa and chocolate, each of which had a huge impact on European diet. And as they consumed more, they produced more, finding a growing market for the tools and clothes, hats and stockings, which colonists increasingly wanted (Solow 1991; Solow and Engerman 1987).

But before turning to those consumers, let us touch upon the diet of those who went to the tropics. In recounting their culinary conquests, many writers sought to entice others to join the new sugar frontier. Ligon's account, like other early travel narratives, is replete with pages of fulsome descriptions of ravishing edibles and the satisfaction of 'the sense of Tasting'. He was particularly impressed by the pineapple, in which the Epicure will find 'all excellent tastes the world has, comprehended in one single fruit':

> Now to close all that can be said of fruits, I must name the Pine[apple], for in that single name, all that is excellent in a superlative degree, for beauty and for taste, is totally and summarily included . . . when it comes to be eaten, nothing of rare taste can be thought on that is not there; nor is it imaginable that so full a Harmony of tastes can be raised, out of many parts, and all distinguishable . . . [and] the Blossome may be said to represent [as] many of the varieties to the sight, which the fruit does to the taste.[13]

The pineapple entered European iconography as a symbol of welcome and hospitality, and also eventually found its way into botanical gardens such as the Chelsea Physic Garden where it was grown in heated pits. Dazzled by flavour, colour, and variety, the Northern palate became enamoured of these sweet fruits of tropical lands. Due to their highly perishable qualities, though, most tropical fruits could only be tasted by going to where they grew. While human bodies were also perishable, they nevertheless travelled more viably than did fruit. Apart from the small elite with access to glass hothouses, tropical fruit for most people maintained a mysterious aura perpetuated in the imaginary realms of textual simulacra. Going to the Caribbean as a sailor, a servant, a colonist, or an overseer became an Epicurean adventure.

Yet making the Caribbean islands into viable sugar-producing colonies required not only the immense transfer of enslaved people from Africa, but also challenging efforts to find sufficient food to feed these multitudes. While certain foods, including many fruits, were borrowed from indigenous peoples, sufficient quantities of starch and protein would have required too high a commitment of time from the enslaved workers whose labour was needed full time to keep the plantations going. This led to not only the large-scale importation of salted cod from the North Atlantic (Kurlansky 1997), but also the offer of prize money which drove Captain Bligh to attempt to bring breadfruit back from Tahiti to the British West Indies, resulting in the famous mutiny on *The Bounty*. Indeed, when North America was barred from trade with the British West Indies following the American War of Independence, it was not simply 'a tremendous commercial loss for New England [but also resulted] in a tragic famine among slaves cut off from their protein supply. Between 1780 and 1787, 15,000 slaves died of hunger in Jamaica' (Kurlansky 1997: 100). Only global movements of ships, people, plants, fish, animals, armed forces, and information could make the Caribbean colonies work – but at what cost? The assemblage of new agrarian networks in the Caribbean took its toll both on the producers of food and on the consumers who put their bodies at risk in new ways.

By the eighteenth century the white settlers of the Caribbean, known as Creoles, had gained a reputation for excessive indulgence in eating and drinking. Typical is the Jamaican diary of Thomas Thistlewood, who recorded that he had dined on 'stewed mudfish, and pickled crabs, stewed hog's head, fried liver, etc., quarter of roast pork with paw paw sauce and Irish potatoes, bread, roast yam, and plantains, a boiled pudding (very good), cheese, musk melon, water melon, oranges, French brandy said to be Cognac, punch and porter' (Hall 1989: 170; cited in Burton 1997: 28–9). Such a hybrid cuisine was suggestive of the planter's own creolization, as he ate a diet invented by African cooks and drawing on the produce of the Americas, Europe, and Africa, later to be joined by Asia as well (Mintz 1996: 38–9). Gluttony symbolised the planter's moral corruption by slavery, and the way in which it got inside him and contributed literally to degeneracy, illness, indigestion, fevers, poisoning, and 'diseases of consumption'. Tasting the sweetness afforded by global trade lured Europeans into risky places and brought corrupting substances into their homes and bodies. Their bodily relation to the Caribbean teetered precipitously on the cusp between luxurious indulgence and gut-wrenching anxieties. As a new world-economy took shape through their actions, the lust for acquisition of new tastes, new islands, and new riches was tempered by an ethics of restraint and abstention played out upon consuming bodies, as I shall argue below. This dilemma of anxious ingestion ensnared British consumers *en masse* as an unceasing craving for sweetened beverages drove forward the engine of slavery, which drove the entire Atlantic economy.

Europe's sweet tooth

Sidney Mintz, in *Sweetness and Power* (1985) and subsequent work, has explored in most depth the changing consumption of West Indian sugar and sweetened imported beverages such as tea and coffee in Europe. He argues that the transformation of sugar from a luxury for the elite to an item of mass consumption for the working classes had a profound impact on the structure of production, processing, shipping, marketing, and consumption. Mass consumption of these Caribbean and Asian commodities fed into – and literally fed – a new capitalist world that tied together far-flung markets and created a new international division of labour, affecting the meaning of work, the definition of self, and the very nature of material things. Consumption, in other words, is never innocent: it changes the consumer. In consuming the Caribbean, to extend the argument, Europe was itself transformed (Mintz 1985). As the Liverpool Maritime Museum puts it in its Transatlantic Slavery Gallery: 'Much of the social life of Western Europe in the Eighteenth Century depended on the products of slave labour. In homes and coffee-houses, people met over coffee, chocolate, or tea, sweetened with Caribbean sugar. They wore clothes made from American cotton and smoked pipes filled with Virginian tobacco. They used furniture made from mahogany and other tropical woods.'[14] As Europeans became more and more attached to these goods, they were sucked into the vortex of slavery and its human-consuming economy.

There were, of course, differences between the consumer cultures of the European states involved in the 'triangular trade' and the colonial systems that were linked to them. In France for example, 'West Indian trade engaged the bulk of eighteenth-century shipping in the Atlantic ports of Nantes, La Rochelle, and Bordeaux'. However, France evidently benefited less than Great Britain from the dynamic growth of its plantation colonies (Solow 1991: 11, 13). While my analysis will touch upon sources dealing with the French, Hispanic, and Dutch Caribbean, the main focus will be on British and Anglo-American consumers. One of the most important debates in modern economic history concerns the extent to which profits from the slave trade and from slave colonies stimulated industrialisation in Britain (Williams 1944; Drescher 1977; Eltis 1987; Solow and Engerman 1987). I cannot present this debate fully here, but will instead focus on the impact of the transatlantic system of slavery on *patterns of consumption*.

The British colonies in North America were also deeply implicated in the slave economy and the consumption possibilities it offered. The British West Indies and the British North American colonies were integrated into a common system of trade. In the eighteenth century, for example, most Jamaican sugar (and rum) went to London and Bristol, but sugar and molasses were exported to North America 'in return for the beef, pork, cheese, corn, pease, staves, plank, pitch and tar, which they have from thence'.[15] David Richardson's work suggests that in 'the final twenty-five years of British rule, growth in New England's overseas trade seems to have rested largely on dealing with slave-based economies in the Caribbean' (Solow 1991: 17). Furthermore, 'the slave colonies contributed significantly to supplying the food needs of New England in the second half of the eighteenth century' (ibid.: 18). Imports of West Indian sugar, rum, and molasses to the Middle Colonies and Upper South allowed New England to pay for imports of food grains, which were in short supply in the North. In short, 'The eighteenth-century British Atlantic world was bound together . . . not simply by ties of language or administration, but also by a shared material culture which was constantly nourished by flows of commodities' (Styles 1994: 527; Breen 1986).

The flow of commodities from the West Indies to Europe and North America indicates that imperialism was not only 'an extension of empire outward', but also 'a kind of swallowing up' (Mintz 1985: 39). Sugar consumption became 'a national habit', argues Mintz, and sugar along with tea came to define English character. It is difficult to imagine English cuisine without sugar, a crucial ingredient in jams and preserves, chutneys and cakes, chocolate and biscuits, not to mention its role in both alcoholic and non-alcoholic beverages. Sugar brought together the domestic realm and the world market, with women playing an especially important role in domesticating this once exotic luxury good. In making preserves, conserves, marzipans, and other sugary confections, elite 'seventeenth-century women participated in a growing movement from a Mediterranean to an Atlantic economy, and made the English home an important part of what Immanuel Wallerstein has called the modern world system' (K. Hall 1996: 169). But what drove this strange attraction, and what implications did it have for the formation of 'consumer society'? How did the flow of sugar from the Tropics to the Temperate zones shape a world market? And how did sugar users come to understand their place in that market? These questions have been explored by a number of writers, and I briefly reprise some of their arguments here.

Initially sugar was used mainly for medicinal purposes, being a key ingredient for making bitter medicines palatable. It was used in marmalades carried on ships to treat scurvy, and one late seventeenth-century doctor described it as 'restorative and good for all diseases of the lungs, as colds, coughs, asthma, hoarseness, and ulcers. It attenuates cuts and cleanses and eases pain.'[16] Besides functioning as a medicine, sugar was also used as a spice or condiment, a decorative material, a sweetener, and a preservative (Mintz 1985: 78). Molasses, a by-product of sugar production, was also the key ingredient for the production of rum.[17] By the turn of the eighteenth century sugar had made the transition to a common household item of consumption. Kenneth Morgan argues that 'there is no doubt that cane sugar from the Caribbean was the most valuable British import in the century and a half down to 1820. English sugar imports increased sevenfold from 430,000 cwt. in 1700 to over 3,000,000 cwt. in 1800.' Per capita sugar consumption in England 'rose from 1 lb. to 25 lbs. between 1670 and 1770', and by '1787–96, English labouring families spent around 10 per cent of their annual food expenditure on treacle, sugar and tea' (Morgan 1993: 184–5; cf. Shammas 1990). The early eighteenth-century British state gained by a strategy of monopolies in trade and taxation of consumption, exemplifying what John Brewer describes as a voraciously expanding 'warfare-welfare state', for which tea and sugar were a kind of 'national addiction' (Lawson 1997: 16).

It has been argued that the momentous shift from an anti-consumerist mercantilist political economy to an unfettered 'free market' world of consumption and consumers began with sugar. Ralph Austen and Woodruff Smith argue that sugar (taken with tea or coffee) became central to new rituals of respectability that 'stimulated and ultimately reshaped the entire pattern of Western consumer demand' (Austen and Smith 1992: 184). Rather than sugar consumption simply being a by-product of the demands and needs of an industrialising economy, they argue that sugar stimulated industrialisation in so far as it played crucial part in the 'active construction of a broader European market for overseas goods in the seventeenth and eighteenth centuries'. European notions of 'respectability' and social virtue came to be culturally constituted through the 'healthy' consumption of sugar with tea (replacing beer), and this new set of consumer practices and meanings 'contributed to the conditions that made industrialisation historically possible' (ibid.: 189, 195). Indeed, Philip Lawson (1997) argues that tea consumption transformed the forms of hospitality and civility, manners and habits, the uses and architecture of personal and public spaces, and women's lives in particular. In both aristocratic and later middle-class culture, drinking these beverages became occasions for self-display. In seventeenth- and eighteenth-century court society such display involved the use of enslaved African children to serve the beverage in domestic settings presided over by wealthy 'cultured' women (Schivelbusch 1992: 20). The drinking of coffee, tea, and cocoa were thus all closely related to new forms of embodied ritual and practice.

If tea played a crucial part in domestic rituals of consumption, over which women presided, coffee was most significant in the coffee-houses where a masculine and bourgeois public sphere first emerged, as Jürgen Habermas (1989) has argued. However, Habermas pays little attention to the fact that coffee-houses were centres of business and social life where the produce of slavery could be consumed, the profits of slavery spent, and enslaved African children could be bought and sold to work as domestic servants in British households. While many critics of his public sphere model have focused on his lack of attention to 'subaltern counterpublics' (Fraser 1992; Emirbayer and Sheller 1999) and the constitutive exclusion of women from the masculine public sphere (Landes 1988; Ryan 1990, 1992), few have noted the Eurocentrism of his understanding of publicity. Habermas's analysis of the bourgeois public sphere is typical of much contemporary social theory inasmuch as his concern with European urban centres and 'bourgeois' culture precludes any discussion of the colonial world in relation to an emerging modernity and forecloses the possibility that the colonies are crucial to modernity.

Yet, as I argued in Chapter 1, urban centres of knowledge and power such as London were already by the early eighteenth century deeply constituted by networks of material and cultural exchange that spanned the world. 'Consuming publics', defined as elements of the public oriented toward a world economy from which a new cornucopia of consumer goods flowed, were the movers and shakers of the bourgeois public sphere. The first London coffee-house was opened in 1687 by Edward Lloyd and by 1700 there were approximately three thousand to serve London's population of 600,000 (Schivelbusch 1992: 49–51). They became, as Schivelbusch puts it, '*the* site for the public life of the eighteenth century middle class, a place where the bourgeoisie developed new forms of commerce and culture' (ibid.: 59). As a meeting place for ships' captains and owners, merchants and insurance brokers, Lloyd's evolved into the largest insurance brokerage in the world in the eighteenth century, the mighty Lloyds of London. Other major banking institutions also grew out of the profits from financing of the slave trade, including the fortunes made by the Heywoods which went into Barclay's Bank, the Leylands which went into the Midland Bank, and Sir Francis Baring (Martin 1999: 55–8). London's dominant position in contemporary financial services and banking thus originates from this underwriting of trade with Africa and the West Indies, adding another dimension to the powerful effects of consumption. As a political public formed within the eighteenth-century coffee-houses, I suggest, this public was also forming new kinds of economic relations to the colonial world: relations of consumption that were premised both on distant imperial trade and on immediate ingestion of colonial commodities.

Coffee became ever more widely available in Britain in the early eighteenth century, when the duty was reduced on imports from British colonies. Although it initially came from Arabia, interruption of trade routes led to efforts to introduce its cultivation into the West Indies. According to a 1785 work on coffee written by Benjamin Moseley, M.D., it was first cultivated by the Dutch in Surinam in 1718, and then introduced by the French into Martinique in 1727, and by the English into Jamaica in 1728. Moseley promoted its health benefits:

> The extraordinary influence that Coffee, judiciously prepared, imparts to the stomach, from its tonic and invigorating qualities, is strongly exemplified by the immediate effect produced on taking it, when the stomach is overloaded with food, or nauseated with surfeit, or debilitated by intemperance. To constitutionally weak stomachs, it affords a pleasing sensation; it accelerates the process of digestion, corrects crudities, and removes the cholic, and flatulencies. Besides its effect in keeping up the harmony of the gastric powers, it diffuses a genial warmth that cherishes the animal spirits, and takes away the listlessness and languor, which so greatly embitter the hours of nervous people, after any deviation to excess, fatigue or irregularity.[18]

Thus coffee was particularly suited to those who wished to engage in excesses of eating and drinking, smoothing consumption. Moseley describes its medicinal uses to relieve headaches, stomach ailments, excess in drinking, and as an antidote to opium abuse. It was also generally recognised to stimulate the mind and arouse mental activity (Schivelbusch 1992: 110), thus contributing towards a certain kind of embodied 'habitus' suitable to a bourgeois disposition (Bourdieu 1984).

Consumer culture, therefore, arose in a context of complex transatlantic flows that depended firstly and finally on the enslavement of Africans in the Americas, not only as bound plantation labourers, but also in urban trades, ports and haulage, the merchant marine, and above all in domestic settings. It is precisely the juxtaposition of the horror of slavery with the everyday mundane goods (and practices) of household consumption that seems to have made the direct linkage of slavery and consumer culture so difficult to contemplate and to write about. From the late seventeenth century on, the 'middling' farmers, tradesmen, and artisans of Britain began to consume 'what were often entirely new household goods, consisting most obviously of clocks, prints, earthenware, cutlery, equipment for drinking tea and coffee, and window curtains' (Styles 1994: 537). To feed this consumer culture expanding colonial trade networks were increasingly integrated, and of greater importance to the British economy. From 1700 to 1773, British imports from its North American and Caribbean colonies rose from 19 to 38 per cent of all British imports, while exports from Britain to its colonies rose from 10 to 38 per cent of total British exports (McFarlane 1994: 226–7). The West Indies surpassed North America and Asia in importance to the British economy in this period. To feed this economy between 1701 and 1780 up to one million slaves were landed in the British Caribbean colonies, with the largest portion destined for the sugar and coffee plantations of Jamaica (ibid.: 230; Curtin 1969).

The colonial plantation economy not only transformed the consumption habits of entire populations, but it also had a massive impact on British urban culture. Cities like London, Liverpool, Bristol, and Lancaster were transformed by West Indian wealth, and this in turn had a knock-on effect on surrounding rural–industrial enterprises and investment in infrastructure. In London, 'No fewer than 15 Lord Mayors, 25 sheriffs and 38 alderman of the City of London were shareholders' in the Royal Africa Company between 1660 and 1690 (Martin 1999: 57). Derrick Knight has shown that returning West India planters were closely connected to the development of Marylebone and Oxford Street in London, and the Georgian building explosion in Bath (Knight 1978). Madge Dresser has argued that families who made their money in the slave trade and related industries drove urban development in Bristol between 1673 and 1820 (Dresser 2000). Lancaster too was built upon the slave trade, as Melinda Elder has shown, its ships supplying slaves to Barbados, Jamaica, South Carolina, and Georgia, and returning with sugar, rum, mahogany and dyewoods for the British market. Slaves were purchased on the West African coast using a wide variety of locally-produced manufactures including textiles, beads, iron bars, copper pans, brassware, guns, and gunpowder (Elder 1992, 1996), stimulating rural industries and supporting British population growth.

The wealth of the West Indian planters and large and small venture capitalists in slavery also contributed to direct investment in Britain. West Indian planters not only built urban townhouses and invested in rural estates in England, they also bought English goods and furniture to send back to their opulent plantation houses in the West Indies.[19] A new sense of middle-class comfort and material opulence of domestic settings was developed by the West Indian planters, and flaunted on their return to Britain, often accompanied by their enslaved servants. The flow of people and material goods between Europe and the Caribbean thus fed a new middle-class consumer culture in multiple ways, via the boom in consumption of sugar and coffee, the new material culture of households and public places, and the newly 'refined' display of cosmopolitan taste.

A closer look at the British port city of Bristol takes us to the heart of the sugar trade. The Merchant Venturers' Wharfage Accounts for the latter half of the seventeenth century show that in the late 1650s there were in Bristol on average 150 importers operating about 22 ships and importing 3,950 hogsheads of muscovado and white sugars per year. By the late 1690s, this had more than doubled to on average 379 importers operating about 55 ships and importing 7,230 hogsheads per year (Jones 1996: 5). This semi-refined sugar had to be refined locally, and 'between 1660 and 1695 the number of sugar [refining] houses in the city grew from two to ten' (ibid.: 10); by 1750 there were twenty refineries in Bristol, more than in any other British port (Morgan 1993: 185). In the eighteenth century 'the world's sugar trade multiplied at a compound rate of 7 percent per year' and Bristol's imports ranged from 10,000 to 22,000 hogsheads per year between 1728 and 1800 (Jones 1996: 12). During this period the main suppliers shifted from Barbados and Nevis to Jamaica. The Bristol sugar industry magnates, with their substantial fortunes, had a crucial impact not only on the city's economy, but also on its social and political circles (Morgan 1993: 186). Between 1633 and 1832, 16 of Bristol's sugar refiners became Mayors of the City, 29 were Sheriffs, and 8 became partners in banks (Jones 1996: 17). The Bristol trade also supported 'tradesmen and artisans of all kinds connected with the repair, equipment, lading and manning of ships', as well as 'woodworkers, cabinet-makers, dyers, timber importers, insurance-brokers and many more who worked in colonial commodities, or in some way were dependent upon their importation and distribution' (MacInnes 1939: 217).

A second phase of massive increase in sugar consumption occurred following the abolition of slavery, when the British government began to reduce sugar duties in 1844–5, and in 1847–8. Between 1844 and 1848 there was an increase in per capita sugar consumption in Britain from 17 lbs. to 23 lbs., and by 1864 it was about 42 lbs.[20] Turning to Liverpool, we can trace the knock-on impact. In 1854, prior to the equalisation of sugar duties, there were seven sugar refineries operating in Liverpool, producing 24,000 tons of crushed sugar; there were 100 resident importers of sugar in the city, 35 brokers, and 9 wholesale grocers. There were a further 36 tea and coffee merchants, 12 brokers, and upwards of 300 tea and coffee dealers.[21] Per capita sugar consumption in Britain rose to a staggering 92 lbs. per head in 1913. This rate of consumption was linked to the development of key sugar-based industries in places like Liverpool, where in the 1920s there were factories producing brewing sugar, golden syrup, edible treacle, toffee, chocolate, sweets, jam and fruit preserves, cake, confectionery, and sweetened mineral waters.[22] These trades and industries employed a workforce of tens of thousands, and contributed immensely to civic pride and development.

Sugar thus transformed European productive capacity by generating profits and new institutional capacities, spawning new food-processing industries and financial service industries, as well as directly increasing the caloric intake of workers. What is crucial about this history, is the way in which slavery touched people in the most intimate ways – in terms of the foods and drinks they ingested and in the making of their domestic environments. At the same time the slave economy shaped civic life in the most public of ways – in terms of the 'men of substance' who became leaders in politics, the economic policies they promoted, and their huge investment in the material fabric of cities and improvements of early industrial infrastructures. Just as the pleasurable tasting of tropical fruits was haunted by images of sin, however, so too was this take-off of a consumer culture grounded in slavery subject to trenchant ethical critique. In the following section I turn to the political history of ethical consumption and fair trade, which first took root in the boycotts of slave-grown produce starting in the 1790s among a new kind of anti-consumerist public. As European consumers began to recognise their direct relation to enslaved workers, they also began to frame a moral discourse in which consuming publics could take responsibility for driving markets through their day-to-day decisions about what to buy and what to eat, or not eat. If the Weberian 'Protestant ethic' drove them towards restrained accumulation of wealth, it also produced a restraint in the literal ingestion of substances seen as luxuries. As Europe's sweet tooth began to bite, the ethical consumer would begin to taste blood.

Sugar boycotts and the free produce movement

If new public modes of consumption produced a new bourgeois habitus, they also produced a new domestic habitat. Consuming publics not only emerged out of the masculine realm of the London coffee-houses, but also in the 'feminine' domestic realm where everyday consumer decisions were made, and consumer fantasies and anxieties played out. In both cases there was a crucial relation between metropolitan consumption and colonial plantation slavery, between home economy and political economy.[23] The politicisation of issues of consumption depended on an explicit recognition of personal responsibility for colonial relations of domination, which came to be powerfully framed by the anti-slavery movement. Rather than discussing public leaders of the anti-slavery movement such as William Wilberforce or Thomas Clarkson, however, I focus here on the female consumers who began to call into question the sugar on their tables and who became concerned with the ways in which slavery poisoned their own bodies and homes.

A new culture of ethical consumption first emerged during the movement to boycott slavery's commodities, spearheaded in England especially by Quaker women's anti-slavery organisations. Sugar boycotts began in the context of the first major abolitionist campaign of the 1790s. Pamphlets were published by Thomas Cooper (1791), William Allen (1792), and William Fox, founder of the Sunday School Society, calling for abstention from slave-grown sugar as a means to ending the slave trade (Deerr 1950: 296). Cooper's 1791 pamphlet, for example, argued that,

> The consumption of Sugar in this country is so immense, that the quantity commonly used by individuals will have an important effect. A family that uses five pounds of Sugar *per week*, with the same proportion of Rum, will, by abstaining from the consumption 21 months, prevent the slavery, or murder, of one fellow creature; eight such families in nineteen years and a half, would prevent the slavery, or murder, of 100; and 38,000 would totally prevent the Slave Trade, by removing the occasion to supply our island – A French writer observes 'That he cannot look upon a piece of Sugar without conceiving it stained with spots of human blood'.[24]

The pamphlet then goes on to describe the hundreds of thousands of Africans murdered, whipped, and mutilated in the regular course of the slave trade. Reaching a crescendo, it argues: 'If sugar were not consumed it would not be imported – if it were not imported it would not be cultivated, if it were not cultivated there would be an end of the Slave Trade, so that the consumer of sugar is really the prime mover – the grand cause of all the horrible injustice which attends the capture, of all the shocking cruelty which accompanies the treatment of the wretched African Slave.'

A most compelling aspect of these arguments was the imagery of sugar soaked in blood. In his famous 1791 'Address to the People of Great Britain, on the Propriety of Abstaining from West India Sugar and Rum', which had reached twenty-six editions by 1793, William Fox argued that,

> The laws of our country may indeed prohibit us the sugar-cane, unless we will receive it through the medium of slavery. They may hold it to our lips, steeped in the blood of our fellow-creatures; but they cannot compel us to accept the loathsome portion. With us it rests, either to receive it and be partners in the crime, or to exonerate ourselves from guilt, by spurning from us the temptation . . . if we purchase the commodity we participate in the crime. The slave-dealer, the slave-holder, and the slave-driver, are virtually the agents of the consumer, and may be considered as employed and hired by him to procure the commodity.[25]

Indeed, 'so necessarily connected are our consumption of the commodity, and the misery resulting from it,' Fox argues, 'that in every pound of sugar used . . . we may be considered as consuming two ounces of human flesh.' Stories circulated that planters sometimes entombed a slave in each sugar cask to impart a better taste to it. The notion of cannibalism took on a strange new life as eating sugar was envisioned as eating human flesh and blood in a high-impact campaign with extensive national publicity.[26]

Morton refers to this as the 'blood sugar *topos*', by which the 'sweetened drinks of tea, coffee, and chocolate are rendered suddenly nauseating by the notion that they are full of the blood of slaves' (Morton 2000a: 173). He links this blood–sugar discourse to wider developments in Romantic aesthetics and ethics, including the movements of vegetarianism and concern for animals. 'The rhetoric of mangling flesh,' he observes, 'was a feature of anti-slavery and animal rights rhetoric, often found together in the same work' (ibid.: 197). Thus the sugar boycotts were part of a wider culture of 'radical food', which has close connections to the contemporary resurgence of ethical consumer movements promoting vegetarianism, animal rights, and fair trade (Morton 2000b). Just as Romanticism contributed to new landscapes of bodily immersion in the Caribbean, as I argued in the previous chapter, it also contributed to a newly embodied sense of proximity to the slave and a feeling of empathy for the downtrodden. By refusing to let the bloodstained, slave-produced sugar pass their lips, white anti-slavery activists dramatised their own moral subjectivity and their feeling of proximity with the slave through relations of tasting and not tasting particular commodities that directly flowed from one body into another body.

Thomas Clarkson computed that there were approximately 300,000 people abstaining from West India Sugar during the 1790s campaign. Besides resorting to bitter drinks, some tried to redirect the world economy toward free labour. China-makers introduced 'East India Sugar Basins' which were labelled in gold letters: 'East India Sugar not made by Slaves' (see Plate 3.1). Thus the campaign entered the private realm of tea service, by which women could politicise the domestic economy through the choice of material objects and commodities which constituted this everyday ritual. Ethical eating was thus performed and enforced within the bosom of the family, and was easily parodied as a kind of tyranny of

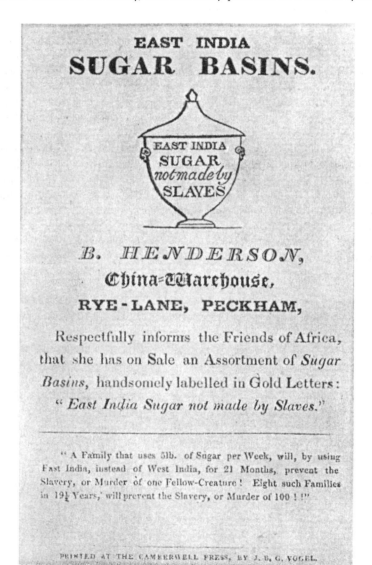

Plate 3.1 Refusing the bitter chalice of slavery.
'East India Sugar Bowl', from Noel Deerr, *The History of Sugar*, Vol. 2 (London, Chapman & Hall Ltd., 1950).

moralistic women. The print satirist James Gillray took a swipe at the 'anti-saccharrites' in his 1792 satirical print of an English family taking tea without sugar (Plate 3.2). It shows a mother exhorting her downcast daughters, 'O, my dear Creatures, do but Taste it! You can't think how nice it is without Sugar, And then consider how much Work you'll save the poor Blackamoors by leaving off the use of it! And above all, remember how much expense it will save your poor Papa.' The family in question was in fact the royal family, as King George III was known for being a spendthrift. Yet his wife's teeth are already blackened with decay, and her coarse hands set them apart from the usual dainty respectability noted above. The question of slavery is here reduced to a matter of 'Taste' and domestic economy. Rather than offering a radical critique of slavery, Morton notes, 'the bourgeois discourses of prudence, economy, and temperance [were precisely] the discourses that supported the plantations' (Morton 2000a: 200). Critics of the abolitionists often contrasted their misplaced concern for slaves in the West Indies against the plight of the 'free' English worker, who was portrayed as the hard-working and deserving beneficiary of cheap sugar supplies. Thus Gillray's parody of the anti-saccharrites pits the shallowness of the anti-slavery scruples of a privileged elite (of women especially) against the economic interests of the working man and his family, in a clash of different kinds of moral economy.

Gillray's 1791 engraving 'Barbarities in the West Indies' (Plate 3.3) further parodies a famous case in which abolitionists charged that slaves were thrown into vats of boiling sugar. Depicting an 'English negro-driver' throwing a slave into a

Plate 3.2 Ethical eating as bourgeois family ritual.
'The Anti-Saccharrites', engraving by James Gillray, 1792, from Noel Deerr, *The History of Sugar*, Vol. 2 (London, Chapman & Hall Ltd., 1950).

Plate 3.3 Cannibalism in reverse?
'Barbarities in the West Indies', engraving by James Gillray, 1791.

'copper of boiling sugar juice', which he stirs with a cat-o'-nine-tails, the print also echoes the cannibalistic imagery of the anti-saccharrite pamphlets of the period. The body of the slave literally is boiled into the sugar, while in the background a human forearm and ears can be seen nailed to the wall alongside birds and rodents (suggesting the link between sympathy for both small animals and slaves). While some read this as a parody of abolitionist claims, Marcus Wood sees it as even more sinisterly 'enacting a fantasy of execution and dismemberment upon an anonymous set of black bodies, a fantasy in which the viewer is invited to participate' (Paulson 1987: 204–5; Wood 2000: 155). The somewhat comic gesture of the hands and feet emerging from the vat turns the eating of 'Negroes' into a joke on barbarity, replacing abolitionist horror with consumerist humour. It undermines the sugar boycott by ridiculing its claims about the abuse of slaves, by visualising 'cannibalism in reverse', and by suggesting that it might even be funny to eat slaves scalded in sugar (cf. Morton 2000a: 181). Yet we could also read this image as representing the contradictions of capitalist consumer culture (Miller 1997). Why should it take revulsion at the *taste* of blood-infused sugar to move middle-class consumers to action, rather than simply revulsion at the inhumanity of slavery? Why does their ethical stance require a demonisation of the less privileged overseer as some kind of monster? Gillray is again pinpointing the problematic moral subjectivity of supposed ethical consumers and suggesting that his own sympathies lie with the English working class who are exploited by these very same bourgeois consumers.

This is not the place for a full account of the abolitionist movement, nor of the extensive debate over its protagonists and causes.[27] The ending of Britain's slave trade in 1807, suffice it to say, was one of the first successful political campaigns waged on behalf of the 'other'. Nevertheless, slavery remained in place in the British colonies until 1834, when it was replaced by an 'apprenticeship' system that finally ended in 1838. Thus following a brief hiatus, the campaign to boycott slave-produce resumed in the 1820s (a period during which sugar from the East Indies was also increasingly available as a 'free produce' substitute). In 1825 the Birmingham Female Society for the Relief of British Negro Slaves was founded with the resolution:

> That this Society, convinced that abstinence from the use of slave cultivated sugar, is one of the best modes to which recourse can be had to express its abhorrence of the system of Colonial Slavery, and that the exclusive consumption of the produce of free labour is the most effectual means of annihilating the existence of that scourge of humanity, not only in our West India Colonies, but also in other parts of the World, – earnestly desires, that its members will endeavour by their influence, as well as by their example, to promote the exclusive use of the productions of free labour in the neighbourhoods in which they reside.[28]

Here we see a significant extension of the movement beyond the British colonies to all 'parts of the World'. Up to 20,000 families were called on to join the boycott from 1825–8 in the Birmingham region alone,[29] and it was also promoted in Nottingham, Leicester, and Brighton. Meanwhile, prominent anti-slavery activists including Brougham, Buxton, Lushington, and Sturge formed a Free Labour Company to establish free-labour sugar plantations in India (Deerr 1950: 297).

Middle-class women were perceived as moral arbiters and guardians of their families, and their consumption habits were also linked to broader temperance movements, which urged restraint. As Paul Glennie argues,

> all nascent capitalism in the early-modern West did experience tensions between increasing commodification, and discourses about consumption's destructive moral and corrosive social effects. . . . In each case, consumption was made morally legitimate through notions of responsible consumption, which defined socially appropriate styles, timings and settings for consumption, and were inflected particularly through moralising about women's roles.
>
> (Glennie 1995: 181)

It was women who presided over the taking of tea, who purchased the sugar that would sweeten it, and the china in which it would be served. As McClintock has argued for a slightly later period, 'the mass-marketing of empire as a global system was intimately wedded to the Western reinvention of domesticity, so that imperialism cannot be understood without a theory of domestic space and its relation to the market' (McClintock 1995: 17). It was the women's anti-slavery movement that first saw these connections.

In their publications, aimed at a female reading public, the Birmingham society argued,

Is it for Christian females to be bribed by the greater *cheapness* of this, or the other article of daily consumption, to lend themselves to the support of a flagrant system of blood-guiltiness, and oppression, which cries to heaven for vengeance? . . . The influence of females in the minor departments (as they are usually deemed) of household affairs is such that, it rests with them to determine whether the luxuries indulged in, and the convenience enjoyed, shall come to them *from the employers of free men, or from the oppressors of British slaves*. When the preference is given to the latter, we see, therefore, with whom the responsibility must mainly rest; – we see at whose door the burden of guilt must lie.[30]

Thus the guilt for slavery and the means of overturning it were placed explicitly in women's hands, in the day-to-day decisions they made in the consumption practices of their households. This was a powerful moral discourse of abstention, linking women to a world market and to economic matters of great import (Midgley 1992; Sussman 2000).

Even after slavery was finally abolished in the British colonies in 1834, sugar was still being imported for British consumption made by enslaved workers on plantations in Cuba and Brazil. The 1846 Sugar Duties Act equalised duties on British free-labour sugar and foreign slave-labour sugar (with full effect in 1854). Between 1845 and 1851 the increase in British sugar imports was made up entirely of foreign sugar, while West Indian free-labour sources declined. In a petition presented to Parliament by Lord Brougham in July 1846, he argued that '[T]he poor man should have plenty of sugar, cheap sugar, and sugar of the most exquisite quality too, but it must be lawfully and honestly come by; and above all, he must not have slave-made or slave-supplied sugar, which he must know is crimsoned with the blood of the African.'[31] In order to avoid this inevitable ethical failure, British anti-slavery activists renewed their efforts to promote free produce, in association with projects to export free produce from the West Indies and the free states of the northern United States.[32]

Following slave emancipation, the Birmingham Female Society for the Relief of British Negro Slaves became the Ladies' Negro's Friend Society. It continued its work both by rejecting sugar grown in the booming slave plantations of Brazil and Cuba and by promoting free produce cotton (in place of that from the American South, where slavery would continue until the end of the Civil War in 1865). They supported the Free Produce Association, and called on Queen Victoria to exclude slave-grown produce from her household and to encourage the growth of free produce cotton in British India.[33] By 1851, there were twenty-six free produce societies in Britain (Temperley 1972: 166; cf. Nuermberger 1942). Free produce stores were set up in cities like London, Manchester, and Birmingham. The supporters of this movement argued on moral grounds for 'non-consent to the consumption of this [slave] produce', based on the logic that 'demand creates supply' and that each consumer has a 'personal responsibility' for the continuation of slavery.[34]

The Sugar Duties Act contributed to the collapse of the sugar plantation economy in the British West Indies, and the post-emancipation 'labouring classes' soon faced a stark existence eked out between subsistence peasant economies and whatever wage labour could be had (see Sheller 2000). Coffee provided one alternative crop for the world market, but real economic growth would not occur until the coming of the new fruit trade in the late nineteenth century, in which the curious relationship between bodies 'here' and bodies 'over there' continued to inform the restructuring of the global market. As we shall see, bananas would enter a strange circuit of exchange between Europe, America, and the Caribbean, in which ethical choices about eating once again came to challenge the interests of huge agro-industrial corporations and even shook the diplomatic status quo of world powers. As Daniel Miller has noted, today 'the links between First World "taste" and Third World suffering are understood by the producing nations and it has become evident that increasingly their destiny has become, in effect, a secondary effect of shifts in First World consumption patterns' (Miller 1995: 3). As global banana consumption shifts at the whim of new trade regimes, social movements have again called attention to the ways in which consumption patterns cause distant suffering.

Banana republics and the banana wars

Throughout most of the nineteenth century it was still necessary for Europeans to go to the Caribbean if they wanted to taste tropical fruits, since most would not keep on the long transatlantic journey. As in the seventeenth century, both tasting and seeing the tropical produce were prominent pleasures of travel. Visiting the markets of Trinidad in 1833, for example, Captain J.E. Alexander describes fruit as part of the scenery:

> [I] saw the treasures, in the shape of vegetables and fruits, which are here bestowed in luxurious abundance by a bountiful nature. Plantains and sweet potatoes, okras, yams and teniers were exposed in baskets before brown or black hucksters, sitting under the shade of umbrellas, whilst the eye delighted to wander over the heaps of pomegranates, guavas, shaddocks, oranges, limes, custard-apples, mangoes, pines, and grenadilloes, which could be purchased for very trifling sums.[35]

Besides the fruits easily available in the open-air markets, the Caribbean was also famed for the feasts and banquets of its upper classes. Lady Emmeline Stuart Wortley wrote of a banquet she attended in Cuba in 1849. After the second course the guests left the table for a promenade in the gardens, and then:

> On their return to the banqueting room, they find an immense profusion of crystal, alabaster, or porcelain vases, and *canastillas* (small baskets) of silver, loaded with a vast variety of fruits. 'Mameys' which says Madame de Merlin, are '*Alimento de las almas bienaventuradas en los valles del otro mundo, segun la creencia de los habitantes de Haiti*' and the '*zapatillas suaves*,' which she declares have a

'*gusto silvestre.*' Then there are *tunas* – a very handsome fruit of a lovely rose-color, about the size of a small pine-apple, the inside of which is excellent, and all of it eatable . . . then there are *guayavos*, and hosts of others. Besides fruits of almost innumerable kinds, and sizes, and shapes, there are crowds of light silver dishes, and *bandejas* or *dulces* – which mean all kinds of sweets . . . and the table, the borders of the dishes, even the glasses are wreathed, and covered, and almost buried in flowers.[36]

Such beauty, profusion, and taste could only be created in the tropics, where not only the fruits and flowers were available, but also the wealth, the social customs, and the setting. The luxurious materials of the vases and bowls match the luxuri-ant fruits. Lady Wortley's use of Spanish to describe these indescribable and innumerable sweets suggests their other-worldliness, their un-Englishness, and their *frisson* of creolization.

If this form of consumption required the European to go to the Caribbean, the relationship between mover and moved would soon be reversed. It was not until the late nineteenth century that fresh tropical fruits could be transported in refrigerated ships, as well as being canned, enabling their mass consumption in Europe for the first time. As one tourist noted in 1885, from Port Antonio, Jamaica, '[f]ast Steamers reach New York in five or six days, and the more south-ern ports of the United States sooner; so that the luscious fruits of the West Indies can be eaten in the less sultry North before the imprisoned sunbeams have had quite time to escape'.[37] Finally, the Northern consumer might rejoice, the taste of the Tropics could travel. The trade in tropical comestibles culminates with the curious history of banana consumption. The story of their massive production and exportation starting in the late nineteenth century (and the concomitant development of 'banana boat' tourism in places like Port Antonio, Jamaica) can be followed through to the recent 'banana wars' between the European Union and the United States. The 'trade war' over preferences and barriers for bananas grown by small Caribbean farmers versus those grown by American corporations in huge Central American plantations involves a complex interplay between local producers, national governments, multinational corporations, fungal diseases, natural disasters, macro-economic policies, transnational organisations, and world diplomacy.

Although there are records of bananas being imported from Havana to New York as early as 1804, it was not until the 1870s that they became generally available and they were featured in the United States Centennial Exhibition in Philadelphia in 1876 (Enloe 1989: 127). Until the late nineteenth century bananas remained a small luxury import supplied to Europe by places like the Canary Islands until transatlantic journey-times were reduced by use of steam-powered ships. Although David Gideon of Port Antonio, Jamaica, first promoted the Jamaica Co-operative Fruit and Trading Company in 1887, international inter-ests quickly squeezed local co-operatives out of the market as soon as it became viable. Jamaica's international banana industry truly began when Lorenzo Dow Baker founded the Boston Fruit Company in 1888, which merged to become the

United Fruit Company (UFC) in 1899, and later was incorporated into Chiquita Brands International. By the mid-1890s bananas were providing twenty per cent of the value of Jamaica's total exports. By 1903 UFC owned or leased 60,000 acres of land around Port Antonio, and employed thousands of workers. They monopolised the market, for example when a combination of growers tried to form the St. Catherine Fruit Trust, in 1904, UFC refused to deal with them (Davies 1990: 61, 145). However from the start of the industry a struggle occurred not only between international corporations and local growers, but also between British and United States interests.

The British market was supplied initially by the Imperial Direct West India Mail Service, whose refrigerated steamers could carry over 30,000 bunches of bananas, 10,000 boxes of oranges, and 1,000 crates of pineapples and mangoes into Bristol. Increasingly 'concerned about U.S. corporate influence in the region', according to Lawrence Grossman, the British government in 1901 'provided a subsidy to the large British shipping firm of Elder Dempster for operation of a refrigerated service linking Jamaica and the United Kingdom' (Grossman 1998: 35). *The Fruit Trade News* reported in December 1901, that bananas could be seen all day wending their way to Covent Garden:

> The stocks in the warehouses must be phenomenal, for never were such quantities sent into London before. Fifty thousand bunches in a week – and such bunches too – are nothing out of the way, for as soon as they are delivered they disappear as if by magic. The buyers seem on the wait for the fruit, and many of the loads are sold without being unloaded.
>
> (cited in Davies 1990: 113–14)

Elders and Fyffes introduced larger steamers to meet the growing demand. In 1905 the *Oracabessa* carried 'the largest cargo of bananas that ever left Jamaica', with 45,000 bunches, and bananas became the 'most popular fruit handled in the British markets'. According to a 1905 guide, 'The total importation of bananas into England for the first six months of 1905 amounted to 2,395,351 bunches, as compared with 1,416, 873 during the same period in 1904'.[38] The cultural impact of the market for bananas can be imagined from this photograph of a Liverpool shop-front from around 1901 claiming to have the 'Largest Show of West Indian Fruit Ever Exhibited' (Plate 3.4). It shows a fruiterer's swathed in grapefruit, oranges, pineapple, and mainly bananas selling for sixpence a dozen, and indicates a 'banana room' upstairs.[39] Tropical fruit had finally come 'home' thanks to a complex mobilisation of transatlantic labour, transportation, marketing, government intervention, and new patterns of consumption.

Bananas became a significant element in the global competition to control huge markets in tropical plantation commodities, including coffee, tea, rubber, palm oil, and sugar. Between 1880 and 1930, as Cynthia Enloe notes, the United States colonised or invaded a number of major plantation crop regions of the world: Hawaii, the Philippines, Puerto Rico, Haiti, the Dominican Republic, Cuba, and Nicaragua (Enloe 1989: 124). In 1932, concerned with United Fruit's grip on the

Plate 3.4 The banana-boats come 'home'.

'Largest Show of West Indian Fruit Ever Exhibited' (1901), from F. Dodsworth, *The Book of the West Indies* (London, G. Routledge & Sons, 1904).

Jamaican industry, 'the British government established the first in a long series of import policies that provided preferential treatment for banana producers within the empire' (Grossman 1998: 37–8). However, American companies operating in Latin America benefited from more advantageous environmental conditions (flat, fertile land with better transport) and economic advantages (economies of scale, vertical integration, lower wage rates). The continuation of the Windward Islands banana industry therefore depended on British tariffs and licences limiting importation of non-empire 'dollar bananas' (ibid.: 41). By 1935, 'with a regularity almost like clockwork, specially equipped modern ships, capable of carrying up to 100,000 bunches, plough their steady way from Caribbean ports across the Atlantic to distribute their cargoes, grown under tropic skies, to well-nigh every country in Europe. . . . [I]t is by such extensive travel that the banana has become a common domestic food in the teeming cities of Europe and North America.'[40]

Such intensive banana cultivation quickly took a toll on the lands of the Caribbean. In the 1920s Claude Wardlaw was sent to the Imperial College of Tropical Agriculture in Trinidad to study a fungal disease called Panama Disease that was devastating huge tracts of banana plantation throughout the circum-Caribbean region. The 'Gros Michel' variety that was grown for the export markets was especially susceptible to the disease. He reported that 'by the end of 1931 upwards of 15,000 acres had gone out of use for banana cultivation [in Jamaica]' and 50,000 acres had been lost in Panama, 50,000 in Costa Rica, and more than 5,000 each in Honduras and Guatemala.[41] Wardlaw described how thousands of acres of virgin forests, populated by monkeys and birds and full of valuable and useful trees and plants, were indiscriminately felled by North American fruit companies, who left the wood to rot. They were then planted over in bananas, only to be abandoned a few years later due to Panama Disease.

Wardlaw blamed this cultivation of 'vast acreages devoted entirely and continuously to one crop' for providing the conditions for epidemic disease. Not only did these practices entail the destruction of giant forests, but once abandoned,

> the deforested land does not revert to its original state, but it is repopulated by an entirely different flora. Once established, the secondary vegetation is not readily displaced from its hold on the land. Secondary forests some twenty-five years old show only a few additional species. . . . Virgin forest land is the raw material of the agricultural pioneer in the tropics. Before it can be exploited to advantage, its value must be truly assessed, otherwise the exploiter may find himself bankrupt while posterity is left with an infinitely poorer heritage.[42]

Wardlaw, like others before him (Grove 1995), recognised that the tropics were not infinitely productive, and that the amazing fantasy of fruitfulness was in fact the result of careful native cultivation and preservation of useful species. 'The vegetable wealth of virgin tropic lands is not, if the truth be told, arrayed before the wayfarer's eyes like the goods in a fruit-shop window,' he observed, 'nor yet like the assemblages of specimens set out in botanic garden hot-houses in sections devoted to utilitarian plants . . . the lavish tropical garden of the imaginative author and armchair adventurer is strictly speaking a synthetic entity derived from many sources.'[43] By the time, he wrote, though, the fantasies driving European and North American profit-seekers had already wreaked 'green havoc'.

On arriving in the Caribbean, Northern tourists often linked together for the first time the foods that they were familiar with eating at home and the bodies of the Caribbean workers producing them. When James Pope-Hennessy arrived for the first time in a Caribbean port in the early 1950s, he noted the brilliant colours and how the people 'were all as static as in a tableau, as authentic and typical as the West Indian people on the label of a rum bottle' (Pope-Hennessy 1954: 19). He then saw workers loading bananas, and remembered that,

> Two weeks before, in Bristol, we had watched the bananas being mechanically unloaded from the ship, placed on a smooth-travelling conveyor belt and stacked into railway trucks by husky Irish navvies . . . Here at Castries [St. Lucia] . . . the place of the mechanical conveyor belt and the muscular navvies was taken by a human chain of negresses of all ages, who carried the heavy hands of bananas from the warehouse to the boat upon their heads. As each of these human pack-animals was loaded, a negro with a cutlass deftly sliced off the projecting stalk of the banana hand above their foreheads. The women would then set off at a brisk jog-trot, the pink soles of their large black feet kicking up the dust as they jostled and wrangled for precedence in the line to the hold. Paid by the piece, it is in their own interests to work as fast as they can.
>
> (Pope-Hennessy 1954: 27–8)

These dehumanised workers present a stark contrast to the image of exotic, fun, tropical femininity projected by a banana-bedecked Carmen Miranda in Hollywood in the 1940s, or the calypso-singing, dancing banana-woman used to market Chiquita Bananas in the 1950s (Enloe 1989: 125–30). 'Between the woman consumer and the fruit,' argues Enloe, 'there now was only a corporation with the friendly face of a bouncy Latin American market woman' (ibid.: 129). Such benign imagery masked the international gender and racial relations that underpinned the banana industry, and helped to hide from view the impoverished women workers described by Pope-Hennessy, or the globally-enmeshed peasant-growers in islands like Dominica described by Michel-Rolph Trouillot (1988).

With ups and downs over the course of the twentieth century, the banana industry managed to survive and expand in both Central America and the Caribbean, as well as in other parts of the world. Fyffes controlled the Jamaican industry while Geest controlled the British Windwards, where it worked with the Windward Islands Banana Growers' Association (WINBAN), which formed in 1958. Following a 'banana war' between the two companies in 1964–6, they agreed to share the market between them and limit supplies to keep prices high in Britain (Grossman 1998: 43, 47). The 'Banana Protocol' in the 1975 Lomé

Convention ensured market protection, and despite some difficulties for the industry in the late 1970s, there was a period of strong growth in the 1980s 'banana boom'. Following the formation of the Single European Market in 1992 the European Union became the world's largest market for bananas (35–40 per cent) and the dismantling of various countries' preferential regimes for bananas became one of the most contentious trade issues. Protected markets for overseas territories and former colonies in the African–Caribbean–Pacific (ACP) countries existed in the United Kingdom, Italy, France, Spain, Portugal, and Greece, making up 38 per cent of European banana imports in 1992. However, 62 per cent of EU imports (into Germany, Belgium, Luxembourg, Ireland, Denmark, and the Netherlands) were 'dollar bananas' produced by the three big US-based transnational corporations, Chiquita, Dole and Del Monte (ibid.: 52–3).

The General Agreement on Tariffs and Trade (GATT) 'Uruguay Round' undermined the new Lomé banana regime that was set for 1993–2002, and in 1996 the United States and Latin American producers lodged a complaint with the World Trade Organisation, which ruled in their favour in 1997. It was well known that the chief executive of Chiquita, Carl H. Lindner, had made substantial political contributions to both the Democrat and Republican parties. The dispute dragged on and led in 1998–9 to the so-called 'banana wars' between the United States and the European Union, which placed the issue on the front page of many newspapers replete with puns such as 'Billion dollar banana split'.[44] The British papers presented it as a case of big corporate interests using their hefty political donations to pressure the Clinton Administration in the United States into retaliating against the European Union's continuing protection of small ACP banana growers (with only 7 per cent of the EU market in any case). US newspapers emphasised the unfairness of European protectionism and the near bankruptcy of Chiquita Brands International. In December 1998, the US announced that it would place 100 per cent import duties on a range of sensitive EU exports, including cashmere sweaters, batteries, plastics, biscuits and cheese, amongst other things. In March 1999 the US Secretary of State Madeleine Albright was dispatched to London for 'crisis talks' with the British Foreign Secretary, Robin Cook, in an attempt to stem the trade war. However, in April 1999 the WTO ruled that the EU banana regime violated global trade rules, and that the US was allowed to impose $191.4 million in sanctions.[45] Following further appeals and negotiations, it was finally announced in April 2001 that the dispute had been settled. Front-page business stories in the *New York Times* described it as 'a victory for the Bush administration in dealing with Europe', with Europe agreeing to phase out all quotas and tariffs by 2006.[46]

The entire incident reflects the complex flows of trade, diplomacy, governance, and historical relationships across the Atlantic world. The debate over 'free trade' is again being shadowed by a debate over 'fair trade'. The contemporary discourse of 'free trade' must be examined in light of the history of the Caribbean's relation to European and American consumers. Where does responsibility for the collapse of Caribbean agricultural economies lie? While bananas may seem a frivolous luxury to some, they are for many a livelihood. Jamaica earns $40 million annually from the banana industry; in St. Lucia more than 60,000 people (one-third of the island's population) depend on bananas for employment; and it is a crucial crop in Dominica, Grenada, St. Vincent and the Grenadines where 70 per cent of the population live either directly or indirectly off the industry.[47] The importance of the crop in these islands is understood to be a legacy of Britain's colonial and postcolonial involvement in the region, for which it is today being held accountable. Moreover, the trade disputes are broadening to encompass not only bananas, but also other key crops such as sugar and rice, trademark protections and intellectual property rights, and 'offshore' financial services and banking. The economic threat to the Caribbean is also linked to political debates surrounding increases in drugs transshipment, criminality, and 'economic' migration. As one global trade flow stops, another less desirable one may emerge.

Consumers are culturally and economically distanced from the social and cultural space of production in which their food originates, and from the temporal rhythms of agricultural seasons in the Caribbean, both subsumed to the frantic time-space of food distribution and shopping in the North. As Miller argues, 'What is required is a "middle-range" morality, which reinscribes on to the surface of commodities their consequences for producers, often from the developing world. . . . The first move has to be a transfer of profits from First World consumers to Third World producers as increased prices for raw materials' (Miller 1995: 48). Ethical issues have become increasingly central to modes of consumption throughout Europe and North America.[48] In Britain something of an ethical stance has emerged in relation to the EU/US trade dispute, with the growing marketing of 'ethical' bananas. Sainsbury's, for example, now sells bananas from the Windward Islands, labelled clearly: 'These bananas are grown on the Commonwealth Islands of Dominica, St. Lucia, St. Vincent and Grenada. They are tended by farmer cooperatives who own their land and are shareholders in the marketing company that ripens and distributes this fruit.'[49] Booth's supermarket likewise promotes 'Caribbean Bananas: specially selected from the traditional banana growing countries of the Caribbean'.[50] These apparently socially responsible (and more expensive) bananas are implicitly contrasted to the Central American banana industry, owned by big multinationals, using higher levels of pesticides, and with lower wages and poorer working conditions. Still, they remain marginal to the overall banana market. In 1998 global imports of organic bananas were estimated by industry sources at approximately 27,000 metric tonnes, and European imports of Fair Trade bananas were approximately 17,366 tonnes, compared with total global banana imports of over 11 million tonnes.[51]

The politicisation of the banana is in fact not as banal as it might at first seem, but rather attests to the re-emerging consciousness of the material relations between natures, landscapes, foods, bodies, and markets. Just as North Atlantic salt cod and grain became a staple in the Caribbean diet during the days of the triangular trade, Caribbean countries today (despite their supposed tropical fecundity) remain highly dependent on imported food (Klak 1998). While the labour, resources, and produce of the Caribbean are voraciously consumed, its markets are unable to sustain self-provisioning: 'The Caribbean produces what it does not consume, and consumes what it does not produce' (Deere *et al.* 1990: 4). Without paying attention to the conditions of consumption within the Caribbean, I suggest, strategies of 'ethical consumption' will fail to recognise the full effects of commodity exchange and will only salve the conscience of those middle-class consumers in the North who can afford to eat 'ethically'. Any ethics of consumption must recognise not only the conditions of production under which some workers are exploited, but also the conditions of consumption under which some consumers enjoy locational privileges, of which they are not even aware, while many others struggle merely to survive.

Conclusion

In this chapter I have argued that embodied relations of mobile consumption are central to the contradictory impulses of capitalist modernity. In contrast to recent studies of consumer culture that have focused on processes internal to Europe, I suggested that the ethical dilemmas of consumer culture must be grounded in the material connections between North Atlantic consuming publics, Caribbean producers, and the articles of pleasure that connect them. We could add that this ethics must also include responsibility toward 'other others' (Ahmed 2000), who are also involved in the production and circulation of tropical commodities. I then tracked these relationships from the early days of colonisation and tasting the Tropics, through the rise of the sugar plantation system, and into the modern fruit trade. In first tasting the Tropics, I argued, European consumers placed their bodies in a risky relation of anxiety-inducing pleasure, driven by the 'sweet of this Trade'. Then their bodies and their domestic realm were swept up in the sugar rush, surging through the public and private spheres, particularly in England where a culture of sweets was created. If anti-slavery consumers first made evident the connections between the barbarities of enslavement in the colonies and the supposed refinements of bourgeois civility, the eating of Third World produce continues to trouble metropolitan consumers, as seen in the case of the banana.

In each section I have highlighted the ethical dilemmas surrounding the consumption of Caribbean goods, ranging from the problem of moral corruption by luxuries, to the ethics of eating slave produce, and finally the current question of fair trade. If there is a lesson to be learned from the nineteenth-century sugar boycotts, it is that ending slavery was not in and of itself enough to challenge the social injustices of the global economy and the forms of cultural consumption that it supported. Those who abstained from sugar constructed their own ethical practices through representing the slave as an abject body without agency. In so far as emancipation implied that slaves were to become 'free labourers', still working to service the European market, abolitionism failed to listen to the demands being made by African-Caribbean people for justice, democratic citizenship, and economic reparation (cf. Sheller 2000). It remains to be seen how these still relevant demands will be dealt with in the twenty-first century, as the ACP group of countries is losing its unity and its special claim on the European Union in the face of new global trade agreements.

In the first half of this book I have considered the ways in which Europeans consumed Caribbean nature, landscapes, natural products, and edible commodities either by travelling to the Caribbean or by bringing things back from the Caribbean. But this is only one-half of the story. When early travel writers framed the landscape of the Caribbean within particular visual regimes, they were also framing the bodies that inhabited those places. When tourists or Northern consumers indulge in eating tropical fruits and tasting the 'spicy' cuisine of the West Indies, they are also consuming the bodies of those who are producing the goods and services that make up tourism. Moreover, the cultural geographies and global markets which constitute the 'circuits of culinary culture' (Cook and Crang 1996) are closely intertwined with the circuits of human mobility during different 'ages of migration'. In the United States, for example, sugar is grown in Florida on sugar plantations owned by Cuban exiles and worked by Haitian cane-cutters, many of whom were expelled from the Dominican Republic when it gained entry into the European market and shifted to banana production.[52] In the rest of this book I turn to the mobilities of travellers and migrants, the visual representation and consumption of the exotic body of Caribbean 'others', and the forms of objectification and enforced localisation of Caribbean people that enable the privileges of travel.

Part II

Bodies and cultural hybridities

4 Orienting the Caribbean

When East is West

The Tropics have long been metaphorically consumed through colonial and imperial travel narratives, fictions, and artistic depictions of far-away places, lush landscapes and exotic others. Yet the Caribbean occupies an ambiguous place in the realm of Western imagined geographies, partaking of the paranoid fantasies of discovery that Anne McClintock identifies as 'both a *poetics* of ambivalence and a *politics* of violence' (McClintock 1995: 28). Euro-American understandings of the Caribbean pivot around what Silvia Spitta, following Edmundo Desnoes, has described as 'a single Manichean political, economic and discursive opposition which was repeated ad nauseam. This opposition, paradise/hell, noble savages/cannibals, has persisted to this day, but now it reads: friendly natives/hostile guerrillas' (Spitta 1997: 160). The interplay of these two discourses in the consumption of the Caribbean creates a sense of excitement and danger, produced through moving closer and distancing, longing and horror, touch and recoil. It is both the site of escapist tourism and the dangerous terrain of criminals, unstable governments, disease, and desperate boat-people. As one recent travel writer ambivalently describes it: 'The first time I went to Jamaica, I didn't know much about the place beyond a vague impression of pirates, palm trees, Noel Coward, ganja and beneath that a sense of intensity, a lurking voluptuous danger.'[1]

In this chapter I seek to unravel Europe's ambivalent relation to the Caribbean through a close reading of Western travel narratives and visual representations, which I argue produce a dual 'Orientalisation' and 'Africanisation' of 'West Indian' places and peoples. The Caribbean, of course, lies literally to the west of Europe. Yet it has always been expunged from the figurative time-space of 'Western modernity' (and from sociological accounts of it) ever since Christopher Columbus gazed upon what he mistook for an outpost of the Great Kublai Khan's Eastern civilisation, as described by Marco Polo. As far as we know from the journals written during his four voyages (two of which were preserved by Bartolomé de Las Casas) Columbus believed that he was near Asia and would soon find the great city of 'Quisay'. He mused that Cuba was perhaps the land of 'Cipangu' (Japan) and thought that he had reached the East until the end of his life.[2] But Columbus's journeys were fraught with doubts and fantasies of the unknown. Underlying his glowing accounts of fertile islands was an inkling that this was not the rich Orient at all, but the savage land of cannibals mentioned in ancient manuscripts: a poor and dangerous place offering nothing but ignominious death (cf. Hulme 1986; Hulme and Whitehead 1992; Barker *et al.* 1998). As McClintock argues, figures of women and cannibals marked the European explorers' fear of engulfment in the unstable liminal spaces of discovery (McClintock 1995: 24–5). In this 'porno-tropics' the crisis of male imperial identity was warded off by naming the unknown as 'cannibal', thereby 'confessing a dread that the unknown might literally rise up and devour the intruder whole' (ibid.: 27).

To be lost, perhaps devoured by 'man-eaters', in an unknown land would certainly be to lose all the potential advantages to be gained there. So Columbus had to return to Europe; and to return he had to keep moving, 'discovering' one island after another, looking for the Orient beyond the Cannibal Islands – going West to find the East. If the Caribbean was a kind of detour on the European route to Eastern riches (and capitalist modernity), it was one made profitable only by return. As Edouard Glissant observes in *Le Discours Antillais* (1981), 'The Detour is not a profitable ploy unless it is fertilised by the Return: not a return to the dream of origin, to some immutable unity of Being, but a return to the point of entanglement, from which we were forcibly turned away; that is where we must ultimately put to work the forces of the Relation, or perish' (Glissant 1981: 36; cf. Dhareshwar 1989; Dash 1989). We can read Glissant as suggesting that Europe's relation to the Caribbean can most profitably be understood if we return to its original entanglement with Asia (and Africa), which led to this Caribbean detour. In the following sections I will 'put to work' these forces by exploring how Anglo-Americans oriented the landscapes and bodies of the West Indies by gauging their similarity to and difference from the 'Oriental' and the 'East Indian', as well as 'the African'. In so doing, it was most importantly their tropical travels, their detours and returns, which enabled them to profit from the Relation (yet also put them at risk).

Ever since Columbus, European travellers have used movement, touch, and the gaze to 'orient' the Caribbean in a number of different senses of the word. As the dictionary definition suggests, European explorers first had to 'align or position (something) relative to the points of a compass or other specified positions'. Yet Columbus mistakenly thought he was in the Orient, i.e. 'situated in or belonging to the east'. In a further meaning, Europeans were orienting the Caribbean as in to 'adjust or tailor (something) to specified circumstances or needs', the dictionary example being 'market-oriented'. They were also orienting themselves as in to 'find one's position in relation to new and strange surroundings'.[3] In so far as orientation means 'the determination of the relative position of something or someone (especially oneself)', European *dis*-orientation in the Caribbean required some kind of relative determination of positions.

I will draw on Sara Ahmed's argument in *Strange Encounters: Embodied Others in Postcoloniality* to explore these various acts of relative determination. Ahmed suggests that 'each time we are faced by an other whom we cannot recognise, we seek to find other ways of achieving recognition, not only by re-reading the body of *this* other who is faced, but by telling the difference between this other, and other others. The encounters we might yet have with other others hence surprise the subject, but they also *reopen the prior histories of encounter that violate and fix others in regimes of difference*' (Ahmed 2000: 8; cf. Levine 2000).[4] Similarly, Duncan and Gregory suggest that 'Within the geographical imaginary of post-Enlightenment Europe, "Asia", "Africa", "America", and "Australia" were each discursively constituted by relations of contradiction and opposition that not only confirmed "Europe" as sovereign subject but also marked out a differentiated and often agonistic space of alterity' (Duncan and Gregory 1999: 5–6; Gregory 1999). The Caribbean became a special point of entanglement in the alignment of these agonistic fields of alterity.

European encounters with the Caribbean were a surprise, but one which was read through histories and memories of its prior (violent) encounters with the Orient and its unfolding violent relation with Africa. Columbus's "America", it has been noted, 'was very much an intertextual invention shaped by Pliny's *Natural History*, Marco Polo's *Travels*, romances of chivalry, and Renaissance epic poems' (Shohat and Stam 2000: 67). As Ella Shohat and Robert Stam suggest, 1492 inaugurates the era of Europe's self-invention both through the *Reconquista*, with its expulsion of Muslims and Jews from Spain, and through the *Conquista*, Europe's expansion into the New World. The elaboration of Europe's reflexive modernity necessitated the purging of the Afro-Asiatic roots of its civilisation (Bernal 1987), and this was achieved in part via its fortuitous entry into a New World where the mythic Savage other could be embodied in new form. Europe defined itself through a comparative operation, which positioned America as like Asia in some ways (a land of luxury, wealth, minimal work, indulgence of the senses) and like Africa in other ways (primitive, dangerous, wild). As this chapter will demonstrate, Europeans produced the idea of the Caribbean via a hybrid Orientalist and Africanist discourse characterised by an unstable logic of East vs. West, tradition vs. modernity, and barbarism vs. civilisation.[5] This effort at producing boundary distinctions has served to 'orient' the West's relationship to the Caribbean from the moment of its 'discovery' until today (while in turn shoring up the ideas of the Orient and of Africa).[6]

While Orientalism has been examined by Edward Said as a discourse within Europe about the East, how did it shift from this geographical referent to take on a wider significance as a generic 'regime of difference' in the Caribbean, understood as another 'Indies'? Said's understanding of Orientalism as 'a discourse for the production and constitution of the Orient as the object of a particular form of colonial power and knowledge', is linked to several different traditions in Occidental thought. These include a theory of despotic power, a theory of social change in which Oriental stagnation is contrasted to Western dynamism, and a theory of sexuality, sensuality, and irrationality associated both with the climate of the region and with femininity (Said 1991 [1978]). As Bryan Turner suggests, 'Orientalism is a discourse which represents the exotic, erotic, strange Orient as a comprehensible, intelligible phenomenon within a network of categories, tables and concepts by which the Orient is simultaneously defined and controlled' (Turner 1994: 21). Each of the tropes of Orientalist discourse can be traced into the discursive construction of the Caribbean in the writings produced by travellers from the North Atlantic. Orientalist discourse took different forms in different European societies, as Said notes in his comments on German or US variants, and as Lisa Lowe demonstrates in her comparative study of French and British Orientalisms (Lowe 1991). Within the various Caribbean colonies of each colonial power there were also differing practices, legislation, and understandings of hybridity, miscegenation, and race (Hoetink 1985). This chapter will focus especially on Anglo-American variants of 'Caribbeanist' discourse, recognising that a full analysis of French, Hispanic, or Dutch variants is beyond the scope of this book.[7] What is particular about the working out of these relations in the Caribbean, as I shall argue below, is the ways in which it was situated as a place of dangerous hybridisation, or intermixing of East and West.

Europeans inscribed Columbus's original misreading of the Caribbean as the Orient through its very naming as the West Indies, a kind of mirror image of the East Indies, and its inhabitants as Indians. But these Indies were also always troubled by the underlying fear of its mysterious inhabitants, who were known both as Caribs (Caribales in some texts) and as cannibals. As Peter Hulme (1986) has shown, the alignment of relative differences began with Columbus's constant efforts to draw a distinction between 'friendly natives' (whom he generally called Arawaks) and 'fierce savages' (whom he called Caribs, and described as man-eaters). In depicting some of the natives as fierce savages, Columbus, who had married into a sugar-planting Madeiran family,[8] was able to justify his effort to enslave some of them (he captured six and brought them back to Europe in chains, and later returned to found a sugar colony on Hispaniola). The alleged practice of anthropophagy (man-eating), which as Hulme shows was entirely fantasised by Columbus, became a crucial legitimisation of Carib enslavement. The conflict between 'good primitive' and 'violent savage' also informed the famous debate between Juan Ginés de Sepúlveda and Bartolomé de Las Casas in the 1550s, with Las Casas defending the 'Indians' as innocent children of nature and calling instead for the enslavement of Africans (Root 1998: 37).

The early conquistadors' motives were to gain an advantage for Spain in world trade, which depended on luxuries from the Far East which were up until then traded via the Moorish empire in the Middle East and North Africa. If Columbus and his men were disappointed that Eastern wealth could not be directly accessed via the western route, they soon consoled themselves that it could be rivalled first via enslavement of indigenes to mine gold and later enslavement and transportation of Africans to the West Indies to grow sugar. Thus the Caribbean was from its inception oriented in relation to Europe's East, as Europe grasped its way toward a new capitalist mode of production that would enable it to outstrip Africa and even overtake Asia in the production of wealth, cities, and surplus accumulation.[9] This history of entanglement introduced an Orientalist vision into the West Indies almost from their inception in European thought. Yet within Orientalist discourses there was a dark side, figured as savagery, wildness, and decay. Such notions of cultural decay were linked to ideas of environmental determinism, 'which suggested that Europeans who remained too long in the tropics would themselves decay and degenerate into hybridity' (Duncan 1999: 159). Such fears were especially prevalent in the Caribbean, as I began to explore in Chapter 2.

As one of the foremost sites for the sexual meeting of once distant populations, the Caribbean has served as a laboratory for European theorisation of 'race' and 'miscegenation'. For Europeans the Caribbean by the late eighteenth century, but especially in the nineteenth century, came to represent a dangerous site of hybridisation and potential 'racial degeneracy' (Banton 1998; Young 1995). It was a special zone open to the re-mixing of previously separate populations and 'racial' substances. Efforts to classify all of the racial permutations in the Caribbean led to arcane typologies such as that of Moreau de Saint-Méry with its 172-odd categories, and debates over the supposed sterility of certain human 'crossbreeds'. It was the very impossibility of such systems of ordering that drove many Europeans to insist upon the fundamental difference of races and to attempt to reinforce and shore up racial boundaries by systems of inequality, discrimination, and segregation. In travelling, white Europeans tried to gauge difference by 'reading' the traces of skin tone, facial features, or gait of various kinds of Caribbean people in order to relocate that which had moved in relation to its place of origin (e.g. Africa, the Orient, Europe), thus fixing racial meanings.

The 'imperialist self' in the West Indies was always at risk of getting lost, never finding a way back to Europe, both literally and metaphorically. The imperialist body is literally vulnerable to losing its bearings and being shipwrecked on a distant wild shore, starving, being eaten by cannibals, or succumbing to disease. Metaphorically, the European is also open to 'going native', to crossing the frontier of another culture, never to return. The idea of 'hybridisation' is one way of expressing this process of transformation. Others have used the term 'transculturation', and Caribbean theorists have favoured the term 'creolization', which I discuss further in Chapter 6. These are all processes not simply of degeneracy, but of cultural creativity and generativity, which disrupt any simple notions of colonisation, imperialism, or cultural hegemony. Forces of creolization in particular may blur the distinction between European and 'native' cultures, making it difficult for the aspiring imperialist to distinguish between what is 'his' and what is 'theirs'. Rather than attributing unlimited power to the European, we can understand these modes of 'consuming' the Caribbean as a two-edged sword by which the consumer is himself or herself consumed (I discuss this further in Chapter 6).

This unstable relation between Europe and the Caribbean returns us to the points of their entanglement. My analysis is based on a reading of Anglo-American literature of exploration, travel, and tourism in the 'West Indies'. Unlike earlier analyses of the complex figuration of this relation in 'high literature', such as the various postcolonial readings of William Shakespeare's treatment of Prospero and Caliban in *The Tempest*,[10] here I light upon some of the most banal and devalued forms of popular documentary and fiction. There was a voracious reading public for these 'real' and fictionalised accounts of various European and Anglo-American 'travel writers'. This chapter focuses in particular on the sentimental personal narratives in which the 'I' takes centre stage, rather than the more 'objective' mode of scientific natural history accounts (Pratt 1992).

In travelling, Anglo-Americans established relative differences among bodies through forms of proximity and distance that depended on the mobility of various bodies into and around the Caribbean, as discussed in Chapter 1. These intersecting mobilities, these detours and returns, inform the 'economies of touch' (Ahmed 2000: 49) by which particular bodies were determined to be either like or unlike other bodies. I will first explore the early imagining of the West Indies as being like the Orient or the Levant. I then consider the arrival of Eastern peoples and cultures in the western hemisphere, and how travel writers imagined that hybridisation. And finally I turn to the Africanist discourse developed especially in relation to Haiti. In each case I will begin to indicate the economies of consumption of human labour and visual representations of the body, which will be more literally explored as actually 'eating bodies' in Chapter 5.

Luxury and decadence: West Indies as Orient/Levant

In spite of the fear of unknown Caribs/cannibals, Columbus's glowing reports on the colony he planted on Hispaniola in 1493 and the enticing myth of El Dorado, a source of gold lost in the jungle, drove Spanish and Portuguese explorers in search of some profit to be turned here. The Dutch and English followed close behind, also eager to gain some advantage in the Tropics (or subtropics). The Tropics hold a special dual meaning because the word 'tropical' is suggestive not only of the region between the Tropic of Cancer and the Tropic of Capricorn, but also of a change of signification, deriving from the Greek *tropikos*, meaning 'turning'. It shares this derivation with the literary term 'trope', 'a figurative or metaphorical use of a word or expression'.[11] Developing this dual meaning, Srinivas Aravamudan suggests a process which he calls 'tropological', based on the early eighteenth-century definition of trope: '*Trope, tropus*, in rhetoric, a word or expression used in a different sense from what it properly signifies. Or, a word changed from its proper and natural signification to another, with some advantage. – Ephraim Chambers, *Cyclopedia*, 1741' (Aravamudan 1999: xi). To what extent was an Orientalist trope used in the Caribbean 'in a different sense from what it properly signifies . . . with some advantage'? How did this Orientalist catachresis (a mistaken usage based on 'abuse or perversion of a trope or metaphor' (Spivak 1999: 14)) enable Europeans to advantageously orient themselves in the New World? Or, were Europeans themselves changed by the Tropics?

The first step in the 'tropological' act is the entry of the European into the tropical zone, driven not only by a search for profits, but also by a desire for pleasures. As Richard Ligon told his readers considering going to Barbados in the 1650s:

> [if one] loves the pleasures of Europe, (or particularly of England) and the great varieties of those, let him never come there [to Barbados]; for they are things he shall be sure to misse. But, if he can finde in himselfe a willingnesse, to change the pleasures which he enjoyed in a Temperate, for such as he shall

finde in a Torrid Zone, he may light upon some that will give him an exchange, with some advantage.[12]

If a European man changes from his proper and natural place in the Temperate zone to a life in the torrid Tropics, Ligon asks, what advantage or profit might he gain? Orienting oneself advantageously in the Tropics is in the first instance a matter of bodily sensation, and Ligon's thoughts dwell on the sensuous body and its pleasures. Bodily mobilities are crucial to gaining this pleasurable position, but such mobility also entails various forms of dangerous proximity and risky co-presence.

Ligon writes that the European man will gain an advantage in the enjoyment of the visual and aural senses from the natural beauty and birdsong of the islands. He will also find pleasure in the sense of smell from the ever-blooming scented flowers of the Tropics; and above all in the sense of taste, from the prolific and heavenly fruits unlike any he has ever tasted. The only sense for which there will be no advantage or pleasure gained in the Tropics, he writes, is feeling through the skin:

> For the sense of feeling, it can be applied but two waies, either in doing or suffering; the poor Negroes and Christian servants, find it perfectly upon their heads and shoulders, by the hands of their severe Overseers; so that little pleasure is given the sense, by this coercive kind of feeling . . . But take it in the highest, and most active way it can be applied, which is upon the skins of women, and they are so sweaty and clammy, as the hand cannot pass over, without being glued and cimented in the passage or motion; and by that means little pleasure is given to, or received by the agent or the patient: and therefore if this sense be neither pleased in doing nor suffering, we may decline it as uselesse in a Country, where down of Swans, or wool of Beaver is wanting.[13]

The Tropics, then, are not a place of touching the other in a caress, yet they are a place in which one's other senses will be beguiled. Troubling thoughts of sadism and sex seem to stick to Ligon's dwelling on the sticky skin. What is it about the whip-suffering or sweaty skins in the Tropics that detract from the potential pleasures? Is it in these sticky situations that the European planter's 'advantage' is most at risk?

The skin can be thought of as a 'locus of social differentiation', as Ahmed argues, which is 'touched differently by different others' (Ahmed 2000: 49, 155; and see Ahmed and Stacey 2001). In the white body's mobility, and its coming into proximity with the enslaved or servile body, the sting of the whip and the sticky caress matter. As Ahmed suggests in considering the 'ethics of touch',

> we could also ask about the different ways in which bodies 'touch' other bodies, and how those differences are ways of forming the bodies of others. We could differentiate, for example, between the caress, the shake, the beating,

and so on . . . in terms of the affect they have on the living out of one's bodily relation to others. We could consider how some forms of touch have been means of subjugating others, or of forming the other as a place of vulnerability and fear (colonial and sexual histories of touch as appropriation, violation and possession).

(Ahmed 2000: 48–9)

So the 'strange encounters' of colonialism are 'tactile as well as visual' and, Ahmed continues, 'some skins are touched as stranger than other skins'. Some are whipped, others are caressed; some are dressed in fine clothes and others are stripped and raped. The 'social body' of a colonial society is formed by these sticky 'economies of touch' through which proximity and distance are managed. Thus careful marking of differences became crucial to resisting the sensual morass and dangerous lethargy of the Tropics, and the whip was used literally as a way of marking other bodies, 'domesticating' the other while maintaining mastery of the self. So the crack of the whip on some (usually black) skins marks them as different from those (white and sometimes non-white) skins which shall not be whipped, but caressed. The marks of race were applied by these variations of touch as much as coded by the gaze. And to gaze and to touch required the white 'agent' to move through the dangerous Tropics, to seek pleasures and gain an advantage by turning 'what might have been an incommensurable and discontinuous other into a domesticated other that consolidates the imperialist self' (Spivak 1999: 130).

In migrating to the Tropics and becoming slave owners white colonists placed their own bodies at risk. Besides the risk of fevers and death, they risked the effects of their unfettered exercise of coercion over enslaved bodies, with all the associated excesses of lust and power. Such excesses, however, could lead to 'miscegenation' or racial hybridisation, through which the very differentiation of bodies on which their advantage and profit rested would be lost. As James Duncan suggests, 'The British who were residents in, rather than visitors to, this picturesque place feared that they were part of the cultural decay of the place' (Duncan 1999: 152). The planter not only lived in fear of Cannibals and of slave uprisings, but through the overly-excessive application of coercion upon servants' and slaves' bodies, or the overly-indulgent exercise of lustful pleasures upon women's bodies, also risked his own body. The planter's embodied energy is gradually sapped; he soon succumbs, so the account goes, to lethargy, profligacy, gluttony, and other deadly sins. In this tropological turn, according to this discursive frame, too much intermingling of moist bodies, too much sweaty self-indulgence, too much blurring of East and West, leads Europeans astray, corrupting their moral compass.

Given these dangers, it is not surprising that European notions of the Orient closely linked the idea of 'luxury' to the imagery of 'corruption' of the mind and body. The popular novelist Tobias Smollett, for example, wrote that the 'Roman Commonwealth of old' fell because 'luxury and profuseness' from the Orient 'led the Way to Indigence and Effeminacy; which prepared the Minds of the People for Corruption; and Corruption for Subjection' (Tchen 1998: 3; cf. Sekora 1977). This notion of luxury was best represented in the practice of gluttony. As Roy

Porter has shown, eighteenth-century medical writers raised concerns about gluttony and over-consumption leading to diseases of consumption. George Cheyne wrote in 1733:

> When Mankind was simple, plain, honest and frugal, there were few or no diseases. Temperance, Exercise, Hunting, Labour, and Industry kept the Juices Sweet and the Solids brac'd. . . . [However,] Since our Wealth has increas'd, and our Navigation has been extended, we have ransack'd all Parts of the *Globe* to bring together its whole stock of Materials for *Riot, Luxury*, and to provoke *Excess* [italics in original].[14]

This idea of excess and corruption became attached to the Caribbean both through the luxury goods that Europeans began to import from the colonies, such as coffee, rum, and tobacco, and through a moral critique of the effects of the institution of slavery on Europeans who went to the Caribbean. Moreover, the racial/cultural mixtures that accompanied global trade were also understood as leading to decadence. By the late eighteenth century the figure of the Mestizo or Mulatto in European thought 'was dreaded by racists as a monster, an infertile hybrid' (Pieterse 1992 [1990]: 360; Young 1995).

Depictions of colonial wealth were tinged with undercurrents of decadence coded as racial degeneracy or sexual hybridisation. The themes of financial cupidity, cross-racial love, and the moral corruption of slavery were taken up repeatedly, for example in the many retellings of the story of Inkle and Yarico. Based on the writings of Richard Ligon about his visit to Barbados in the late 1640s and popularised by Richard Steele's version in *The Spectator* in 1711, the story was retold in poems, plays, opera, song, prints, and engravings over the next century. It centres on an Indian 'virgin' (or in some cases 'Negro') woman, Yarico, who saved a shipwrecked young Englishman, Inkle, with whom she fell in love. But he betrayed her when instead of taking her back to England as he had promised, he sold her into slavery, despite knowing that she was pregnant with his child. While Ligon's account included many details of the harsh treatment of slaves and servants by Barbados planters, this story caught the imagination in so far as the young man's lust for wealth exceeded his love for the Native woman.[15]

The story of Inkle and Yarico epitomised the immorality of the slave system even while dispensing with a 'hybrid' love that could never have been acceptable.[16] Indeed it was the very impossibility of such 'love' within a context of slavery that served to both underline and conceal the moral and sexual corruption of the European in the West Indies. In an amusing reading of a poetic version of the story, published in 1726/38, Derek Walcott lights into Inkle, after his line 'I needed not for such a prize to roam/ There are a thousand doating maids at home':

> Inkle! Inkle! After the juicy mangoes and the crystal streams, diet and regular, after the tiger-skin crib and the you-know-what of these coupling couplets, that's the best you can do? More, because he sells Yarico into slavery. Besides,

she's pregnant. But without a tear's twinkle, Inkle gets aboard the ship and leaves her there. The first tourist. Cf. 'Jamaica Farewell' by H. Belafonte.[17]

So, the (sex) tourist leaves behind his 'little girl' and his unborn child, and makes money from selling them to boot. We shall return to these themes in Chapter 5, but first let's consider whether Inkle the tourist leaves with no inkling of his own transformation by this encounter with Yarico, no kinship with his unborn 'hybrid' child.

The unfolding of hybridity and 'miscegenation' in the Caribbean colonies became a topic of fascination in eighteenth-century Europe, where efforts at scientific ordering and classifying of humanity were already underway. European painters such as Agostino Brunias (*c.* 1730–96) took a great interest in representing 'Mulattoes' in scenes painted for wealthy white patrons. Brunias's well-known paintings of Dominica, for example, concentrate on the 'hybrid culture' of the 'Mulatto, born from the mixture of European, African, and Carib races. Hence his fascination in the nineteenth century for French ethnologists such as Hamy', who benefited from Brunias's ethnographic eye for 'the diverse aspects of exotic humanity'.[18] His paintings furnished Europeans with examples of how the 'Free Coloured People' dressed and socialised, attending dances dressed in sumptuous fashion, with characteristic bright colours, elaborate head ties, and much jewellery. Engravings based on his pictures were used to illustrate Bryan Edwards's *The History, Civil and Commercial of the British Colonies in the West Indies* (London, 1807), thus reaching a wide audience. Such efforts at collecting ethnographic material on the Caribbean followed in the footsteps of botanical collectors like Hans Sloane, who had collected samples and accurate images of flora and fauna (along with occasional human evidence). As art historian Veerle Poupeye suggests, Brunias's 'sensualist preoccupation with the exotic "other", especially the coloured woman, prefigures orientalism and Gauguin's primitivism' (Poupeye 1998: 32).

The figure of the 'mulatta' or 'quadroon' served to raise questions of human difference through a discourse of cupidity, immorality, sexual corruption, and tropicalization. As Robert Young suggests, the 'cultural construction of race has always been fuelled by the corrupt conjunction of such hybridised sexual and economic discourses' (Young 1995: 158). In William Blake's much reproduced illustration of 'A Surinam Planter in his Morning Dress' for John G. Stedman's 1796 narrative (see Plate 4.1),[19] we see the signs of the planter's bodily pleasures: his pipe for smoking tobacco, his drink being poured by a young bare-breasted slave. Her small, delicate figure in the background inclines toward his, her gaze set on his face, with only the pipe, the precariously balanced drink, and a distant house, like a doll's house, coming between them. Against an empty sky, his much larger figure fills the foreground, noticeably posed in loose clothing, gazing into the unseen distance. Yet his informal clothing, open collar, and unusual broad-brimmed hat might also hint to the European viewer that this dissolute man has been 'tropicalized', he has been re-formed by his tropical environment, even corrupted by the substances he ingests and the slaves he sexually possesses. Stedman's text describes the image in the following terms:

Plate 4.1 Planter tropicalization as domestic corruption.
William Blake, 'A Surinam Planter in His Morning Dress' from Captain John G. Stedman,
Narrative of a Five Years' Expedition Against the Revolted Negroes of Surinam (London, 1796).
Reproduced courtesy of the Library Company of Philadelphia.

His Worship Sa[u]nters Out in his Morning Dress Which Consists in a pair
of the Finest holland Trowsers, White Silk Stockings, and red or Yellow
Morocco Slippers, the Neck of his Shirt open & Nothing Over it, A Loose
flowing Night-Gown of the Finest India Chintz Excepted – on his head is a
Cotton Night Cap, As thin as a Cobweb, and Over that an Enormous Beaver
Hat, to Keep Covered his Meagre Visage from the Sun, Which is Already the

Colour of Mahogany, While his Whole Carcase Seldom Weigh'd above 8, or 10 Stone, being Generally Exhausted to the Climate and Dicipation, And to Give a better idea of this fine Gentleman, I here Represent him to the Reader, With a pipe in his Cheeck/ Which Almost Every Where keeps him Company/ And receiving a Glass of Madeira and Water, from a female Quaderoon Slave to Refresh him During his Walk.[20]

Dressed in luxury goods from around the world (silk, beaver, fine chintz), his body given over to dissipation, this figure epitomises the 'tropicalization' of the European. Blake's engraving organises this story visually into the triangle formed by the pipe, the slave pouring alcohol, and the planter's dissipated body. The alchemy of changing skin-colour is performed by the triangular trade of material goods which adorn his body, the ingestion of narcotic substances, and the sexual intimacy implicit in the 'quadroon' slave, already the result of more than one generation of interracial union.[21] The house between them suggests the dangerous erotics by which the slave is lightened, and the master darkened.

Stedman's narrative focuses on the brutal treatment of slaves in Surinam, and on his own love for a 'mulatta' slave called Joanna, whom he marries but who in the end refuses to accompany him back to England. It is another version of Inkle and Yarico's tale of the pitfalls and pain of crossing over the tropical natural and racial boundary. Aravamudan compares tropicalization to what Mary Louise Pratt calls transculturation, 'acts of cultural transformation, or "going native", in various colonial "contact zones"' (Aravamudan 1999: 6; Pratt 1992). Pratt herself borrowed the concept from the Cuban sociologist Fernando Ortiz (Ortiz 1940 [1947]). As used by these theorists it refers both to Europeans themselves going native, and to European ideas being seized and transformed by tropical subaltern agents, in acts of rhetorical reappropriation and discursive redeployment by those whom Aravamudan calls 'tropicopolitans'. Here I focus on the transformation of the European in the Caribbean, and the effects of consuming the Caribbean in Europe. The particular form of transculturation in the Caribbean, also theorised as 'creolization' (Brathwaite 1971), held the potential of 'hybridisation' and miscegenation, which put the white advantage at risk. The detour into tropical luxuriance must remain only that, lest the European not return. In innumerable narratives 'Europeans visit the colony and promptly die, go crazy, go native, drown in alcohol or sex – the list goes on. . . . It seems that Westerners are only safe if they strictly maintain their position of colonial or racial authority' (Root 1998: 44).

Tropicalization can also be thought of as a moral danger inherent in the climate itself, and in the proximity of 'different' bodies. As one traveller put it in 1804, 'I am afraid also, from the mean and disingenuous behaviour of some of the inferior white inhabitants of the town, that the climate, and perhaps their association with the blacks, have not a little relaxed in them the strength and integrity of the British moral character'.[22] Thus in entering the Tropics, the European gained certain advantages, but also risked being permanently changed. This degeneracy was, in a way, a kind of disorientation, a loss of moral bearings, purpose, and direction. Spanish planters, in particular, were viewed in British culture as having gone too far in hybridisation, or 'creolization'. As Edward Long remarked in his *History of Jamaica*, 'Let any man turn his eyes to the Spanish American dominions, and behold what a vicious, brutal, and degenerate breed of mongrels has been there produced, between Spaniards, Blacks, Indians, and their mixed progeny'.[23] In an 1820 illustration on the same theme we see a typical 'Spanish Planter of Porto Rico, Luxuriating in his Hammock' (Plate 4.2),[24] again smoking and being served a drink by a slave. Resting in his hammock (an Arawak invention and practice), he is immersed in lush tropical flora with giant leaves crowding in on the scene, a pineapple and mangoes in easy reach. With delicately drawn facial features, he too looks away from the smiling male slave, who steps forward with bare feet, gazing upon the planter's face as if happy to serve him. The 'strange' (non-European) tropical fruits and drinks that he ingests, the close service of a slave, the very habit of his luxuriating in a hammock are all suggestive of the power of the Caribbean to engulf the European. His active mastery has given way to torpor, self-indulgence, and consumption of luxuries.

It was not only male travellers who indulged in the sensual fantasies and bodily risks of the West Indies. In a romantic novel set in the French colony of Saint Domingue, but written shortly after the revolution that brought the richest colony in the world to a sticky end, the North American writer Eleanor Sansay conjured up the white Creole woman's luxuries and more ticklish pleasures of the skin:

> I should repose beneath the shade of orange groves; walk on carpets of rose leaves and frenchipone; be fanned to sleep by silent slaves, or have my feet tickled into extacy [*sic*] by the soft hand of a female attendant. Such were the pleasures of the Creole ladies whose time was divided between the bath, the table, the toilette and the lover. What a delightful existence! Thus to pass away life in the arms of voluptuous indolence; to wander over flowery fields of unfading verdure, or through forests of majestic palm-trees, sit by a fountain bursting from a savage rock frequented only by the cooing dove, and indulge in these enchanting solitudes all the reveries of an exalted imagination.[25]

Combining imagery of the Caribbean with familiar tropes from Orientalist depictions of harems (being fanned by slaves, 'voluptuous indolence'), Sansay sexualises Creole existence with a kind of polymorphous perversity. This was a world of Creole pleasures that was destroyed by the time she published in 1808, the planters and debauched mistresses of Saint Domingue slaughtered in the uprising of their slaves. The enchantment of the Creole existence was perhaps so great that the masters failed to detect the coming uprising of their slaves.

The luxuriant 'hothouse' of tropical nature again casts its damp shadow into this vision of Creole debauchery and self-indulgent luxuriance, a kind of corrupting sink of sin, lethargy, and despotism.[26] This parallels Orientalist discourse, which as Said found, associates corruption both with excesses of wealth and with

Plate 4.2 The European engulfed by tropical luxury.
'A Spanish Planter of Porto Rico, Luxuriating in his Hammock', in John A. Waller, *A Voyage in the West Indies* (London, 1820). Reproduced courtesy of the British Library.

the excessive profusion of nature, both figured through feminine corruption. As Walcott describes engravings of scenes from this era, they exude 'the sickly sweet fragrance of molasses':

> Strange that these engravings should still look so sinister, their feathery heraldic fountains of palm and bamboo arching over shallow, rippling brooks, their light, always of mid-afternoon, suggesting languor, and beyond them the estate house with its jalousie windows and an empty verandah sad in its vacancy, or other pastorals, of Creole beauties in costume, or panniered donkeys prodded home by straw-hatted peasants, the donkey's hooves plodding to the meter of an era, a languorous, condescending prose.
>
> (Walcott 2000: 57)

Today we see such images from an historical distance, thinking we are free of their colonial condescension, yet much within them is still sculpted into the living landscape of Caribbean resorts with their 'colonial-style' buildings and languorous gardens, some even with picturesque 'chattel houses' tucked away in the corner. Colonial luxury and countrified quaintness occur side by side in the invented contexts of Caribbean tourism.

The Anglo-American fantasy of the Caribbean thus combines a fascination with primeval nature and a compulsion to seek the pleasures of cosmopolitan wealth and power, just as primitive cannibalism and civilised China loomed side by side in Columbus's imagination. An English captain visiting Surinam in the early 1830s typically cites the doubly magnetic pull of primeval forests and haunting El Dorado:

> I remained but a short time in Stabroek, for I was impatient to plunge into the primeval forests of the interior – to navigate the mighty rivers fertilizing regions unexplored by European travelers – to visit the nameless creeks overshadowed by the gloomy, though rich and luxuriant vegetation – to tread the soil of that country, ever famous since the days of Sir Walter Raleigh, as containing the magnificent city of Eldorado, which 'for greatness, riches, and the excellent seat, far exceeded any city in the world, and founded on an inland sea two hundred leagues long, like unto the Mare Caspium'.[27]

In depicting this convergence of primeval nature and urban magnificence (cited via the Old World), each act of exploration is an act of quotation. Alexander quotes Raleigh's text, Raleigh quotes Las Casas, Las Casas quotes Columbus, Columbus quotes Marco Polo, and so on in a never-ending *mise-en-abyme* in which Europe chases its own tale.

In the Tropics the 'gloomy, though rich' excesses of nature engulf the European, leaving him or her lost in a land of uncivilised cannibals, without a map. But the dream of Oriental luxury passed down from one travel account to the next guides each one onwards in the quest for unlimited riches and unimaginable wealth, beyond the dense jungles. They must only survive and return, and writing itself operates as a means of 'staying in touch' during their detour. Through their Caribbean narratives Anglo-American travellers constituted a reading public in the North Atlantic for whom the Tropics became 'second nature' (Franklin *et al.* 2000), known through its cultural representations, a nature made to do certain kinds of work to assist a fantasy of the 'untouched' primeval. Caribbean nature must be staged to always perform as Paradise. It is a simulated world in which imperialist fantasies are played out again and again, and in which 'certain Western literary protocols have become so naturalised as to be almost invisible' (Root 1998: 61).[28]

Ultimately, a deeply Orientalist tourism has been instituted in the West Indies, founded on the 'global' exoticism of the cruise ships, like *The Levant*, that ply the warm tropical waters and materially encoded in generic tropical resorts with 'Moorish' architecture and pan-Indian names like 'The Taj'. Such Eastern fantasies are closely tied to ideas of luxury, indulgence, and excessive wealth. Especially in celebrity havens like Mustique there are numerous homes designed to impose a fantasy Orient in the Caribbean. The British theatre set designer Oliver Messel designed a series of villas there that 'are built along Japanese lines or in the Spirit of Bali, with names like Moongate, Obsidian and Sleeping Dragon'; David Bowie once owned one called 'Mandalay', while Mick Jagger has a 'Japanese-style' one. As a recent travel writer typically observes in defence of this 'pleasure island': 'The Caribbean is, after all, about indulging the senses: eating, sunbathing, sleeping and, of course, snorkelling. You don't exactly go there for the culture.'[29] Especially when the only culture to be found has been bent to the whims of colonialist fantasy. 'Balinese-style' villas in the Caribbean are taken to the ultimate on Richard Branson's $14,000-a-day Necker Island in the British Virgin Islands. Escapist, 'placeless places' such as these serve to naturalise the 'pleasure island' as a hybrid of East and West, while expelling the dangerous African-Caribbean primitive from paradise. But Asia and Africa entered the Caribbean in more literal ways, which were not so easily manipulated; in the following sections I trace first the entrance of Asia into the Caribbean, and then the appearance of a displaced Africa.

Asia in the Caribbean

These tropes of luxury, decadence, and the rediscovery of paradise have a long cultural pedigree. As noted in Chapter 2, European views of Caribbean islands present a fascination with a particular type of tropical landscape and particular kinds of 'natural' and 'cultivated' scenery. Here I want to focus more closely on the Orientalist inflections of European perceptions of the Caribbean. Mary Louise Pratt argues that Alexander von Humboldt in his widely read account of his travels of 1799–1804 applied a new discourse of the sublime in nature to describe the 'luxuriant' and 'exuberant vegetation' of South America and the Caribbean. Since that time, in trying to make sense of what they saw in the West Indies, Europeans have drawn on romantic imagery of the East. Seeking words to describe the dazzling sunrise in Grenada, for example,

Captain Alexander can only manage borrowed accounts and images from Arabia and Italy:

> on coming on deck before it was light, the island appeared like a mighty wall against the grey horizon, and the clouds which floated round the highest ridges were as black as the smoke from some dreadful conflagration, reminding one of the mountain of adamant of the Arabian Nights, towards which luckless vessels were irresistibly impelled. Gradually a light rosy tint overspread the horizon ... through a break in the mountain a blood-red ray darted from the as yet invisible sun; ... and then he burst forth in the full glories of his splendour, revealing a scene of purely Italian character.[30]

Mixing Homeric language with Arabian imagery, the Caribbean landscape is here seen through 'Old World' eyes, often drawn from Greek and Roman poetry and European imagery of the Orient and the Levant. Somehow the scene becomes 'purely Italian' in this displaced Mediterranean. When the Orientalist genre of painting took hold in Europe in the 1830s, following the French invasion of Algeria (Root 1998: 163), its set pieces and protocols also became increasingly influential in depictions of the Caribbean.

Charles William Day, arriving in Bridgetown, Barbados in the 1850s, described it in terms of the Levant, which he knew through his own travels: 'To one who like myself has been in the Levant, Bridgetown did not by any means seem so strange. . . . It is not unlike the Frank quarter of a Mohammedan city, though the general character of the town is more or less Italian, modified by something that reminds one of the East.'[31] He travelled with pre-formed literary ideas of the 'scene' he expected to see, and matched his experience to these models, especially when describing the people to whom he referred as 'brownies': 'how perfect do they render the scene! Their outlandish jabber, their tawdry rags, brimless hats, and in the case of the females, often fine forms, how perfectly in unison with our impressions of "Incle and Yarico", "Paul and Virginia", and the "Cruise of the Midge".'[32] Rather than simply passing over these citations as literary licence or derivative imitation, we can read them as significant tropes of cross-racial imagination and hybrid Levantinization by which Europeans oriented themselves in the West Indies and thereby 'oriented' the Caribbean.[33] Travel through the Caribbean is deeply invested in these sexual romances and romanticised landscapes, which materialise racial and scenic hybrids of East and West.

Instability in the terms of reference is notable in all such tropological writing. As Homi Bhabha has pointed out, colonial discourse is 'a form of knowledge and identification that vacillates between what is always "in place", already known, and something that must be anxiously repeated' (Bhabha 1983: 18). The Caribbean is a site of constant repetition, as each writer-in-motion anxiously tries to fix the unstable, non-locatable, shifting context in place. Lola Young argues that,

> [This] necessity for vacillation is occasioned because the discourse attempts to fix and stabilise that which is not static. The desire for scientism, exemplified

in the valorization of systematic categorization based on empiricism, inevit-
ably produces some instances which refuse to be contained by the conceptual
boundaries established. In these cases the lines of demarcation have to be re-
ordered or the exceptions denied, and this is why stereotypes are protean
rather than stable.

(Young 1986: 56)

I suggest that the discourse of Levantinism became a way of expressing something that exceeded the categories of Oriental versus African. There was a state
of flux in the Caribbean, a protean racial crucible, disturbing European attempts
at ordering. Thus specific understandings of the amalgamation of East and West
were closely linked to ideas of sexual mixture and proximate and distant kinship,
which were refined through gazing upon and symbolically ordering East Asians
and 'Mulattas' in the West Indies.

On arriving in Port of Spain, Trinidad, Captain Alexander wrote: 'the
coloured women here are uncommonly handsome; Spanish blood they say
amalgamates better than British with African, and really I saw some faces and
figures that reminded me of the healthy olive cheeks and cypress waists of the
East. Now the brown creoles of the old English islands have not such characteristics, neither do they dress so well.'[34] As in many travellers' tales, Alexander's
dream of Eastern riches and Italianate landscape transmutes into an Orientalism
read onto the bodies of Caribbean women (an updated 'porno-tropics'). Women's
bodies are used here to figure the relative distances between places, and to orient
the male traveller, while fantasies of sexual 'amalgamation' inform his adventures.
The notion that Spanish 'blood' amalgamates better with African builds on the
British criticism of Spanish planters noted above, for becoming too 'Creole'.
Here, though, it is expressed literally in the progeny of mixed parentage, whose
bodies come to substantiate theories of cultural mixture. Adding Spaniard to
African, the Englishman calculates a Middle Eastern mean.

Levantinization becomes a mode for expressing this in-between or indeter-
minate status, the Levant lying between the East and the West proper. As Said
demonstrates, Near Eastern Orientalism is linked to notions of despotism, sexual
excess, and failure of self-regulation, all of which were read onto and *marked on* the
bodies of West Indian women. The celebrated twentieth-century Irish travel
writer Patrick Leigh Fermor could write in similar terms of Martinican women
in the 1950s:

> This girl seemed the epitome of Antillean beauty, and of all the grace, charm
> and elegance for which the islands are so celebrated . . . Her skin was about
> the same colour as a dark Greek girl's or a southern Italian's . . . Negro
> women ought always to wear bright colours and compact, dashingly tied
> turbans. Mulatto girls should affect a sort of Italo-Iberian swank.[35]

Such Levantine imagery (spanning from Arabia via Moorish influence to Spain
and parts of the Mediterranean) became a code for reading the hybrid 'Mulatta',

while inflaming sexual passions coded as intermingling of 'races'. The Spanish Creoles themselves had far more complex systems of naming and tracking all the possible 'racial' mixtures (Hoetink 1973, 1985; Young 1995), but they were equally anxious in their efforts to order and fix in place every last drop of these impure 'bloodlines'. Nevertheless, as Duncan and Gregory suggest, travel writing 'spins webs of colonizing power' which involve 'the play of fantasy and desire, and the possibility of transgression' (Duncan and Gregory 1999: 3). Fantasies of transgressing racial boundaries thus became central to processes of drawing those boundaries in the first place. The lure and allure of the Caribbean as a place of hybridisation, embodied in its beautiful brown women, elicited efforts at stabilisation of racial boundaries in so far as it put whiteness (and colonial power) at risk.

European calculations of racial difference could hardly bear the weight of the complex mixtures to be found in the Caribbean. When people from Asia arrived in the Caribbean in the nineteenth century, a new dimension was added to Caribbeanist travel writing. Having begun as a discourse about Caribbean inhabitants as 'Indians', by the mid-nineteenth century, Asia came to the Caribbean in the form of indentured workers from India and China. The British colonial project, founded upon the East India Company and the Royal Africa Company, had always been oriented towards both the East and the West at once, and the British Caribbean became the crossroads at which the East Indies and West Indies met. British colonies such as Trinidad, British Guiana, and to a lesser extent Jamaica took in an 'Eastern' culture. As one European traveller noted in 1888, 'Walking through the cooly quarter of San Fernando [Trinidad] I could scarcely realize that I had not been transported from the Western to the Eastern hemisphere by the mysterious art of an occultist sorcerer'.[36] The 'coolies are emigrants, it is true,' he observed, 'but they appear to have brought their country with them; they *orientalize* (if I may use the term) that part of the New World into which they come – they are not *new-worldified* by crossing the seas'.[37] This curious intertwining of 'West Indies' and 'East Indies' in the 'contact zones' of European colonisation has been little examined, yet has deeply influenced the formation of Euro-American self-identity. The relative place of the racialisation of the 'Oriental' or the 'Asian' in relation to the 'white' and the 'Negro' has recently attracted greater study in the United States (Ryan 1997; Jacobson 1998; Lee 1999; Tchen 1999), but remains far less studied in the Caribbean.

As May Joseph notes in her study *Nomadic Identities* (1999), there is a complex history of contact between Indians and Africans organised around both the transatlantic flows of enslaved African labour and Indian contract labour to the Caribbean, and the trans-Indian Ocean maritime economy linking the East African coast, Mauritius, the Seychelles, Zanzibar, and the Maldives. 'Under the burden of plantation economies,' she argues, the laws governing the rights of colonised peoples within the British Empire 'inflected Indians and Africans differently . . . Articulated as Hindu versus indigenous African, transient labor versus settler/slave, customary practice versus common law, subtle relationships to local legitimacy divided these communities of exploited labor in the interest of colonial hegemony' (Joseph 1999: 73). Joseph's important commentary on the making of a hybrid 'Afro-Indo-Arab culture with Anglophone, Lusophone, and Franco-phone inflexions' helps explain the emergence of anticolonial movements and forms of subaltern agency that crossed national boundaries. Here, however, I want to concentrate on the ways in which colonial projects reinforced distinctions between these two communities in the Caribbean by reading embodied difference through Orientalist and Africanist tropes.

While Said suggests that the formations of Near Eastern Orientalism which he first identified may be extended to many other parts of the colonised world, the specificity of the peculiarly disorienting vortex of Caribbean Orientalism requires greater elaboration. Lisa Lowe (1991) has identified differences between French and British Orientalist discourses, but we might ask not only how Orientalism differs in its point of origin but also how it shifts in different points of destination. The trope of Oriental luxury was picked up, for example, by Creoles themselves who decorated their homes in 'Oriental' fashion. As Lady Emmeline Wortley noted on her visit to Cuba in 1859 (by which time there were many Chinese indentured labourers coming into Cuba), there was 'a splendid house in the city [of Havana], in which, I hear, there is a *boudoir* representing the apartment of a mandarin and mandariness in far Pekin, which is declared to be in the *Chinesest* taste imaginable, and more Pekinish than the Chinese junk itself'.[38] How, then, does Levantine Orientalism relate to Far Eastern Orientalism as both are implicated in the West Indies? How are differences between Near East and Far East calibrated as a way of gauging differences within the West Indies?

Because the reading and writing public were exposed to 'classic' travel accounts before ever embarking on their journeys (many note having imbibed them as children, which fed their desire to travel to the Tropics), the Orientalist references remain remarkably uniform over centuries. Charles Kingsley, in his famous novel, *At Last: A Christmas in the West Indies* (1871), made much of the fact that after forty years of reading, 'at last, I was about to compare books with facts, and judge for myself of the reported wonders of the Earthly Paradise'. Crucial to his comparative project was to see the people of the West Indies: 'When you have ceased looking – even staring – at the black women and their ways, you become aware of the strange variety of races which people the city [of Port of Spain].' He felt a sense of kinship with the 'Hindoos', writing that their 'every attitude, gesture, tone, was full of grace; of ease, courtesy, self-restraint, dignity . . . which draws the European to them and them to the European'.[39] He was neither the first nor the last to describe this sense of racial kinship, and the practice of observing, recording, and visually representing degrees of racial difference was a crucial part of the tour in the West Indies.

Visitors like William Agnew Paton (whom we met in Chapter 2, on his 'Voyage in the Caribbees') were especially taken with the Hindu women, such as those in Demerara, who wore their native dress (Plate 4.3):

> Her little feet were bare; nevertheless she trod firmly, stepping lightly, with graceful poise . . . I was enabled to inspect, with approving criticism, the

Plate 4.3 Paton's mahogany-skinned 'Aryan kinswoman'.
'A Hindu Cooly Belle', frontispiece of Edward Agnew Paton, *Down the Islands: A Voyage in the Caribbees* (London, Kegan Paul, Trench & Co., 1888). Reproduced courtesy of the Schomburg Center, New York Public Library.

object of my admiration from tip to toe, and from every point of view. In time I made a mental catalogue of the bewildering items of her apparel and ornaments, taking memoranda that would enable an ingenious artist to paint from my description a full-length picture of her . . . And now, alas! I must confess it, this Aryan kinswoman of mine was as brown as any Hindu cooly girl in Georgetown, and all of her East Indian sisters are as dusky as richest rosewood, as brown and dark as rarest mahogany.[40]

Once again the male traveller uses the female body to gauge relative placements, distances, and orientations. In the idealised engraving, her gaze is turned not only away from the viewer (even though the position of the viewer seems to block her progress down the middle of a road), but heavenward, her loose robes imbuing her with a kind of celestial halo. Paton uses the tropical hardwoods that had made their way into Euro-American homes as furniture to index this tropical woman's skin colour; she embodies nature and the surface of her skin can be objectified within an apparently appreciative natural trope. Yet despite Paton's sense of 'kinship' with this entrancing figure (drawing on racial formations of the Aryan in European philology and ethnology (Banton 1998; Bernal 1987)), her 'mahogany' skin distances her from him.

Paton also photographed women (see Plates 4.4 and 4.5) to illustrate racial 'types' such as 'A Cooly Woman' or 'A Martinique Belle', whose forms were often contrasted against each other. Yet the 'Cooly Woman' in the photograph also appears different from the one in the drawing. She gazes steadfastly at the camera, she lifts her long hair provocatively, with hand on hip, and her skin tone is darker and features less delicate. We can see more clearly how his 'ingenious artist' transformed Paton's mental catalogue into a more palatable vision of exotic femininity. Paton's photographic eye aligns the Coolie woman alongside the similarly posed Martinican woman, who serves as a point of reference so that their differences can be compared. The crucial points of comparison for him are their clothing, jewellery, skin tone, facial features, and style of movement. Like the natural specimens collected by seventeenth-century scientists, these images serve as a catalogue of human diversity, representing aspects of the 'family of man' (McClintock 1995). If the trace of Aryan kinship drew Paton closer to the object of his gaze above, such mythic kinship is not possible with the descendants of Africa in the Caribbean (though the women's choices of floral prints are surprisingly similar!).

To be able to make such racial comparisons authoritatively became one of the central purposes of Anglo-American travel through the West Indies. As Peter James has noted of such images in the Birmingham City Archive,

Just as there was a trade in people's labour through the slave trade, there was also a trade in people's likenesses especially taken for anthropologists and ethnographers in Britain . . . [such as Sir Benjamin Stone's] print 'Negress of the West Indies' [which] appears in his album, 'Types and Races of Mankind'. The presence of such uncontextualised images in a public

Plate 4.4 Returning the tourist gaze?
'A Cooly Woman', photograph in Edward Agnew Paton, *Down the Islands: A Voyage in the Caribbees* (London, Kegan Paul, Trench & Co., 1888). Reproduced courtesy of the Schomburg Center, New York Public Library.

Plate 4.5 Absent presence in the photographic archive.
'A Martinique Belle', photograph in Edward Agnew Paton, *Down the Islands: A Voyage in the Caribbees* (London, Kegan Paul, Trench & Co., 1888). Reproduced courtesy of the Schomburg Center, New York Public Library.

institution serving a culturally diverse community, viewed from a post-colonial perspective, could best be expressed as perhaps 'problematic'.

(James 1998: 30)

The troubling 'presence and absence' of these subaltern 'likenesses' in the archives tell us more about the viewer, and the relations of viewing, than about the objectified Caribbean people they construct as objects and then purport to 'show'. I return to these modes of visually 'consuming bodies' in Chapter 5, to show in more detail how the tourist gaze informs economies of bodily touch and exchange of 'services'.

It is the longevity of these modes of seeing and representing that is so striking. Fermor, in his acclaimed book of 1950, describes Port of Spain, Trinidad, in terms quite similar to Kingsley's in 1873 and Paton's in 1888, and again picks up the self-consciously Orientalist imagery of the *Arabian Nights* in describing a scene in Trinidad:

> It is a large and startlingly cosmopolitan town. The streets blaze with milk-bars, drug stores, joints and picture-places. . . . Songs in Hindustani – plaintive little tunes in the oriental minor mode – float into the air from upper windows which the flag of the Indian republic adorns, while opposing windows fly the colours of Pakistan. The Moslem banner also flutters from the walls of a great snow-white mosque which raises onion-shaped domes and minarets and crescents high above the mean surrounding streets. Against the flamboyance of the Trinidadian sunset, these pearly cylinders and spheres possess the exaggerated orientalism of European illustrations to Omar Khayyam or the Arabian Nights.[41]

It is precisely this exaggerated cartoon-like character of Orientalist imagery and literature in Europe that makes it so applicable to the Caribbean. It is an invention, a foil for Europe itself, and its very inventedness becomes ever more apparent in the West Indies as it threatens to collapse under its own absurd weight. Fermor also describes seeing swimmers as 'severed Asiatic heads, whose features appeared delicate and frail after the robuster cast of the Negroes. We felt that we had wandered by mistake into the middle of a religious ceremony in Benares.'[42] His gaze violently severs the swimmers' heads, while his own body can wander freely, in the mind's eye, from Trinidad to Benares, India.

Fermor explicitly links this Orientalist vision of the Caribbean to the originary mistake of Columbus, noting that the 'region of Antillia existed in the minds of Europeans long before the Antilles were discovered . . . Columbus, landing on Guanahani and the northern coasts of Hispaniola, was convinced that the Arawaks were akin to the Indians of the Orient and the Chinese. Cathay and Hindustan, he felt sure, were not far off (oddly enough, time has lent some colour to his adumbrations; for now, after four centuries, Chinese and East Indians abound in Cuba).'[43] Thus history seems to have vindicated the Columbian vision. Fermor also traces the amalgamation of East and West through an odd historical detail to be found in Kingston, Jamaica. Following a fire in 1882 that destroyed Kingston's synagogues, this became the first known instance of the joining together of a Sephardic and Ashkenazic Jewish community. 'So these two branches of Jewry,' writes Fermor, 'which separated so many centuries ago in the Levant . . . have at last met and amalgamated in this West Indian Island. Only here among the coconut palms and the mangoes, does a Henriquez or a de Cordova bow down in worship beside an Eisenstein or a Weintraub.'[44] Thus he hints at a kind of tropological process, an amalgam of East and West performed through the alchemy of tropical nature.

White female tourists also gauged their own white femininity via comparisons of 'coolies' and 'Negroes'. Sady Brassey, an English woman who toured the Caribbean in 1885 (accompanied by her two black poodles) wrote of Trinidad that,

> the coolie traders, with their dark-brown skins, fine smooth black hair, and lithe figures swathed in bright-coloured shawls, their arms and legs heavy with jewelry, the produce of their spouses' wealth, were quiet and graceful in voice and action; and presented a striking contrast to the buxom black negresses, with their thick lips, gay turbans, merry laughter, and somewhat aggressive curiosity.[45]

Such descriptions combine elements of racialisation and gendering, blurring 'essential' physiological traits with 'superficial' cultural adornments, all of which are aligned from the unmarked position of the privileged white female. Similarly, a North American tourist, Susan de Forest Day, contrasted African and Indian when she described 'an old Indian coolie, whose aristocratic features and delicate skin are a joy after the retreating forehead and flat noses of the dusky African'.[46] A joy in what sense, we must ask; what comfort does this white woman derive from the practice of racial classification?

She too links skin and facial features to notions of aristocracy and the primitive. Day was disturbed when she saw some children who, for her, embodied racial mixture that crossed the Levantine and the African:

> I say the children were black, but they had flaxen hair tied with pink ribbons, and their little features were distinctly and unpleasantly Jewish. But the flaxen hair had the telltale kink, which is the infallible sign of negro blood, and their red-brown eyes, thick lips and slightly hooked Semitic noses, were sickening evidences of a mixture of races which cannot but result in demoralization.[47]

As Said noted in introducing his study of Orientalism, it shares a secret history of resemblance with Western anti-Semitism (Said 1991 [1978]: 27–8). For Day the 'signs' of Jewishness stand for evidence of racial degeneracy and implicit erosion of whiteness in the hybridised contact zones of the West Indies; she further links this cross-breeding with 'demoralization', as if 'mixture of races' itself implies moral corruption.[48] If Paton was entranced by the potential to touch the mahogany skin of the Coolie girls, for Day too much intermixture of 'races' in the Tropics poses a threat of hybridisation. As the essence of one gets thoroughly amalgamated into the other, racial distinctions are lost, morals are threatened, and white femininity is put at risk.

Her views derive from racial theories of the mid-nineteenth century such as those of Josiah Nott and George Gliddon, who argued against hybridisation:

> It seems . . . in human physical history, that the superior race must inevitably become deteriorated by an intermixture with the inferior . . . through the operation of the laws of Hybridity alone, the human family might possibly become exterminated by a thorough amalgamation of all the various types of mankind now existing on earth.
>
> (Cited in Young 1995: 133)

To guard against such 'degeneration' the white tourist had to resist amalgamation by always marking the differences between 'races'. They found it necessary to police racial boundaries by getting close enough to say what was one thing and what was another. Travel became a way of producing a sufficient knowledge of many others in order to fix each one in the right place. Creolization and its lurking dangers of miscegenation threatened the loss of such fixed markers, leaving the traveller without a map of the racial order and the gender order, which necessarily underpinned their enjoyment of privileges.

Yet it was in their very transgression that such borders could be made and unmade. The transgression of racial boundaries and its very dangers were what attracted many travellers to the Caribbean in the first place. Charles Stoddard, a North American visitor to Guadeloupe in the 1890s, was entranced by the Creole women he saw in the market, which he described as a 'novel and exciting scene':

> Several hundred women – black, yellow, quadroon, and octoroon, with very little negro blood and hardly any negro features – were chattering and chaffering, screaming and gesticulating like monkeys, over little piles of fruit and vegetables and roots and meats and bouquets of flowers. They wore loose and flowing gowns of gaudy and brilliant prints, which they held half-way up to their waists as they walked in the market-place. On their heads were turbans which equalled anything in Damascus or Assouan, formed of Madras handkerchiefs, rolled and twisted . . . All the women wore jewels, necklaces of huge beads, great hoops and cylinders of gold in their ears, bracelets and rings without number.[49]

Again the Levant is used as a gauge of difference, while a Caribbean imagery of animality and linguistic babble is introduced. Stoddard is entranced by this scene of hybridity, excited by the mixtures of East and West, human and animal, black and white, skin and jewellery. He favourably contrasts these women, with their 'fine complexions', 'dark and lustrous eyes', 'pearly teeth', 'coral lips', and 'beautifully shaped hands and feet', against the 'large-limbed and broad-shouldered black women', once again demonstrating the comparison of different others against each other.

'Spanish' Creoles, as noted above, could appear slightly more 'tropicalized' to the English or North American in the Caribbean than 'whiter' Anglo-Saxon cultures. The US Consul in Haiti in 1898, for example, described the women of Cuba along with the natural products of the land:

> The Cuban senorita is always a subject of interest, because she is generally pretty. She has languishing black eyes and sweeping lashes, a small mouth with luscious red lips, and two rows of perfect teeth. Her complexion is olive, and her cheeks have a healthy tinge of pink. She smiles bewitchingly, and her whole face lights up as she talks. She is of ordinary height, has a shapely form, graceful, undulating gait, and her hands and feet are small and exquisitely shaped. What she lacks in book learning she makes up with mother wit. At twelve years she merges into maidenhood; she marries at fifteen or seventeen, has considerable of a family by thirty, and in later years is given to obesity.[50]

Such observations generalise particular women's faces and bodies as indicators of a total climate and culture of their island. The 'Creole Belle' or the 'Cuban Senorita' became ideals of the 'interest' white male travellers might find in the island Tropics. In contrast to such sexualised 'brown' and 'olive' coloured women, black women were often 'unsexed'. The de-feminisation of Afro-Caribbean women was a crucial aspect of the practice of securing white femininity, and establishing a 'natural' hierarchy of human distinction, and continues to inform racial discourses today.[51] In the following section I consider how Africanist discourses read onto Caribbean landscapes and bodies continue to inform tourist consumption of the Caribbean today.

Africa in the Caribbean

In order to maintain the relative distinctions of 'race' in the unstable Caribbean context Euro-American writers often fell back on the underlying trope of the Cannibal, the risky primitive within the West Indies. Beneath the serenity of the Orientalist dream of the tropical paradise lurked a troubling savage, who reappears insistently in travel accounts. These stories are suggestive of a far greater complexity to the racial and spatial orientation of the Northern 'white' traveller within the Tropics than simple white/black dichotomies would reveal. Many tried to orient themselves in the Tropics both with a glance to the 'Old World' of the East, a glance to the 'New World' of the Americas, and a glance 'down' at barbaric Africa. The cannibalistic undercurrent in Northern imagery of the Caribbean came to be coded in relation to an Africanist discourse of primitivism which became more pronounced in the late nineteenth century as European projects of colonisation of Africa took hold.

In the 1880s, for example, James Anthony Froude called for an expansion of the white population in the British West Indies, since the 'natural superiority of the white would assert itself without difficulty'. Black self-rule was doomed, he wrote, because,

> Where the disproportion is so enormous as it is in Jamaica, where intelligence and property are in a miserable minority, and a half-reclaimed race of savages, cannibals not long ago, and capable, as the state of Hayti shows, of reverting to cannibalism again, are living beside them as their political equals, such panics arise from the nature of things, and will themselves cause the catastrophe from the dread of which they arise.[52]

By generalising from Haitian 'reversion' to cannibalism, Froude tried to justify white rule in the British Caribbean. 'These beautiful West Indian islands were intended to be the homes for the overflowing numbers of our own race, and the few that have gone there are being crowded out by the blacks from Jamaica and the Antilles.'[53] The West Indian writer N. Darnell Davis quickly identified Froude as a cynical sensationalist who had spent very little time in the West Indies:

> And what is the outcome of Mr. Froude's seven weeks' pic-nic in the British West Indies? . . . It is clear as the day that Mr. Froude brought out his dread of *Haytia*, ready made, with him from England. . . . Knowing nothing of the West Indian man of colour, of either the mulatto or the negro, our Tourist fears that, if these be allowed to vote for some of the members of the Colonial Councils, the end will be *Haytia*, or a relapse into barbarism.[54]

He calls Froude a Cook's Tourist because, like so many other writers, he travelled through the Caribbean by mail steamer, making only short stops. Thus the ignorance of many of the writers who claimed expertise on the Caribbean was the result of a touristic outlook in which hearsay was used to reinforce racist beliefs in African barbarism. Each tourist went in search of barbarism and cannibalism, perpetuating previous myths.

By moving through the Tropics, viewing the objectified bodies of various 'exotics', and making comparisons between different others, the white traveller came to gauge his or her own whiteness and to fix in place the differences between the 'strange' others encountered there (Ahmed 2000). In Barbados in 1900, for example, a British tourist described the street scene:

> The streets were densely packed, black women filing past us in twos and threes dressed in white calico, with handkerchiefs tied round their heads, and carrying all manner of produce on the top of their skulls . . . Their faces are almost always repulsive, the thick lips and wide nostrils being fatal to European ideas of beauty, but the figure and carriage are splendid.[55]

His inscription of these 'black' bodies stands in clear contrast to the Orientalised women described above, and indicates the crude contours of the Africanist discourse. In referring to European ideas of beauty he is clearly reinforcing the superiority of white femininity, while suggesting a kind of primitive 'naturalness' of the black woman's 'carriage'.

Other forms of Africanist discourse mobilised scenery within geographies of difference. In illustrating her visit to Dominica in 1899, for example, Susan Day uses a photograph of a home and garden (Plate 4.6), captioned, 'In an hour we seem as though transported to Darkest Africa'.[56] Through her framing of what she sees as 'African' she imbues it with a deep cultural essentialism. Such 'negro-huts' were standard fare in the depiction of Caribbean landscapes, as we have seen in Chapter 2. Their 'picturesque' thatch, kitchen gardens, and shady fruit trees served to underline the supposed ease of living in the tropical Caribbean. In the foreground of the photograph is the road, over which Day moves as she is transported both physically through the Caribbean and imaginatively back to 'Darkest Africa'. Constructing their own superior subjectivity in the northern hemisphere, travel writers like Day survey all around them by moving through it, gazing, tasting, touching, sketching, photographing, and recording the details for others at home to read and see.

These texts represent the black body from a safe distance, where it cannot touch the consumer/reader, but they also incite others to take part by joining them in travel, for these books were in effect guidebooks, and some of them were immensely popular. Most of the writers did not stay in one island, but travelled by boat 'through' the islands, as many of their titles indicate, and on arrival at each port they also described their journeys across or around particular islands. These movements then shape the itinerary of tourists who followed in their footsteps. Thinking of the movement of some people as a means of fixing others offers a compelling way to think about travel in the Tropics in relation to questions of racial boundary marking. As Ahmed has argued, movement can often become a means by which boundaries are enforced rather than undone (Ahmed 2001; and see Ahmed *et al.*, forthcoming). Anglo-American practices of mobility, border-crossing, and dabbling in hybridity in the West Indies are precisely such projects of enforcing boundaries. By moving through, across, and about 'the islands' the travellers establish measures of similarity and difference, proximity and distance, progress and stasis, by which they mark both their own 'home' position (as modern, liberal, dynamic) and the differences between various strange others (as more or less backward, uncivilised, primitive).

European and North American travel writers especially employed Africanist discourses in relation to Haiti, the only independent 'Black Republic' in the colonial era, and long feared by Europeans. Placed under a kind of political quarantine, Haiti was explicitly associated with cannibalism and African barbarism in the kind of sensational nineteenth-century travel literature popularised by James Anthony Froude and Spencer St. John, which I have analysed more fully elsewhere (Sheller 1999; cf. Antoine 1978; Dash 1997; Plummer 1988: 70–5).

Plate 4.6 'Darkest Africa' discovered in Dominica.
'Dominica', photograph in Susan de Forest Day, *The Cruise of the Scythian in the West Indies* (London, New York, and Chicago, F. Tennyson Neely, 1899). Reproduced courtesy of the Schomburg Center, New York Public Library.

Subsequent accounts of visits to Haiti linger on the black bodies, which stood as a signifier of darkness, irrationality, and terror, as in this account by Hesketh Prichard in 1900:

> Darkness had come on by the time I recrossed the market-place. The scene was weird. Among the ruinous wooden booths a few fluttering flames cut into the blackness of the night, and from the gloom around came the indescribable screeching babble of negro voices. Here and there in the dim light I saw pale-palmed hands twisting in gesticulation, or wide mouths that flashed white teeth over slips of sugar-cane. And so the busy unseen night-life, which the dark-skin loves, went on under the dense sky.[57]

Here the irrationality and primitivism of Haiti is figuratively lodged in the skin itself, as the dark body and its 'unseen' activities merge with the darkness of the night. Prichard and others connected their accounts of the failure of Haitian government to stories of Voodoo, but to do so they also made imaginative journeys and comparisons between Africa, the Caribbean, and India.

Again making reference to his knowledge of other places through which he had travelled, he concludes,

> as long as Hayti retains an entirely negro Government, at least so long will the shadow of the Papaloi loom large in the land, for Africa transplanted is Africa still, and she is so conservative that the passage of uncounted years finds her ever the same . . . [The Voodoo priest] is dirtier than an Indian fakir, without that excuse [of godliness;] he is filthy, because to be clean is troublesome. And the Papaloi possesses a treble share of the universal laziness of the children of Ham.[58]

Thus he links failure of government with Voodoo with Africa with uncleanliness with laziness; and this is measured against the Indian versions of the same, but in the Indian case it is mitigated by a certain kind of godliness which the European recognises. It is perhaps also the 'Aryan' kinship of the European and Indian that places him higher on the scale of humanity or Family Tree of Man (McClintock 1995). Travel to Haiti thus became an ethnological enterprise, with many anthropologists going there to search out African 'survivals' in the New World. The 'Africanization' of Haiti also became crucial to projects of nation-building in the Dominican Republic, which differentiates itself from its neighbour by claiming an 'Indio' racial identity (Hoetink 1973; Howard 2001).

Construction of an African barbarism in the Caribbean was continually gauged against an Eastern exoticism. Trying to make sense of what he saw in Haiti, another North American, Blair Niles, compared the dancing of Vodoo worshippers to those he knew from the Orient:

> I am familiar with the measured posturing dances of Japan, of India, Java and Burma. I have watched the head-hunting dance of the Dyaks of Borneo.

That was savage enough, primitive enough . . . But savage as it was, that too had been in a way sophisticated; it was dramatization, and to impersonate is more sophisticated than to express surging emotion, such as we watched under the Haitian moon . . . It was the dance of the sixth day of creation: a strange and unforgettable sight, sweeping back the tide of life to the beginning of us all.[59]

Although gauging its strangeness, Niles nevertheless links what he discovers to the beginning 'of us all', trying to share some primitive kinship. Others were less willing to embrace the primitive within.

In some cases the Orientalist and the Africanist discourses merged, and together were used to justify American interventions, such as the occupation of Haiti. John Houston Craige opens his book *Black Bagdad* (1933), an account of the US occupation of Haiti, which he characterises as an 'Arabian Nights Adventure', with this story: 'These people are still living in the days of the Arabian Nights. You may meet Haroun al Raschid and Giafer, his Grand Wazir, any day, walking arm in arm in the street. You may hear tales as amazing as any Sheherezade ever told. You may see woolly-headed cannibals and silk-hatted savants side by side.'[60] Echoes of Columbus's original dichotomy again emerge in the peculiarly Caribbean juxtaposition of primitive cannibals with sophisticated urbane others. If Paton's and Day's accounts of the Caribbean were infused with a sense of the pleasures (and potential dangers) of the flesh, Prichard, Craige and other North Americans wrote from a military perspective concerned with defining a pathological despotism. His concern is with the necessary exercise of coercion upon 'primitive' black bodies, in order to discipline and civilise them, in the unruly island-states of the Tropics.

By the early twentieth century, the mixing and morphing of Oriental despotism into the story of African barbarism had become a doubly powerful trope in accounts of Caribbean failures of self-government. It was used to justify military intervention through the 'feminisation' of weak island-states, and served to excuse US support of authoritarian political cultures and violent dictatorships in the region's so-called 'banana republics'. The violent 'fixing of others' was achieved by moving into Caribbean territories, moving over and across them, opening their interiors through 'improvements' to harbours, airstrips, and roads. The attitudes enacted in military occupation can be seen in Craige's dehumanising views of Haitian people's bodies. Craige, describing himself as a 'sort of white Emir to command the black troops of a province . . . A sort of West Indian version of . . . the Punjab Border Patrol', began his command over his servant: 'Destine was my new Number One Boy – my first venture in black ivory. He was short, slim, bullet-headed, jet-black, with a nose like a squashed tomato and lips so thick they gave him the appearance of having a bill like a duck. A true Congo type.'[61]

Repulsively objectifying the bodies of those around him, he describes one 'tiny naked girl, black and shiny as an ebony doll', and describes a 14-year-old giving birth in a ditch beside the road in the cruellest of terms:

She was young, a *tiefie* of fourteen or fifteen years, with tiny pointed breasts and a skin like polished obsidian. She writhed and moaned fitfully. The old woman kept up a continued stream of mumbled incantations. Presently the fingers tightened on the iron-wood roots until the blood sprang from beneath the nails. Eyes turned upwards until only the whites were visible. The suffering body ached and labored in a supreme spasm. Then a tiny strange strangling cough announced the arrival of a new life. The mother closed her eyes and relaxed. Soon she opened them again with the utter calm and unconcern of one awakening from a restful sleep. She yawned nonchalantly, then grinned and reached for the tiny negrillon.[62]

There is no sense of a human being in his depiction, just the figuratively dismembered fingers, bloody nails, eyes, suffering body. And the 'new life' is never named as a human infant, a baby, but is only a 'tiny negrillon', like some exotic tropical animal. The description of the girl's obsidian-like skin implies a certain kind of touch – the touching of an object that one polishes, and therefore possesses.

Other visitors similarly objectify and animalise Caribbean men and women, blending their bodies into the tropical landscape through a 'tourist gaze' (Urry 1991). In 1932, John Van Dyke wrote 'sketches' of the people and landscape of Jamaica. He begins with an awe-struck vision of the landscape, drawing on the Romantic genre:

These sketches of the Caribbean and its shores should interest those who perhaps agree with me in thinking the West Indies the most beautiful islands in any sea, and the sea itself the most beautiful in the world. That is a superlative statement at the start, but the Caribbean and its islands are superlative themes. Chemistry cannot turn out bright enough colors, nor dictionaries sufficient of winged words to tell the splendor of these islands. The glory of their light, the rose and violet of their atmosphere, the high key of their color cannot be exaggerated. Pictorially, they are intangible dreams, fantasies that the retina records confusedly, and the hand grasps feebly.[63]

Again the Caribbean is seen to somehow exceed reality, and is thereby constructed as real yet fantastic, the viewer as awake yet dreaming. As he loses his way here, Van Dyke's body itself seems to become fragmented into a recording retina and a grasping hand. Yet in his fantasy he seeks to grasp not only the land, but also the people, who for him form a crucial part of 'the picture',

Seen along the Jamaica roads, under the broken sunlight filtered through palm and bamboo, the black is decidedly picturesque. He has the fine line and movement of an animal, the dark skin born of a tropical sun, and the female of the species comes in to help out the picture with the glow of bright clothing. Male and female after their kind they belong to the landscape as much as the waving palm or the flowering bougainvillea or the gay hibiscus.

They are exotic, tropical, indigenous, and fit in the picture perfectly, keeping their place without the slightest note of discord.[64]

Thus the objectified body and the orientalised landscape become one, each 'keeping their place' relative to the moving viewer, who gazes upon these people shamelessly, as if they were animals. This is the Ur-tropics 'in which the inhabitants are identified with the natural world of luxuriant growth and fecundity' (Root 1998: 62). Describing the 'West Indian fieldhand' as 'little more than an animal', Van Dyke's dehumanisation of West Indians serves a new American imperialism, grasping the 'renaturalised' Caribbean islands through adventure tourism, as discussed in Chapter 2.

Other tourists used references to Africa to conjure up a sense of evil lingering in the Caribbean. James Pope-Hennessy, a British tourist in the early 1950s, wrote: 'No scenery in my experience is as malevolent as that of the West Indies . . . the air seemed charged with evil forces . . . it needed no whispered tales of obeah practices to persuade one that the innate malice of the islands was being constantly reinforced by non-Christian beliefs and invocations, brought long ago from Africa with the cruel misery of the old slave ships.'[65] This *frisson* of evil and sorcery both frightens off tourists, and compels them onwards, much as stories of danger and drug trading, Voodoo and gunmen, are used to add a thrill to jaded travel today. By the twentieth century ethnographers were combing Haiti in search of real 'evidence' of zombies and cannibalistic practices. Their accounts often blend genres of ethnography, autobiography, and fiction (e.g. Hurston 1990 [1938]; Davis 1986), and they continue to inspire a particular sub-genre of journalistic writing on Haiti. This fascination with the dark side of the Caribbean has become a cultural touchstone in a range of Caribbeanist writing, from novels like Graham Greene's *The Comedians* (1966), to more recent journalistic accounts like Chris Salewicz's *Rude Boy: Once Upon A Time in Jamaica* (2000). In every case the narrator becomes a kind of guide, telling a story but also leading the reader on a surreal journey into the inferno. Many contemporary writers and journalists who travel to Haiti, for example, cite Greene's use of the Oloffson Hotel in his novel, and refer to meeting Auberlin Joliecoeur there, the man on whom Greene based one of his more shady characters, Petit Pierre. As one journalist writes: 'On the edge of Port-au-Prince, the Oloffson is a place of shadow and light, madness and mystique. It's a hulking mansion of gables, turrets and doily trimmings, all in faded wedding-dress white; at its back are mountains that sometimes echo at night to voodoo drums, and to the front is a garden of palms in which lurk papier mâché voodoo spirits and black turkey cocks with molten red faces.'[66] Here the Haitian fantasy teeters between 'the glamour of the 1950s and the evil of the 1960s', with a dose of Hollywood zombies for good measure.[67]

In this chapter, in sum, I have argued that in these travel guides the fantasy and practice of Anglo-American mobility become crucial to efforts to 'fix' others both in space and in time. By fixing each 'strange' body encountered in relation to various others, partly through practices of literary citation, these travellers are able to position themselves by 'orienting' those around them, and by orientalising the place itself. By then linking Caribbean landscape and scenery to a shadowy primitive past, they also Africanise the West Indies as a place in which time somehow stands still. Projecting their own moral debauchery onto the bodies of those around them, white travellers construct their own cultural 'modernity', 'civility', and 'whiteness' by what might be called 'proximate distance' from these juxtaposed others, that is to say a distance constructed by getting closer. Blending together the tropes of Orientalism, Levantism, and Africanism, they mark out not just 'an other', but relative and carefully calibrated distinctions of some others from 'other others'. The blending of the East and West in the Caribbean thus does not serve to dissolve racial boundaries, but rather enables mobile Western subjects to distance from themselves those who may be all too close. The movement of empowered subjects, the transgression of racial and moral boundaries, and 'playing in the dark' (Morrison 1992) therefore serve to *reproduce* difference and reinforce the constitution of the geographies of belonging and exclusion that have long excised the Caribbean from Western modernity. In the following chapters I will further chart this spatio-temporal interplay of distance and proximity, orientation and disorientation, desire and fear, through the movement of bodies in circuits of global migration, enslavement, disease, tourism, and creolization.

5 Eating others

Of cannibals, vampires, and zombies

Cannibalism, the literal ingestion of one human by another, haunts the foundational moment of European presence in the Caribbean islands, as seen in early visual portrayals of this liminal zone of encounter as a site of human dismemberment and cooking (see Plate 5.1).[1] This chapter builds in part on recent explorations of cannibalism by Peter Hulme, Francis Barker, and others of the interlocking meanings of 'Carib' and 'cannibal' ever since the time of Columbus's arrival in the New World (Hulme 1986; Barker *et al.* 1998). Many have asked of this seminal moment and of all that has followed from it: who was eating whom? Was the Caribbean truly a place where Europeans were at risk of being eaten? Or were they in fact the ones who posed a threat to the bodies, health, and lives of the indigenous people of the region, and later to the enslaved and indentured workers who were consumed in the system of plantation slavery and colonial capitalism? From the founding myths of European 'discovery', to the blood-sugar *topos* of the abolitionists, and finally to the popular folk cultures of the Caribbean in their responses to capitalist exploitation, stories of the literal dismembering and eating of others have circulated for centuries in the Caribbean.

Plate 5.1 Consuming cannibals: who ate whom?
'Columbus's Fleet Attacked by Cannibals', Honorius Philoponus (1621).

What happens when we think about bodies not as consuming food, but as becoming food for others? In what sense can one human body be 'eaten' by another? And how does consumption of the human body function as a boundary limit for consumer excess? For Elspeth Probyn, 'the present preoccupation with cannibalism and appetite' expresses a concern with the limits of humanity and perhaps the limits of our capacity to consume (Probyn 2000: 81). Her somewhat counter-intuitive reading of the 'figure of the cannibal' casts it not only as 'a historicised spectre of Western appetite' but also as an interrogative figure pointing toward the possibility of 'an ethics and practice of restraint' (ibid.: 99). Her search for a 'gut ethics' in the face of excess is helpful in returning us to the questions of ethical consumption raised in earlier chapters. However, she uses 'the figure' of the cannibal in a reified and ahistorical way, simply as a metaphor, which prevents any deeper analysis of its colonial and postcolonial implications. What if we instead try to locate cannibalism in relation to the very specific set of violent bodily relations through which the Caribbean was (and continues to be) formed?

If we understand ethics as a particular relation to others which involves 'intimate responsibility for the other' (Ahmed 2000: 137), then we can begin to ask how that responsibility gets mediated through different forms of intimacy. As Chapter 3 suggested, commodity objects may intervene between bodies in world systems of colonial trade, yet some consumers may still recognise an ethics of responsibility for distant others who produce the commodities that they consume. In this chapter I want to consider more direct relations between bodies, constituted by practices of travel, tourism, and infection. This chapter hinges on questions of ethics, morality, and disease, which entwine working bodies and consuming bodies in intimate relations of political and sexual domination and subordination. My main concern is with the embodied effects of material relations of consumption: What does it mean to eat another? What turns our stomachs and why? In what sense can restraint be practised in consuming the bodies of others? Can there ever be an ethical relation of consumption?

A number of cultural theorists have analysed the 'commodification of Otherness' as a form of 'eating the other' (hooks 1992). Here Western (or Northern) cultures visually and metaphorically 'eat' or consume racially marked bodies as a kind of spice or condiment to flavour the bland whiteness of mainstream culture or to enact an expansive 'global culture' (Ahmed 2000; Stacey 2000). As hooks argues, 'the commodification of difference promotes paradigms of consumption wherein whatever difference the Other inhabits is eradicated, via exchange, by a consumer cannibalism that not only displaces the Other but denies the significance of that Other's history through a process of decontextualization' (hooks 1992: 31). As I have argued in previous chapters, consuming the Caribbean occurs first through its displacement from the narrative of Western modernity (decontextualisation), followed by its recontextualisation as an 'Other' to serve the purposes of Western fantasy. The longing for an unattainable pleasure, argues hooks, 'has led the white west to sustain a romantic fantasy of the "primitive" and the concrete search for a primitive paradise, whether that location be a country or a body, a dark continent or dark flesh, perceived as the perfect embodiment of that possibility' (ibid.: 27). Caribbean islands and Caribbean bodies have been made to work as sites for seeking pleasure, in the form of 'consumer cannibalism' of Caribbean 'difference'.

Beyond the system of commodity consumption, however, hooks's analysis suggests that we can also consider the consumption of racialised and sexualised bodies. In this chapter I am concerned especially with body-to-body relations of 'pleasurable' consumption which lead to the actual bleeding, illness, dismemberment, or death of particular, embodied, others. Thus I refer not to 'eating the Other' (in which 'the Other' operates as a disembodied and generalised symbolic figure) but to 'eating others'. I want to begin, though, by expanding upon our understanding of the meanings of eating and being eaten. Within Caribbean Creole languages there are multivalent meanings of the words equivalent to eat/ eating/eaten. The Jamaican words *nyam*[2] and 'mashing up', the Haitian word *manjé* (Stevens 1995) and their description of the rich as '*gro manjeurs*' (big eaters) and the poor as 'eaten', give an especially vivid sense of the forces of power and violence involved in eating. The Vodou practice of 'feeding' the *loas* also suggests the duality of the corporeal and spiritual powers of eating and serving food. These various material and spiritual understandings of consumption can allow us to focus on the relation between ingestion, incorporation, appropriation, sacrifice, and various forms of using up and wasting away bodies. If the figure of the cannibal represents European anxieties around the boundaries of consumption, then the Haitian 'zombi' – a 'living-dead' slave deprived of will and physically controlled by a sorcerer – is the ultimate representation of the psychic state of one whose body/spirit is consumed.

The dialectics of eating and being eaten pertain as much to the hollowing out of human agency by degraded forms of labour (the zombie) as to the actual appropriation, objectification, fragmentation, and ingestion of the physical body itself (to be cannibalised). Joan Dayan suggests that the 'dead-alive' zombie 'haunts Haitians as the most powerful emblem of apathy, anonymity and loss. . . . [It is an] incarnation of negation or vacancy' (Dayan 1998: 37). She goes on to explain that,

> The phantasm of the zombi – a soulless husk deprived of freedom – is the ultimate sign of loss and dispossession. In Haiti, memories of servitude are transposed into a new idiom that both reproduces and dismantles a twentieth-century history of forced labor and denigration that became particularly acute during the American occupation of Haiti. As Haitians were forced to build roads, and thousands of peasants were brutalized and massacred, tales of zombis proliferated in the United States. The film *White Zombie* (1932) and books like William Seabrook's *The Magic Island* (1929) and John Huston [*sic*] Craige's *Black Bagdad* (1933) helped to justify the 'civilizing' presence of the marines in 'barbaric' Haiti. This reimagined zombi has now been absorbed into the texture of previous oral traditions, structurally reproducing the idea of slavery in a new context.
>
> (Dayan 1998: 37–8)

Here we see a strange currency in zombies, as they shift from a dread memory of slavery into a new idiom of forced labour, and then from a ghoulish monster in Hollywood movies they slip back into Haitian understandings of the US occupation. Thus occupation and the American cultural consumption of the uprooted figure of the zombie serve to reinforce its power, as it is re-grounded in contemporary Haitian culture.[3]

Initial incorporation of Haiti into North American popular culture drew on earlier travel writing to create a cinematic version of Haiti steeped in Africanist imagery of 'voodoo' sorcery and terror. Even in the nineteenth century, as Paul Farmer notes, the British envoy to Haiti Sir Spencer St. John 'delighted his audience with tales of voodoo and cannibalism, including the "practice of eating young children and digging up freshly buried corpses for brutal ceremonies or food"'(Farmer 1994: 228; cf. Sheller 1999). Hollywood zombie movies brought the ethnological sensationalism of travel in Haiti to the big screen, and the zombie entered North American and European culture as a creature more terrifying than even the cannibal had been. One of the first zombie movies, *White Zombie* (1932), starring Bela Lugosi, was actually set in Haiti and concerned sugar workers who had been turned into zombies working as slaves for a greedy sugarmill owner. The zombie reached its zenith in George Romero's *Night of the Living Dead* (1968), followed by the 1978 sequel *Dawn of the Dead*. The former, set in a Pittsburgh suburb, introduced the idea of the flesh-eating zombie (a kind of cannibal-zombie hybrid), while the latter, set in a shopping mall infested with zombies, has been read as a satire of consumer society. Wes Craven's 1988 film *The Serpent and the Rainbow*, based on the book by Wade Davis (1986), was again set in Haiti, but concerns a Harvard anthropologist seeking a sample of the natural drug used in zombification, which a US company planned to develop into a revolutionary new anaesthetic. Each film thus deals with issues of consumption through the liminal figure of the zombie. However, the locale shifts from concern with the industrial labour that went into sugar production in the Caribbean, to the horrors of consumer society 'at home' (the zombie within), and finally to new forms of medical research that consume Caribbean 'ethnopharmacological' substances. In each case Haiti serves as a primeval and deeply exoticised 'Other' to Western modernity, a place set apart in both space and time.

The distancing and 'othering' of Haiti is closely related to North American cultural discourses around Haitians as carriers of AIDS, which I return to in the conclusion of this chapter. In linking stories of zombies and AIDS, I want to suggest that there is a close relation between fantasies of the primitive and fantasies surrounding what bell hooks refers to as the 'willingness to transgress racial boundaries within the realm of the sexual' (hooks 1992: 22). Both the fear of Haitian zombies and the fear of supposedly infectious bodies from Haiti arise out of the racialised sexual encounters and sexualised racial encounters of (post)colonialism, which I shall analyse in more detail through specific examples in this chapter. As hooks suggests, such border-crossing encounters serve to reaffirm the power of the dominant and to reconstitute the boundaries between Western self and Caribbean other. Or, as Ahmed puts it, 'The proximity of strangers within the nation space . . . is a mechanism for the demarcation of the national body, a way of defining borders within it, rather than just between it and an imagined or exterior other' (Ahmed 2000: 100).

In the first section I consider how human beings and their labour power were directly consumed in the colonisation of the Caribbean and in the system of slavery. My analysis builds on the discussion of the anti-saccharrites in Chapter 3. This movement recognised for the first time that the sugar they were eating had been produced through a horrific process that also produced certain types of labouring bodies: bodies that were whipped, mutilated, branded, injured, scarred, tortured, and suffering. Here I take a closer look at the direct effects of colonial relations of domination on the bodies of indigenous and enslaved people in the Caribbean, both in terms of the disease environment by which they were killed and the sexual relations by which they were exploited. However, I also consider the forms of resistance that emerged to counter those processes of destroying and using up bodies, focusing in particular on the notions of 'slackness' and 'erotic autonomy' as theorised by Carolyn Cooper and M. Jacqui Alexander, respectively.

In spite of the momentous achievement of the abolition of slavery in one colonial sphere after another during the nineteenth century, 'emancipation' nevertheless drove the formerly enslaved working classes to continue to bend their bodies to hard labour, servicing the faraway consumers of tropical produce in Europe and North America. Not only did Northern consumers continue to 'eat' them from a distance, but they increasingly came to consume them up close as tourists. While Caribbean comestibles like sugar, bananas, and rum flowed into Northern markets, Northern tourists found an equal enjoyment, or at least interest, in watching the labouring bodies of people in the Caribbean. They drew, photographed, painted, and described in writing the 'picturesque' scenes that these labouring bodies constituted. In the second section I turn again to popular tourist literature in order to consider how touristic forms of voyeurism and sexual interest consumed the labouring bodies of Caribbean people. Expanding on the argument in Chapter 4 on the objectification of exotic bodies via the tourist gaze, here I consider how Caribbean bodies have come to be 'sexed' and 'unsexed' under the tourist gaze.

This leads in the third section into a discussion of the actual exchanges and touches between bodies as material 'things', physiologically linked by the flow of sexual touches, disease vectors, and medical practices. Recalling the story of Sir Hans Sloane, body parts and body fluids again emerge as crucial 'flows' within global commodity production and consumption in which some medical practices, substances, and knowledges have taken on strange shapes in parts of the Caribbean. I also consider how fears of Caribbean 'infection' have produced the reactionary imagery of the violent Jamaican 'posse' in America and 'Yardies' in Britain, marking Caribbean bodies as carriers of pathological disorder. Moving between the imagery of cannibals, vampires, and zombies, we can question the eating of others not only in terms of symbolic forms of commodity consumption, but also in terms of the actual material relations through which bodies in one place unethically touch bodies in another place.

Killing, enslaving, torturing, and touching bodies

The original narrative of Caribbean cannibalism in Columbus's journals rested on a distinction between those who would work docilely for European colonisers, and those 'cannibals' who staged resistance and could thus be enslaved or killed. The belief that the Caribs dismembered and ate their enemies was prevalent throughout European accounts of the New World in the sixteenth century. Such stories were widely disseminated in early Spanish and Italian accounts of the New World, in which the Caribs came to represent the 'monstrous savage' par excellence and were called 'pests of humanity . . . the nastiest, cruelest, lustful, lying . . . abominable people in the world' (Boucher 2000: 104–5). These writers contrasted an Arcadian vision of the Americas (inhabited by 'peaceful' Arawaks) against the ignoble savagery of the cannibal Caribs. As Lola Young argues, the attribution 'of cannibalism to savage Others serves at once as justification for taming those savages, as a confirmation of white European supremacy and as a screen onto which to project guilty repression of the knowledge that it is the white oppressor who behaves in a cannibalistic manner' (Young 1986: 74). It is a 'useful metaphor for colonial exploitation' because it so literally spells out the suppressed relation of European colonisers to indigenous others.

Practices of cannibalism have also been used to describe Western consumer culture in general as a culture of excessive consumption and insatiable hunger, feeding off human bodies for profit (Forbes 1992; Root 1998). Deborah Root, for example, argues in *Cannibal Culture*, that contemporary capitalist cultures literally demand blood sacrifice, consuming human bodies in acts of violence. 'People are consumed, their bodies devoured by other, more rapacious people in many different ways, some of the most obvious being in systems of slave labor, in pointless and destructive wars undertaken for profit, and in the killing of people to "free" their land for development projects' (Root 1998: 10–11). Following Native American understandings of white men's greed and consumerism, she interprets this capitalist cannibalism as a warped 'approach to reality' or a sick 'state of mind' that is obsessed with limitless consumption. Thus she calls for a refusal of the cannibal within. This generalisation of cannibalism to the entire culture of capitalism, however, still leaves intact the disavowal of cannibalism, which as Claude Lévi-Strauss observed, 'of all the savage practices, is without doubt the one that inspires in us the greatest horror and disgust' (Lévi-Strauss 1976 [1955]: 347–8).

Lévi-Strauss takes another tack, which is to place cannibalism in relative perspective to Western attitudes and practices that might be equally repellant to an outside observer. He explains ritual cannibalism as the practice of eating either an ascendant or the fragment of the body of an enemy, in order 'to permit the incorporation of his virtues or the neutralisation of his power' (Lévi-Strauss 1955: 348). Both practices are of the same nature as Western beliefs in resurrection or spirit–body dualism. Inasmuch as we find such anthropophagy disgusting, he suggests that our own judicial and penal customs constitute an equally repulsive form of 'anthropoemie' (from the Greek *emein*, meaning to vomit). Some societies (anthropophagic) absorb the liminal, the evil, or the enemy into the social body in order to control their power, while others (anthropoemic) expel or emit such problematic entities through customs of isolation, segregation, and social death. Thus he sees symmetry in such cultural practices, and each appears barbaric in the worldview of the other. Although he appears to overcome his own cultural biases, however, his relativism is achieved through the practice of ethnographic travel and travel writing (*Tristes Tropiques*), which paradoxically reinforces his own Western superiority in knowledge and mobility. Only he can 'translate' cannibal cultures for 'us' at home.

An alternative, but still culturally relative approach, is that of the Brazilian modernists of the 1920s who played with the literal and metaphoric meanings of cannibalism. They 'made the trope of cannibalism the basis of an insurgent esthetic, calling for a creative synthesis of European avant-gardism and Brazilian "cannibalism," and invoking an "anthropophagic" devouring of the techniques and information of the superdeveloped countries the better to struggle against domination' (Shohat and Stam 2000 [1994]: 307). Rather than disavowing the cannibal, by devouring foreign culture in a 'cordial mastication', Brazilian publications such as the *Cannibalistic Review* in the 1920s and Oswald de Andrade's 'Anthropophagic Manifesto' (1928) valorised the aboriginal Carib and Tupinamba cultures of the New World. The cannibal, then, has come to stand for a number of different ways in which relations between colonising and colonised bodies and nations might be imagined. The individual body is projected onto the social body or polity such that metaphors of eating, ingesting, and vomiting come to describe international relations of empowerment and disempowerment.

More recently, May Joseph adapts this 'notion of ideological cannibalism as postcolonial critical practice' (Joseph 1999: 131) in her reading of the character of Sycorax in Shakespeare's *The Tempest*. Written in 1611, almost a decade before English colonisation of the Caribbean began, *The Tempest* has been interpreted as associating the semi-human but animal-like Caliban (whose name is thought to be an anagram of cannibal) with the European imagination of the indigenous people of the Caribbean (Hulme and Sherman 2000). His mother, Sycorax, from Algeria, is described as a hag, a sorceress, and a maleficent power, according to Joseph, and her pregnant, maternal body is animalised like the bestial natives we have met in other texts (cf. Fanon 1968: 42, 55). 'She emerges cannibalized by the systems of capital through which her enslaved pregnant black body is consumed as free labor. She is the expendable commodity of an unmarked island in the outer peripheries of Europe's imagination' (Joseph 1999: 131–2). As Joseph explains,

> Prospero must project onto Sycorax all that he fears in himself and his modernity. He reads Sycorax as cannibal to enable his own cannibalizing logic of devouring indigenous rights to the Island-Nation. By scarring, torturing, incarcerating, demonizing, mythologizing, and projecting onto the native

bodies of Sycorax and Caliban the barbarism of European modernity, Prospero inscribes European law onto his stolen territory. His system of governmentality is replete with the punitive regimes of torture, incarceration, and surveillance on colonial terms.

(Joseph 1999: 132)

Joseph argues that Sycorax can be read as the taken-for-granted native woman whose corporeality serves as the backdrop for masculine state-building projects, whether colonial or postcolonial. The 'sonic intransigence' of her scream echoes in the heads of the slave women who killed their own children, and more recently in the experience of the Haitian women who have served as a research population for the contraceptive device Norplant, discussed below. The torture of these women's bodies indicates the corporeal violence of sexual consumption in the practices of (neo)colonialism, and as I shall argue below there is a close relationship between the policing of sexual practices and the policing of national boundaries.[4]

Returning, then, to this original site of transatlantic violence, I will begin from the material relations of European, Indigenous, and African bodies in the Caribbean. We can first ask, how many were 'eaten'? How many natives were violently dispatched? The best estimates we have for the native population of the Caribbean prior to 1492 are those of Las Casas. For the island of Hispaniola alone, with which he was most familiar, he believed there to have been between 1.1 and 3 million 'Indians' originally (depending on which of his texts we use), who were already reduced to only 30,000 to 60,000 by 1508–10 (Watts 1990: 73; cf. Henige 1978). It was not until 1518, though, that smallpox was introduced from Europe, and yellow fever and malaria from Africa (Watts 1990: 111), followed by typhoid and measles. This pathogenic killing off of entire populations marks the beginning of the violent consumption of the New World via invasion. With the loss of this local source of forced labour, the Spanish and Portuguese colonisers turned to Africa where a slave trade already existed.

Total African arrivals in the New World during the existence of slavery are estimated to be nine to ten million people. Another ten million are figured to have been killed in the process of capture. Furthermore, the disease environment of the Caribbean meant that death-rates there were much higher than in North America, as is evident in the failure of the slave population to reproduce itself in the West Indies. For example, Richard Dunn has shown that between 1708 and 1735 'the Barbadians imported 85,000 new slaves in order to lift the black population on this island from 42,000 to 46,000. By 1790 Barbados, Jamaica, and the Leewards had taken a total of some 1,230,000 slaves from Africa in order to achieve a collective black population of about 387,000' (Dunn 1972: 314). Other colonial spheres in the Caribbean suffered equally devastating patterns of what Dunn calls 'human spoliation'.

As Kenneth Kiple has pointed out, following Philip Curtin, the Caribbean islands 'received' over 40 per cent of all slaves brought into the Western hemisphere, yet as of the mid-twentieth century they contained only 20 per cent of the hemisphere's black population. The United States, in contrast, 'received' (stole? took? devoured?) less than 5 per cent of the slave trade's victims, yet ended up with one-third of the population of African heritage in the Americas (Curtin 1969; Kiple 1984: 105). Efforts to calculate and find explanations for the 'missing' population of the Caribbean indicate that colonies like Barbados suffered net natural decrease in the slave population of 4 to 5 per cent per annum during the eighteenth century, and Jamaica 3 to 3.5 per cent per annum (ibid.: 106). Infant mortality ran from 25 per cent to a staggering 50 per cent in some cases, probably due to severe maternal malnutrition and vitamin deficiencies (ibid.: 117), as well as proximate causes such as infection and dehydration. Causes of slave infant mortality included tetanus/tetany, beriberi, protein energy malnutrition, infectious diseases, and vulnerability associated with premature birth and low birth weight. The disease environment in the United States was far less killing, and maternal nutrition was somewhat better due to greater access to protein (especially pork). As Richard Sheridan suggests, 'The concentration of people, plants, and animals in lowland tropical areas suited to cane sugar production opened a Pandora's box of debilitating and lethal pathogens and their vectors to prey on the black and white inhabitants. . . . Compared with other societies in the New World, the Caribbean plantations stand out as the most destructive to life and limb' (Sheridan 1985: xvii, 327). His detailed medical and demographic history of the British West Indies concludes that 'sugar and slavery had taken a terrible toll on the black people in the West Indies'.

But the consumption of African bodies in the Caribbean goes beyond the disease environment, and must be placed in the context of social relations of slavery. Orlando Patterson has analysed the master–slave relation as a parasitic one, in which the master feeds off the slave, the dominator in effect becoming dependent on the dominated. The slave, he argues, understood this well, as seen in the response of an eighteenth-century slave to his master's disingenuous offer to set him free: ' "Master," the withered slave demurred, "you eated me when I was meat, and now you must pick me when I am bone" ' (Patterson 1982: 340). The slave's body was literally consumed by capture, forced transport, 'seasoning', work regimes, physical punishment, mutilation, disease, sexual exploitation, and the appropriation of children from their parents. The master–slave relationship occurs as a crucial political metaphor in the work of thinkers such as Hegel, Marx, and Nietzsche in so far as it embodies and makes proximate the idea of exploitation, which exists between people in more distantly mediated forms. Marx, for example, described industrial capitalism as vampiristic, parasitically living off the blood of workers. Commodities are fetishised materialisations of alienated labour, literally the living flesh turned into a dead object, in the consuming of which the producer's life force (or 'blood') is sucked dry.

What does it mean to eat another? If slaves were not literally eaten (though perhaps some may have been), then in what sense was their 'blood' feeding the flow of commodity capitalism? We have already seen how the anti-slavery movement utilised the imagery of cannibalisation of the slave to inspire revulsion and boycott of the products of slavery. The imagery of blood-soaked sugar used in the political pamphlets of the anti-slavery movement's sugar boycotts and in the visual images of political satirists suggested that a vomiting nausea could be induced by the literalisation of the commodity. Visual representations of the blood-sugar nexus put the body back into the commodity. To eat someone would literally require certain types of violent touching: to cut up the body, perhaps to cook it, to chew it, or to drain the blood and swallow it. And true enough, slaves' bodies were touched in extremely violent ways. Most significantly, enslaved bodies were literally touched by 'owners' and 'overseers' in two main ways: either by whipping, branding, and other forms of torture that left scars on the body, or by sexual relations that left their mark in physical violence, psychic scarring, and offspring. These forms of touching were also forms of consuming the enslaved body, which required getting close to the slave, and hence also put the slave-exploiter's body at risk.

Anxieties over this violent touching of black bodies increasingly became a central topic of European visual culture (and a key concern of anti-slavery consuming publics). As Marcus Wood suggests, by the late eighteenth century, 'the representation of the black body had become a [key] site of cultural contestation' in social and political satire (Wood 2000: 154). The cruel satires of James Gillray or William Hogarth (Dabydeen1987), the engravings of scenes of slavery by William Blake, the paintings of slave society by Brunias, and the popular imagery used in abolitionist writings, all depicted black bodies as a contested terrain of racial and sexual politics. Representations of black bodies and slave sexuality brought the West Indies and the black body into the domestic and public realm of European consumer society, feeding into voyeuristic interest in the scene of colonial immorality and violation. For example, a colonial genre of eighteenth-century poetry such as that recorded by J.B. Moreton or Bryan Edwards fixated especially on the sexual relations between masters and slaves. As Carolyn Cooper argues in her reading of their apologetic presentations of little erotic songs or poems from Jamaica,

> The pornographic impulse to simultaneously expose and conceal the pruriently exotic facts of native life is barely suppressed. Travel-writing of this age is essentially a colonising fiction, civilising savage landscapes – but only so far. Domesticating difference by making the strange intimately 'familiar' and acceptable, the travel-writer feeds the eroticised *conquistador* fantasies of the *voy(ag)eur/* reader safe at home, and tames the feminised alien landscape.
>
> (Cooper 1993: 21)

While British viewers were being titillated by such poetry, or by abolitionist imagery of slave torture in the 1820s–30s, the French were fascinated with Orientalist paintings of harems, barbaric Muslim tortures, and 'grotesque displays of power, especially over women' (Root 1998: 164). In both cases, argues Root, such displays 'accentuated the colony as a bizarre spectacle existing to delight or horrify the European viewer'.

What was seen as most unethical about slavery in many instances was its sexual practices: the sexual access masters had to slaves, the unnatural breaking of parental and conjugal bonds among slaves, and the associated corruption of all human morals. As Barbara Bush argues, white men in colonial slave societies were understood as desiring black slave women despite a supposed disgust at their bodies:

> According to plantocratic commentators like Bryan Edwards slave women were free of any restrictive moral codes, 'refused to confine themselves to a single connexion with the other sex' and boldly disposed themselves sexually 'according to their own will and pleasure'. . . . Edward Long fulminated about the conniving and licentious ways of the black woman while Emma Carmichael . . . blamed the moral ruin of white men in the West Indies upon the seductive capabilities of the black woman.
>
> (Bush 1990: 17–18; cf. Cooper 1993: 27)

The inhumanity and immorality of slavery were expressed in terms of a moral corruption of those who engaged in its practice, and as we have seen, this became linked to wider moral concerns with over-consumption and the need for restraint. Owning slaves was associated with moral degeneracy, indulgence in luxuries, and gluttony, while the mercurial wealth of colonial commerce came with the risk of tropical enticement and corruption. It was only through controlling black women's sexuality that these dangerous erotics could be safely and profitably contained.

As Young argues, 'There is also in evidence in these anxious repetitions of colonial tropes, the fear of being re-absorbed into the dark, articulated as a fear of the dark or being swallowed, or ingested by the Other. In order to exercise "mastery" over that "darkness", to pre-empt the retaliation that they guiltily fear will be enacted against them, acts of violation are perpetrated such as rapine penetration, and genocide' (Young 1986: 74). Through both rape of slave women and the mutilation and killing of slaves, slave owners sought to allay their own fears. Enslaved women's bodies were sites of both physical torture and sexual exploitation. They were both publicly traded and privately kept. They were seen both as distant objects and intimate companions. In some cases their children were recognised by white fathers, inheriting property from them, in other cases they were disavowed and sold as human commodities (like Inkle's unborn child). It was at this dense juncture of capital investment, kinship, and familial legacy that the consuming of slave bodies was most paradoxical and painful.

Such intimate violences, I suggest, continue to inform the racial and sexual politics of contemporary consumer culture. As bell hooks argues in her reading of consumer cannibalism:

> To make oneself vulnerable to the seduction of difference, to seek an encounter with the Other, does not require that one relinquish forever one's mainstream positionality. When race and ethnicity become commodified as resources for pleasure, the culture of specific groups, as well as the bodies

of individuals, can be seen as constituting an alternative playground where members of dominating races, genders, sexual practices affirm their power-over in intimate relations with the Other.

(hooks 1992: 23)

Thus getting close to dark Others (whether slaves or contemporary service workers) is a way of affirming and exercising domination, even as it is figured as seduction by the excessive and uncontrolled 'natural' sexuality of the Other. This typical Caribbean narrative of seduction, powerlessness, and moral corruption of those in positions of 'mastery' is, therefore, a crucial part of the act of domination.

Nevertheless, it is also important to recognise that enslaved men and women in the past and 'service workers' today, were and are able to exercise embodied resistance by staking a claim in their own bodies. In the case of slaves, this ranged from suicide and abortion to running away, self-mutilation, and working slowly, and more positively to forms of liberating sexuality, dance, dress, and spirituality. For women in particular such resistance challenged European definitions of the distinctions between self-harm and self-liberation, death and life (Bush 1990; Morrissey 1989). As Hilary Beckles argues, 'the role of gender to an understanding of [an] individual's relationship to their "body" is critical to the study of slavery. . . . The notion of slavery as the "using up" of the body – day and night – had clearly differentiated sex and gender implications' (Beckles 1999: 158). While male slaves could run away, cut off their own hands, or make themselves ill, enslaved women 'extended their resistance network into bio-social zones associated with maternity. Child-bearing became politicised', as enslaved women declared 'gynaecological warfare upon slavery' (ibid.: 159). Such a form of 'resistance', of course, was at best a two-edged sword.

While it is arguable that the high rate of infant mortality in the West Indies was due to maternal malnutrition, anaemia, infant dysentery, and other diseases, it was nonetheless perceived to be a problem by white plantation managers, who charged slave women with using abortifacients and outright infanticide. Even taking into account the medical arguments of Kiple and others, Bush still argues for recognition of a greater degree of agency among enslaved women. She points out that slave women had cultural knowledge of plants that could be used to induce abortion (including manioc, yam, papaya, mango, lime, and frangipani) and indicates that 'women in the modern Caribbean still buy herbal concoctions from old women to induce abortion' (Bush 1996: 206). Infanticide or 'encouraging' infants to die was also not unthinkable, Bush suggests, thus 'slave women's responses to childbirth may be viewed as part of a wider pattern of resistance informed by African cultural practices and the personal and institutional relations which developed in slave societies' (ibid.: 210). These forms of embodied resistance unmask the enslaver as consumer of bodies, demonstrating, through their very brutality and horrible claim upon the flesh, the master's fiction of erotic seduction or pleasure in sharing white sexuality as attributed to the slave.

In a kind of displacement of these literal facts of the master's relation to the slave, Europeans in the Caribbean fixated upon their own bodily risk through imaginary fears of cannibalism, of poisoning, and of the ever-expected violence of slave rebellions. Innumerable depictions of white bodies being slaughtered and dismembered, stories of white planters and their families being poisoned, and tales of white women being raped shaped the white Creole imagination. It was often said that rebel slaves ate the hearts and tongues of murdered whites (e.g. Beckles 1999: 56). These fears of cannibalism were used to legitimise the continuing power to consume slave bodies, and to normalise the very practices of torture and mutilation that Europeans were themselves carrying out on slaves. The branding of slaves was simply a matter of course, as Marcus Wood argues, while the metal chains, collars, masks, and other grotesque instruments of torture were mundane everyday objects of control (Wood 2000).

Against such tortures, enslaved people had to find freedom within their own bodies. Reclaiming one's own body and sexuality have become crucial elements of a culture of freedom in post-slavery societies. Even in 'emancipation', the body has remained a contested terrain. As Cooper argues in relation to the contemporary stylistics of 'slackness' in Jamaican Dancehall culture,

> it can be seen to represent in part a radical, underground confrontation with the patriarchal ideology and the pious morality of fundamentalist Jamaican society. . . . Slackness is potentially a politics of subversion. For slackness is not mere sexual looseness – though it certainly is that. Slackness is a metaphorical revolt against law and order; an undermining of consensual standards of decency. It is the antithesis of Culture.
>
> (Cooper 1993: 141)

Against the forces of a world economy that commodified black bodies, sucked the marrow from their bones, and tried to turn them into will-less workers, resistance took the form of staking a claim in one's own body. Using one's own sexuality for personal gain and profiting from the sexual display of oneself are ways of 'turning a trick'. In contrast, to work for another, to become an object controlled by forces outside oneself suggests a disciplined body, a body without agency, a zombie.

M. Jacqui Alexander has posed the same issue in relation to the contemporary neocolonial (or 'recolonised') state in terms of what she calls 'erotic autonomy':

> Women's sexual agency, our sexual and our erotic autonomy have always been troublesome for the state. They pose a challenge to the ideological anchor of an originary nuclear family, a source of legitimation for the state, which perpetuates the fiction that the family is the cornerstone of society. Erotic autonomy signals danger to the heterosexual family and to the nation . . . operating outside the boundaries of law and, therefore, poised to be disciplined and punished within it.
>
> (Alexander 1997: 64–5)

Alexander's close reading of legislation on domestic violence and criminalised homosexuality in the Bahamas demonstrates the conjuncture of bodily erotics and the national 'body' in the neocolonial Caribbean. Women's erotic autonomy as lesbian or prostitute is policed by the 'recolonised' state in order to enable the 'unequal incorporation of the Bahamas into an international political economy on the basis of serviceability (e.g. tourism)' (ibid.: 67). Tourism, based on the advertising slogan 'It's better in the Bahamas', mobilises the population as 'loyal sexualised citizens to service heterosexuality, tourism, and the nation simultaneously' (ibid.: 90). Most importantly,

> the significance of tourism lies in its ability to draw together powerful processes of (sexual) commodification and (sexual) citizenship. The state institutionalization of economic viability through heterosexual sex for pleasure links important economic and psychic elements for both the imperial tourist (the invisible subject of colonial law) and for a presumably 'servile' population whom the state is bent on renativizing. . . . The state actively socializes loyal heterosexual citizens into tourism, its primary strategy of economic modernization[,] by sexualizing them and positioning them as commodities.
>
> (Alexander 1997: 67–9)

Alexander's analysis calls into question the extent to which the autonomous eroticism of something like Jamaican Dancehall culture can be emancipatory, given the ease of its recontextualisation as a commodified raunchy and primitive 'black' sexuality serving the needs of the national tourism and music industries. In the following section I want to return to the late nineteenth-century origins of related forms of imperial sex tourism, and trace the ways in which the production of the Caribbean as a site of pleasure ('natural paradise') rests on the organisation of tourism through a violent sexual gaze.

Viewing 'free labour': working bodies as tourist scenery

The ongoing politics of racialised sexual confrontation in the Caribbean suggest that the abolition of slavery did not end the importance of this arena of conflict over bodily control. Alongside the economy of producing the goods that would fuel North Atlantic industrialisation, a new form of touristic consumption was developing in the late nineteenth century, which reconstituted power relations of bodily proximity and domination. Western consumption of 'black' and 'brown' bodies continued in newly mediated forms, which can be traced from nineteenth-century tours 'through the islands' into contemporary forms ranging from package holidays to sex tourism. If previous chapters have followed the commodities that linked Caribbean producers to Northern consumers, here I focus on the consuming body in proximity with the consumed body. The consumer now goes to the Caribbean to use embodied services in direct co-presence with the labouring body, rather than alienated labour being transferred in the form of a mobile commodity. In some respects this is a return to the co-presence of consumption exemplified by the direct abuse of the slave's body by the European colonist, but the tourist touches and consumes 'others' in different ways. In this section I consider several examples of objectification of Caribbean working bodies in the gaze (and writing) of Anglo-American tourist/consumers, connecting these practices over the course of the twentieth century to contemporary forms of sex tourism.

In Chapter 4 I observed how the viewing of bodies as part of the scenery of tropical landscapes involved various kinds of animalisation and objectification of 'black' bodies. Here I want to consider other forms of objectification, through the visualisation of bodies as edible commodities and as sexual objects. Forms of proximate consumption of black/brown 'exotic' bodies continued unabated, if in newly mediated forms, in the late nineteenth century. Tourists voyeuristically gazed upon the black working body as an exotic object, as in this 1888 account by William Agnew Paton:

> I was much interested in watching the darkies at their work [in the sugar mill]. The rags that hung in tatters on powerful forms scarcely served to conceal the muscular limbs of the men, who exerted their strength awkwardly, but with right goodwill. The women bore their part right *manfully*, if I may be permitted the expression, in all the hard work, being evidently unsexed, not to say brutalized, by their unwomanly occupation. . . . Nevertheless, all the groups of laborers, male or female, were picturesque, awakening little pity for their raggedness . . . [which instead] lent a variety of blended coloring to a picture full of sunlight. . . . [F]rom their matted woolly pates down to the soles of their plantigrade feet they were so daubed over and smeared – if not literally clothed, at least coated – with a sugary glaze, that each darky looked for all the world like a life-sized animated chocolate figure.
>
> (Paton 1888: 69)

What does it mean for a woman to be 'unsexed' by her work? Why does Paton view this labour as picturesque? What optics of imperialism can turn working people into imagined chocolate figurines? In this slippage from human to chocolate, Paton inadvertently hints at the cannibalism inherent in the tourist gazing directly upon the labouring body. Yet Paton feels no disgust at the prospect of bloodied-sugar; he tastes only the imagined sweetness of chocolate bodies (reconnecting milk chocolate with its Jamaican origins).

Just as eighteenth-century travellers enjoyed views of slaves working in the cane-fields, late nineteenth-century tourists found it interesting to watch higglers, washerwomen, and other 'Negroes', 'coolies', and 'Mulattas' at work. Children's bodies were also appropriated for the picturesque. The English tourist Sady Brassey noted in 1885 'a little Madrasee boy, bearing on his shoulder a huge bundle of sugar-canes . . . his little naked figure standing out in strong relief against the sunset sky, formed quite a pretty picture'.[5] In 1895 Charles Augustus Stoddard enjoyed watching women unloading coal from a British steamer in St. Thomas. Balancing hundred-pound baskets of coal on their heads as they walked up and down a plank to the ship, he describes them as: 'Black, rough, coarse in face and feature beyond description, they seemed like huge human beasts of burden. With long arms, great prehensile hands and fingers, large, misshapen, and unshod feet, with dirty turbans on their heads, bare breasts, and rags half-concealing their nakedness, they marched up and down the planks for hours, a weird and disgusting spectacle'.[6] In contrast to the orientalised imagery of brown and olive women met with in the previous chapter, the description of these working women alludes to the Africanist discourse of primitivism and animality in the Caribbean imaginary. Their 'nakedness' is half-concealed, their faces are rough and coarse, their bodies somehow huge and out of proportion. Yet Stoddard never associates their degraded state and 'disgusting spectacle' with his own access to the West Indies on the steamer that they are loading. His proximity to these 'weird' women only reinforces his distance from them.

Susan de Forest Day likewise took great interest in the coaling of steamships in St. Lucia in 1899:

> Coaling in the West Indies is indeed a strange sight. The coal is piled in great black hills on the shore, and around these heaps stand the women who are to coal the boat. They are chattering and jabbering like monkeys, with turbaned heads, grimy skirts well tucked up to their knees, and baskets in their hands. . . . There is a continuous stream of these women, and as their faces grow smutchy with the coal dust, and the perspiration trickles in unbecoming drops down their noses, it is impossible to distinguish one from the other. They are like gnomes bringing their wares from the bowels of the earth, to return when their work is done. It is not in any way a good moral, but it is none the less true, that the only really degraded looking people we saw during our trip were these same hard-working women, with their grimy features, muscular legs and hard, unsexed faces.[7]

Once again the women workers are perceived as 'unsexed' and inhuman, monkeys and gnomes, without language or feeling. Yet their work makes an interesting 'sight', and never do these tourists connect the labour they are watching to the fact that it is fuelling the means of transport that has brought them to view this scene. The steamships seem so fast, so modern, so clean – they exist in another world of blue-sparkling seas and leisured whites, detached from this dirty manual labour by degraded masculine women.

Such objectification extended to men, women, and children, at work or at play, in cities and in the countryside. All were available for the touristic sightseer. E.A. Hastings Jay, for example, observed people he saw during his visit to Barbados in 1900:

> In a few minutes, the bay was alive with boats rowed by brawny-looking negroes in slouched hats and calico shirts and trousers, all pulling lustily towards us. They swarmed round the steamer like flies round a horse's head, the boatmen shouting and gesticulating wildly to the passengers on deck.

These were soon joined by a fleet of little copper-coloured negro boys, in canoes made of matchwood, who dived after silver coins and brought them to the surface with a wonderful rapidity, their woolly heads looking, if any-thing, drier than before the immersion. . . . On landing I found myself in the midst of perfect pandemonium, negroes with grotesque faces screeching and yelling on every side of me, while there was scarcely a white face to be seen.[8]

His words drip disgust and loathing at every turn, the people reduced to swarms of flies, a colour of skin, a 'woolly' head, or a grotesque face. Descriptions of voices as screeching and yelling dehumanise them, and it is the lack of a 'white face' that sums up his view of this scene of difference. Viewing people as objecti-fied scenery became a crucial tourist practice and remains so today. Such urban scenes, however, with their noise and crowded streets, continue to inspire fear in travellers to the Caribbean, who prefer to find the well-worn icons of the empty beach, the palm tree, and the green tropical forest. As noted earlier, tourist resorts are designed to provide only the conveniences of 'civilised' luxury while cutting off tourists from the 'real life' of the streets and urban areas.

Natives are safe only in so far as they can be incorporated into the natural landscape. In Trinidad, Jay enjoyed immersing himself in the storybook forests where he could enjoy an uninterrupted view of the natives from a safer distance and slower tempo:

The ground is covered with all kinds of magnificent ferns, wild palms, grasses, and innumerable species of undergrowth, whilst masses of creepers cover even the tallest trees, climbing the trunks and spreading over the branches, then falling in festoons to the ground. . . . Sitting on a rock at the side of the water, I gazed long upon the scene before me. Some coolies were bathing in a beautiful pool at the bend of the river, their bronze colouring making a fine contrast to the green of the forest behind them. Presently they disappear, and a little mulatto boy comes to fill a bucket at the river. . . . Now quite a stream of coolies with flowing hair and moustaches begin to pour down towards the river-bank, with buckets balanced across their shoulders by a pole, to fetch and sell water. They chatter to each other in a jargon which is unintelligible . . . there suddenly appears a little band of boys and girls. Some of them have a scanty covering of cloth or cotton, others are as nature made them. They all plunge in just as they are into the cool water . . . I tore myself away at last, eager to explore farther into the heart of the forest.[9]

Here Kingsley-esque landscapes are experienced through viewing 'bronze' bodies against the greenery and gazing upon scantily clad children playing in water. The tourist's eager eyes seek out Caribbean bodies, and especially bared skin, for his viewing pleasure. The unintelligible 'jargon' allows him to feel a distance from these woodland nymphs, who are naturalised as part of the scenery, and the viewer imagines himself as an explorer discovering the 'heart' of the tropical forest. Yet these scenic bodies are also working – fetching water for sale – and their labour once again becomes a source of touristic consumption as picturesque.

Despite efforts to stage scenes in which to consume the people, the enjoyment of a holiday in the Caribbean was often disrupted by tense encounters with local people. The 'quiet, soothing influence of the Rio Cobre Hotel,' Jay wrote, 'was very welcome, and there my nervous system gradually regained its normal condition'; yet, he complained,

> Even in this beautiful spot we were found out and shadowed by a growing squadron of little black boys, who at length drove us back to the hotel. They stared at our faces, clothes, and boots, and more than ever at R.B.'s camera, which he had brought out in search of subjects. We differed somewhat as to the attitude which should be adopted. I was in favour of strong measures, being at the time not a little influenced by the attentions of sundry mosquitoes and sand-flies. R.B., on the other hand, counselled a policy of indifference. He was accustomed to the tropics; mosquitoes did not bite him; and he regarded little nigger boys as beneath his notice.[10]

Throughout his travels around Jamaica and other islands Jay was perturbed by the 'niggers' who returned his gaze (though he had no shame in staring at them). His companion's camera sought out subjects who would become objects, passively posing for his lens. Jay also experienced discomfort in relation to the service workers in his hotels, in this case the Moneague:

> There was something absolutely grotesque in the appearance of a shabby-looking black boy in his shirt sleeves, with a dirty cap on his head, who came to bring me my early tea in the morning, in the midst of all this magnificence. . . . A strong white manager is a necessity to keep the black servants up to the mark . . . but they are very unfit for positions of any responsibility.[11]

Such racist comments demonstrate the asymmetries of power at a personal level, which were implicit in the tourist–servant relation and which continue to inform the tourist industry in the Caribbean.[12] 'Grotesque' reminders of African primitivism undermine Jay's Orientalist expectations of holiday luxury and consumable brown bodies.

In touring through the islands, moving from one to another, the ideas of ease, luxury, and relaxation were crucial. The patterns of when and where bodily proximity between 'white' European and 'black' West Indian would occur were changing. As noted in Chapter 2, the tourist immersed his or her body in a tropical experience of sights, scents, and tastes in which nature was understood to be more bountiful, more colourful, with more flowers, exotic fruits, and leafy greenery. At the same time it was a place where others did all the labour and living would be easy, where tourists engaged in sensuous abandon, indulging in overeating and enjoying substances like alcohol and tobacco. Thus the fantasies of tropical nature came to be closely allied with experiences of transgression and intoxication, often linked with sexual encounters with the exotic 'others' who inhabit these island worlds-apart. As hooks suggests, such transgressions serve only to absorb and control primitive 'difference' and reconfirm the boundaries of domination (hooks 1992: 25). The cover of a 1901 guide to Jamaica (Plate 5.2), for example, depicts a dark-skinned boy lying by a flowery pool of water in a feminine and sexualised pose, his hat turned up beside him, brimming over with tropical fruit. The allure of travel was often expressed through the sexualisation of Caribbean bodies, particularly those of children. While seemingly innocent, when placed alongside accounts of child prostitution in the Caribbean the image may be read in a more disturbing way, as is true of contemporary imagery of Caribbean children used in promoting tourism destinations.

Objectification of 'naturalised' black bodies in travel writing is quite explicitly linked to sexual interest in them. Lucian Freud's elegant image illustrating James Pope-Hennessy's 1952 trip on a banana boat from Bristol to Dominica shows how the black body becomes an almost invisible part of the lush tropical landscape (Plate 5.3). The face of a young black man or boy (is it a striped school cap he wears?) can just be made out, deeply wrapped into the leafy profusion of a banana tree, becoming an inviting part of the 'natural' scenery. The boy's lips are parted; he looks frightened. Something seems sinister, a kind of tropical excessiveness is hinted at. Pope-Hennessy writes of his arrival in Castries, St. Lucia, that 'boys and girls stand about in the streets of Castries, drinking rum when they can afford it, and vaguely offering themselves or their young sisters, or little brothers, to the crews of passing ships'.[13] The image, then, seems to imply the

Plate 5.2 Embodied tourism as the sexualisation of children.
Cover of Thomas Rhodes, *Jamaica and the Imperial Direct West India Mail Service* (London, George Philip & Son, 1901). Reproduced courtesy of Liverpool City Library.

Plate 5.3 Freud's fruit: the banana boy.
Frontispiece by Lucian Freud, for James Pope-Hennessy, *The Baths of Absalom: A Footnote to Froude* (London, Allan Wingate, 1954). Reproduced courtesy of Lucian Freud.

dual consumption of Caribbean landscapes and young bodies in the practice of tourism. Both are on offer to the tourist who seeks out a colonial fantasy of domination in the Caribbean (as suggested by the book's subtitle, referring to the nineteenth-century writer, James Anthony Froude, famed for his blatant racism and anti-Haitian attitudes).

Prostitution of course has a long history in the Caribbean going back to the commercialisation of slave women's sexuality (Beckles 1999: 22–37; Bush 1990). In the early twentieth century, though, the combination of US military presence in the Caribbean, the increased access of tourism, and the gender relations of plantation economies set the stage for new international relations of sexual exploitation. In economic terms, 'Foreign sun-seekers replace bananas. Hiltons replace sugar mills' and tourism has become the top foreign-exchange earner in many Caribbean countries (Enloe 1989: 30–1). As Enloe compellingly argues, bananas, beaches, and bases are all connected by the international exercise of gendered sexual power. Both military bases and plantation economies have long been accompanied by prostitution, 'permitted in order to control . . . the largely male plantation workforce' and by sexual harassment used to control women workers (Enloe 1989: 140). Sex tourism developed initially in regions that had served as 'rest and recreation' sites for the American military (ibid.: 36), including around bases, open ports, or occupied countries in the Caribbean. The famous Calypso 'Rum and Coca-Cola' was written by Lord Invader in 1943 to protest the increasing degree of prostitution in Trinidad due to the presence of US military personnel (Segal 1995: 392):

> Since the Yankees came to Trinidad
> They have the young girls going mad
> The young girls say they treat them nice
> And they give them a better price
>
> They buy rum and Coca-Cola
> Go down to Point Cumana
> Both mother and daughter
> Working for the Yankee dollar

When the Andrews Sisters recorded a version in 1944, it was banned from the major US networks and became one of the most popular hits in the country. If the words seem clear enough in print, few who hum along to the tune today seem to notice that 'working for the Yankee dollar' means prostitution.

The North American craze for all things Latin in the 1950s brought another image of the Caribbean to both the big screen and to television: the fun-loving, singing, dancing, Latin lover. Pre-revolution Havana's night clubs and voluptuous entertainment were the epitome of tropical decadence and pleasure (a reputation also enjoyed at different times by Port-au-Prince, Haiti and Kingston, Jamaica). Ernest Hemingway captured Cuba's macho allures of cigars, rum, and deep-sea fishing, and remains a key touchstone on the tourist circuit.[14] In the 1990s Cuba was resurrected as a travel destination, trading on the crumbling colonial past, the 1950s American cars, the macho aura of Hemingway, and a romantic nostalgia for the revolutionary Che Guevara and the seemingly dying days of state communism. Despite the continuing US embargo against Cuba, dollar-wielding tourists have welcomed Fidel Castro's desperate measures of the 'Special Period' (necessitated by the collapse of the Soviet Union and loss of Eastern Bloc trade partners). The surreal overlay of an economy based on dollars onto a population still living on pesos has produced a marketing dream: the close yet unattainable, the illicit embrace of the taboo island, the sexually charged meeting of packed wallets and poor brown women. Consuming Cuba has become a bonanza, with Cuba Libre bars springing up, a new fad for cigars thriving, and a growing popularity to the pursuit of sex tourism. One typical recent book is illustrated with copious pictures of 'brown' women in skimpy cabaret costumes. The text easily slides from the *belle époque* days when Havana was 'the Paris of the Caribbean' to a tawdry invitation to enjoy Havana's twenty-first century 'smells of tobacco, rum and lovely girls' (Lechthaler *et al.* 1997: 75, 92).

While Enloe emphasises female prostitution, more recent research points to the equally prevalent practice of male prostitution in many Caribbean countries, where working-class men and boys are disempowered *vis-à-vis* wealthier foreign tourists, whether men or women. Even a respected travel writer like Patrick Leigh Fermor could express interest in the young men seen on his Caribbean travels in the 1950s, describing their bodies thus:

> The young men are nearly all beautifully built, and look their best when they are working without their shirts, and displaying magnificent shoulders and torsos that taper down to flat stomachs and phenomenally narrow waists. Their bodies have the symmetry and perfection of machines. Muscles and joints melt smoothly into each other under skin which shines like a seal's or an otter's.[15]

It becomes clear in his account, and others, that some of these lithe bodies (including those of children) are available for sexual hire, as tourism shifts easily into sex tourism. The sexualisation of young 'exotic' bodies, male and female, has become a standard tool of Caribbean tourist promotion, from hotel brochures to magazine advertising and guidebooks. Certain regions even specialise in the selling of particular kinds of bodies, from the dark-skinned 'African' rent-a-dread in Jamaica to the 'hybrid' light brown mulatta woman in the Dominican Republic or Cuba (Sánchez Taylor 1999).

As Jacqueline Sánchez Taylor has shown, sex tourism packages Caribbean people as 'embodied commodities' by turning the long history of sexual exploitation of women (and men) under colonial rule into a 'lived colonial fantasy' available for the mass tourist consumer. 'A key component of sex tourism', she argues, 'is the objectification of a sexualised racialised "Other"', available at a low price (Sánchez Taylor 1999: 42; Clift and Carter 1999; Kempadoo 1999). The sugar-coated tourist gaze is once again evident in the sex tourist's views recorded by Sánchez Taylor: 'You think of those incredible . . . women, ranging in colour from white chocolate to dark chocolate, available to you at the subtle nod of your head or touch-of-your-hat' (cited in Sánchez Taylor 1999: 42). The forms of 'chocolate' these sex workers embody underlines their commodity status as tropical pleasures produced for Euro-American markets. Informal service workers are not simply selling their labour power, but also their racially marked bodies; the 'commodification of difference' makes it possible for people to market their bodies and for tourists to purchase different forms of 'embodied racisms' according to Sánchez Taylor (ibid.: 51). These 'embodied racisms' draw on the long history of objectification through the tourist gaze and the circulation of travel texts that I have traced above. These texts are not simply historical documentation of the colonial relation, then, but are the narrative and imaginative subtext to contemporary forms of relation between Northern consumers and Caribbean (sex) workers.

Many of the writers cited here were in effect writing guidebooks for subsequent travellers, and some of them were immensely popular. Their movements, rhetoric, and imagery shaped not only the itineraries but also the fantasies and perceptions of the tourists who followed in their footsteps. Jamaica, for example, also became an escape for the rich and famous in the 1950s. As Diane Austin-Broos describes it, the construction of 'gay nights' in Kingston began around the turn of the twentieth century and reached its height of 'exoticization' in the 1950s. Noël Coward, known for his lifestyle of 'hedonism and glamour', entertained guests like Errol Flynn, Bette Davis, and Laurence Olivier at his north coast homes Blue Harbour and Firefly.[16] 'Conspicuous consumption in the early nineteenth century, along with conspicuous revelry, were the practices on which a tourist trade could draw in painting Kingston and Jamaica as exotic haven of the metropolitan world. The haven that was beyond the modern, even as modernity created it; the haven as distant from its own people's space as it was from the North American metropolis' (Austin-Broos 1995: 155). In this space of juxtapositions of wealth and poverty, of side-by-side fantasy retreats and gritty ghettos, an alternative modernity could be imagined, a Caribbean modernity set apart from the time-space of Western modernity.

In the post-independence period, as the glamour faded, Jamaican tourism came to be associated especially with relaxation and chilling out. It was, as one travel writer puts it, the 'one hopeful beacon that shines out of the sunny Caribbean into our lives and says "Yo, tek it easy man, kick back, chop ten, everyting gonna be all right". . . . Jamaicans have become the world's jesters, the nation we turn to when we find ourselves tired of life, the place we visit when we need a shot of pure relaxation. And it rarely disappoints'.[17] Today advertising campaigns for various products such as soft drinks and alcoholic drinks constantly keep before the public the equation of the Caribbean with fun, relaxation, and taking life easy. The deep layering and reiteration of such representations of the Caribbean tends to reinforce an imaginary geography in which it becomes a carnivalesque site for hedonistic consumption of illicit substances (raunchy dancing, sex with 'black' or 'mulatto' others, smoking ganja). These hedonistic practices of holiday abandon today serve to mark 'the islands' as places differing from the tourist's point of origin. The West Indies are inscribed as 'resorts' beyond civilisation, places where the normal rules of civility can be suspended, especially at the all-inclusive hotel complexes like Jamaica's infamous 'Hedonism II'. Thus the transgression of racial and moral boundaries serves to reinforce the constitution of geographies of difference that define Europe or North America as 'civilised' and the Caribbean as a chain of 'unreal' fantasy islands. These fantasies reflect a long history of the inscription of corruption onto the landscapes and inhabitants of these 'Paradise isles'.

Now '*voy(ag)eurs*' can again consume Caribbean sexuality vicariously from a distance. A revived prurient interest in Jamaican culture surrounds the phenomenon of Dancehall, which first seems to have come to the notice of the British media with the 1997 Jamaican-made film *Dancehall Queen* (directed by Don Letts and Rick Elgood). While the film dealt with the lives of a mother and daughter who became involved in Dancehall in order to 'put food on the table', the lifestyle has been mythologised on British television. Broadcasts by Channel Four such as 'Dance Hall Queens' and 'Exotic Dancers' have shown the 'inside story' of sexual exhibitionism in Jamaica, complemented by series like 'Caribbean Uncovered' on Channel Four and 'Pleasure Island' on ITV, which show the sexual antics of tourists on their Jamaican holidays. A whole series of programmes on Jamaican popular culture in Channel Four's 'Caribbean Summer' programming in July and August 2000 tied into a media build-up of books and releases of Jamaican music. These appropriations of Caribbean culture have depended significantly on particular constructs of Black sexuality and gender relations as not only dangerous and dysfunctional, but also 'wild' and uncontrolled (although it is the tourists themselves who engage in wild sexual practices). Again it is the perception of 'excess' in Caribbean culture, a kind of 'natural' carnivalesque vibrancy, which justifies continuing relations of consumption – the apparent inexhaustibility of the Caribbean incites the tourist to further consumption. As I have argued in previous chapters, though, there is always a set of risks, dangers, and anxieties associated with such consumption; in the following section I turn to the fears of disease and violence through which the Caribbean has entered Western metropolitan culture.

Disease vectors, blood suckers, and body snatchers

Mobilities of bodies are closely related to various 'pathologies of travel' (Wrigley and Revill 2000). While such approaches recognise the close connections between health and travel, they focus mainly on the health of the traveller, or the traveller's relation to health and illness. There has been less attention to the ways in which diseases, bodies, body parts, and substances injected or implanted into bodies also all travel. In this section I turn to these forms of travel including both disease vectors and the networks of medical research and health promotion which test or impose new medical technologies on Caribbean bodies. Just as slavery existed in a context of pathological circulation of tortured bodies, infections, and efforts to gather knowledge of diseases and substances for their treatment, so too does the contemporary global economy involve disturbingly asymmetrical bodily flows, disease vectors, and knowledge-gathering projects connecting the North and the South.

As bodies circulate globally, they become crucial vectors of disease, transferring bacterial and viral agents from continent to continent. I have already noted the collapse of Amerindian populations in the sixteenth century. Here I concentrate on those who entered the Caribbean from elsewhere. In creating a 'plantation', of course, the planter also put his own body at great risk. He had to move to the Torrid zone where the heat was excessive, fever was rampant, and death by disease and misadventure were ever present. Nibbled by mosquitoes, burnt by the sun, weakened by dehydration, and in an unfamiliar environment, the white planter, the missionary, and the indentured servant alike suffered in the Tropics. While European-carried infectious diseases and enslavement laid waste to the bodies of Caribbean peoples, European bodies were also highly vulnerable to disease in the Tropics. The journey across the Atlantic was itself a killer, with 'death rates of 20 to 25 percent among both its white sailor and black slave participants alike', according to Watts, due to epidemic disease, dysentery, and the effects of poor diet and scurvy (Watts 1990: 274). For the region as a whole, Watts estimates that in the late seventeenth century the mean life expectancy for Europeans 'could have been no more than 35', with the 'main diseases of the period being malaria . . . yellow fever, dysentery, dropsy, leprosy, yaws, hookworm and elephantiasis, aided and abetted by sometimes poor nutrition and an abysmal standard of hygiene' (Watts 1990: 357).

Sexually transmitted diseases were also extremely common in the plantation setting. As Beckles observes of the frank diary of slave-owner Thomas Thistlewood (who recorded twenty-seven different slave women as sexual partners in 1759–60 alone), it is a long litany of sexual encounters, 'and everyone it seemed, was being infected with venereal disease . . . The "clap", it seemed, held them all together in a pathogenic family' (Beckles 1999: 48). However, by the nineteenth century there was a profound demographic revolution evidenced in the dramatic drop in death-rates of Europeans in the tropics. 'When those death rates dropped,' argues Philip Curtin, 'Europeans were free to move into the tropical world at far less risk than ever before' (Curtin 1989: 1). A far better understanding of water-borne diseases and how to prevent them led to a dramatic improvement in European survival in the Caribbean in the 1850s, perhaps helping to open the way for tourism.

In contrast, health conditions for slaves had been especially devastating throughout much of the Caribbean, where a stable self-reproducing slave population was never established (in contrast to North America). Slaves were not only susceptible to all of the diseases that killed Europeans, but were also weakened by poor nutrition, overwork, and injury at the hands of slave owners and overseers. The sheer decline in slave population year on year, despite equal sex ratios and fairly high rates of fertility in some areas, indicates a staggering population deficit. Even after emancipation, disease continued to wend its destructive way through

African-Caribbean populations. In the nineteenth century cholera made its first appearance in the Caribbean, carried from Asia, with a serious epidemic hitting Cuba as early as 1833. Severe cholera broke out in Cartagena in 1849, and then spread to Cuba (1850), Jamaica (1850), Nevis (1853), and St. Kitt's, St. Vincent, Barbados, and Trinidad in 1854. In Jamaica, from October 1850, 'eighteen successive months of cholera killed between 25,000 and 30,000 people, or *circa* 8 percent of the total population . . . No sooner had this epidemic ended, than smallpox broke out, to be followed by yet another spell of cholera during 1854' (Watts 1990: 462). In the 1854 cholera epidemic close to 15,000 died in St. Vincent, over 20,700 in Barbados, and up to 6 per cent of the total population of Trinidad (ibid.: 467–8).

Given this context of disease and mortality, plantation labour (whether as slave, indentured or nominally 'free' labourer) came to be understood as turning people into expendable things. Significantly, in contrast to the European fear of cannibalism, the fulcrum of Caribbean popular fear is not the cannibal, but the body snatcher, which takes the living body but destroys its soul. Dayan describes well these Haitian folk beliefs in evil spirits, understood as 'the surfeit or remnants of an institution that turned humans into things, beasts, or mongrels' (Dayan 1998: 258). On the one hand there are the *lougawou* (vampires), *djables* (she-devils), and *soucriants* (suckers), which are said to 'eat' their victims by sucking their blood (ibid.: 264). Then there are the *zobops*, *kochons gri* (grey pigs), and secret sects of *san pwel* (hairless), *san po* (skinless), and *bizango*, spirits which 'are known by their hunger for humans, usually children (called *kabri san kon*, or hornless goats)', which are thought to be called for in sacrifices. These bodies, relocalised as spirits, are like 'consumers, taking up space, greedy for goods, services, and attention' (ibid.: 258). Dayan connects this 'oppressive magic' with the 'remembered torture' of slavery, when slaves in Saint Domingue had their skin flayed off and rubbed with pepper, salt, lemon, and ashes (ibid.: 265). These beliefs also seem to reiterate the sheer sense of loss, death, and pathological dismemberment of the slave system.

In what sense, then, does the contemporary global economy continue to consume Haitian bodies? As the oft-repeated 'poorest country in the Western hemisphere' Haiti has become a 'poster child' for the ills of poverty, disease, ecological crisis, and political catastrophe. However real these concerns might be, they also fit into an established pattern of pathologising Haiti. In 1920, according to Farmer, a *National Geographic* article made claims that 87 per cent of the Haitian population 'were infected with contagious diseases'. He argues that 'AIDS is merely the most recent in a long series of plagues attributed to Haiti. . . . In the sixteenth century Europeans insisted that syphilis originated in Haiti, and was brought back by Columbus's sailors. (The converse now appears to have been the case)' (Farmer 1994: 229). In contrast to claims that HIV/AIDS may have originated in Haiti, as first suggested by the US Center for Disease Control in the early 1990s, there is significant evidence that it was introduced into Haiti via sex tourism, which proliferated in the 1970s throughout the Caribbean. For example, a 1984 study found that 'a large number of the early cases of HIV among Haitians involved those who had sexual contact with US tourists' (Farmer 1994). Thus it is likely that the high incidence of Haitian HIV was closely related to its popularity as a sex-tourist destination, yet the powerful discourse of 'African primitivism' and weird Haitian religious practices contributed to the stigmatisation of Haitians. The US state shores up its own borders by ignoring sex tourism and instead policing the sexuality of fantasised dark Others in the Caribbean through a narrative of transnational infection. As Alexander suggests, 'the organization of tourism is presented so as to erase the complicity of the tourist in the production of tourism' (Alexander 1997: 94), and we could add, the complicity of the tourist in the production of sexual infection.

Another kind of demonisation of Caribbean people occurs around the movements of drugs from the Caribbean into Europe and North America, and the associated migration of violence, especially from Jamaica. The representation of Caribbean migrants in the North took a sinister turn in the 1980s when the crack trade brought Jamaican 'posses' to the streets of New York. Laurie Gunst followed the routes of these seasoned gunmen from their lairs in the ghettos of Kingston into the crackhouses of Brooklyn:

> The U.S. Bureau of Alcohol, Tobacco and Firearms has been tracking the posses since their mainland debut in the early 1980s, and it now reports that the gangs have killed forty-five hundred people in the United States since then. . . . They brought with them a killer enthusiasm honed by years of warfare with one another and the police, and when they came onto America's mean streets they were afraid of no one. . . . They are a Caribbean cultural hybrid: tropical bad guys acting out fantasies from the spaghetti westerns, kung fu flicks, *Rambo* sequels, and *Godfather* spin-offs that play nightly in Kingston's funky movie palaces and flicker constantly behind young men's eyes.
>
> (Gunst 1995: xv)

The globalization of Hollywood violence came with an unexpected hidden instruction: return-to-sender. Gunst suggests that it was in part the US 'war on drugs', with its crackdown on cannabis growers in Jamaica, that led criminal syndicates to switch into cocaine trafficking. Eventually the Jamaican police were turned loose in the Kingston ghettos 'to execute their former paladins. The reign of terror sent posse men by the hundreds on the run to the United States' (ibid.: xv).

The apparently unintended consequence of this dense interchange of weaponry and wickedness was the unleashing of crack in a wave of crime and violence on the streets of American cities. Criminal migrants from the Caribbean and the associated traffic in drugs and guns triggered the US government to launch new initiatives to control Caribbean migration more tightly. In Britain, Scotland Yard also believed it was facing the onslaught of the Jamaican 'Yardies' who were said to be behind much of the violent crime in London in the late 1980s and early 1990s. Yet as Leone Ross points out in the 'Afterword' to Gunst's book, the myth of the Yardie in Britain was a misrepresentation, a 'media-created folk devil' that whipped up police hostility towards Black British communities (ibid.: 252). Prominent white crime families controlled most of the crack trade and Jamaican posses made little impact in the UK. Many of the apparent 'Yardies' were not even from the Caribbean, but were 'black British youth who have deliberately taken on the look, the accent, and the attitude' (ibid.: 253).

Given the images of transgression and rebellion associated with Jamaica, it is not surprising that urban youth cultures in Britain simulate the tough language and hard image of Caribbean masculinity for their own processes of cosmopolitan signification and subaltern commodification (Back 1999). Reggae, we are informed, 'was born on the mean streets of '50s Kingston . . . amid gunslinging gang battles and knife fights in the dancehalls'.[18] Popular figures like the character Ivan (played by Jimmy Cliff) in *The Harder They Come* (1972) or more recently the character Wonie in *Third World Cop* (2000), whatever the merits of their efforts to reflect Jamaican reality, nevertheless reinforce imagery of Jamaica as violent and lawless. Meanwhile, the 'slack' lyrics of Yellowman, Shabba Ranks, and Buju Banton add a dimension of sexual excess to the violence, and Beenie Man, Bounty Killer, and Ninjaman take lyrical violence to new extremes. As one Sunday supplement trumpeted, 'Violent lyrics abound in ragga music, an edgy mix of rap and reggae. Now that gunmen are bringing Jamaican-style executions to the streets of London, can we blame the new sound for inciting anarchy in the UK?' Barbara Browning has noted the use of the metaphor of 'infectious rhythm' to describe the ways in which African-Caribbean music gets into 'white' bodies, like a virus, thus connecting positive attitudes toward music with a more subtle negativity towards immigrants and the dangers they might carry with them (Browning 1998).

Imagery of the Jamaican 'Yardie' gangster in Britain and the 'war on drugs' in North America exploits the image of the Caribbean as a lawless zone of disorder in need of global policing, legitimising greater external control over the movements of its 'infectious' people. Beyond Gunst's account of the 'Jamaican posse underworld' in *Born fi' Dead* (1995), publishers have embraced other journalistic extended travelogues or memoirs such as Chris Salewicz's *Rude Boy: Once Upon A Time in Jamaica* (2000). Such books give currency to widely circulating representations of Jamaica as a place of violence, drugs, and gunmen, without actually offering much in the way of explanation for those phenomena. What is distinctive about this genre of writing is the way in which it rests on the authority of an outsider-insider, that is, a Northerner who has infiltrated the ghettos of Kingston and can speak the lingo. When violence again swept Kingston and nearby areas in early July 2001, with twenty-five killed over one weekend, the world press turned to such commentators to help them explain the political turf wars between the supporters of Edward Seaga's Jamaica Labour Party and the ruling People's National Party.

Such projects of 'translation' of the 'real' Jamaica build on the traditions of travel writing that we have considered in previous chapters. However sympathetic the authors might consider themselves, they are essentially extending a form of fascination with the fundamental dualities of Caribbean culture and its 'poor sufferahs'. The authors draw on the easily available contrast between noble 'natives' and an inexplicably violent gun culture of criminality and corruption. They slip into 'Patwa' to demonstrate their own mastery of the local culture, translating its more exotic aspects for the armchair tourist-reader. Excerpts from Salewicz's book concerning a violent robbery, for example, were published in a Sunday newspaper supplement, along with night-time and daytime photographs of a hammock on the verandah of a villa overlooking a mountainous landscape.[19] This imagery and the tone of the writing both play on the contrast between Jamaica as a pleasure island and the 'natural' violence inscribed onto its mountainous interior landscape and by extension its 'rude' people.

Most significantly, though, these books fail to identify any reason for the violence in Jamaica, or any cause for the migration of Caribbean people to Britain and North America. Economic instability in the Caribbean (such as that being caused by the dismantling of the sugar industry and the shift in the banana regime) is linked in media accounts to the potential danger of waves of criminal migrants leaving the islands to wreak havoc in the North. The drugs that infect the populace of America like a disease have been trafficked through the Caribbean and carry with them the gun-toting badmen who poison 'our' cities with extreme, brutal, inhuman violence. As in the days of slavery, we are again beset with stories of people having their skin flayed off by acid, bodies slashed to pieces, babies torn from their mother's wombs. The gunmen and gangsters have become one of the most violent incarnations of savage violence against innocent victims, and the Northern consumer continues to be 'infected' by the disease of decadent intercourse with dangerous others.

Returning to the 'infectious' bodies of Haitians, we could consider how they have countered these endless foreign distortions of their culture with their own understanding of the bodily dimensions of their relation to the North. If mythic figurations of dismemberment have been passed down over generations in Haitian folk beliefs, more recently they have taken on a new form in stories of people whose bodies have been 'taken' by powerful Northern interests in a number of different ways. In these cases, though, it is easier to find evidence for the actual 'consumption' of blood and body parts than it is to find evidence of zombies. We already saw in Chapter 1 how Sir Hans Sloane collected body parts in Jamaica for 'scientific' purposes in the seventeenth century. How far has Western science advanced since then? Recent human rights campaigns have highlighted how poor people in disadvantaged countries have been used unethically by foreign medical and research institutions, often with state support. Do these bodily relations constitute a new form of cannibalism?

In an odd twist on the history of slavery as a kind of cannibalism, poor populations in some Caribbean countries have literally had their blood sucked and their bodies cut up 'for science'. Medical consumers in much wealthier countries like the United States have benefited from medical research carried out on poor women. Haiti in particular has been used for medical research and experiments, such as trial runs of the birth control implant Norplant (Auguste 1995), for the export of blood rich in antibodies for use in US hospitals, and even the export of cadavers for use in US medical schools (Abbott 1988). As Abbott notes, the Hemocaribian company, owned by Luckner Cambronne, a leading supporter of the dictator François Duvalier, made great profits in the late 1970s shipping 'five tons of plasma a month to American laboratories directed by Armour Pharmaceutical, Cutter Laboratories, Dow Chemical and others' (Abbott 1988). Ironically, while Haitians suffer poor nutrition and high rates of disease, their blood is rich in antibodies and their dead bodies' lack of fat offers easier access to the inner organs for trainee doctors. The United States Agency for International Development (USAID) has also been instrumental in facilitating the testing of the controversial contraceptive Norplant on poor Black women both in the 'Third World' and in the United States itself.[20]

Tests of the device on Third World women in the mid-1980s, including in Haiti, led to its approval by the US Federal Drug Administration in 1990. In 1991, according to Rose-Anne Auguste, reports were published in New York giving testimonies from Haitian women who had suffered severe migraines, dizziness, nausea, high blood pressure, hair loss, and in some cases continuous haemorrhaging for an entire month (Auguste 1995). As Jacqui Alexander notes, feminist organisations within the Caribbean, such as DAWN (Developing Alternatives for Women Now), mobilised against the introduction of Norplant:

> The state had acquiesced to the unexamined introduction and diffusion of Norplant, an invasive birth-control procedure, without the knowledge or consent of women, enabling and reinforcing the metropolitan ideology of backward Third-World women as silent, yet willing receptacles of the technologies of development and modernity.
>
> (Alexander 1997: 72)

Nevertheless, USAID promoted Norplant as a key method of contraception to be distributed in 'aid' programmes, with Haiti identified in 1993 as set to become the 'largest USAID-funded Norplant program worldwide'. Haitian women who have suffered from continuous bleeding due to Norplant have had great difficulty and expense in getting the implant removed, while delivery of 'family planning' programmes has increasingly been 'demedicalized' in order to encourage 'access'.[21] One of the private clinics contracted by USAID to administer Norplant in the Port-au-Prince slum Cité Soleil was also involved in other medical scandals. In the early 1990s the clinic administered a measles vaccine in mistaken dosages, which 'resulted in a higher than expected death rate' and in 1996 a toxic impurity in a children's cold medicine directly caused the deaths of sixty children.[22] Once again the literal bleeding to death of bodies in the Caribbean is directly linked to macro-level structural inequalities that have been produced by Haiti's troubled political relationship with the United States (cf. Farmer 1992, 1994, 1999).

In sum my reading of embodied relations of consumption in this chapter demonstrates a number of different ways in which the violences of the master–slave relation and the eroticised politics of colonial domination have continued to inform contemporary practices of tourism, immigration, and relations between nations. In imagining the proximities between bodies and between nations as forms of 'eating others' I have argued that the Northern consumer's desire to get close to exotic others in the Caribbean, and to seek out pleasures of excess consumption, operates to reconstitute boundaries of difference between dominant and subordinate positions. Through the ingestion of embodied commodities (such as slaves, scenic labourers, service workers, and sex workers), apparent 'intimacy' operates not as a relation of responsibility toward others, but as an unethical relation of violent domination. In the next chapter I will expand on this argument as I consider the ways in which discourses of 'creolization' have been mobilised in the name of 'global culture'.

6 Creolization in global culture

The Caribbean has long been at the forefront of 'globalization'. Many of the defining features of what is understood as globality have long been present here, including transnational flows of trade and investment, mass migration to and from far-flung parts of the world, intermixture of many ethnic, linguistic, and cultural groups, and dynamic processes of 'creolization'. It has become a prime location for the emergence of transnationalism, both in terms of its uprooted people and its hybrid texts, spoken languages, diasporas, and music travelling across world markets. Not only does each Caribbean society embody and encompass a rich mixture of genealogies, linguistic innovations, syncretistic religions, complex cuisine, and musical cultures, but these 'repeating islands' (Benítez-Rojo 1996 [1992]) have also exported their dynamic multicultures abroad, where they have recombined and generated new diasporic forms. The processes described as 'creolization' are crucial to understanding the contemporary expansive discourse of 'globalization', and in this chapter I consider the many different meanings of creolization in relation to a self-asserting 'global culture' that has arisen as the latest discursive construction of Western modernity.

As I have argued in previous chapters, symbolically the Caribbean as a whole acts at once as a place of promising possibility (whether for profit or for pleasure) and as a risky and 'dangerous crossroads' (the trope of cannibals, pirates, and gunmen). The metaphor of the crossroads is often used in association with Haiti, where it has special connotations in the religion of Vodou.[1] As Barbara Browning explains,

> In Vodou belief, the crossroads are the domain of Legba – known elsewhere in the diaspora as Eṣu, Eṣu-Elegbara, Exu, Echu-Elegua, Papa-LaBas. Legba is part of the Yoruba-Dahomean pantheon ... [and] is the principle of communication (this is why he is found at intersections) – the mercurial dispatcher and receptor of messages – and it is this function which also makes him the principle of confusion. Any communication is potentially a miscommunication.
>
> (Browning 1998: 35)

Legba is the intermediary between the worlds of humans and of gods, related to the Roman/Greek messenger figure Mercury/Hermes and symbolised by the

Christian cross, or an old man standing at a crossroads with a cane or staff. The Caribbean, figured as a dangerous crossroads, is the place where East and West, North and South, Third World and First World, capitalism and communism, global high tech and local poverty, tourists and drug runners, all collide. In this 'trafficking' it becomes increasingly less clear what is inside and what is outside, what is pure and what is impure, what is North and what is South, what is local and what is global.

In view of the dangers of the Caribbean as a crossroads on the way to European modernity, it would be alluring to argue that the Caribbean can never be simply consumed, swallowed, disposed of, and discarded. It forever gets inside the consumer and extends its own 'infectious' counterflows through ever-shifting global scapes (Browning 1998). Nevertheless, as we have seen above, the models of bodily infection, boundary transgression, and racial and cultural hybridisation are already part and parcel of the mythic fantasy of the Caribbean. Any notion of the Caribbean as a 'dangerous crossroads' can serve to reproduce and enforce the boundaries that set it apart as a dark 'Other' to the more stable West, and can be fed right back into the discursive production of its 'difference'. This chapter focuses on the processes of creolization that stand for the Caribbean crossroads and constitute both their creative opening and their alleged danger. Rather than simply celebrating creolization as some kind of assertion of Caribbean agency, however, I want to more carefully question how the idea of creolization has come to be incorporated into discourses of 'global culture'. As Browning's understanding of the crossroads suggests, they are as much a place of miscommunication as of communication. What miscommunications have taken place in the translation of Caribbean 'creole' languages and cultures into the self-constituting ideas of mainstream Western postmodernity?

I begin with some of the histories of migration that have made the Caribbean a prime site of 'transnationality', border crossing, and 'colonisation in reverse'. From the processes of indigenisation by which 'creole cultures' formed within the Caribbean, to their re-localisation in a global diaspora, I consider how Caribbean culture has travelled. In the second section I begin to track some of the contested meanings and complex usage of the concept of creolization, beginning with linguistics, to show how Caribbean language and literature has been consumed in the metropolitan centre. In these two sections my aim is to show how the metropolitan centre has in many ways embraced 'creole cultures', getting close to them, letting them in, taking pleasure in consuming their exotic flavour. This pleasure in consuming the creole Caribbean, I argue, suggests that the embrace of theories of creolization in recent discourses of global culture is not about an expansive letting go of purity and privilege, but may instead serve a highly problematic function of reconstituting relations of consumption.

In the second half of the chapter I turn more directly to the question of the appropriation of the concept of creolization by theorists of global culture. Here my concern is with the way in which a set of cultural practices and a theory of those practices which originated in the Caribbean and which was popularised by Caribbean theorists 'travelled' around the world. While the Caribbean is the original site of Western theorisation of hybridity and creolization, these terms have been taken up in a more general sense in the theorisation of contemporary global culture and postmodernity. I trace the convoluted travels of the concept of creolization as it first arose within the Caribbean, and then left the Caribbean with diasporic theorists, and finally seemed to take on a life of its own. Finally, in concluding, I use this critique of the consumption of creolization in global culture to reflect on the place of this book itself in networks of Caribbean representation and 'area studies'. I hope to demonstrate that an ethical relation of responsibility towards others first and foremost requires recognition of one's own location of privilege, before any attempt can be made to 'touch' (or to feel) those others.

Colonisation in reverse

If the early forms of mass tourism explored in the last chapter suggested a shift in the spatial and temporal relationship between consuming and consumed bodies (with the consumer going to the Caribbean to consume it close up), it soon became obvious that the flow of bodies is always two-way. Having followed tourist bodies on their travels through the Caribbean, here I want to turn to the travels of Caribbean bodies and cultures into the Northern 'centre'. Especially in the post Second World War period, Caribbean people began a 'counterflow' into the metropolitan centres in a process of migration sometimes referred to as 'colonisation in reverse'. These migrations have reconfigured ideas of home and belonging, contributing to the transnational projects and theories of diaspora which have destabilised national boundaries and identities. In what sense and to what degree are consumer cultures troubled by the counterflow of Caribbean bodies, which breaks the sharp distinction between 'here' and 'there', colony and metropole, producers and consumers, Third World and First World?

In the 1940s there was still a sharp division between 'tropical paradise' and the homes of the tourists who came to visit it. It was assumed that traffic would not be in the opposite direction. But the voyage of the Empire Windrush in 1948 was already changing all that; the more that the Caribbean sugar and banana industries struggled, the more people there were on the boats making the journey to the 'motherland'. Given the post-war decline in 'manpower' such colonial migrations were initially devised to help fill particular job niches, whether as bus drivers, nurses, or garbage collectors. Popular English ignorance about West Indian migrants to England in the 1950s was common:

> during the last dozen years, Jamaica has been exporting for some reason, along with the bananas and the sugar, a tide of immigrants, blacks, who talk a high, monotonous, sing-song English that might just as well be Bantu for all one understands of it, who are sending property-values down wherever they live, and who caused all that trouble in Notting Gate. The ordinary Englishman can't imagine why they don't stay at home in their tropical paradise. 'Jamaica', says Mr. Alec Waugh, 'is one vast playground'. Who

would prefer emptying dustbins in an English November to bathing on the palm-beaches on the various coral strands at his disposal? Why do they leave their 'Island in the Sun' to flood the labour-market here? The ordinary Englishman much prefers the good old days when the colonies were far-away places where administrative types made their careers and investors their profits.[2]

Here we see a connection drawn between the commodities flowing from the Caribbean into Britain, and the 'tide' of people who followed them. As in nineteenth-century travel literature, their mode of speech is made to seem primitive through an association with Africa and incomprehensibility. The Caribbean itself, we are reminded, is a 'tropical paradise', and the 'Englishman' prefers it to be a faraway storybook land, not too close to home. In following the flow of commodities from the Caribbean into Europe, therefore, Caribbean people confronted Europeans with their embodied existence not as slaves or distant labour taking commodity form, but as neighbours and service providers. As the postcolonial slogan goes, 'We're over here because you were over there'.

West Indians celebrated, laughed at, and took a new view of the Caribbean following their arrival in 'Mother England'. Cooper wryly observes how Louise Bennett's satirical poem 'Colonization in Reverse', 'gleefully celebrates the transforming power of Jamaican culture as it implants itself on British soil in a parodic gesture of "colonization". History is turned upside down as the "margins" move to the "centre" and irreparably dislocate that centre' (Cooper 1993: 175). As in Samuel Selvon's *The Lonely Londoners* (1956) and George Lamming's *The Pleasures of Exile* (1960), the moment of arrival in England becomes a significant act of decolonisation both through the embrace of Creole language as the powerful transformation of English and through the Caribbean infiltration of England. May Joseph suggests that, 'The anthropophagic logic of modernity that consumed slave bodies also devoured the master's language, spewing forth chattel language, babu english, slave idiom, and coolie pidgin' (Joseph 1999: 136). The very presence of these speaking bodies in England enacts a colonisation in reverse, posing a threat to the power of the 'centre' by getting into its innermost zones, even teaching its children to speak a new 'London Jamaican' patois (Hewitt 1986; Back 1999).

Many Caribbean theorists have described this Caribbean migration as a form of colonisation in reverse or a spewing back of what Europe had emitted (and omitted). As Stuart Hall eloquently expresses his Caribbean origin:

> People like me who came to England in the 1950s have been there for centuries; symbolically, we have been there for centuries. I was coming home. I am the sugar at the bottom of the English cup of tea. I am the sweet tooth, the sugar plantations that rotted generations of English children's teeth. There are thousands of others beside me that are, you know, the cup of tea itself. Because they don't grow it in Lancashire, you know. . . . That is the

outside history that is inside the history of the English. There is no English history without that other history.

(Hall 1991: 48)

So the Caribbean is already within, and to consume it is really to regurgitate what is already there. Hall claims Englishness as his own, England as home, and the 'Others' of empire as that which makes English history possible, while England, in its anthropoemic way, keeps trying to spit out the Caribbean, to reject those who claim to belong to it. Yet as I shall consider further below, what if Britain and other colonising nation-states were to take an anthropophagic turn? What if they started to enthusiastically embrace, lick, and devour postcolonial migrants, cultures, and theorists? As Ahmed argues, when the nation-space is imagined as a body, the problematic of letting 'strangers' into the nation is not a simple matter of letting in or keeping out strange others. Instead, 'the definition of the nation as a space, body, or house *requires the proximity of "strangers" within that space*, whether or not that proximity is deemed threatening (monoculturalism) or is welcomed (multiculturalism)' (Ahmed 2000: 100, italics in original). The proximity of Caribbean bodies within the British national 'body', therefore, serves to shore up certain notions of national identity whether or not those 'strangers' are reviled or rejoiced.

Although the arrival of Caribbean migrants in Britain, the United States, and Canada, was initially perceived through models of ethnic 'assimilation' and racial 'integration', it soon became the catalyst for fracturing such homogenising models. Indeed theorists of Caribbean origin have played a key role in the theorisation of diaspora and the imagining of 'outer-national' formations such as the 'Black Atlantic' (Hall 1990; Gilroy 1993). The scale of migration was huge. Between 1950 and 1980,

> about 4 million persons left the Caribbean to establish permanent residence elsewhere, principally in Europe and North America . . . [representing] 5 to 10 percent of the total population of nearly every Caribbean society, a higher proportion [of migrants] than for any other world area. . . . [In the mid-1970s], 16 percent of the total population of Jamaica and 25 percent of the populations of Puerto Rico and Surinam, were living abroad.
>
> (Chaney 1987: 8–9)

These recent migrations have been driven by changes in the global economy and especially changes in agricultural regimes. The flow of Caribbean migrants into the United States, for example, is closely related to the historical recruitment of workers to work in the agricultural sector beginning during the Second World War. Temporary labour recruitment programmes such as the British West Indies' Temporary Foreign Worker Programme and the H-2A programme of the 1990s 'helped set in motion the massive northward flows of legal and illegal immigrants from Latin American and the Caribbean to the USA and Canada' (Castles and Miller 1998: 136).

In addition to the sheer numbers, there was also the back and forth eddies of

Caribbean migration 'streams'. The maintenance of ties to the Caribbean and the politicisation of a pan-Caribbean identity in North America became the original prototype for theories of 'transmigration' and 'transnationalism' (Georges 1990; Schiller *et al.* 1992; Basch *et al.* 1994). As Elsa Chaney puts it, 'Caribbean life in New York City is the product of the continuous circular movements of people, cash, material goods, culture and lifestyles, and ideas to and from New York City and the islands and mainland territories of the English- and Spanish-speaking Caribbean and, in recent times, the island of Haiti' (Chaney 1987: 3). Constance Sutton refers to the economic and cultural 'Caribbeanization of New York City', which she describes as 'the Caribbean cross-roads of the world' and 'the largest Caribbean city in the world' (Sutton 1987: 19), symbolised by imagery of green palm trees sprouting up amongst the grey skyscrapers of Lower Manhattan. This has been accompanied by a 'tropicalization' of US cuisine. The explosion of Dominican, Cuban, and other Caribbean restaurants in New York, Miami, and several other US cities is creating new culinary cultures based on rice, beans, and plantains in North America. Border-crossing by Caribbean people is thus twinned with border-crossing by Caribbean culinary cultures, as both get 'inside' the United States and transform it from within.[3] There has been a 'creolization' of culinary cultures throughout the Northern metropolitan centres, where restaurants serving versions of Caribbean rice and beans, plantains and mangoes, jerked pork and Cubano sandwiches are now commonplace. Even without going anywhere, then, Europeans and North Americans are increasingly represented as exposed to the creole cultures of the Caribbean, which are infiltrating the metropolis. The music young people listen to, the Jamaican-influenced 'patois' spoken on the streets, the significance of Caribbean carnivals in many major metropolitan areas, all point towards a 'Caribbeanization' of global culture.

Inasmuch as globalization is said to be producing diversification, localisation, and a proliferation of 'hybrid' or 'syncretistic' cultures (Featherstone 1995), Caribbean cultures have been key elements within this flow of 'the exotic' into Western culture. As Mary Chamberlain argues, Caribbean people are engaged in a kind of 'globalization from below':

> Moving and manoeuvring, ducking and weaving in the narratives and debates on globalization are, and have been, actual or potential migrants, slipping through the one-way traffic of globalization by the cultural backroads, absorbing and transforming the global agenda into that of their own, at the same time transforming the cultures and societies into which they enter, momentarily or for ever. A form, as Vertovec observes, of 'globalization from below' (Vertovec 1997). . . . The culture of the Caribbean continues its globalizing mission in the person of its migrants, its transnationals (Basch *et al.* 1994), who traffic freely in and through the culture of the Caribbean, as they have done for five hundred years or so, absorbing what they encounter as much as being absorbed by it, changing and being changed, indigenizing the new as well as the old.
>
> (Chamberlain 1998: 4–5)

Chamberlain here suggests a certain amount of agency on the part of Caribbean people, to absorb and change 'the global', turning it into their own. At the same time, Caribbean culture has increasingly been consumed in the 'cosmopolitan' North through appropriations of styles of music, dance, fashion, foods, and language. To take just one example, we could consider Caribbean musical cultures as a prime example of the transnational implementation of a creolization process.

Whether consumed by travelling visitors or injected directly into the heart of metropolitan centres like London and New York, or other important capitals like Lagos and Nairobi, Caribbean musical cultures transcend any fixed place. As Peter Manuel notes in his introduction to a book on the 'currents' of Caribbean music,

> immigrants mingle with one another and with longtime locals, developing intricate multiple senses of identity reflected in the most eclectic musical tastes. Meanwhile, musical styles and influences cross-pollinate and multiply, spawning every conceivable sort of fusion, from Spanish-language reggae to merengues in Hindi. As creolization reaches a new level and the internal and external musical borders of the region dissolve, any book attempting to take stock of the contemporary music scene is doomed to rapid obsolescence.
>
> (Manuel 1995: 16)

The globalization of various genres of Caribbean music enables the tourist or virtual visitor to slide more easily into the local context, where the sounds instantly produce a sense of holiday fun, relaxation, and dance. Such fluid musical mixtures, with their 'infectious rhythms', have become symbolic of 'global culture' and the newly proclaimed porosity and permeability of cultures throughout the world (Browning 1998). Some even claim that the displacement of people and the mobilities of music are bringing about a world of 'poly-lateral relations across countries and cultures' that enable popular public spheres to become 'as dynamic and as mobile as the forces of capital' (Lipsitz 1994: 16).

Jamaica in particular is epitomised by reggae music and the nearly deified figure of Robert Nesta Marley, who is claimed today as 'part of the very fabric of global culture' (Salewicz 2001: 44). Marley's 1980 concert in the San Siro football stadium in Milan attracted 110,000 people, at the time the largest audience ever for a musical event. In the 1990s explosion of 'world music' there was another wave of musical interest in the roots of Jamaican music with a proliferation of new musical histories and CD collections.[4] In 2000, *Time* magazine named Bob Marley's *Exodus* Album of the Millennium. According to Paul Gilroy, however, Marley's commodification is not simply another Northern consumption of the Caribbean. His work not only marks the beginning of 'world music' as a marketing category, but also brought something more to the world:

> Bob became, in effect, a planetary figure. His music was pirated in Eastern Europe and became intertwined with the longing for freedom right across Africa, the Pacific, and Latin America. Captured into commodities, his music

traveled and found new audiences. . . . In Bob Marley's image there is something more than domestication of the other and the accommodation of insubordinate Third Worldism within corporate multiculturalism. Something remains even when we dismiss the presentation of difference as a spectacle and a powerful marketing device in the global business of selling records, tapes, CDs, videos and associated merchandise

(Gilroy 2000: 131–2)

Gilroy here suggests that as much as Caribbean culture has been commodified, marketed, and consumed in the North, something remains that exceeds this consumption. 'What are wrongly believed to be simple cultural commodities,' argues Gilroy, 'have been used to communicate a powerful ethical and political commentary on rights, justice, and democracy that articulates but also transcends criticism of modern racial typology and the ideologies of white supremacy' (ibid.: 130). Just as Marley, in Gilroy's reading, exceeds his consumption and the commodification of his music, we might ask whether something of the Caribbean also exceeds the consumption of its lands, plants, people, and cultures.

Are consumers at risk of *being moved* by that which they consume? Can consumption of the Caribbean never be complete, something always remaining beyond the consumerist grasp? And is there an underlying ethical and political commentary, as Gilroy suggests, inherent in the post-slavery Afro-Caribbean cultures of the New World? While Gilroy's reading of some modicum of redemption within commodity culture is tempting, I want to explore other avenues. The problematic that concerns me is not commodification *per se*, nor questions of 'authenticity', but the question of how embracing or 'eating' the 'creole cultures' of the Caribbean operates to elide or bypass any ethical engagement with responsibility towards others. In getting closer to Caribbean cultures, in 'becoming Creole', does metropolitan culture in fact again reproduce its domination, reconstitute its centres of knowledge and power, and erase the (neo)colonial relations of violence that enable this proximity in the first place?

Consuming Caribbean language and literature

Before taking stock of the contemporary meanings of creolization, we can first return to its origins in the Caribbean. While its etymological origins remain murky, the Spanish term *criollo* was first used in the sixteenth-century Caribbean to refer to people of Iberian descent who were born in the Americas, in order to set them apart from the *peninsulares* who were sent out from Spain. It was also applied to locally born and bred 'livestock and slaves' (usually placed in the same category on colonial property inventories), as distinguished from imports of European stock or 'salt-water' slaves. *Criollos*, whether human or animal, had survived the seasoning process of entering a new disease environment, and were thus seen as better suited to local conditions than in-comers. But it also came more importantly to refer to a hybridisation of cultures and a turning away from metropolitan Iberian culture:

It was a matter of enterprising people, *mestizos* and *mulatos* in large measure who, because they lived far from the cities, stayed outside of the orbit of the colonial bureaucracy, the military garrisons, and the Church's watchful eye. . . . [They] subsisted in a self-sufficient manner, with their backs turned to the mother country and the island's capital; they ate from English plates, they used French knives, and they dressed in fine Holland shirts; they imported wines, furniture, tools, arms, fashions, and many other objects, and they read 'heretical' books, including Bibles that were translated into Spanish by expert Flemish Jews. . . . In this society with its free habits, under the common interest of its contraband trading and separated from the centers of colonial power by distance and by mountain ranges, the people properly called creoles (*criollos*) and also, significantly, people of the land (*gente de la tierra*) started to emerge.

(Benítez-Rojo 1996 [1992]: 45–6)

Rather than focusing on the sea-borne commerce flowing back towards Iberia, these 'people of the land' became rooted in the New World and turned their attentions to cattle ranching and contraband. This was now their home, and their economic interests shifted the centre of gravity of their lives to the Antilles. It was precisely such Criollos, both white and *mestizo*, who would later lead the independence movements against Spain.

In the French territories the term Creole was also used to refer to locally born white populations, while in the British territories it was predominantly used to refer to populations of mixed African and European descent who had developed a local 'creole culture' that was a hybrid or mixture.[5] In every case, though, the word carries the connotation of what could be called an achieved indigeneity. That is to say, it refers to a process of being uprooted from one place and re-grounded in another such that one's point of origin loses its significance and one's place of arrival becomes 'home'. Thus it implies the falling away of a previous home and the claiming of a new place of belonging. At the same time it also carries the connotation of a mobility and mixture of peoples, cultures, languages, and cuisines. Creolization (becoming Creole) can therefore be understood as a process of achieving an indigenous status of belonging to a locale through the migration and recombination of diverse elements that have been loosed from previous attachments and have reattached themselves to a new place of belonging.

The modern academic usage of the term 'creole' originates in the field of linguistics, where there has been a longstanding interest in a range of languages that arose especially in the context of the Atlantic slave trade (but also in parts of the Indian Ocean and other plantation societies). These 'creole languages' are thought to have arisen from some sort of mixture of European languages with various African languages and other non-European languages, although the original mechanism for their evolution remains empirically unsupported. One commonly accepted hypothesis (cf. Alleyne 1980; Le Page and Tabouret-Keller 1985; Sebba 1997) is that in these special contact zones between radically different linguistic groups in situations of social inequality there first developed a simplified language of convenience known as a 'pidgin'. People in these areas (especially those who were enslaved and removed from their communities of origin) suffered a radical break in transmission of their native languages and came to speak only the pidgin for most purposes. When the pidgin became extensive enough that a generation of children were brought up speaking it as their mother tongue, it is then thought to have gone through a process of 'complexification', in which it was re-elaborated into a more fully-fledged language, known as a creole language.

As in the case of people becoming 'Creoles', these theories of creole genesis also rest on processes of involuntary migration and subsequent re-indigenization, or we might say, denaturalisation and renaturalisation. In this sense creoles are said to be 'new' languages, evolutionarily 'younger' than non-creole languages, which have developed gradually and organically over centuries without any radical breaks in transmission from one generation to the next. 'In this view', suggests Michel DeGraff, 'Creoles are linguistic neonates whose morphologies lack the features that characterize "older", more "mature" languages' (DeGraff 2001: 54). This theory of language genesis, however, remains highly contested and unproven. In a devastating critique of the commonly accepted story of creole genesis, DeGraff has argued that current theories rest on a set of invalid empirical assumptions and ideologically suspect theoretical suppositions. Drawing on his own extensive knowledge as a native Haitian creole-speaker and as a trained linguist, he demonstrates step by step that each assumption about the 'difference' of creoles from other languages is unsupported by the empirical evidence. While it would be inappropriate to use the specialised terminology of linguistics in this context, I would like to try to summarise some of his main conclusions in the most general terms.

First, DeGraff shows that the basic generalisations and predictions of the creole prototype as proposed in McWhorter (1998) and in traditional 'catastrophic' creole genesis scenarios are 'disconfirmed' by the evidence from Haitian creole, which is considered to be one of the most classic cases of a creole (DeGraff 2001: 87). Haitian creole is not lacking in the linguistic features and complexities that are usually attributed to 'more mature' languages. Second, he demonstrates that there is a preconception permeating creole studies, from before the nineteenth century until today, that creoles are somehow non-'normal' or non-'regular' languages 'intrinsically marked by one or both of the following related genetic factors:'

> (1) their catastrophic genesis as emergency (thus 'simple' and 'optimal') solutions to communicative problems in plurilingual communities; (2) their genesis as failures on the part of 'inferior' beings to acquire 'superior' languages.
>
> (DeGraff 2001: 90)

While the second supposition is clearly racist, the first one also carries with it ideological baggage that has been extremely detrimental to contemporary creole speakers and to the language and education policies in creole-speaking societies. The notion that creoles are morphologically simple or simplified languages (and have had less time to 'develop' than 'normal' languages) is, argues DeGraff, 'empirically untenable, theoretically unfounded, and methodologically bizarre' (ibid.: 97). Yet because of these notions 'Creoles remain among the most stigmatized and undervalued languages of the world, even among self-styled progressive intellectuals, including linguists' (ibid.: 98).

To return, then, to the wider processes of inventing a new hybrid culture and Creole people, we may need to ask whether the theory of cultural creolization has imported any of the assumptions of creole linguistics from which its central concepts have been borrowed. Certainly the term creole has at times carried derogatory connotations, for example when used by British travellers, as we have seen in previous chapters, to pass judgement on the 'degeneracy' of the people of the Hispanic Antilles. It has also been used in the context of Black Power or Pan-African movements by Caribbean people of African origin to insult 'Afro-Creoles' who were resented for abandoning their 'own' culture and trying to become European in manners and customs. More recently, though, it continues to imply a kind of novelty within culture, a dynamic of constant invention, a shifting and morphing which suggests a youthfulness and, dare we say it, immaturity of creole cultures in comparison to more conservative, stable, steady 'Old World' cultures. In so far as creole languages are largely regarded as oral idioms, lacking in a literature, a history, and even, according to some, the ability to develop 'abstract concepts', they are thought to be highly mutable, open to change, and even vulnerable to 'decreolization' under the influence of the 'standard' language. Although these characteristics of dynamism are sometimes cast in a positive light, they may nevertheless carry with them a set of unwarranted assumptions about underlying cultural differences.

If we turn to literature, and the ways in which Caribbean literary texts have been consumed in metropolitan centres, we can begin to see the far-reaching effects of theories of creole genesis on interpretations of contemporary Caribbean culture. Caribbean literature has taken on a markedly prominent role in metropolitan literary studies and publishing worlds since the 1980s, when it became increasingly fashionable to read postcolonial and non-Western literatures.[6] With St. Lucian poet Derek Walcott receiving the Nobel Prize for Literature in 1992 and Martinican novelist Patrick Chamoiseau winning the Prix Goncourt in 1993, there was a growing canonisation of classics of Caribbean literature and poetry. New editions and anthologies appeared bringing new attention to authors such as Claude McKay, E. Kamau Brathwaite, Jean Rhys, Jamaica Kincaid, George Lamming, Samuel Selvon, Caryl Phillips, Maryse Condé, Alejo Carpentier, Juan Bosch, and young diaspora writers like Edwidge Danticat, to name but a few. University courses appeared on 'Caribbean Women Writers' and conferences on related themes proliferated in the 1980s and 1990s. There was also a growing interest in 'dub poetry' and the oral verse of Jamaican poets like Louise Bennett and Lynton Kwesi Johnson. Then in 2001 V.S. Naipaul (of Trinidadian origin) was awarded the Nobel Prize for Literature, further crowning Caribbean literature with the metropolitan seal of approval. But how are these literatures being consumed in the metropolitan centres?

Crucial to the reception of Caribbean literature in French and Anglo-American literary studies has been the idea that they have in them something which is 'creole', native to the Caribbean, even if they are written in French, English, Spanish, or Dutch. They are described as hybrid literatures, born of the New World, Antillean, rhythmic, and polyphonic. Antonio Benítez-Rojo, for example, suggests that,

> The literature of the Caribbean can be read as a *mestizo* text, but also as a stream of texts in flight, in intense differentiation among themselves and within whose complex coexistence there are vague regularities, usually paradoxical. The Caribbean poem and novel are ... projects that communicate their own turbulence, their own clash, and their own void, the swirling black hole of social violence produced by the *encomienda* and the plantation, that is, their otherness, their peripheral asymmetry with regard to the West. Thus Caribbean literature cannot free itself totally from the multiethnic society upon which it floats, and it tells us of its fragmentation and instability.
>
> (Benítez-Rojo 1996 [1992]: 27)

These 'polyrhythmic' texts are thus counterpoised against the West, just as Creole languages are contrasted to 'older' languages: Caribbean language and literature is perceived as being more dynamic, chaotic, improvised, musical, and impure without the clear rules, grammars, and stabilising features of 'mature' languages and literatures. While for Benítez-Rojo this is part of its beauty and grandeur, in view of DeGraff's argument this postmodern praise may also have more troubling implications.

By positing an essential difference of Caribbean literature, rooted in its *créolité*, it is treated something like the way in which European Surrealists such as André Breton treated Caribbean painting: it opens up access to the primitive, the natural, the magical, the feminine, the wells of poetic inspiration.[7] Such interpretations of *créolité* as civilisation's 'other' and dark mirror are extended to entire cultures and peoples, as can be seen in typical travel journalism on the region. The French Caribbean, in particular, has been characterised as a tropical transmutation of France:

> French is what Guadeloupe is, but it is France carried 3,000 miles in a leaky bag and dropped into a subtropical archipelago: a hot, steamy, volcanic France, beach-frilled, sun-fried and rain-forested, yet for all that, inexorably a sprig of the old country. ... French, yes, but West Indian of course to its core. ... Thus, blended with French finesse is a winsome Caribbean artlessness, a hot, splashy, noisy directness. Women's clothes are primary-colour bright. Flowers, wild or garden, are big and brashly hued ... Fruits like melons, breadfruit and papayas are cannonballs on branches, and their

fall can maim. Names tend to be elemental: Basse-Terre, Grande-Terre, Grosse-Montagne, Grand-Bourg, Petit-Bourg.[8]

In this leaky France, parochial artlessness and brash colours replace civilisation's finesse and sophistication. There is a metonymic slippage from the volcanic and hot landscape, to the noisy and colourful people, to the elemental and direct language. The writer finds the 'clackety french patois' to be 'Twes twes cuwieux'. And lurking behind the alluring charms and childish palette, even the high-calibre fruit is dangerous.

Indeed food and language are close companions in the metropolitan consumption of creole cultures. As Celia Britton has shown in relation to the consumption of French Caribbean literature, if in the past exotic fruit was the main export of the French Antilles, now 'the metropolitan French readership consumes Caribbean novels as food'. French Caribbean 'novels are marketed as food' through the use of 'gustatory metaphors' which describe the 'taste' of the language as savoury (Britton 1996: 16). 'The trick' of this tasting, suggests Britton, 'is to make the reader feel that s/he is in unmediated contact with the authentic living "voices" of this exotic culture' (ibid.: 18–19). The writing of Chamoiseau, for example, is described in the *New York Times Book Review* as Rabelaisian, but with a story 'driven by an African beat, its syncopation measured like the percussive claps of its music. Just as you *hear* his sentences, you must *hear* the whole book, the differing intensities in the flows of its story, its "nonlinear" history, add complexity to the melodic line'. Reading is imagined as a form of close contact with 'the other' through the production of an illusion of hearing spoken creole or hints of the oral 'folk' culture. Other reviewers describe his language as 'lush and colorful', or a 'colorful and exciting patchwork, filled with the sights, sounds, and smells of its exotic locale'.[9] In so far as 'creole *speech* is the source of the stylistic peculiarities of the novels' discourse' (in comparison to metropolitan French novels), as Britton argues, the reader can get closer to the 'exotic' through vicariously consuming the *créolité* of writing as if it were being heard, smelled, and tasted.[10]

By 'eating their words', Britton argues, French readers are engaged in a particular kind of (un)ethical relation to this exoticised culture. Consuming the products of different cultures 'raise[s] the problem of the *ethics* of understanding. The "alien" object, whether it is a text, as in this case, or some other artefact, offers a resistance to our attempts to understand it' (ibid.: 19). Whereas Caribbean theorists like Edouard Glissant have argued that the 'opacity' of language is a positive characteristic 'signifying the resistance which the oppressed put up against being understood, which is equated with being objectified and appropriated' (ibid.: 19), the use of the gustatory metaphor 'short-circuits' this resistance. It allows the consumer to taste an 'alien' object and savour its difference, without recognising his or her own lack of understanding and objectification of subaltern difference. Britton argues that if 'what we are invited to do to the text is in effect to *eat* it, then its resistance – its alien or even incomprehensible quality – is simply reduced to part of its exotic, picturesque "saveur"; it becomes something to "get your teeth into"' (ibid.: 19–20). As we have seen with the descriptive literature of travel and the drawing and photographing of Caribbean people and landscapes, such objectification facilitates its distant consumption. Ultimately Caribbean literature (like its digitised 'world music') becomes a commodity valued for its 'flavour' while the first-world subject is positioned and consolidated '*as a consumer*' (ibid.: 21; cf. hooks 1992: 21).

One way in which creole oral cultures have resisted this commodification and consumption is through their 'rawness'. There has been a movement among some Caribbean (and African) writers to write in their own Nation Language, which requires translation for speakers of so-called 'standard' languages like English or French. If the language is 'raw' enough (e.g. 'deep' on the 'creole continuum', vulgar, rough, crude, sexual, violent, harsh on the ear) it will repel any who might potentially 'eat' it. Only when cooked up in literary form is it 'palatable' to the metropolitan gourmand. As Carolyn Cooper argues in her study of Jamaican vernacular texts, *Noises in the Blood,*

> The vulgar body of knowledge produced by the people . . . is devalued. In all domains, the 'vulgar' is that which can be traced to 'Africa'; the 'refined' is that which can be traced to 'Europe'. . . . In the domain of language and verbal creativity, English is 'refined' and Jamaican is 'vulgar'; oral texts are 'vulgar'; written texts are 'refined'. . . . The subjects of this study are, for the most part, bastard oral texts . . . products of illicit procreation . . . perverse invasions of the tightly-closed orifices of the Great Tradition.
>
> (Cooper 1993: 8–9)

Her own theoretical discourse promotes a transgressive 'oraliteracy' which 'attempts to cross the divide between Slackness and Culture, between Jamaican and English, between the oral and the scribal traditions' (ibid.: 12). Taking a stand on the literary consumption of Caribbean texts, she states that her decision '*not* to translate into English all of the Jamaican texts analysed in this study is part of this reverse colonisation project. For non-Jamaicans, the apparent inscrutability of these texts is an invitation to engage in the rehumanising act of learning a new language' (ibid.: 193).

The use of Nation Language in the writing of theory can achieve a certain amount of resistance to metropolitan consumption. Several other Caribbean academics have experimented with publishing non-literary works in creole languages (e.g. Trouillot 1977) and systems of writing and dictionaries of Caribbean English have appeared. Creole usage, especially in so far as it continues to be stigmatised, remains a tactic against metropolitan consumption *and* an invitation to 'folk up' theory (Cooper 1993: 14). Of course, to pitch one's camp on the subaltern side one needs to have sufficient oraliteracy to stand at this crossroads, and that usually requires having one foot in that camp already, being in other words 'between camps' (Gilroy 2000). But it is not only Caribbean literature that has been in vogue recently, but also Caribbean theory. In so far as these theorists are also between camps, in what sense might their theories either be consumed or resist consumption? Can a theory of creolization grounded in the vernacular cultures of the Caribbean stand up to global consumption?

Theoretical piracy on the high seas of global culture

Caribbean theoretical concepts have increasingly been appropriated into discourses of 'global culture' produced in Western academic institutions and media publics. If the Caribbean was once erased from the time-space of Western modernity, it has now been voraciously sucked into the vortex of 'global culture'. Creolization is today posited as a condition that we are 'all' experiencing in a context of 'globalization', defined as the increasingly rapid interchange of capital, information, people, and cultural objects between far-flung parts of the world, and a reflexive consciousness of that interconnectedness (Robertson 1992; Beck 2000; Urry 2000). I am specifically concerned with the way in which contemporary claims to mobility, hybridity, and creative cultural adaptation draw on Caribbean antecedents of 'creolization', borrowed via the work of Caribbean diaspora theorists, but gutted of many of the original connotations of the term. How has the concept of creolization moved from the periphery to the centre? How do (non-Caribbean) 'postmodern' and 'postcolonial' theorists consume figurations of intermixture to claim the Caribbean for 'global culture'? And what is lost (by some) and gained (by others) in taking creolization as simply shorthand for cultural mixing, linguistic hybridisation, and fluidity of identities?

Earlier generations of Caribbean intellectuals invented theoretical terms such as 'transculturation' (Ortiz 1947 [1940]; cf. Spitta 1997), 'creolization' (Brathwaite 1971; cf. Nettleford 1978), and 'transversality' (Glissant 1981) to craft powerful tools for intellectual critique of Western colonialism and imperialism, tools appropriate to a specific context and grounded in Caribbean realities. Here I will first consider those theorists who used the concept in the context of national independence movements in the 1960s and early 1970s. Then I turn to the Caribbean diaspora theorists who in the 1980s re-worked the concept of creolization into a tool capable of challenging nationalist projects. Finally, I will consider how theorists of global culture have appropriated the term in the 1990s, prying it loose from its Caribbean location.

The Jamaican historian and poet Edward Kamau Brathwaite was one of the most significant early theorists of creolization. As Glen Richards notes, his work was part of the post-independence nation-building projects of the 1960s which 'developed partly in response to the legacy of racist thought that had helped to shape the written history of the region' (Richards 2001: 10). Cultural anthropology of the Caribbean in the mid-twentieth century was deeply influenced by the 'plural society' thesis, which posited that there were separate cultural strands within each Caribbean society, a lack of any indigenous local culture, and only the broken remnants of African cultures (Smith 1965). In contrast, anthropologists like Melville Herskovits (and later Sidney Mintz and Richard Price) argued that there were African 'survivals' across the New World, which informed a particularly Caribbean cultural formation (Herskovits 1964; Mintz and Price 1992 [1976]). Brathwaite likewise rejected the idea that Africans had been stripped of their culture in the process of enslavement and transportation to the West Indies, to be remade in a (failed) European mould. Instead he argued that 'African cultural norms had played a decisive role in the formation of the culture of the local population in the Anglophone Caribbean and that this culture was not merely a poor imitation of Europe's but a new "Creole" culture' (Richards 2001: 10; Brathwaite 1971).

In so far as creolization refers specifically to the process by which descendants of Africans forged a new Caribbean culture out of the melange of available (and imposed) cultures, it retained a sense of dynamic critique and strategic rearticulation in the 1970s. For example, Rex Nettleford in 1978 wrote that the 'two-pronged phenomenon of decolonisation and creolisation (or indigenisation) represents that awesome process actualised in simultaneous acts of negating and affirming, demolishing and constructing, rejecting and reshaping' (Nettleford 1978: 181). Nettleford further clarifies that creolization 'refers to the agonising process of renewal and growth that marks the new order of men and women who came originally from different Old World cultures (whether European, African, Levantine or Oriental) and met in conflict or otherwise on foreign soil . . . The operative word here is "conflict" ' (Nettleford 1978: 2). As this history suggests, creolization is not simply about moving and mixing elements, but is more precisely about processes of cultural 'regrounding' following experiences of violent uprooting from one's culture of origin. It is deeply embedded in situations of coerced transport, racial terror, and subaltern survival.

While grounded in the specificity of Caribbean realities, Caribbean intellectuals in different kinds of locations have developed the meaning of 'creolization' and 'creole societies' in a wide range of ways (see useful reviews in Bolland 1992 and Burton 1997). Most importantly, though, as Nigel Bolland argues and Richard Burton seconds, 'the portrayal of creolization as a "blending" process, a mixing of cultures that occurs without reference to structural contradictions and social conflicts' is not sufficient. This reduction 'obfuscates the tension and conflict that existed, and still exists, between the Africans and Europeans who were the bearers of these traditions' (Bolland 1992: 64; Burton 1997: 6). Creolization, they insist, is 'a process of *contention*'. Unlike the more biologistic and racially-inflected idea of 'hybridisation' (cf. Young 1995), then, it suggests a political process expressed through a subaltern oppositional culture. However, one effect of this nationalist-oriented anti-colonial contention, as Richards notes, was that it tended to prioritise African-Caribbean culture at the expense of Indo-Caribbean, Chinese-Caribbean, or other elements. It was only in the 1980s that theorists across the wider Caribbean diaspora began to extend usage of the concept of creolization as a subversive force in a way that began to free it of its nationalist and essentialist connotations. While nationalism may have been necessary to the Caribbean postcolonial transition, diaspora theorists began to widen the project of creolization to become an 'outer-national' force, as Gilroy puts it (Gilroy 1993), that went beyond any nationalist efforts at containment.

Gilroy has argued that the 'theorisation of creolisation, métissage, mestizaje, and hybridity' remain 'manifestly inadequate' to the stereophonic and bifocal cultural processes of the black diaspora (Gilroy 1993: 2, 15). Nevertheless, he holds onto the possibilities of 'creolized, syncretized, hybridized, and chronically impure cultural forms' (Gilroy 2000: 129). While such projects remain anti-hegemonic, they have been freed of their nationalist connotations to inform a more global process of postcolonial contention. His work has been influential in spreading these concepts throughout cultural studies. Diasporic formations represent for him a ceaseless reprocessing of a politics and poetics of self-making in the face of racialised terror. 'Invariably promiscuous, diaspora and the politics of com-memoration it specifies challenge us to apprehend mutable forms that can redefine the idea of culture through a reconciliation with movement and complex, dynamic variation' (ibid.: 129–30). Notable here, though, is the way in which Gilroy appropriates the racialised and sexualised language of hybridity, impurity, and promiscuity, which as I have argued in previous chapters were key tropes in the construction of white domination in practices of Caribbean travel and tourism (cf. Young 1995). This should perhaps alert us to a problem in the use of theories that blur together hybridity and creolization as effective modes of popular resistance.

Stuart Hall, as a prime voice both of the Caribbean (Jamaican) diaspora and of cultural studies in Britain, explains Caribbean identity in terms of a position-ing that is not only dialogic, but also conflictual. What is uniquely 'essentially' Caribbean, according to Hall, is 'precisely the mixes of colour, pigmentation, physiognomic type; the "blends" of tastes that is Caribbean cuisine; the aesthetics of the 'cross-overs', of 'cut-and-mix' to borrow Dick Hebdige's telling phrase, which is the heart and soul of black music' (Hall 1990: 235–6). Crucially, however, he observes that Caribbean culture negotiates a 'doubleness' that is simul-taneously grounded by continuity with the past (the cultural, linguistic, musical, and culinary traces and bodily practices of Africa), yet always ruptured by difference and discontinuity, arising from the historical traumas of displacement, dismemberment, and transportation. As Helen Thomas summarises,

> Creolisation is thus a response to crisis and extreme upheaval, which operates upon a series of linguistic, psychological and ontological levels. In essence it attests to the overriding will to survive, a paradoxical process which endeavours towards expansion at the moment of reduction; towards speech at the moment of silence; and towards history at the moment a cultural continuum is broken.
>
> (Thomas 2000: 11)

Thus Hall uses the concept of creolization in a complex way, suggesting that it can express creativity in the face of destruction, dislocation, and loss, rather than a simple conjoining of cultures. Kobena Mercer also suggests that 'across a whole range of [African diaspora] cultural forms there is a "syncretic" dynamic which critically appropriates elements from the master-codes of the dominant culture and "creolises" them, disarticulating given signs and re-articulating their symbolic meaning' (Mercer 1988: 57). This is a useful definition of the work of creolization because it clearly differentiates it from notions of 'hybridity' as a non-conflictual cultural process that is somehow 'natural' to Afro-Caribbean cultures.

The Cuban-American literary theorist Antonio Benítez-Rojo also attempts to articulate ideas of historical disruption and paradoxical speech in Caribbean literature. He interprets Caribbean literature as a postmodern expression of unresolved fragmentation, instability, lack, noise, and chaos (rather than synthesis, acculturation, or miscegenation) (Benítez-Rojo 1989, 1996 [1992]; cf. Spitta 1997: 166–7). In an overflow of terminology he describes the Caribbean itself as a 'meta-archipelago' in which there was 'an extraordinary collision of races and cultures' in processes of 'syncretism, acculturation, transculturation, assimilation, deculturation, indigenization, creolization, cultural *mestizaje*, cultural *cimarronaje*, cultural miscegenation, cultural resistance, etc.' (Benítez-Rojo 1996 [1992]: 37). Given the excision of the Caribbean from the time-space of Western modernity, however, his analysis raises questions about the positing of the Caribbean as 'postmodern *avant la lettre*'. As Silvia Spitta asks, if 'postmodernism [is] yet another unacknowledged western cannibalization of the "Third World" . . . where does that leave Benítez-Rojo's argument, indebted as it is to postmodernism, and coming as it does from a very specifically Cuban context *in* the United States?' (Spitta 1997: 170).

And, we could add, what of Gilroy's or Hall's location in Britain? Benítez-Rojo creates a strange dynamic between postcolonial Caribbean diaspora theorists and metropolitan theories of postmodernity. Spitta suggests that,

> what we are seeing is the development of two distinct yet at times overlapping modes of conceptualizing the border. The first is oppositional, explosive, politically engaged . . . the second corresponds to the internationalization of the border (i.e., it attempts to systematize the consciousness of displacement) where . . . any encounter between people of different cultures constitutes a 'border experience'.
>
> (Spitta 1997: 176)

While the idea of the 'border experience' has been central to postcolonial theory, and suggests a way of moving beyond national and ethnic essentialism, it nevertheless leaves us with a less located politics. The explosive, politically engaged, and conflictual mode of conceptualizing creolization in the nationalist period of the 1970s has been met with a later usage, from a different (metropolitan) location, in which creolization refers to *any* encounter and mixing of dislocated cultures. This dislocation has enabled non-Caribbean metropolitan theorists to pirate the terminology of creolization for their own projects of de-centring and 'global' mobility.

The value of diasporic theories of creolization is in their capacity to address questions of 'hybridity, syncretism, of cultural undecidability and the complexities of diasporic identification which interrupt any "return" to ethnically closed and "centred" original histories' (Hall 1996: 250). While there have been clear gains – theoretically and politically – in the move to destabilise the borders and boundaries of global modernity, the slippage of theoretical terms from the periphery to the centre may have some unintended consequences brought about by 'the inescapable power-geometries of time-space' (Massey 1999). As theories become mobile there is a risk that they will be consumed within the mainstream culture and stripped of their oppositional meanings. I suggest that this is precisely what has happened to the concept of creolization in global culture.

Starting in the 1980s, the concept of creolization began to be pried loose from its specific grounding and taken up in a more general sense in the theorisation of the cultural fluidity of postmodernity and contemporary forms of globalization. Transcending the specific context of creole societies, the Caribbean has apparently bequeathed its culture to the world, part of a general embrace of postcolonial 'counterflow, from periphery to center' (Hannerz 2000: 14). Yet there has been little reflection on the dynamics of such counterflows and how they might operate in the reconfiguration and redeployment of metropolitan culture. What happens when postmodern and postcolonial theorists consume figurations of intermixture and subaltern agency to claim the Caribbean for global culture? In what ways does the appropriation of the metaphor of creolization within sites of contemporary metropolitan self-theory, erase the specificity of Caribbean processes of creolization and of their historical, political, cultural, and economic roots? What is lost in taking creolization as simply a play on language or shorthand for cultural mixing and what implications does this have for the future of Caribbean theoretical projects?

In a 1987 article entitled 'The World in Creolisation' the anthropologist Ulf Hannerz argued for a new macro-anthropology of culture that would encompass both the 'Third World' and 'metropolitan' culture. Recognising the cosmopolitan connections of all 'local' cultures and drawing on creole linguistics, he defined creole cultures as 'those which draw in some way on two or more historical sources, often originally widely different. They have had some time to develop and integrate, and to become elaborate and pervasive'. The 'complexity and fluidity' of the world system, he concluded, suggested that '[in] the end, it seems, we are all being creolised' (Hannerz 1987: 552, 557). He went on to use the concept of creolization as a 'root metaphor' and 'keyword' in much of his subsequent work (Hannerz 1989, 1996, 2000), using it as a device to free anthropological description from ideas of cultural integration within homogenous communities. He proposes, for example, that,

> here we are now, with hybridity, collage, mélange, hotchpotch, montage, synergy, bricolage, creolization, mestizaje, mongrelization, syncretism, transculturation, third cultures and what have you; some terms used perhaps only in passing as summary metaphors, others with claims to more analytical status, and others again with more regional or thematic strongholds.
>
> (Hannerz 2000: 13)

Hannerz himself prefers the term creolization as being more precise and restricted than the other terms. But what does it mean to be 'with' all of these things, and who is the 'we' who is 'now' with them? Is not this feeling of getting closer to 'difference' very similar to the colonial and imperial practices of travel as a way of getting close to exotic others that we have considered in previous chapters?

Having claimed that 'we are all being creolised', Hannerz also admits that 'some cultures are more creole than others' (ibid.: 14). Are the more 'mature', standard, non-creole cultures, then, only slightly creole, just dabbling? Drawing an explicit analogy with linguistics, Hannerz suggests that 'a creolist view is particularly applicable to processes of cultural confluence within a more or less open continuum of diversity, stretched out along a structure of center-periphery relationships which may well extend transnationally, and which is characterized also by inequality in power, prestige and material resource terms' (ibid.: 14). And yet, given such inequalities, nowhere does he consider on whose terms 'we' are 'with creolization' only *now*. Others, presumably, have long been creole, yet have not been considered more 'modern' (or postmodern). So their creolization is not like 'ours', but rather is something that 'we' can get closer to. Thus his ('*our*') becoming creole functions as a way of getting closer to 'the other', of taking in a little piece of difference (Ahmed 2000; Stacey 2000), but only within strictly controlled situations in which the terms of creolization are drawn up in relation to a mobile centre of power. The current desire for creolization is clearly something like what bell hooks calls 'eating the other' (hooks 1992), not only eating their words, but taking in and cannibalising their literary imagery, cultural dynamics, and theoretical concepts.

Shortly after Hannerz, the influential North American anthropologist James Clifford also claimed that 'We are all Caribbeans now in our urban archipelagos . . . hybrid and heteroglot' (Clifford 1992). 'Throughout contemporary Euro-American criticism from the late '70s to the present,' notes Caren Kaplan, 'a universalized concept of creolization or hybridity has come to reflect a post-modern turn in cultural criticism' (Kaplan 1996: 129). Hybridity has since become a key concept across a range of anti-essentialist theories of identity, which draw on Caribbean histories of *mestizaje*, creolization, or syncretism (cf. Young 1995). For Homi Bhabha (1994), for example, the hybridity of language, with its Bakhtinian heteroglossia, draws attention to the ever-present potential for subversion and destabilisation of colonial authority. And Gilroy, as we have seen, employs a similar set of terms to describe diasporic identities and counter nationalisms. But in some cases the concept of creolization has been used in a more general sense, with even less attention to structural inequalities. In cultural studies, what is now called 'the creolization paradigm' (Howes 1996) is employed to describe the ways in which cultural consumers throughout the world creatively adapt in-flowing goods, thereby localising the global and indigenising the universal. Mike Featherstone, for example, speaks of creolization in global culture as a process of mixture, incorporation, and syncretism (Featherstone 1995).

This embrace of cultural hybridisation is more widely linked to a cluster of other ideas of the mobile or fluid. This family of concepts includes 'deterritorialization' and 'nomadism' (Deleuze and Guattari 1992; Braidotti 1994;

Joseph 1999), 'traveling theory' (Clifford and Dhareshwar 1989), 'global fluids' (Urry 2000), and 'liquid modernity' (Bauman 2000). Although differing in their specifics, these concepts can all be seen as symptomatic of an effort to escape the limits of time and space imposed by earlier structural metaphors of modernity. Beyond the mobilities of things, people, texts, and representations, these theorists have elicited a growing interest in the mobility of concepts and theories within differently located academic arenas and publics. Sociology itself, it is argued, must become more 'mobile' (Urry 2000). While some, like May Joseph, are more attentive to the actual sovereignties and struggles for citizenship involved in such mobilities, most of these metropolitan theorists of (post)modernity write from a 'universal' perspective which assumes a 'Western' subject who is described as becoming other, becoming mobile, becoming fluid, becoming creole. Ironically, despite their embrace of creolization and transculturation, such theories continue the historical amnesia that has excised the Caribbean from the time-space of Western modernity.

In sum, creolization has transmogrified from a politically engaged term used by Caribbean theorists located in the Caribbean in the 1970s, to one used by Caribbean diaspora theorists located outside of the Caribbean in the 1980s, and finally to non-Caribbean 'global' theorists in the 1990s. While this move enabled a shift from an anti-colonial nationalism to a post-essentialist transnationalism, it also made the theory of creolization less 'raw'; it was removed from its Caribbean location and cooked up for easier metropolitan consumption. As in any process of translation, crucial elements of its meaning have been lost. Creolization was originally theorised not only in terms of mixture and mobility, but also in terms of conflict, trauma, rupture, and the violence of uprooting. In contrast, current usage in 'global' theories not located in the Caribbean centres on creative bricolage, cultural blending, and symbolic reshaping, with little to say about negating, demolishing, and rejecting. This failure to recognise the more critical implications of the term as used by Caribbean theorists leaves the current 'creolization paradigm' with little to contribute to an operative theory of conflict and unequal power relations.

Clifford, unlike many others, at least cites the Caribbean sources from which his ideas originate. He adopted Aimé Césaire as a 'forerunner of postmodern hybridity', according to Kaplan, by focusing on his use of language, in particular its 'radical indeterminacy' and 'resistance to easy translation', which 'constitutes a "Caribbean" practice of pastiche' (Kaplan 1996: 128–9; see Clifford 1988). In his 1990 essay on 'Traveling Cultures' Clifford mentions some Caribbean paragons of the analysis of travel and displacement, including C.L.R. James, V.S. Naipaul, Edouard Glissant, Alejandro Carpentier, Paulette Nardal, and Jamaica Kincaid. He further mentions the work of Paul Gilroy and Stuart Hall, refers to the transnationality of migrants to the US from Haiti, Puerto Rico, and the Dominican Republic, and alludes to the 'Caribbeanization' of New York City as part of his own biography (Clifford 1997). Yet his claim to the Caribbeanness of 'us all' raises a number of thorny questions. What happens to the specificity of Caribbean cultural identity if the whole world is said to be Caribbean? What is lost in taking 'creolization' as *simply* a kind of cultural mixing in which 'we' – the urban, hybrid, heteroglot – all share? If creolization has its origins in Caribbean cultures of resistance, in what sense can postmodern metropolitan culture possibly share in its dynamic?

In so far as creolization has, finally, been wrested from its Caribbean location and appropriated as a free-floating signifier of the border-transcending encounters of globalization, it would seem now simply to serve the hegemonic logic of 'globalization'. What gets left behind (and what gets taken) when Caribbean theories – and theorists – travel on the high seas of global culture? How do uprooted or deracinated theoretical terms differ from more located political usages, such as those that understand 'creolising practices' as counter-appropriations of 'master-codes of the dominant culture' in order to destabilise them (Mercer 1988; Aravamudan 1999)? In so far as cultural terms, theory, and theorists all 'travel', what homing instincts and regroundings might be developed to counter the footloose free trade of theoretical piracy? If some borders are dissolving in the 'world in creolization', it should not go without saying that others are being kept in place. It is precisely the questions of what can move, who can move, where they can move, and when, that marks the not-so-fluid boundaries between wealth and poverty in the 'creolized' world of global capitalism.

Frances Aparicio and Susana Chávez-Silverman draw a useful contrast between 'tropicalizations', which can serve 'the transformative cultural agency of the subaltern subject' and 'hegemonic tropicalization', which represents particular spaces and mythic places through the trope of the exotic, primitive Other (Aparicio and Chávez-Silverman 1997: 2). Likewise something like 'hegemonic creolization' has become a mode of 'becoming (the) other'. As Ahmed argues, in such cases, 'Hybridisation becomes, not a means of transgression, but a technique for getting closer to strangers which allows the reassertion of the agency of the dominant subject' (Ahmed 2000: 123). The language of universality and 'we-ness' used by these theorists to describe the 'new' conditions of creolization with which we are 'all' now said to be living belies a specifically located (Western, metropolitan, privileged) position of those using the concept in this way. Current forms of postmodern 'nomadism' and being-in-travel, envisioned as a disavowal of roots, and dwelling in a fluid state of creole becoming, are in fact exercises of power through which global theorists establish an unmarked position of locational invisibility.

Who is able to become mobile and to claim creolization as a new state of becoming? The seemingly inclusive gesture towards rootlessness brings with it unacknowledged locational privileges, much in the way that critical race theorists have argued 'whiteness' operates as an unmarked yet dominant position in racial discourses (Dyer 1997; Frankenberg 1993). A generic and dislocated notion of creolization denies the very rootedness that has enabled creole cultures to recreate homes away from home in the face of colonial dislocation and racial terror. It is oblivious to (or, more cynically, purposefully disavowing of) its (post)colonial positioning, and is thus incapable of locating any grounding for an oppositional politics. If we pay greater attention not to mobility in general, but to specific practices of cultural travel and transportation, border crossing and return, symbolic visas and restrictions on movement, we can remember the structural parameters of creolization in different times and places.

Faced with the rise of 'the South', James Clifford has observed that the movements that matter most now are those of postcolonial intellectuals, who, he says,

> move theories in and out of discrepant contexts, addressing different audiences, working their different 'borderlands'. Theirs is not a condition of exile, of critical 'distance', but rather a place of *betweenness*, a hybridity composed of distinct, historically-connected postcolonial spaces. . . . Theory is always written from some 'where', and that 'where' is less a place than *itineraries*: different, concrete histories of dwelling, immigration, exile, migration.
>
> (Clifford 1989: 184–5)

These itineraries and histories of dwelling are re-writing the story of the Caribbean, touching it in different ways. As Carolyn Cooper argues, native Caribbean intellectuals are today 'remapping the boundaries of "margin" and "centre"' by reclaiming 'a body of subversive knowledge that originates in the centres of consciousness of the historically dehumanised peoples of the region' (Cooper 1993: 174). It matters who is speaking, where they have come from, where they are going, and who has stayed put in order to enable their movement (cf. Ahmed 2000). In returning to the Caribbean roots of the concept of creolization, regrounding it in its specific social and cultural itineraries, we might recover the political meanings and subaltern agency that have been barred entry by the free-floating gatekeepers of 'global' culture.

Power and positionality in Caribbean research

This brings us finally to a more reflexive analysis of how academic disciplines consume the Caribbean through the production of knowing discourses and bodies of knowledge. This book itself has taken its own itinerary through Caribbean history, collecting, compiling, ordering, and displaying a wide range of textual and visual information about the Caribbean. From eighteenth-century scientific collection, to nineteenth-century travel literature, ethnographic writing, and anthropological investigation, and finally twentieth-century popular journalism and academic 'area studies', the Caribbean has been and continues to be an object of study produced in Northern centres. This book itself is situated in the circuit of cultural commodities consumed as 'knowledge' about the Caribbean. Such practices of cultural consumption are based on unequal structures of institutional support, research funding, archival collection, and academic publishing, all of which enable the production, packaging, promotion, and consumption of this book from a certain (non-Caribbean) location.

Traditional modes of research, patterns of academic networking and funding, and trajectories of peer review and publication are all centred in the North and remain difficult to challenge. Funding is available for Northern researchers to visit the Caribbean and carry out their research, or to travel back and forth to attend professional conferences, even as the very archives they use are crumbling before they can even get to them. Inward investment in Caribbean archives, libraries, universities, publishing ventures, and local educational initiatives is badly lacking in many cases. The process of academic consumption of the Caribbean is further linked to the formation of asymmetrical global policy networks and the role of non-governmental organisations in the region. Just as colonial knowledge projects produced reams of missionary writing and government reports and inquiries, today those concerned with advancing democracy and development in the region produce another flood of facts and reports. Just as independent researchers in the nineteenth century produced monographs on the political or economic history of various colonial possessions, today doctoral dissertations and monographs continue to be churned out, though most will have little impact (or even availability) in the region. The extensive writings of abolitionists likewise foreshadow the more 'engaged' writers of today, those with an interest in supporting grassroots organisations such as women's groups, environmental groups, or peasant political organisations.

The critique of 'colonising discourses' in postcolonial theory and Third World feminist thought (e.g. Mohanty 1991) offers an opportunity to reflect on the making of 'area studies' as a branch of knowledge. Northern academic publics interested in knowledge about the Caribbean emerged from the reading publics who consumed fictional tales and factual 'knowledge' about the Caribbean starting as early as the sixteenth century. The policy debates surrounding the abolition of slavery in the late eighteenth to early nineteenth century then produced a glut of factual knowledge and 'real' representations of a wide range of slave societies in the Caribbean. The texts produced in this process of authentication of antislavery claims and pro-slavery counter-claims have become the archive on which a great deal of Caribbean history has been built. At this stage 'knowing' the Caribbean was largely a European colonial project, with contributions from prominent white Creole historians, who lived in the West Indies and could claim to know its culture more closely. Occasionally free people of colour were called upon (or impelled by circumstances) to contribute to these debates, thus laying the foundations for an indigenous intellectual stance and history of ideas (Lewis 1987; Richards and Shepherd, forthcoming).

Later in the nineteenth century it was the new imperial interests of the United States in the region that led to a consolidation of the Caribbean as a single knowledge region. Unlike earlier colonial writers, North Americans had interests in more than one colonial zone and saw the entire Caribbean as their 'backyard', as I noted in some of the military writings discussed in Chapter 2. With deepening US military engagement in the region following the Spanish-American war and throughout the first third of the twentieth-century (e.g. in Haiti, the Dominican Republic, Puerto Rico, Cuba) a North American school of Caribbean anthropology and area studies emerged. As the region became radicalised in the 1960s, following the Cuban revolution, competing economic interests led to the elaboration of schools of economic thought that incorporated the Caribbean as a key example within a macro world history, ranging from modernisation theory to models of dependent development and world-systems theory. Later US interests in the region and concerns with suppressing popular left-wing revolutions again reinforced a consolidated notion of 'the Caribbean basin' as a single area, as in President Ronald Reagan's Caribbean Basin Initiative. From all of these perspectives, though, study of the region was framed from an all-encompassing outside perspective that gave little attention to the agency or actions of people within the region.

Those working within the Caribbean in the 1970s came increasingly to recognise the need for a local history that empowered Caribbean people. A new concern with Maroon societies (Price 1973; Heuman 1986), slave rebellion and revolution (Genovese 1979; Craton 1982; Okihiro 1986), and forms of everyday resistance (Beckles 1989a; Bush 1990) came to characterise Caribbean historiography (cf. Higman 1999). But only a few challenged the prevailing methodologies, which remained distanced from actual Caribbean people. In some instances historians turned towards methods such as oral history, life histories, autobiography, and testimonial, as ways to foreground questions of agency in the creation of history and memory. This work drew partly on existing forms of life history and self-narration as an ethnographic method, e.g. Sidney Mintz's seminal life history of a Puerto Rican sugar worker, *Worker in the Cane* (1960), but has more recently also been influenced by feminist methodologies (Brereton 1995; Chamberlain 1995). Oral histories are a narrative framework in which the past is constantly retold, revised, and reconstructed, thus they depend on very different conceptualisations of what the past is, how we come to know it, and for what purposes. Honor Ford-Smith's work with the Sistren theatre collective in Jamaica engaged a women's group in portraying issues that they felt were important within their own lives through consciousness raising, life history, and fictionalised oral performances (Sistren 1986). Yet any translation of oral cultures into academic text remains highly problematic, as noted by theorists like Cooper who deal with the relation between high culture and low culture, the academic and the folk.

Another strategy for writing Caribbean agency into Caribbean studies is a self-limiting, perhaps more humble historiography that makes fewer great claims to narrative omniscience and power, and instead highlights the power and positionality inherent in all history. A few writers have experimented with alternative methods that engage more reflexively in situating their own voice in relation to the voices of Caribbean people. This might involve subaltern histories with contrapuntal voices interrupting the smooth flow of the authorial voice and disrupting the Western conception of historical temporality (a very good example being Richard Price's *First-Time* (1983)). Like subaltern studies more widely, such a historical anthropology involves a healthy scepticism towards colonial archives, and a gathering of fragments from other perspectives, which cannot be fully comprehended, reconstructed, or represented. Alternatively, such a broken history might focus on the 'silencing of the past' (Trouillot 1995), and foreground the importance of acts of commemoration. Commemoration involves the recognition of the importance of 'performing' history for a living community, as opposed to the 'recording' of history for academic purposes. This raises the question of who is the audience for knowledge about the Caribbean, and suggests that a closer embedding in local contexts would be beneficial not only for historians, but for other academic fields as well. Along these lines, for example, DeGraff argues that 'Having Creolophones read what creolists write will provide useful checks and balances, and so will having Creolophones write what creolists read. Such collaboration is beneficial to the international linguistics community' (DeGraff 2001: 102).

If experts have travelled 'there' to research and write on the Caribbean, intellectuals of Caribbean origin have also long sought training in metropolitan educational institutions and outlets for publication. Many of these travelling Caribbean theorists have in fact been lionised within recent metropolitan theory, from Frantz Fanon and C.L.R. James to more recently Glissant and Benítez-Rojo. Yet one wonders to what extent their words are simply being 'eaten' for the more piquant flavour they offer to a moribund postmodernism.[11] Even those diasporic intellectuals like Gilroy and Hall who have taken hold of the very centres of production of cultural theory in several key instances have to some extent been incorporated into metropolitan theory as interesting creolised spin-offs from the mainstream, and harbingers of a creole world to come. Caribbean writers and theorists have intervened repeatedly in the projects of 'imaginative work' which have produced the Caribbean, but they cannot stop the train of outside interests who produce books about the Caribbean for their own purposes. While there are some lines of communication opening up across the Caribbean, linking together sites which, in the past, were mainly linked via metropolitan centres, they remain marginal and unable to compete with powerful metropolitan flows of knowledge, power, and capital.

I first began studying the Caribbean while undertaking a Masters degree at the New School for Social Research in New York City, and then completing a Ph.D., which was a comparative historical study of peasant rebellions in post-emancipation Jamaica and post-independence Haiti (Sheller 2000). My own motives were to understand the transatlantic world in which I was living, and the legacies of slavery in the United States, but to do so from a 'decentred' perspective that stepped outside of the parochial and insular views of 'American' (US) history. In the process I moved to Britain and became more interested in British colonial history in the Caribbean. I also became increasingly aware of my connection to a field called 'Caribbean Studies', which was closely linked to British and North American colonial and neo-colonial interests and military and business involvement in the region. In adding to this body of literature, I am acutely aware that I too am 'consuming' the Caribbean, by mobilising a wide range of information attached to this place and using it to tell a story, to sell a book, and to build a scholarly reputation.

People often ask me whether I am from the Caribbean or have family there. The answer is no, and as I think back over my personal ties to the Caribbean now, it only makes my position more compromised: an outsider who has consumed the Caribbean as a tourist, a cultural consumer, and an academic. I grew up in Philadelphia where many Caribbean migrants settled, joining the mosaic of other immigrant populations (including my own family who had come from Eastern Europe around the turn of the century). As a child I was very privileged to have family holidays in places like St. Martin, Guadeloupe, St. Barthélémy, Cozumel, and Curaçao. So I was very aware of the peculiarity of distinctive histories and cultures, languages, and cuisine in various Caribbean locations, as well as the painful relation of tourists to the inhabitants of these tourist destinations. Like many young people in Philadelphia I listened to reggae music and was fascinated by Rastafarians; somewhere in the mists of memory I remember thinking that Jamaica was an island somewhere near Africa. I enjoyed Caribbean restaurants, Caribbean accents, Caribbean holidays, and reading Caribbean literature.

As a university student I lived in Caribbean neighbourhoods in Brooklyn and in Dalston, London, where I could buy Jamaican ackee and saltfish, Trinidadian rotis and good curried goat with rice and peas. I went to Dominica for my honeymoon, immersed in the rainforest eco-paradise of waterfalls and volcanic springs. But I also did several months of dissertation research amongst the gritty urban realities of Kingston, Jamaica (catching the bus downtown from Crossroads to the Parade each day, with fearful warnings from my hosts ringing in my ears). Perhaps I consumed the Caribbean, but I was also consumed by it. Later I went on a study tour of Haiti with the London-based Haiti Support Group, to learn what I could of the popular struggle against poverty, violence, and injustice in that troubled country. Finally, as an academic I not only learned from reading widely in Caribbean history, sociology, and anthropology, including the works of many Caribbean writers, but also had the privilege of attending professional conferences of the Society for Caribbean Studies, the Association of Caribbean Historians, and the Latin American Studies Association. These various opportunities brought me to places as wide-ranging as Miami, Cuba, Barbados, Trinidad and Tobago, while also finding important archives for Caribbean research in 'Black Atlantic' locations including London, Bristol, Liverpool, New York, and even back home in Philadelphia.

Now at home in the north of England, feeling far away from the Caribbean, I scan the papers for snippets of news and search the web for Caribbean sites. I cook jerked chicken and buy Windward Island bananas; my Tate and Lyle cane sugar must come from the West Indies, though it doesn't say so on the label, and perhaps my local roads are made from Trinidadian asphalt. I listen to recorded music by artists from Jamaica, Haiti, Cuba, and their diasporas. I will undoubtedly again visit the Caribbean, and continue to buy Caribbean commodities. I have in my home woodcarvings from Dominica, paintings from Cuba, pottery from Barbados, hot sauce from Jamaica, tapes of music from Haiti. I consume the Caribbean. I am far away, yet I have been licensed to write about the Caribbean, to represent it to others, or in this case to write about how others have represented it. That is why I say this is not a book about the Caribbean, but is one about 'The Caribbean' – the invention, the fantasy, the idea, the context for my writing. Yet I write this knowing all along (it is impossible to ignore) the material effects of all that has been said about and done in the name of this Caribbean.

All of this is, of course, academic, when measured up against the far more powerful flows of popular culture that shape representations and perceptions of the Caribbean both within and outside of the region, and the migrants, tourists, and transnationals who carry those cultures around the world. However much the Caribbean is repeatedly invented, consumed, and eaten, it is never eaten up. As I have argued in previous chapters, there are multiple forces at work, including desires and attachments that lure consumers onto new grounds, invisible agents that get within and 'infect' the consuming subject, and confusions and disorientations at the dangerous crossroads. The key question for those in the North remains how to foster a more ethical relation with the Caribbean. By proposing a new kind of attention to the changing mobilities of consumption over the past five hundred years, I hope this book has contributed to the foundations for building a more ethical relationship based on acknowledging complicity in relations of domination and with that an intimate responsibility for others.

Conclusion

I have argued that by tracking the continuities in certain forms of consumption that have sustained the inequalities and violence of the Atlantic system for centuries, we can better understand how power is exercised within subtly shifting kinds of proximity and distanciation, mobility and immobility, mutability and immutability. I considered the mobilities of plants, commodities, and material objects in Part I, and the texts and visual images that represented those natures and objects. Developing a framework for analysing different forms of mobile consumption and their interaction, I argued in Chapter 1 that one could re-narrate the history of the West in terms of the flows of some objects, people, information, and culture across the Atlantic world, and the stabilisation and recontextualisation of others. A key argument in this chapter (building on the theoretical work of Sara Ahmed) was that the mobilities of some things and people require the immobility of others. The very technologies (both material and social) which enable the mobility of those in positions of privilege also fix in place locations of disadvantage.

In Chapter 2 I suggested that one of the seemingly most innocent of pleasures, a holiday on a tropical beach fanned by palm trees, is deeply implicated in a long history of metropolitan consumption of the nature, landscape, and scenery of the Caribbean. Tracing the development of changing visual regimes, from the early modern era up to the early twentieth century, I showed how earlier modes of consuming Caribbean nature and landscape continue to inform contemporary relations of neo-imperialism. The image of the Caribbean island remains a powerful icon within the imaginary of global culture. Here again we saw how movement 'through the islands' operated as a reiteration of the 'rhetoric of presence' through visual mastery. Yet one also detected an increasingly emotional engagement with the tropical landscape, and hints that the European body was at risk of certain kinds of dangers in the Tropics. The mover, it seems, could be moved.

In Chapter 3 I argued that the consumption of 'articles of pleasure' and edible commodities from the Caribbean had a massive impact on European consumer cultures. Sugar consumption, in particular, led to deep ethical anxieties over the foreign substances that entered European bodies, and the possible 'blood' with which such commodities were tainted. Here a key argument was that the Caribbean could get inside Europe, and that in consuming the Caribbean the consumer could also be consumed by it. The anxieties of consumption revolved around the ways in which exotic and foreign substances entered the homes and bodies of consumers, eating away at them from within. Women played a crucial part in this domestication of the world economy and also to some extent led the way in the articulation of a 'gut ethics' of refusal of slave-produced products, which I suggested is closely linked to the contemporary fair trade movement.

In Part II I turned my attention to the ways in which bodies and representations of bodies are consumed through various practices of imperialist subjectivity, the tourist gaze, and getting closer to and 'eating' others. In each chapter I highlighted both the power and the risks inherent in this proximity, and suggested that the consuming body is always vulnerable to a shifting context in which home may be lost. Just as the mover could be moved and the consumer consumed, in getting close to the Caribbean the tourist or traveller risks being swallowed up by it. In Chapter 4 I considered these processes in relation to the intersection of gender formations, racial orders, and class hierarchies. Once again I explored how moving through and gazing upon the Caribbean and its people enabled travellers to shore up white privilege and construct their own whiteness by gauging the differences of a variety of exotic 'others'. I also demonstrated how the interplay of a dual Orientalist and Africanist discourse helped to invent the Caribbean as a place apart from the West, and a field of Western fears and fantasies of hybridisation.

In Chapter 5 these themes were explored through a closer look at embodied relations, extending the concept of consumption to more metaphorical modes of consuming bodies through cannibalisation and zombification. The key argument here was that a pleasurable touch can also be the touch that causes pain to another, and that a sense of proximity can also be that which produces relations of domination in which the subaltern is 'eaten' by those in positions of power. Echoing the story of Sir Hans Sloane, we saw again how Western medical and scientific technologies draw 'natural' and human substances from the Caribbean in order to reconstitute them as Western technologies of knowledge and power, as well as sources of capital accumulation and cultural capital. The very constitution of such centres of power and knowledge depends on embodied relations of domination by which the periphery is used, abused, and devoured, though not without leaving the empowered with an anxious sense of their own mortality and morbidity.

In concluding with the topic of creolization I have tried to consider how language, literature, and theory itself are all subject to these same processes of mobile but risky consumption. Through the very processes of getting closer to 'others' Western colonisers, consumers, tourists, and theorists have exercised forms of 'othering' which enable the consumption of difference. The contradictions of capitalist modernity continue to be materially inscribed in and through the mobile flows of people, plants, and objects, which constitute the Caribbean and its diaspora. Although creolization has become a keyword for processes of dynamic creation, agency, and self-making in the imagery of global culture, I have argued that there is a sense in which the theory of creolization was displaced from its Caribbean context. In that dislocation it was emptied of its resonance as a project of subaltern resistance. I have also suggested the necessity of tracking the itineraries of theories and theorists, just as we tracked the biographies of objects and travel of symbols, and I have put my own work on the table as equally implicated in the processes of consuming (and being consumed by) the Caribbean. Rather than consuming the Caribbean as a place of difference, I conclude, it is time that historians and theorists of Western culture begin to recognise its centrality in the making of 'our' modernity.

Appendix

Chronology of key dates in Caribbean relations with Europe and the United States

1492	Columbus's First Voyage. After wreck of the *Santa Maria* near Hispaniola, Columbus establishes first European settlement in New World.
1493	Second Voyage of Columbus, sighting many islands between Dominica and Puerto Rico.
1498	Third Voyage of Columbus, visiting Cuba and 'discovering' Grenada, St. Vincent, Trinidad, and the Guyana coastline.
1502	Fourth and final voyage of Columbus, landing at Martinique; later marooned on the north shore of Jamaica with 115 men.
1508	Juan Ponce de Léon officially settles Puerto Rico.
1509	Juan de Esquivel settles Jamaica. First sugar mills started on Hispaniola.
1515	First exports of Caribbean sugar to Spain.
1567–8	Francis Drake accompanies John Hawkins on New World slaving voyages.
1577–80	Francis Drake circumnavigates the world.
1621	Dutch West India Company formally established.
1624	English settle Barbados and St. Kitts; Dutch settle Berbice.
1630s	Dutch establish themselves on Curaçao, Saba, St. Martin, St. Eustatius.
	English settle Antigua, Montserrat, St. Lucia.
	French settle Martinique and Guadeloupe.
1641	Sugar cultivation introduced into Barbados by Dutch merchants from Brazil.
1647	First Barbados sugar sent to England.
1652	First Anglo-Dutch War.
1666	Second Anglo-Dutch War. Treaty of Breda (1667) gives Surinam to Dutch in exchange for Manhattan Island, New York.
1672–8	Third Anglo-Dutch War.
1673	Chelsea Physic Garden founded.

1687	Sir Hans Sloane visits Jamaica. The first coffee-house established in London by Edward Lloyd (later to become the insurance brokerage Lloyd's of London).
1695	Sloane marries Elizabeth Langley, widow of Fulk Rose of Jamaica.
1734	First Maroon War in Jamaica.
1739–63	Wars between European powers over Caribbean commerce and possessions.
1772	English chief justice, Lord Mansfield, declares slavery illegal in England.
1790s	First English mobilisation to boycott slave-grown sugar.
1791	Slave revolt in the French colony of Saint Domingue marks the beginning of the Haitian Revolution.
1793	Breadfruit tree introduced to Jamaica from Tahiti. British Navy captures Martinique, Guadeloupe, and St. Lucia.
1794	French National Assembly temporarily abolishes slavery.
1795	Second Maroon War in Jamaica.
1797	British capture Trinidad.
1804	Haitian Independence declared.
1808	Great Britain and the United States abolish the trade in slaves, followed by Sweden (1813), France and Holland (1818), and Spain (1820).
1820s	Second English mobilisation to boycott slave-grown sugar.
1833	Emancipation Act passed by British Parliament initiating apprenticeship system in British Antilles effective 1834.
1838	Slavery fully abolished in British Antilles.
1848	Slavery abolished in French and Danish Antilles. French Antilles given direct representation in the National Assembly (suspended in 1871).
1864	British sugar consumption approximately 42 lbs. per head annually.
1869	Puerto Rico made a province of Spain.
1873	Puerto Rico abolishes slavery.
1886	Cuba abolishes slavery, finally ending legal slavery in the Caribbean.
1888	Lorenzo Dow Baker founds Boston Fruit Company, which becomes United Fruit Company in 1899, eventually merging into Chiquita Brands Intl.
1899	Treaty of Paris: Spain cedes Cuba, Puerto Rico, and the Philippines to the United States. US military occupies Cuba until 1902.
1900	Puerto Rico becomes a US territory.
1902	Republic of Cuba established, but Platt Amendment gives US the right to intervene in Cuban affairs and to establish a naval base at Guantánamo Bay.
1906	Second US military intervention in Cuba (until 1909).
1915	US occupies Haiti (until 1934).
1916	US occupies the Dominican Republic (until 1924).
1917	Danish Antilles sold to US.

1941	Anglo-American agreement grants military bases to US throughout the British West Indies.
1944	Universal adult suffrage granted to Jamaica, with limited self-government.
1954	Dutch Antilles and Suriname made autonomous and equal with the Netherlands.
1959	Fidel Castro comes to power in the Cuban Revolution.
1962	Jamaica and Trinidad and Tobago become independent.
1965	US invades Dominican Republic with troops from the Organization of American States.
1966	Barbados and Guyana gain independence.
1974	Grenada gains independence.
1977–9	St. Lucia, Dominica, St. Vincent and the Grenadines gain independence.
1980	Mariel boatlift brings 125,000 Cubans to the US.
1981	Antigua and Barbuda, and Belize gain independence.
1983	St. Kitts-Nevis gains independence. US invades Grenada.
1999	'Banana Wars' trade dispute between US and EU.
2004	Bicentennial of Haitian Independence.

Notes

Introduction

1 Some tourists (especially African-Americans) are starting to explore the sites of the 'Black Atlantic' not only on the West Coast of Africa, but also in the United States and Britain. For example, there are city walking tours of sites associated with slavery and the slave trade in Bristol (Dresser *et al.* 1998) and pilgrimages to sites like 'Sambo's grave', a lonely outpost on the far coast of Lancashire where an African was buried on unsanctified ground in the eighteenth century.

2 A Middle Passage Monument Project was launched in July 1999 in the US, which involved the symbolic burial of a monument in the Atlantic to commemorate the transatlantic slave trade, and there have also been a number of significant travelling exhibitions on slavery and abolition (Oostindie 2001: 102–12). The US Congress has recently approved plans to build a National Museum of African-American History in Washington, DC, and there are also plans to build a museum of slavery in Charleston, South Carolina.

3 A Channel Four television production on 'Britain's Slave Trade', broadcast in 2000, highlighted the importance of the slave trade for Britain. A book published in conjunction with the series notes that 'The impact that this barbaric human trafficking had on Britain is unquestionable, yet in perhaps the single greatest act of collective amnesia in British history, it is rarely acknowledged' (Martin 1999).

4 By 'post-slavery societies' I refer to all of the states historically engaged in slavery or affected by slavery, including not only many parts of Africa, all of the Caribbean, parts of Central America and Brazil, but also Portugal, Spain, the Netherlands, France, Britain, Denmark, and the United States.

5 I want to thank Sara Ahmed, Anne-Marie Fortier, Claudia Castañeda and participants in the Uprootings/Regroundings seminar series and day school at Lancaster University for helping me to think about issues of movement and 'fixity'. Thanks also to John Urry and members of the Mobility Group for discussions of ideas of mobility and immobility.

6 In a deeply moving exploration of the meaning of 'ethical encounters', Ahmed (2000, Ch. 7) builds on the work of Emmanuel Levinas to develop what I would call a postcolonial feminist ethics. Such a project is beyond the scope of this book, but has been suggestive in guiding me towards a more reflective consideration of my own position in the 'field' of Caribbean studies, which I will discuss at length in Chapter 6.

1 The binding mobilities of consumption

1 Hans Sloane, M.D., Fellow of the College of Physicians and Secretary of the Royal Society, *A Voyage to the Islands of Madera, Barbados, Nieves, St. Christophers and Jamaica, with the*

Natural History of the herbs and trees, four-footed beasts, fishes, birds, insects, reptiles, etc. of the last of those islands, 2 vols (London: Printed by B.M. for the Author, 1707), Vol. I, Preface.

2 Michael Day 'Humana: Anatomical, pathological and curious human specimens in Sloane's museum', pp. 69–76 in Arthur MacGregor (ed.) *Sir Hans Sloane: Collector, Scientist, Antiquary, Founding Father of the British Museum* (Published for the Trustees of the British Museum, London: British Museum Press with Alistair McAlpine, 1994), pp. 69, 71.

3 Quotation and other biographical details from Alexander Chalmer's *General Biographical Dictionary* (London, 1816), Vol. 28, pp. 63–9.

4 Besides Moyra in Ireland, other sites where his collection was grown include: 'by the order of the Right Rev. Dr. Henry Compton, Bishop of London, at Fulham; at Chelsea by Mr. Doudy; and Enfield by the Rev. Dr. Robert Uvedale; and in the Botanic Gardens of Amsterdam, Leyden, Leipsick [i.e. Leipzig], Upsal, etc., but especially at Badminton in Glocester-shire, where they are not only raised some few handfuls high, but come to perfection, flower and produce ripe Fruits, even to my Admiration; and that, by the direction of her Grace the Duchess of Beaufort, who at her leisure Hours, from her more serious Affairs, has taken pleasure to command the raising of Plants in her Garden, where, by means of Stoves and Infirmaries, many of them have come to greater Perfection than in any Part of Europe' (Sloane, Preface, Vol. I).

5 A nostalgic mock-historical version is marketed today by the Chelsea Physic Garden as 'Sir Hans Sloane Chocolate'. See Cox (1992) on the history of chocolate more generally.

6 The cinchona plant from which quinine is derived grew only in the Andean regions of Peru, Bolivia, and Ecuador, but there was great confusion over the actual source of quinine in the eighteenth century (Haggis 1941). Sloane's illustration of 'Quinquina' in his Herbarium is actually not Cinchona at all, but appears to be a salt-marsh shrub that grows in the Caribbean, which was sometimes sold as 'Jesuit's bark' to treat fevers and was often confused with Cinchona (ibid.: 456).

7 These accounts also gloss over the ways in which marriage served as a transfer of property from one man to another, the 'wife' being a crucial route for the accumulation of colonial wealth. See Minter, *The Apothecaries' Garden*, p. 13; *Caribbeana, being Miscellaneous Papers Relating to the History, Genealogy, Topography and Antiquities of the British West Indies* (London: Mitchell Hughes & Clarke), Vol. II, 1911–12, 'List of Deeds Relating to the West Indies', p. 329; and idem, 'Rose of Jamaica', *Caribbeana*, Vol. 5, pt. iv (1917), pp. 130–9.

8 William Woodville, *Medical Botany: Containing Systematic and general Descriptions with Plates of all the Medicinal Plants, Indigenous and Exotic, Comprehended in the Materia Medica as published by the Royal Colleges of Physicians of London and Edinburgh*, 4 vols (London: William Phillips, 1810); and *Medical Botany: Or, History of Plants in the Materia Medica of the London, Edinburgh, and Dublin Pharmacopoeias, Arranged According to the Linnaian System*, 2 vols (London: E. Cox & Son, 1821, 1823).

9 In a caption to a photograph of 'Hybrid cotton growing in modern-day Barbados', Minter notes that American visitors to the Garden today often ask 'Did this seed reinforce slavery?' (p. 37). She does not venture to answer the question, nor does she comment on slavery or colonial trade when noting that 'Sloane's extraordinary later success pivoted around his several connections with Jamaica' (p. 11).

10 Sue Minter, Curator of the Chelsea Physic Garden, 'Garden of World Medicine' pamphlet (The Chelsea Physic Garden Company, 1998), p. 3; *The Chelsea Physic Garden*, 1980, p. 9–10.

11 Another strategy for thinking Europe 'together with' the Caribbean is the effort to retrace the history of black people in Europe. In Britain especially historians have begun to reconstruct the forgotten history of black settlers, from the Roman legions of the second century to the large African population of eighteenth-century London (Fryer 1984; Segal 1995; Gerzina 1995). As I shall discuss in Chapter 6, postcolonial theorists

of Caribbean origin such as Stuart Hall and Paul Gilroy have also posed a challenge to British national identities which seek to exclude black populations from belonging.

12 The usual reference points for the now commonplace critique of Eurocentric or universalistic theories of 'unfettered' mobility and nomadism include Deleuze and Guattari 1992; Braidotti 1994; Lash and Urry 1994; and Hannerz 1996. A somewhat more nuanced perspective informed by understandings of spatial unevenness or complexity can be found in Clifford 1992, 1997; Urry 2000; Cresswell 2001; and Sheller and Urry 2002. Here, however, I am especially interested in critical perspectives on mobility and immobility informed by postcolonial and feminist theory, as seen in Young 1995; Kaplan 1996; Lury 1997; Ahmed 2000; Fortier 2000; and Ahmed *et al.* forthcoming.

13 For example, freed people's strategies to survive high unemployment and low wages following the abolition of slavery could lead either to situations of share-cropping which tied people to the land, or it could equally lead to the necessity for migration. Thousands of Jamaican men migrated (both permanently and temporarily) in the mid-nineteenth century to clear land to build the trans-Isthmus railway and later the Panama Canal; to cut wood in Belize; to cut cane in Trinidad and Cuba; and to work on the banana plantations along the Central American coasts. Such options were not available to women.

14 Caribbean Executive Conference, 21–4 June 2001, Half Moon Hotel, Montego Bay, Jamaica; The 7th Annual Caribbean Business Conference, 15–16 June 2001, Grand Beach Resort, Grenada.

15 'We're changing the way the world looks at Barbados', *Caribbean Week*, Nov.–Dec. 1998, p. 63. Sponsored by the Director of International Business, Ministry of International Trade and Business, The Business Centre, Upton, St. Michael, Barbados.

16 It has also come to light how global corporations like British American Tobacco have used small islands like Aruba to avoid high tobacco duties and expand their market by allowing (perhaps colluding in) the smuggling of their own cigarettes into South America ('Clarke Company Faces New Smuggling Claims', *The Guardian*, 22 August 2001, p. 1).

17 Port St. Charles property sales promotion, in *The Ins and Outs of Barbados* (The Barbados Tourism Authority 2001), pp. 58–63 (see also insandouts-barbados.com).

18 There is a far wider field of Caribbean tourism studies that I will not be able to deal with fully here. See, e.g. Goodrich and Gayle 1993; Pattullo 1996; Collinson 1996; Momsen 1998; and Klak 1998.

19 The Crane Private Residence Resort sales promotion, in *The Ins and Outs of Barbados* (The Barbados Tourism Authority 2001), pp. 256–7 (see also insandouts-barbados.com).

20 The Caribbean neither fits comfortably into the category 'non-Western', given its Western location and origins, nor 'Southern', since it is well north of the Equator and has many regions which enjoy relatively high standards of living. I discuss these 'disorientations' in greater detail in Chapter 4.

2 Iconic islands

1 Here again it is imperative to reiterate that people from various locations within the Caribbean have their own ways of seeing the places they inhabit, which draw on quite different visual traditions and cultural schemas. It is beyond the scope of this work to track Caribbean literary and artistic depictions of their native lands, but it is a project that would necessarily complement and amplify by contrasts the work undertaken here.

2 On the very curious loss of this manuscript, its rediscovery in 1983, and publication by the Pierpont Morgan Library in 1996, see the foreword by Charles E. Pierce Jr and introduction by Verlyn Klinkenborg to *The Drake Manuscript in the Pierpont Morgan Library: Histoire Naturelle des Indes* (London: Andre Deutsch Ltd., 1996). The remarkably naïve introduction states that 'All early visions of the New World have the power to haunt us.

We search them for signs of innocence, for an Edenic imagining of a world we know too well, just as we continue to consult mirrors for lingering traces of our childhood. This trait is less a measure of nostalgia for a lost world, a time when several continents remained undiscovered, than it is a measure of faith that when Europeans first saw the New World they responded as we imagine ourselves responding – with aesthetic joy and a sense of moral promise' (p. xvii). Klinkenborg seems almost apologetic that we will not find 'virginal' New World scenes within the manuscript, but far more brutal scenes of economic exploitation, enslavement, and invasion of indigenous lands.

3   William Reed, *The History of Sugar and Sugar Yielding Plants* (London: Longmans, Green & Co., 1866), p. 8.

4   [Alexander Exquemelin], *The History of the Bucaniers: being an impartial relation of all the battels, sieges, and other most eminent assaults committed for several years upon the coasts of the West Indies by the Pirates of Jamaica and Tortuga* (London: printed for Tho. Malthus, 1684 [originally published in Dutch, 1678]), pp. 178–9.

5   Beer and wine were at this time the staple beverages of northern and southern Europeans, respectively, in an age when water was generally unsafe to drink and the hot drinks of tea and coffee were yet to come (we will turn to these in the next chapter).

6   Arawak-derived words that remain in our vocabulary include barbecue, canoe, hammock, hurricane, savanna, manioc, papaya, guava, cocoa, iguana, and place names such as Jamaica, Haiti, and Bahamas.

7   'The beginning and Proceedings of the new plantation of St. Christopher by Captain Warner' in *The True Travels, Adventures and Observations of Captain John Smith in Europe, Asia, Africke, and America, beginning about the yeere 1593, and continued to this present 1629,* 2 vols. Reprint from the London edition of 1629 (Richmond, VA: Franklin Press, 1819), p. 273.

8   Père Pierre-François-Xavier de Charlevoix, *A Voyage to North America; Undertaken by command of the present King of France, Containing . . . A Description and Natural History of the Islands of the West Indies belonging to the different powers of Europe,* 2 vols (Dublin: John Exshaw and James Potts, 1766), Vol. I, pp. 309–10.

9   One of the earliest English advocates of tree planting and conservation was John Evelyn, who wrote in his diary of his visit to Sir Hans Sloane's Jamaican collection, which made a great impression on him. His book *Sylva* was sponsored by the Royal Society and was especially influential in France (Grove 1995).

10 A crucial influence on English conceptions of landscape were the writings of William Gilpin, e.g. *Three Essays: On Picturesque Beauty, On Picturesque Travel, and On Sketching Landscape* (London, 1803).

11 Charlevoix, *A Voyage to North America,* p. 319.

12 Daniel McKinnen, *A Tour Through the British West Indies in the Years 1802 and 1803, giving a particular account of the Bahama Islands* (London: J. White; R. Taylor, 1804), pp. 6, 16.

13 Ibid., pp. 18–19.

14 Ibid., pp. 56–7.

15 Ibid., pp. 88–9.

16 Captain J.E. Alexander, *Transatlantic Sketches, comprising visits to the most interesting scenes in North and South America and the West Indies, With notes on Negro slavery and Canadian emigration,* 2 vols (London: Richard Bentley, 1833), Vol. I, p. 244.

17 Granier de Cassagnac, *Voyage aux Antilles Françaises, Anglaises, Danoises, Espagnoles, à Saint-Domingue et aux États-Unis d'Amerique,* 2 vols (Paris: Au Comptoir des Imprimeurs Unis, 1843), Vol. 1, p. 87–9 [my translation].

18 Charles Kingsley, *At Last: A Christmas in the West Indies,* new edn, (London: Macmillan & Co., 1873), p. 126–7.

19 Ibid., pp. 26–7.

20 William Agnew Paton, *Down the Islands: A Voyage in the Caribbees* (London: Kegan Paul, Trench & Co., 1888), pp. 220–1. Peter Hulme (2000: 27) describes this as 'one of the first modern travel-books about the Caribbean'.

21 Ibid., p. 95.
22 Pulaski F. Hyatt (US Consul, Santiago de Cuba) and John T. Hyatt (Vice-consul), *Cuba: Its resources and Opportunities. Valuable Information for American investors, manufacturers, exporters, importers, lumber and mine operators, wholesale and retail merchants, employment seekers, prospective planters, professional men, sportsmen, travelers, railroad men, and others* (New York: J.S. Ogilvie Publishing Co., 1898), pp. 49–50, 74.
23 Charles Morris, *Our Island Empire: A Hand-Book of Cuba, Porto Rico, Hawaii, and the Philippine Islands* (Philadelphia: J.P. Lippincott 1899), p. xi. By the Treaty of Paris, Spain ceded these islands to the US in 1899. The US occupied Cuba until 1902, and then by the Platt Amendment maintained the right to intervene in Cuban affairs and to establish a naval base at Guantánamo Bay. Puerto Rico became a US territory in 1900.
24 Ibid., pp. *xii*, 124.
25 Stuart McCook makes the important point that Creole elites in the independent republics of the Spanish Caribbean also 'used science to nationalize nature, [and] to extend state power over the natural world. . . . [They] funded plant inventories, botanical maps, and botanical gardens to define and control their political territory and to identify plants that might contribute to economic growth' (McCook 2002: 11–12). Yet Spanish Caribbean and Latin American naturalists had to travel to the metropolis to learn about their native plants, while scientific research in the region 'concentrated on export crops rather than food crops' (ibid.: 19–20, 24). Thus local agricultural research was deeply tied to metropolitan interests, despite efforts at 'repatriating, translating, synthesizing, and therefore reappropriating foreign research' (ibid.: 45).
26 Sady Brassey, *In the Trades, the Tropics, and the Roaring Forties* (London: Longman's, Green & Co., 1885), p. 146.
27 Paton, *Down the Islands*, p. 66.
28 Owen T. Bulkeley, *The Lesser Antilles: A Guide for Settlers in the British West Indies, and Tourists' Companion* (London: Sampson Low & Co., 1889), p. 6.
29 Ibid., pp. 22–3.
30 Ibid., pp. 24, 33.
31 Charles Augustus Stoddard, *Cruising Among the Caribbees: Summer Days in Winter Months* (London: Kegan Paul, Trench and Trubner & Co., 1895), pp. 29, 85.
32 Ibid., p. 113.
33 Ibid., p. 163.
34 *Tours in the West Indies*, by the Royal Mail Steam Packet Company (n.p., 1901), p. 6.
35 E.A. Hastings Jay, LL.B., F.R.G.S., *A Glimpse of the Tropics, Or, Four Months Cruising in the West Indies* (London: Sampson Low, Marston & Co., 1900), pp. 34–5.
36 Ibid., pp. 63–4.
37 Susan de Forest Day, *The Cruise of the Scythian in the West Indies* (London, New York, and Chicago: F. Tennyson Neely, 1899), pp. 8, 28–9.
38 James Johnston, M.D., *Jamaica: . . . The New Riviera. A pictorial Description of the Island and its Attractions* (London: Cassell & Co., 1903), p. 10.
39 Stephen Bonsal, *The American Mediterranean* (New York: Moffat, Yard & Co., 1912), p. 20 (cited in Hulme 2000: 92).
40 Contrary to some theorists of globalization (e.g. Featherstone 1995), therefore, I would argue that the image of 'planet earth' from outer space was not the first time in which the fragility and environmental limits of the global totality were realised. The fragility of nature suggested by the 'blue planet' viewed from outerspace can be read as an updating of the image of the tropical island surrounded by blue sea, which Grove (1995) argues was the first indicator of global environmental consciousness among European scientific explorers in the early modern period.
41 Other kinds of trees were also revered in Caribbean societies. Jean Besson has written that 'For the slaves and their descendants trees had a spiritual dimension and, like the eternal land, symbolized the continuity of kinship groups and communities' (Besson 1995: 93). From the sacred Kindah tree of the Accompong Maroons in Jamaica to the

great Silk Cotton trees venerated as places of the spirits in Haiti and Trinidad, the tree has special meaning within African-Caribbean cultures. The tree at the heart of family land, as the repository of the ancestors' spirits, is symbolic of the 'family tree' (Maurer 1997). North American economic interest in trees as resources is fundamentally at odds with this Afro-Caribbean investment in trees as spiritual repositories.

42 From itinerary of the Noble Caledonian Ltd. 'West Indies: Hidden Treasures', 14-night cruise on the *Levant*, 8 to 23 February 2002, as advertised in *The Financial Times*. Other stops include Bequia, 'A place of pure escapism in a charming old world atmosphere with some of the best beaches in the Caribbean'; Grenada, 'a lush and verdant island with spice plantations, tropical forests and secluded coves'; and Tobago, 'One of the natural jewels of the Caribbean, covered with lush rain forest and ringed by picturesque bays and unspoiled beaches'.

43 Guy Kennaway, 'Road to a new Eden (with plenty of temptations along the way)', *High Life*, March 2000, p. 114.

44 Derek Walcott, 'A Frowsty Fragrance', *The New York Review*, 15 June 2000, p. 61. (Review of Thomas W. Krise, ed., *Caribbeana: An Anthology of English Literature on the West Indies, 1657–1777*, University of Chicago Press).

3 Tasting the Tropics

1 The concept of 'consuming publics' is suggested as a critical intervention in the literature on the 'bourgeois public sphere' (Habermas 1989; and see Emirbayer and Sheller 1999), which has generally ignored the colonial connections of the new kinds of public places in which political publics formed. Public spaces of consumption such as London's coffee-houses were dedicated both to the consumption of colonial goods and to the discussion and transaction of colonial trade. They also stand in relation to the more 'feminine' arena of domestic consumption of tea and sugar, out of which I argue an equally important political public arose during the boycotts of slave-produced sugar.

2 Agnew's idea of including the 'men and women whose class, race or religion' left them out of consumer culture focuses on 'immigrants' and 'ethnic' groups in the United States. Though he mentions the work of historians of slavery like Herbert Gutman and Thomas Haskell in relation to wider issues of capitalist culture, 'black communities' are relegated to a footnote observing that they have been little considered in work on consumer goods and consumption (Agnew 1994: 37 n. 40).

3 As Anne McClintock suggests in her analysis of Victorian 'commodity spectacle', 'Imperialism suffused the Victorian cult of domesticity and the historic separation of the private and the public, which took shape around colonialism and the idea of race. At the same time, colonialism took shape around the Victorian invention of domesticity and the idea of the home' (McClintock 1995: 36). My analysis of women's sugar boycotts extends her analysis through an exploration of a (public) social movement that emerged out of the conjunction of colonialism and domesticity. The conjoining of the embodied experiences of female consumers and Caribbean slaves through the mobility of the sweet commodity of sugar first bridged the chasm between 'home' and 'empire'.

4 See, for example, Tullis and Hollist 1986; Marsden and Little 1990; Goodman and Redclift 1991; Bonanno *et al.* 1994; Goodman and Watts 1997.

5 A similar argument can be found in John Berger's *Ways of Seeing*, in which he proposes that 'To have a thing painted and put on a canvas is not unlike buying it and putting it in your house . . . [M]any oil paintings were themselves simple demonstrations of what gold or money could buy. Merchandise became the actual subject-matter of works of art' (Berger 1972: 83, 99).

6 *The Drake Manuscript in the Pierpont Morgan Library: Histoire Naturelle des Indes* (London: Andre Deutsch Ltd., 1996) f.4v, translation of text p. 253.

7 Spanish explorers of the West Indies first brought tobacco back to Europe in the

sixteenth century, having found it extensively cultivated in Cuba especially. It rapidly made the transition from elite luxury to item of mass consumption; however it will not be my main focus here because production of tobacco largely shifted from the Caribbean to the southern United States by the eighteenth century. Nevertheless, the story of tobacco also epitomises the ambivalence of a colonial consumer culture that continues to have massive impacts on ethical debates today.

8 'The beginning and Proceedings of the new plantation of St. Christopher by Captain Warner' in *The True Travels, Adventures and Observations of Captain John Smith in Europe, Asia, Africke, and America, beginning about the yeere 1593, and continued to this present 1629,* 2 vols. Reprint from the London edition of 1629 (Richmond, VA: Franklin Press, 1819), p. 273.

9 Richard Ligon, *A True and Exact History of the Island of Barbados* (London: Humphrey Moseley, 1657), pp. 30, 54.

10 Thanks to Hilary Hinds of Lancaster University for bringing this article to my attention.

11 Ligon, *A True and Exact History*, p. 24.

12 William Reed, *The History of Sugar and Sugar Yielding Plants* (London: Longmans, Green & Co., 1866), p. 6.

13 Ligon, *A True and Exact History*, pp. 82–3, 107.

14 The extent to which Britain and other slaving nations recognise the significance of slavery and the West Indian trade as the basis of their contemporary wealth remains contested (cf. Martin 1999). While maritime museums in Liverpool, Bristol, and Lancaster have begun to explore this history, it remains a rather marginal facet of their presentation of British maritime history, symbolically hidden away in basement galleries or side galleries, which can be difficult even to locate. Bristol at least offers an interesting map for a walking tour of the city's sites connected with the slave trade.

15 Père Pierre-François-Xavier de Charlevoix, *A Voyage to North America; Undertaken by command of the present King of France, Containing . . . A Description and Natural History of the Islands of the West Indies belonging to the different powers of Europe,* 2 vols (Dublin: John Exshaw and James Potts, 1766), Vol. I, p. 310.

16 *Pharmacopiae Londoniensis, or the New London Dispensary* (printed 1696), liber 1, p. 171, as cited in I.V. Hall, 'A History of the Sugar Trade in England, with Special Attention to the Sugar Trade of Bristol' (MA thesis, University of Bristol, 1925), p. 66.

17 West Indian rum became central to British naval power, being issued daily to sailors in the West Indies from the 1740s on, as an alternative to beer, which did not keep well in the tropical heat. Consumed in the form of Grog, by 1831 the daily rum ration of a quarter pint a day was standard throughout the navy (Pack 1982: 21, 71, 75).

18 Benjamin Moseley, M.D. *A Treatise Concerning the Properties and Effects of Coffee,* 3rd edn (London: John Stockdale, 1785), pp. 30–1.

19 The Gillow furniture makers of Lancaster, for example, opened a retail store in London's Oxford Street in 1760, which arranged outward shipments of mahogany flat-packed furniture to the West Indies, along with 'billiard tables, dressing glasses, neat tick mattresses and bolsters, Leicester goods and Kendal cottons, felt hats and white thread gloves' (Barty-King and Massel 1983). Once again, though, the Gillow's museum in Lancaster today makes little of these colonial connections.

20 Reed, *History of Sugar*, pp. 202–3.

21 Braithwaite Poole, *The Commerce of Liverpool* (London: Longman & Co.; Liverpool: Thomas Baines, 1854), pp. 74, 78.

22 *The Ambassador of Commerce for the City and Port of Liverpool and the adjoining Boroughs: An Exposition of Merseyside's Commercial and Industrial Greatness.* Supplement to the *Liverpool Daily Post and Mercury*, 7 July 1924.

23 Anne McClintock has identified the 'commodity spectacle' of the Victorian era as crucial to this invasion of the home by imperial bric-à-brac, 'from milk cartons to sauce

bottles, tobacco tins to whiskey bottles, assorted biscuits to toothpaste, toffee boxes to baking powder' (1995: 219). I would suggest that this process of domestication of the empire had already begun in the late eighteenth to early nineteenth century not only through the consumption of coffee, tobacco, tea, and sugar, but also through the changes that colonial wealth brought to the English home and its domestic rituals.

24 *Considerations of the Slave Trade and the Consumption of West Indian Produce* (London: Darton & Harvey, 1791) [extracted from T. Cooper, *Letters on the Slave Trade*].

25 [William Fox] *An Address to the People of Great Britain on the Propriety of Abstaining from West India Sugar and Rum*, 10th edn (Birmingham: Swinney & Walker, 1791), p. 2.

26 On the wider tactics of the anti-slavery movement and its innovative role in developing new forms of publicity and national political campaigns see Drescher 1982 and 1987.

27 For an introduction to some of the key debates see Williams 1944; Anstey 1975; Davis 1975; Drescher 1987; Solow and Engerman 1987; Blackburn 1988; and Oldfield 1995. I have discussed some of this work more extensively in Sheller 2000. For some of the key dates relating to the abolition of the slave trade and slavery see the Appendix.

28 Birmingham City Archives, microfilm 96615, *The First Report of the Female Society for the Relief of British Negro Slaves, etc., etc.* [1825–26], Resolution 11.

29 Birmingham City Archives, microfilm 96615, *The Twenty-Eighth Report of the Ladies' Negro's Friend Society* [1853], p. 17.

30 Birmingham City Archives, microfilm 96615, *The Second Report of the Female Society for the Relief of British Negro Slaves, etc., etc.* [1826–27], pp. 15–16.

31 William Edmonstone Lendrick, *Sugar-trade and Slave-trade. The West Indian Question Considered* (London: Saunders & Otley, 1853), pp. 78–9, 30–1.

32 In 1847 the Quaker anti-slavery activist Joseph Sturge (1793–1859) contributed five hundred dollars to the Philadelphia Free Produce Association, which promoted trade in goods that were guaranteed not to be made by slaves. Various Americans were dispatched to England to promote the association, including Samuel Rhoads, Elihu Burritt, and Frederick Douglass.

33 Birmingham City Archives, microfilm 96615, *The Twenty-Fourth Report of the Ladies' Negro's Friend Society* [1849], pp. 8–10; *The Twenty-Fifth Report of the Ladies' Negro's Friend Society* [1850]. In 1849 an 'Anti-Slavery Petition from the Women of Great Britain' was presented to the Queen with 59,686 signatures, of which 9,393 were from Birmingham. It was presented on a mahogany roller with a velvet cover lined with calico made from free grown cotton.

34 Anon., '*Bread Upon the Waters', or Letter, Illustrative, Moral and Practical, Addressed generally to the Women of Great Britain and Ireland* . . . (London: W. and F.G. Cash; Dublin: J.B. Gilpin; Edinburgh: John Menzies, 1853), pp. 53, 89.

35 Captain J.E. Alexander, *Transatlantic Sketches* (London: Richard Bentley, 1833), p. 200.

36 Lady Emmeline Stuart Wortley, *Travels in the United States, etc. During 1849 and 1850* (New York: Harper & Brothers Publishers, 1851), p. 259.

37 Sady Brassey, *In the Trades, the Tropics, and the Roaring Forties* (London: Longman's, Green & Co., 1885), p. 281.

38 James Johnston, M.D., *Jamaica: The New Riviera. A pictorial Description of the Island and Its Attractions* (London: Cassell & Co., 1903 [1905]), p. 27; and see *The Fruit Trade Mail*, 6 January 1906, cited in Davies, *Fyffes and the Banana*, p. 116.

39 Francis Dodsworth, *The Book of the West Indies* (London: G. Routledge & Sons, 1904). The book's title-page is faced by an advertisement for 'Bananine Bread' which claims that 'One pound of Bananine Bread contains more nourishment and energy-producing material than one pound of the best beef-steak, and is much more digestible and is less than one-sixth the price'.

40 Claude Wilson Wardlaw, *Green Havoc in the Lands of the Caribbean* (Edinburgh and London: William Blackwood & Sons Ltd. 1935), pp. 32–3.

41 Ibid., p. 37.

42 Ibid., pp. 175–6.

43 Ibid., pp. 183, 185.

44 See, for example, Charlotte Denny, 'Bad Break for the Borders: What Links Bananas to Cashmere Sweaters?' *The Guardian*, 30 January 1999, p. 26; Larry Elliott, Mark Milner, and Mark Atkinson, 'Stakes are Raised in Trade War: Albright Flies in for Crisis Talks with Cook', *The Guardian*, 6 March 1999, p. 1; Stephen Bates, 'Billion Dollar Banana Split', ibid., p. 9; Andrew Marshall, 'The End of a Beautiful Friendship? Firms Hit as Banana War Sours Anglo–US Relations', *The Independent on Sunday*, 7 March 1999, p. 14.

45 The details of these disputes and many of the issues they raise for Caribbean states have been more fully reported on by David Jessop, Executive Director of the Caribbean Council for Europe, in a series of electronic reports titled 'The Week in Europe'.

46 Anthony DePalma, 'U.S. and Europeans Agree on Deal to End Banana Trade War', *New York Times*, 12 April 2001, p. C1 with leader on A1.

47 Earl Moxam, 'Caribbean Bands Together in Banana Dispute', Reuters News Service, 27 January 1999.

48 In Britain from the 1960s alternative agro-food networks were promoted by Oxfam, later joined by Twin Trading, Traidcraft, and Equal Exchange Trading Limited. The Fairtrade Foundation formed in the early 1990s and the British Association of Fair Trade Shops in the late 1990s (Whatmore and Thorne 1997). Fairtrade claims to give producers 'fair prices for their produce, better terms of trade, access to markets and credit'; they encourage organic production and offer support and emergency assistance for growers.

49 Sainsbury's banana label, 21 January 2001. See also www.sainsburys.co.uk.

50 Booth's banana label, 26 April 2001. Booth's is a supermarket chain in the north of England.

51 Intergovernmental Group on Bananas and on Tropical Fruits, 'The Market for "Organic" and "Fair-Trade" Bananas', United Nations Food and Agricultural Organization Committee on Commodity Problems, Meeting in Gold Coast, Australia, May 1999 (www.fao.org/docrep/meeting/X1149E.htm).

52 Protection of US sugar growers from competition with foreign producers is today estimated to cost American consumers $2 billion a year. Excess production led sugar prices to fall in 1999 to their lowest level in twenty years; while some producers filed for bankruptcy, government stockpiles of sugar cost $1.4 million per month simply for storage (David Barboza, 'Sugar Rules Defy Free-Trade Logic', *New York Times*, Business Section, 6 May 2001).

4 Orienting the Caribbean

1 Amy Jenkins, 'Lust for Life', *The Guardian*, Travel Section, 17 February 2001, p. 6.

2 Christopher Columbus, *Journal of the First Voyage, 1492*, ed., trans., intro. and notes by B.W. Ife (Warmington, England: Aris & Phillips Ltd., 1990), pp. 53, 55. For contemporary versions of the Columbus myth in the United States, see Ella Shohat and Robert Stam, 'Formations of Colonialist Discourse' in *Unthinking Eurocentrism: Multiculturalism and the Media* (London and New York: Routledge, 2000 [1994]).

3 *The New Oxford Dictionary of English* (Oxford: Clarendon Press, 1998).

4 For helping me to think through this aspect of my argument I would like to thank Sara Ahmed, Claudia Castañeda, Anne Cronin, Anne-Marie Fortier, and Imogen Tyler.

5 Indeed, many of the stereotypes that we associate with Africanist discourse were actually developed first in the Caribbean, in the context of the development of racial 'science' in slave societies. Only later in the nineteenth century were they applied more directly to Africa, in the context of colonialism. Thus in some sense ideas of African primitivism were initially elaborated through the ideological work done to justify European enslavement of Africans in the Caribbean. Wheeler (1999: 17) argues that the

luxury/cannibalism opposition that originated in the Caribbean was subsequently imposed on the interior of Africa. On Africanist discourse more generally see Mudimbe 1988; Miller 1985; Young 1986; and Yelvington forthcoming.

6 And it is precisely such boundary distinctions, produced in nineteenth-century social theory concerned with the origins of modernity, which continue to inform certain branches of contemporary social theory.

7 On racial ideologies and 'primitive narratives' in France see, for example, Miller 1985 and Sharpley-Whiting 1999; on Spanish racial ideologies in the Caribbean see Hoetink 1985 and Martinez-Alier 1989; on colonial Dutch formations of race and gender see Stoler 1991 (on Dutch East Asia) and McClintock 1995 (on South Africa). Related patterns of Orientalist and Africanist colonial discourse can also be found operating in other colonial zones, such as the Pacific Islands or the East Indies, but I will not be able to explore these comparisons here.

8 On the transfer of the sugar plantation-slavery model from the Old World to the New World, via Madeira, see William D. Phillips, Jr 'The Old World Background of Slavery in the Americas' in Barbara L. Solow (ed.) *Slavery and the Rise of the Atlantic System* (Cambridge: Cambridge University Press, 1991), pp. 43–61.

9 European theorists began to position European capitalist modernity in contrast to two pre-capitalist modes of production: the Asiatic mode of production and the African tribal mode of production, in the same way that they positioned European democracy in relation to these two 'traditional' cultures of despotism. In *The Spirit of the Law* (1746), Montesquieu first theorised 'oriental despotism' in relation to land and climate, thus associating 'torrid climes' with imperial systems and servile people (see Brendan O'Leary, *The Asiatic Mode of Production* (London: Basil Blackwell, 1989)). The system of African enslavement in the Caribbean thus functions paradoxically both as that which enabled European capitalism to break away from Asia, and that which underwrites Europe's narrative of its own modernity founded on the ideology of 'freedom'.

10 Besides the innumerable critical writings on William Shakespeare's *The Tempest* (1612), see the significant re-workings of the Caliban myth by Ernest Renan, *Caliban: Suite de 'La Tempête.' Drame Philosophique* [Caliban: 'The Tempest' Suite. A philosophical Drama] (Paris, 1878); Octave Mannoni, *Prospero and Caliban: The Psychology of Colonization*, trans. Pamela Powesland (Ann Arbor: University of Michigan Press, 1990); Aimé Césaire, *Une Tempête: Adaptation de 'La Tempête' de Shakespeare pour un théâtre nègre* [A Tempest: An Adaptation of Shakespeare's 'The Tempest' for a Black Theater] (Paris, 1969); Edward Brathwaite, *Islands* (London, 1969); Roberto Fernandez Retamar, *Caliban and Other Essays*, trans. Edward Baker (Minneapolis: University of Minnesota Press, 1989); Peter Hulme and William Sherman (eds) *'The Tempest' and Its Travels* (London: Reaktion Books, 2000); Jyotsna G. Singh, 'Caliban versus Miranda: Race and Gender Conflicts in Postcolonial Rewritings of *The Tempest*', in Valerie Traub *et al.* (eds) *Feminist Readings of Early Modern Culture* (Cambridge: Cambridge University Press, 1996); and see my discussion of the critical literature on Sycorax in Chapter 5 below.

11 *The New Oxford Dictionary of English* (Oxford: Clarendon Press, 1998).

12 Richard Ligon, *A True and Exact History of the Island of Barbados* (London: Humphrey Moseley, 1657), p. 104.

13 Ibid., p. 107.

14 George Cheyne, 'The English Malady; or, A Treatise of Nervous Diseases' (London: G. Strahan, 1733; reprinted London: Routledge, 1991), as cited in Porter 1994: 63–4.

15 This discussion draws on the primary texts and commentary in Frank Felsenstein (ed.) *English Trader, Indian Maid: Representing Gender, Race, and Slavery in the New World, An Inkle and Yarico Reader* (Baltimore and London: Johns Hopkins University Press, 1999).

16 Similar themes of sexual romance in Surinam are dealt with in Aphra Behn's 'Oroonoko, or, The Royal Slave' (1688), which has recently attracted the attention of postcolonial and feminist literary critics (e.g. Ferguson 1991). See Aphra Behn, *Oroonoko*

and Other Writings, ed., intro. and notes by Paul Salzman (Oxford and New York: Oxford University Press, 1998).

17 Derek Walcott, 'A Frowsty Fragrance', *New York Review*, 15 June 2000, p. 58. (A review of Thomas W. Krise, ed., *Caribbeana: An Anthology of English Literature on the West Indies, 1657–1777*, University of Chicago Press).

18 This description draws on a Christie's sale catalogue for *Topographical Pictures* (London, 6 June 1996), pp. 41–3, in which Brunias's paintings are listed with guide prices of around $150,000. Thanks to Anne Walmsley for bringing this to my attention.

19 'A Surinam Planter in His Morning Dress' from Captain John G. Stedman, *Narrative of a Five Years' Expedition Against the Revolted Negroes of Surinam* [London, 1796], ed., intro. and notes by Richard Price and Sally Price (Baltimore and London: Johns Hopkins University Press, 1988), p. 365. In this fascinating analysis of William Blake's illustrations of slave torture in Stedman's narrative, Marcus Wood (2000) does not analyse this image, but an interesting plagiarised version can be seen in his Plate 5.18.

20 Stedman, *Narrative of a Five Years' Expedition*, pp. 363–4.

21 Although Blake himself was politically aligned with abolitionism, his illustrations blurred the boundaries between desire and revulsion to such an extent that some of his images of slave society (and especially torture) seem to have circulated as forms of pornography. Thus it remains difficult to impute any single reading to them. Eighteenth-century dramatists like Isaac Bickerstaffe also experimented with exotic settings to depict characters like a Creole orphan in *Love in the City* (1767); Roxalana, a female slave freed from a seraglio, in *The Sultan* (1775); or *The Captive* (1769), which concerns the rebellious daughter of 'an avaricious *cadi*' in Spain. While Oldfield reads these plays as showing 'a deep sympathy with outsiders, often women or blacks' (Oldfield 1995: 28), it was in part the underlying erotic content that drew audiences.

22 Daniel McKinnen, *A Tour Through the British West Indies in the Years 1802 and 1803, giving a particular account of the Bahama Islands* (London: J. White and R. Taylor, 1804), pp. 30–1.

23 Edward Long, *The History of Jamaica. Or, General Survey of the Ancient and Modern State of that Island; with Reflections on its Situation, Settlements, Inhabitants, Climate, Products, Commerce, Laws, And Government*, 3 vols (London: Lowndes, 1774), II, p. 327. Cited in Young, *Colonial Desire*, p. 175.

24 'A Spanish Planter of Porto Rico, Luxuriating in his Hammock', in John A. Waller, *A Voyage in the West Indies* (London, 1820).

25 Eleanor Sansay, *Secret History, or the Horrors of St. Domingo* (Philadelphia, n.p., 1808), p. 25.

26 Another well-known account of the creolization of European women in the West Indies is the pro-slavery Mrs. A. C. Carmichael's *Domestic Manners and Social Condition of the White, Coloured, and Negro Population of the West Indies*, 2 vols, 1833 (New York: Negro Universities Press, 1969). As Hilary Beckles points out, Carmichael described women in St. Vincent as listless, meagre conversationalists, suffering constant domestic drudgery and felt that 'many white women were abandoned by modernity and stranded among negroes – left to decay morally and culturally' (Beckles 1999: 119).

27 Captain J.E. Alexander, *Transatlantic Sketches, comprising visits to the most interesting scenes in North and South America and the West Indies. With notes on Negro slavery and Canadian emigration*, 2 vols (London: Richard Bentley, 1833), Vol. 1, pp. 32–3.

28 Such an ambivalent imagery is not limited to the Caribbean. It also continues to appear in European imagery of the exotic allures and dangers of 'Araby' in the nineteenth century and of the Americas generally in the twentieth century. Mexico especially, according to Root, materialised for Europeans such as Sergei Eisenstein, Georges Bataille, and Antonin Artaud the paradoxical juxtaposition of 'blood and wealth, flowers and flies . . . [it] appears as a kind of collage, both violent and luxurious, barbaric and refined' (Root 1998: 58).

29 Andy Pietrasik, 'Pleasure Island', *The Guardian*, Travel Section, 11 August 2001, pp. 12–13.

30 Alexander, *Transatlantic Sketches*, p. 239.

31 Charles William Day, *Five Years' Residence in the West Indies*, 2 vols (London: Colburn & Co., 1853), Vol. 1, p. 10.

32 Ibid., p. 20.

33 Aravamudan also explores the notion of Levantinization as 'a creative response to orientalisms as a plural rather than a singular category and the specifically dynamic interactions of European culture with Islamic ones that go back at least to the Crusades' (Aravamudan 1999: 19). Nevertheless, his analysis of this phenomenon is restricted to writings on the Levant itself (the Mediterranean, Asia Minor, and North Africa).

34 Alexander, *Transatlantic Sketches*, p. 199.

35 Patrick Leigh Fermor, *The Traveller's Tree: A Journey Through the Caribbean Islands* (London: John Murray, Reprint 1955 [1950]). This book won critical acclaim and two literary prizes, establishing Fermor's reputation 'as the finest travel-writer of the last half-century' (Hulme and Whitehead 1992: 281).

36 Edward Agnew Paton, *Down the Islands: A Voyage in the Caribbees* (London: Kegan Paul, Trench & Co., 1888), pp. 197–8.

37 Ibid., p. 206.

38 Lady Emmeline Stuart Wortley, *Travels in the United States, etc. During 1849 and 1850* (New York: Harper & Brothers Publishers, 1851), p. 257.

39 Charles Kingsley, *At Last: A Christmas in the West Indies*, new edn (London: Macmillan & Co., 1873), pp. 1, 89, 123–4.

40 Paton, *Down the Islands*, pp. 177–8.

41 Fermor, *The Traveller's Tree*, pp. 154–5.

42 Ibid., p. 168.

43 Ibid., p. 243.

44 Ibid., pp. 339–40. See Levine (2000: 9) on British colonial views on 'Asiatic Jewesses' in India.

45 Sady Brassey, *In the Trades, the Tropics, and the Roaring Forties* (London: Longman's, Green & Co., 1885), p. 120.

46 Susan de Forest Day, *The Cruise of the Scythian in the West Indies* (London, New York and Chicago: F. Tennyson Neely, 1899), p. 148.

47 Ibid., p. 166.

48 For an interesting discussion of the history of the racial marking of the Jewish body, in particular the 'Semitic' nose, and its relation to whiteness, see Jacobsen 1998.

49 Charles Augustus Stoddard, *Cruising Among the Caribbees: Summer Days in Winter Months* (London: Kegan Paul, Trench and Trubner & Co., 1895), pp. 101–2.

50 Pulaski F. Hyatt (US Consul, Santiago de Cuba) and John T. Hyatt (Vice-consul), *Cuba: Its resources and Opportunities. Valuable Information for American investors, manufacturers, exporters, importers, lumber and mine operators, wholesale and retail merchants, employment seekers, prospective planters, professional men, sportsmen, travelers, railroad men, and others* (New York: J.S. Ogilvie Publishing Co., 1898), pp. 27–8.

51 Such processes apply to the construction of masculinity as much as femininity. In his ethnography of racism among young people in London, Les Back (1999 [1996]) has also explored the articulation between gender and racism in processes of 'race–gender othering'. He shows how young white men's attraction to blackness occurs around racialised definitions of masculinity which associate black masculinity with being 'hard' or 'bad'. This, in turn, is contrasted to 'Oriental' masculinity, which is viewed as 'vulnerable, soft and effeminate' (Back 1999 [1996]: 68–9).

52 James Anthony Froude, *The English in the West Indies, or, the Bow of Ulysses* (New York: Charles Scribner's Sons, 1888), pp. 261–2.

53 Ibid., pp. 348, 362.

54 N. Darnell Davis, *Mr. Froude's Negrophobia, or Don Quixote as a Cook's Tourist* (Demerara: The Argosy Press, 1888 [reprinted from 'Timehri' Vol. 2, part 1]), pp. 36–8.

55 E.A. Hastings Jay, LL.B., F.R.G.S., *A Glimpse of the Tropics, Or, Four Months Cruising in the West Indies* (London: Sampson Low, Marston & Co., 1900), p. 29.

56 Day, *op. cit.*, p. 107.
57 Hesketh Prichard, *Where Black Rules White: A Journey Across and About Haiti* (New York: Charles Scribner's Sons, 1900), p. 12.
58 Ibid., pp. 94–5.
59 Blair Niles, *Black Haiti: A Biography of Africa's Eldest Daughter* (New York and London: G.P. Putnam's Sons, The Knickerbocker Press, 1926), pp. 26–7.
60 John Houston Craige, *Black Bagdad: The Arabian Nights Adventure of a Marine Captain in Haiti* (New York: Minton, Balch & Co.; and London: Stanley Paul & Co., 1933), p. 1.
61 Ibid., pp. 1, 4.
62 Ibid., pp. 65, 68.
63 John C. Van Dyke, *In the West Indies: Sketches and Studies in Tropic Seas and Islands* (New York and London: Charles Scribner's Sons, 1932), pp. vii–viii.
64 Ibid., pp. 23–4.
65 James Pope-Hennessy, *The Baths of Absalom: A Footnote to Froude* (London: Allan Wingate, 1954), pp. 41–2.
66 Max Anderson, 'Love and Haiti', *The Sunday Times*, Travel Section, 23 July 2000. In fact, I myself met Joliecoeur, dressed in a crisp suit and carrying a silver-handled cane, at the Oloffson Hotel during a study tour of Haiti, while my colleagues whispered of Tonton Macoute and Greene's novel.
67 The same thrill runs through more academic accounts of Haiti; see Hurston 1990 [1938], Davis 1986, 1988, and critiques by Hurbon 1995; Dash 1997; Dayan 1998; and Sheller 1999.

5 Eating others

1 See McClintock (1995) for discussion of a related image of Columbus's arrival on the shores of a Caribbean island, based on a 1575 drawing by Jan van der Straet, in which his apparently peaceful encounter with a native is shadowed by a scene of cannibal dismemberment in the background. McClintock reads the use of women as imperial boundary markers as part of the construction of a 'porno-tropics' in which the 'erotics of imperial conquest were also an erotics of engulfment' (McClintock 1995: 24–5).
2 The Jamaican word *nyam* derives from the Wolof terms *nyam* or *nyami*, the latter a verb meaning 'to eat'. On the West African coast the main food provided to slaves for the long transatlantic voyage was yams, a word which derives from the same Wolof origin via the Portuguese *inhame* and the Spanish *(i)ñame* (R. Hall 1991: 165).
3 Recently, in another appropriation of Haitian culture, some European theorists have adopted the term 'zombie' to describe the 'zombie categories' and 'zombie institutions' of modernity, which are glossed as 'dead and still alive' (Ulrich Beck cited by Bauman 2000: 6, 8). Following on from North American popular misusage of the Haitian religion of Vodou to disparagingly describe everything from 'voodoo economics' to 'voodoo science', we now see the same kind of theft of the term zombie in 'high' theory, an issue that I will pursue further in Chapter 6. I use the creole spelling of 'Vodou' in order to set it apart from the US-American appropriations of the term ('voodoo'), which distort and belittle its function as a religion in Haiti, West Africa, Louisiana, and elsewhere (cf. Brown 1991).
4 This analysis draws inspiration from a wide range of feminist work on the intersection of gender orders and national formations, including Alexander 1997, which I discuss below, as well as Enloe 1989; Parker 1991; McClintock 1995; Kaplan *et al.* 1999; and Ahmed 2000. Thanks especially to Sara Ahmed, whose thoughtful comments helped me to clarify my argument in this chapter.
5 Sady Brassey, *In the Trades, the Tropics, and the Roaring Forties* (London: Longman's, Green & Co., 1885), p. 134.

6 Charles Augustus Stoddard, *Cruising Among the Caribbees: Summer Days in Winter Months* (London: Kegan Paul, Trench and Trubner & Co., 1895), pp. 30–1.

7 Susan de Forest Day, *The Cruise of the Scythian in the West Indies* (London, New York, and Chicago: F. Tennyson Neely, 1899), pp. 163–4.

8 E.A. Hastings Jay, LL.B., F.R.G.S., *A Glimpse of the Tropics, Or, Four Months Cruising in the West Indies* (London: Sampson Low, Marston & Co., 1900), pp. 26–9.

9 Ibid., pp. 84–6.

10 Ibid., pp. 212–11, 216.

11 Ibid., pp. 224–5.

12 Today the training of hotel workers in the Caribbean includes lessons in dress, personal hygiene, and elocution, to help avoid such awkward moments. Tourists are protected from encounters with non-servile natives, and many visitors are specifically told not to explore 'the dangerous interior' of islands like Jamaica.

13 James Pope-Hennessy, *The Baths of Absalom: A Footnote to Froude* (London: Allan Wingate, 1954), p. 21. Both Pope-Hennessy and Patrick Leigh Fermor also describe the 'Saga-boys' (or 'Swagger-boys') of Trinidad as being involved in prostitution or pimping, clearly linked to the prevalence of US naval ships in the region during the Second World War.

14 On Hemingway's 'discovery' of Bimini, in the Bahamas, Alexander suggests that in 'his construction of Bimini as a "blank, empty space," and his view of the "serviceability of Black people," Hemingway continued the imperial narrative that preceded him. Accordingly, nature figures as raw material for American (European) creative expansiveness, nature is positioned to collude in phantasmic represen-tations of Black people, the very rhetorical strategies that state and private corporations utilize to market Bahamians and the Bahamas to the rest of the world' (1997: 93–4).

15 Patrick Leigh Fermor, *The Traveller's Tree: A Journey Through the Caribbean Islands* (London: John Murray, reprint 1955 [1950]), p. 15.

16 Philip Hoare, 'A Englishman Abroad', *The Independent on Sunday Magazine*, 23 April 2000.

17 Guy Kennaway, 'Road to a New Eden (With Plenty of Temptation Along the Way)', *High Life* (British Airways Magazine), March 2000, p. 111.

18 'Guns, Knives and Sound Systems: Prince Buster and the Birth of Reggae', *The Guardian*, Friday Review, 18 August 2000, p. 2, headline based on excerpts from Lloyd Bradley's *Bass Culture* (Penguin, 2001).

19 'Fear and Loathing in Jamaica', *Independent on Sunday*, 5 November 2000, pp. 28–32.

20 Norplant is a form of contraception based on the insertion of silicone rods under the skin of the arm, which slowly release a hormonal contraceptive for a period of five years. It is associated with a wide range of side effects and risks, including prolonged and heavy menstrual bleeding, and is the subject of major class action law suits in the United States.

21 John Canham-Clyne and Worth Cooley-Prost, 'U.S. AID Go Home!', *In These Times*, 8 January 1998, p. 24.

22 'The Health of Nations', *Haiti Support Group Briefing*, no. 35, September 1999.

6 Creolization in global culture

1 'Kalfou Danjere' [Haitian Creole for 'dangerous crossroads'] was the title of a 1992 single by the Haitian band Boukman Eksperyans. It also appeared in the title of a book by George Lipsitz, *Dangerous Crossroads: Popular Music, Postmodernism and the Poetics of Place* (New York: Verso, 1994), and in a 1995 book edited by NACLA, *Haiti: Dangerous Crossroads* (Boston, MA: South End Press).

2 Marjorie Hughes, *The Fairest Island* (London: Victor Gollancz, 1962), pp. 10–11.

3 Though see Cook and Harrison (2001) on the difficulties of actually marketing

Caribbean-made products such as hot sauces in the UK market, which they describe as 'not eating the other'.

4 Timothy White's *Catch a Fire: The Life of Bob Marley* (1983), opened up a spate of new biographies and histories of Caribbean music, e.g. Bradley 2001, CD collections like Tuff Gong's *Bob Marley Songs of Freedom*, and Island Records' *Tougher than Tough: The Story of Jamaican Music* (1993).

5 Contemporary usage varies. In some Caribbean countries the term creole is not used at all. In Trinidad, it may be used to designate all Trinidadians except those of Asian origin. In Suriname, a creole is a person of African origin, while in French Guyana a creole is a person who has adopted a European way of life.

6 An equally significant development, which I will not deal with directly here, was the recognition of a 'West Indian' presence already within English canonical literature. See especially Edward Said's influential postcolonial reading of works such as Jane Austen's *Mansfield Park* in his *Culture and Imperialism* (1993).

7 André Breton, the leader of the Surrealist movement travelled in the Caribbean where he was very influenced by the 'primitive' style of painting seen there, and the African influences in some artists' work, especially in Haiti. He was accompanied on his trip by the Cuban painter Wilfredo Lam, who was one of the few Caribbean artists to be accepted as part of the European avant-garde (Poupeye 1998).

8 Brendan Lehane, 'Q: What's French for Caribbean? A: Guadeloupe', *The Independent on Sunday*, Travel Section, 14 October 2001, p. 21.

9 Various reviews are available on the amazon.com site selling Chamoiseau's novel *Texaco*.

10 Thanks to Andrew Stafford of Lancaster University for bringing this article to my attention.

11 Paul Gilroy makes much of the fact that Glissant's references to the work of Deleuze and Guattari were cut from the English translation (Dash 1989) of his 1981 book *Le discours antillais*, 'presumably because to acknowledge this exchange would somehow violate the aura of Caribbean authenticity that is a desirable frame around the work' (Gilroy 1993: 31). One of the most celebrated theories of the 'creole' Caribbean, it seems, would betray its exotic 'saveur' if it were found to be already metropolitan in its self-theorisation. By holding Glissant apart from French post-structuralism, he can then be consumed as 'indigenous' by Anglo-American metropolitan theorists of postmodernity.

Bibliography

Primary sources

d'Alaux, Gustave [pseud. Maxime Reybaud], *L'Empereur Soulouque et son empire*, Paris: Michel Lévy frères, 1856 [2nd edn, 1860].

Alcott, William A., *Tea and Coffee*, Boston and New York: George W. Light, 1839.

Alexander, Captain J.E., *Transatlantic Sketches, comprising visits to the most interesting scenes in North and South America and the West Indies. With notes on Negro slavery and Canadian emigration*, 2 vols, London: Richard Bentley, 1833.

Anon. *'Bread Upon the Waters', or Letter, Illustrative, Moral and Practical, Addressed generally to the Women of Great Britain and Ireland*, London: W. and F.G. Cash; Dublin: J.B. Gilpin; Edinburgh: John Menzies, 1853.

Behn, Aphra, 'Oroonoko, or, The Royal Slave. A True History' [1688], in *Oroonoko and Other Writings*, ed., intro. and notes by Paul Salzman, Oxford and New York: Oxford University Press, 1998.

Benezet, Anthony, *A Caution and a Warning to Great Britain and her Colonies in a short representation of the calamitous state of the Enslaved Negroes in the British Dominions*, Philadelphia, 1766.

Bonsal, Stephen, *The American Mediterranean*, New York: Moffat, Yard & Co., 1912.

Brassey, Sady, *In the Trades, the Tropics, and the Roaring Forties*, London: Longman's, Green & Co., 1885.

Brown, Jonathan, *The History and Present Condition of St. Domingue*, 2 vols, Philadelphia: William Marshall, 1837. Reprint London: Frank Cass, 1972.

Bulkeley, Owen T., *The Lesser Antilles: A Guide for Settlers in the British West Indies, and Tourists' Companion*, London: Sampson Low & Co., 1889.

Candler, John, *Brief Notices of Hayti: with its conditions, resources, and Prospects*, London: Ward, 1842.

Caribbeana, being Miscellaneous Papers Relating to the History, Genealogy, Topography and Antiquities of the British West Indies, London: Mitchell Hughes and Clarke.

Carmichael, Mrs A.C., *Domestic Manners and Social Condition of the White, Coloured, and Negro Population of the West Indies*, 2 vols, 1833, New York: Negro Universities Press, 1969.

Cassagnac, P. Granier de, *Voyage aux Antilles Françaises, Anglaises, Danoises, Espagnoles, à Saint-Domingue et aux Etats-Unis d'Amerique*, 2 vols, Paris: Au Comptoir des Imprimeurs Unis, Vol. 1: 1843, Vol. 2: 1844.

Chalmers, A., *The General Biographical Dictionary*, Vol. 28, London: n.p., 1816, new edn, pp. 63–9.

Charlevoix, Père Pierre-François-Xavier de, *Histoire de l'isle Espagnole ou de St. Domingue*, 2 vols, Paris: Chez François Barois, 1730.

—— *A Voyage to North America; Undertaken by command of the present King of France, Containing . . . A Description and Natural History of the Islands of the West Indies belonging to the different powers of Europe*, 2 vols, Dublin: John Exshaw and James Potts, 1766.

Clark, Benjamin C., *A Geographical Sketch of St. Domingo, Cuba, and Nicaragua, with remarks on the past and present policy of Great Britain affecting those countries. By a Traveller*, Boston: Eastburn's Press, 1850.

Columbus, Christopher, *Journal of the First Voyage*, 1492, ed. and trans. B.W. Ife, Warmington, England: Aris & Phillips Ltd., 1990. See also *The Log of Christopher Columbus*, trans. Robert H. Fuson, Camden, Maine, 1987.

[Cooper, T. Esq.], *Considerations on the Slave Trade and the Consumption of West Indian Produce*, London: Darton & Harvey, 1791 [extracted from *Letters on the Slave Trade*, by T. Cooper, Esq.].

Craige, John Houston, *Black Bagdad: The Arabian Nights Adventure of a Marine Captain in Haiti*, New York: Minton, Balch & Co.; London: Stanley Paul & Co., 1933.

—— *Cannibal Cousins*, New York: Minton, Balch & Co., 1934.

Davis, Harold P., *Black Democracy: The Story of Haiti*, New York: Lincoln MacVeagh, The Dial Press, 1928.

Davis, N. Darnell, *Mr. Froude's Negrophobia, or Don Quixote as a Cook's Tourist*, Demerara: The Argosy Press, 1888 [reprinted from 'Timehri' Vol. 2, part 1].

Day, Charles William, *Five Years' Residence in the West Indies*, 2 vols, London: Colburn & Co., 1853.

Day, Susan de Forest, *The Cruise of the Scythian in the West Indies*, London, New York, and Chicago: F. Tennyson Neely, 1899.

Deren, Maya, *Divine Horsemen. The living gods of Haiti*, London and New York: Thames & Hudson, 1953.

Descourtilz, Michel Étienne, *Voyage d'un naturaliste en Haïti, 1799–1803*, Paris: Jacques Bouleger, 1935 [1809].

Dodsworth, Francis, *The Book of the West Indies*, London: G. Routledge & Sons, 1904.

The Drake Manuscript in the Pierpont Morgan Library: Histoire Naturelle des Indes, intro. V. Klinkenborg, London: Andre Deutsch Ltd, 1996.

Edwards, Bryan, *An Historical Survey of the French Colony in the Island of St. Domingo: comprehending a short account of its ancient government, political state, population, productions, and exports; a narrative of the calamities which have desolated the country ever since the year 1789 . . . and a detail of the military transactions of the British army in that island to the end of 1794*, London: J. Stockdale, 1797 [French edn, Paris: Pierre Blanchard, 1812].

Exquemelin, Alexander O., *The History of the Bucaniers: being an impartial relation of all the battels, sieges, and other most eminent assaults committed for several years upon the coasts of the West Indies by the Pirates of Jamaica and Tortuga*, London: Thomas Malthus, 1684 [originally published in Dutch, 1678].

Fermor, Patrick Leigh, *The Traveller's Tree: A Journey Through the Caribbean Islands*, London: John Murray, reprint 1955 [1950].

[Fox, William], *An Address to the People of Great Britain, on the Propriety of Abstaining from West India Sugar and Rum*, 10th edn, Birmingham: Swinney & Walker, 1791.

Franklin, James, *The Present State of Hayti (Saint Domingo), with remarks on its agriculture, commerce, laws, religion, finances, and population, etc*, London: J. Murray, 1828 [Reprint Westport, CT: Negro Universities Press, 1970].

Froude, James Anthony, *The English in the West Indies, or, the Bow of Ulysses*, New York: Charles Scribner's Sons, 1888.

Gilpin, William, *Three Essays: On Picturesque Beauty, On Picturesque Travel, and On Sketching Landscape*, London, 1803.

Halliday, Sir Andrew (Deputy Inspector General of Army Hospitals), *The West Indies: The Natural and Physical History of the Windward and Leeward Colonies; with some account of the moral, social, and political condition of their inhabitants, immediately before and after the abolition of negro slavery*, London: John William Parker, 1837.

Harris, J.D., *A Summer on the Borders of the Caribbean Sea*, New York: A.B. Burdick, 1860.

Harvey, William W., *Sketches of Hayti: from the Expulsion of the French to the death of Christophe*, London: L.B. Seeley & Son, 1827 [Reprint Westport, CT: Negro Universities Press, 1970].

Hughes, Marjorie, *The Fairest Island*, London: Victor Gollancz, 1962.

Hyatt, Pulaski F. (US Consul, Santiago de Cuba) and John T. Hyatt (Vice-consul), *Cuba: Its resources and Opportunities*, New York: J.S. Ogilvie Publishing Co., 1898.

Humboldt, Alexander von (and Aimé Bonpland), *Personal Narrative of Travels to the Equinoctial Regions of America, during the years 1799–1804*, trans. from French and ed. by Thomasina Ross, 3 vols, London: Henry G. Bohn, 1852.

Jay, E.A. Hastings, LL.B., F.R.G.S., *A Glimpse of the Tropics, Or, Four Months Cruising in the West Indies*, London: Sampson Low, Marston & Co., 1900.

Johnston, James, M.D., *Jamaica: . . . The New Riviera. A pictorial Description of the Island and its Attractions*, London: Cassell & Co., 1903.

Kingsley, Charles, *At Last: A Christmas in the West Indies*, London: Macmillan & Co., 1871 [new edn, 1873].

Labat, Père Jean Baptiste, *Nouveaux Voyages aux Isles Françaises d'Amerique* (1722), trans. and abridged by John Eaden, *The Memoirs of Père Labat, 1693–1705*, London: Constable, 1931.

Lendrick, William Edmonstone, *Sugar-trade and Slave-trade. The West Indian Question Considered*, London: Saunders & Otley, 1853.

Ligon, Richard, *A True and Exact Hisory of the Island of Barbados, Illustrated with a Mapp of the Island, as also the Principall Trees and Plants there . . . Together with the Ingenio that makes the Sugar, with the plots of the severall Houses, Roomes, and other places, that are used in the whole processe of Sugar-making . . .*, London: Humphrey Moseley, 1657.

Long, Edward, *The History of Jamaica*, 3 vols, London: Lowndes, 1774.

Mackenzie, Charles, *Notes on Haiti, made During a Residence in that Republic*, 2 vols, London: H. Colburn & R. Bentley, 1830 [Reprint, London: Frank Cass & Co., 1971].

McKinnen, Daniel, Esq., *A Tour Through the British West Indies in the Years 1802 and 1803, giving a particular account of the Bahama Islands*, London: J. White & R. Taylor, 1804.

Medical Botany: Or, History of Plants in the Materia Medica of the London, Edinburgh, and Dublin Pharmacopoeias, Arranged According to the Linnaean System, 2 vols, London: E. Cox & Son, 1821.

Moreau de Saint-Méry, Médéric-Louis-Elie, *Description topographique, physique, civile, politique et historique de la partie française de l'île de Saint-Domingue*, trans. and ed. Ivor Spencer, London: University Press of America, 1985 [Philadelphia, 1797–8].

Moreton, J.B., *West India Customs and Manners*, 2nd edn., London: J. Parsons, 1793.

Morris, Charles, *Our Island Empire: A Hand-Book of Cuba, Porto Rico, Hawaii, and the Philippine Islands*, Philadelphia: J.P. Lippincott C. 1899.

Moseley, Benjamin, M.D., *A Treatise Concerning the Properties and Effects of Coffee*, 3rd edn, London: John Stockdale, 1785.

Niles, Blair, *Black Haiti: A Biography of Africa's Eldest Daughter*, New York and London: G.P. Putnam's Sons, The Knickerbocker Press, 1926.

Ober, Frederick, *In the Wake of Columbus*, Boston: Lothrop & Co., 1893.

Paton, William Agnew, *Down the Islands: A Voyage in the Caribbees*, London: Kegan Paul, Trench & Co., 1888.

Poole, Braithwaite, *The Commerce of Liverpool*, London: Longman & Co.; Liverpool: Thomas Baines, 1854.

Pope-Hennessy, James, *The Baths of Absalom: A Footnote to Froude*, London: Allan Wingate, 1954.

Prichard, Hesketh, *Where Black Rules White: A Journey Across and About Haiti*, New York: Charles Scribner's Sons, 1900.

Reboux, Paul [pseud. Paul Amillet], *Blancs et noirs; carnet de voyage: Haïti, Cuba, Jamaïque, États-unis, Texte illustré de nombreuses photographies prises par l'auteur*, Paris: E. Flammarion, 1915 [*c.* 1919].

Redpath, James, *A Guide to Hayti*, Boston: Thayer & Eldridge, 1860.

Reed, William, *The History of Sugar and Sugar Yielding Plants*, London: Longmans, Green & Co., 1866.

Rhodes, Thomas, *Jamaica and the Imperial Direct West India Mail Service*, London: George Philip & Son, 1901.

Robinson, Sir William (Governor of Trinidad and Tobago), *Tobacco: Its Ups and Downs in England and How to Cultivate and Cure it in the West Indies*, Port-of-Spain, Trinidad: Government Printing Office, 1886.

Royal Mail Steam Packet Company, *Tours in the West Indies*, London: n.p., 1901.

St. John, Spencer Buckingham, *Hayti, or the Black Republic*, 2nd edn, London: Smith, Elder & Co. 1884, 1889 [Reprint, London: Frank Cass, 1971].

Saint-Venant, M. [Jean] Barré, *Des Colonies Modernes sous La Zone Torride, et particulièrement de celle de Saint-Domingue*, Paris: Brochot Pere et Co., An X [1802].

Sansay, Eleanor, *Secret History, or the Horrors of St. Domingo*, Philadelphia, 1808.

Schoelcher, Victor, *Colonies Étrangères et Haïti: Résultats de l'Émancipation Anglaise*, Paris: Pagnerre, 1843.

Scott, Sir Sibbald David, *To Jamaica and Back*, London: Chapman & Hall, 1876.

Seabrook, William B., *The Magic Island*, New York: Harcourt, Brace & Co., 1929.

Sloane, Hans, M.D., Fellow of the College of Physicians and Secretary of the Royal Society, *A Voyage to the Islands of Madera, Barbados, Nieves, St. Christophers and Jamaica, with the Natural History of the herbs and trees, four-footed beasts, fishes, birds, insects, reptiles, etc. of the last of those islands*, 2 vols, London: Printed by B.M. for the Author, 1707.

Smith, John, *The True Travels, Adventures and Observations of Captain John Smith in Europe, Asia, Africke, and America, beginning about the yeere 1593, and continued to this present 1629*, 2 vols, from the London edition of 1629. Reprint, Richmond, VA: Franklin Press, 1819.

Stedman, J.G., *Narrative of a Five Years' Expedition Against the Revolted Negroes of Surinam*, London, 1796.

Stoddard, Charles Augustus, *Cruising Among the Caribbees: Summer Days in Winter Months*, London: Kegan Paul, Trench and Trubner & Co., 1895.

Taft, Edna, *A Puritan in Voodoo-land*, Philadelphia: Penn Publishing Co., [1938].

Thompson, Ian, *Bonjour Blanc: A Journey Through Haiti*, Harmondsworth: Penguin, 1992.

Van Dyke, John C., *In the West Indies: Sketches and Studies in Tropic Seas and Islands*, New York and London: Charles Scribner's Sons, 1932.

Waller, John A., *A Voyage in the West Indies*, London, 1820.

Ward, Edward, 'A Trip to Jamaica', in *Five Travel Scripts Commonly Attributed to Edward Ward*, notes by Howard W. Troyer, New York: Facsimile Text Society, ser. 1, vol. 7, 1933 [1698].

Wardlaw, Claude Wilson, *Green Havoc in the Lands of the Caribbean*, Edinburgh and London: William Blackwood & Sons Ltd., 1935.

Waugh, Alexander R., *Hot Countries [The Coloured Countries]*, London: Pan Books, 1948.

Wilcox, Ella Wheeler, *Sailing sunny seas: a story of travel in Jamaica, Honolulu, Haiti, Santo Domingo, Porto Rico, St. Thomas, Dominica, Martinique, Trinidad and the West Indies*, Chicago: W.B. Conkey, 1909.

Wirkus, Lt. Faustin, *The White King of La Gonave*, New York: Doubleday, Doran & Co., 1931.

Woodville, William, *Medical Botany: Containing Systematic and general Descriptions with Plates of all the Medicinal Plants, Indigenous and Exotic, Comprehended in the Materia Medica as published by the Royal College of Physicians of London and Edinburgh*, 4 vols, London: William Phillips, 1810.

Wortley, Lady Emmeline Stuart, *Travels in the United States, etc. During 1849 and 1850*, New York: Harper & Brothers Publishers, 1851.

Secondary works cited

Abbott, E. (1988) *Haiti: The Duvaliers and Their Legacy*, New York: McGraw-Hill.

Agnew, J. (1994) 'Consumer Culture in Historical Perspective', in J. Brewer and R. Porter (eds) *Consumption and the World of Goods*, London and New York: Routledge.

Ahmed, S. (2000) *Strange Encounters: Embodied Others in Postcoloniality*, New York and London: Routledge.

—— (2001) 'Communities that Feel: Intensity, Difference and Attachment', in A. Koivunen and S. Paasonen (eds) *Affective Encounters*, University of Turku: School of Arts, Literature and Music Publication Series.

Ahmed, S., Castañeda, C., Fortier, A., and Sheller, M. (eds), (forthcoming) *Uprootings/Regroundings: Questions of Home and Migration*, Oxford and New York: Berg.

Ahmed, S. and Stacey, J. (eds) (2001) *Thinking Through the Skin*, New York and London: Routledge.

Alexander, M.J. (1997) 'Erotic Autonomy as a Politics of Decolonization: An Anatomy of Feminist and State Practices in the Bahamas Tourist Economy', in J. Alexander and C. Mohanty (eds) *Feminist Genealogies, Colonial Legacies, Democratic Futures*, New York: Routledge.

Alleyne, M. (1980) *Comparative Afro-American: An Historical-Comparative Study of English-based Afro-American Dialects of the New World*, Ann Arbor: Karoma Publishers.

Anstey, R. (1975) *The Atlantic Slave Trade and British Abolition, 1760–1810*, London: Macmillan.

Antoine, R. (1978) *Les Ecrivains français et les antilles*, Paris: G.P. Maisonneuve et Larose.

Aparicio, F. and Chávez-Silverman, S. (eds) (1997) *Tropicalizations: Transcultural Representations of Latinidad*, Hanover and London: University Press of New England.

Appadurai, A. (1996) *Modernity at Large: Cultural Dimensions of Globalization*, Minneapolis: University of Minnesota Press.

Aravamudan, S. (1999) *Tropicopolitans: Colonialism and Agency, 1688–1804*, Durham, NC and London: Duke University Press.

Ashworth, W. (1990) 'Natural History and the Emblematic World View', in D. Lindberg and R. Westman (eds) *Reappraisals of the Scientific Revolution*, Cambridge and New York: Cambridge University Press.

Auguste, R. (1995) 'Health, Population and Family Planning', *Roots*, 1, 3.

Austen, R. and Smith, W. (1992) 'Private Tooth Decay as Public Economic Virtue: The Slave-Sugar triangle, Consumerism, and European Industrialization', in J.E. Inikori and S. Engerman (eds) *The Atlantic Slave Trade: Effects on Economies, Societies and Peoples in Africa, the Americas, and Europe*, Durham, NC and London: Duke University Press.

Austin-Broos, D. (1995) 'Gay Nights and Kingston Town: Representations of Kingston, Jamaica', in S. Watson and K. Gibson (eds) *Postmodern Cities and Spaces*, Cambridge, MA and Oxford: Blackwell.

Back, L. (1999) *New Ethnicities and Urban Culture: Racisms and Multiculture in Young Lives*, London: UCL Press, reprint [1996].

Banton, M. (1998) *Racial Theories*, 2nd edn, Cambridge: Cambridge University Press.

Barker, F., Hulme, P., and Iverson, M. (eds) (1998) *Cannibalism and the Colonial World*, Cambridge: Cambridge University Press.

Barrow, C. (ed.) (1998) *Caribbean Portraits: Essays on Gender Ideologies and Identities*, Jamaica: Ian Randle.

Barry, T., Wood, B., and Preusch, D. (1984) *The Other Side of Paradise: Foreign Control in the Caribbean*, New York: Grove Press.

Barty-King, H. and Massel, A. (1983) *Rum: Yesterday and Today*, London: Heinemann.

Basch, L., Glick Schiller, N., and Szanton Blanc, C. (1994) *Nations Unbound: Transnational Projects, Postcolonial Predicaments, and Deterritorialized Nation-States*, Amsterdam: Gordon & Breach.

Bauman, Z. (2000) *Liquid Modernity*, Cambridge: Polity.

Beck, U. (1992) *Risk Society: Towards a New Modernity*, trans. Mark Ritter, London: Sage.

—— (2000) *What is Globalization?* Cambridge: Polity.

Beckles, H. (1989a) *Natural Rebels: A Social History of Enslaved Black Women in Barbados*, London: Zed Books.

—— (1989b) *White Servitude and Black Slavery in Barbados, 1627–1715*, Knoxville: University of Tennessee Press.

—— (1999) *Centering Woman: Gender Discourses in Caribbean Slave Society*, Kingston: Ian Randle; Princeton: Markus Weiner; Oxford: James Currey.

Benítez-Rojo, A. (1989) *La isla que se repite. El caribe y la perspectiva posmoderna*, Hanover: Ediciones del Norte.

—— (1996 [1992]) *The Repeating Island: The Caribbean and the Postmodern Perspective*, 2nd edn, trans. J.E. Maraniss, Durham, NC and London: Duke University Press.

Berger, J. (1972) *Ways of Seeing*, London: British Broadcasting Corporation and Penguin Books.

Bermingham, A. (1986) *Landscape and Ideology: The English Rustic Tradition, 1740–1860*, Berkeley: University of California Press.

—— (1995) 'Introduction: Image, Object, Text', in A. Bermingham and J. Brewer (eds) *The Consumption of Culture, 1600–1800: Image, Object, Text*, London and New York: Routledge.

Bermingham, A. and Brewer, J. (eds) (1995) *The Consumption of Culture, 1600–1800: Image, Object, Text*, London and New York: Routledge.

Bernal, M. (1987) *Black Athena: The Afroasiatic Roots of Classical Civilization*, London: Vintage.

Berry, C. (1994) *The Idea of Luxury: A Conceptual and Historical Investigation*, Cambridge and New York: Cambridge University Press.

Besson, J. (1995) 'Land. Kinship and Community in the Post-Emancipation Caribbean: A Regional View of the Leewards', in K.F. Olwig (ed.) *Small Islands, Large Questions: Society, Culture and Resistance in the Post-Emancipation Caribbean*, London: Frank Cass.

Bhabha, H. (1983) 'The Other Question . . .', *Screen*, 24, 6 (Nov./Dec.): 18–36.

—— (1994) *The Location of Culture*, London and New York: Routledge.

Blackburn, R. (1988) *The Overthrow of Colonial Slavery, 1776–1848*, London: Verso.

Bolland, N. (1992) 'Creolization and Creole Societies: A Cultural Nationalist View of Caribbean Social History', in A. Hennessey (ed.) *Intellectuals in the Twentieth-Century Caribbean*, Vol. I, London: Macmillan.

Bonanno, A., Busch, L., Freidland, W., Gouveia, L. and Mingione, E. (eds) (1994) *From Columbus to ConAgra: The Globalization of Agriculture and Food*, Lawrence, KS: University of Kansas Press.

Boucher, P. (2000) 'First Impressions: Europeans and Island Caribs in the Pre-colonial Era, 1492–1623', in V. Shepherd and H. Beckles (eds) *Caribbean Slavery in the Atlantic World*, Kingston: Ian Randle; Oxford: James Currey; Princeton: Marcus Weiner.

Bourdieu, P. (1984) *Distinction: A Social Critique of the Judgement of Taste*, London: Routledge & Kegan Paul.

Bradley, L. (2001) *Bass Culture: When Reggae was King*, London and New York: Penguin Books [Viking].

Braidotti, R. (1994) *Nomadic Subjects: Embodiment and Sexual Difference in Contemporary Feminist Theory*, New York: Columbia University Press.

Brathwaite, E.K. (1971) *The Development of Creole Society in Jamaica 1770–1820*, Oxford: Clarendon Press.

Breen, T.H. (1986) 'An Empire of Goods: The Anglicization of Colonial America, 1690–1776', *Journal of British Studies*, 25: 467–99.

Brereton, B. (1995) 'Text, Testimony and Gender: An Examination of Some Texts by Women in the English-speaking Caribbean, from the 1770s to the 1920s', in V. Shepherd *et al.* (eds) *Engendering History: Caribbean Women in Historical Perspective*, Kingston: Ian Randle; London: James Currey.

Brewer, J. and Porter, R. (eds) (1994) *Consumption and the World of Goods*, London and New York: Routledge.

Bridenbaugh, C. and Bridenbaugh, R. (1972) *No Peace Beyond the Line: The English in the Caribbean, 1624–1690*, London: Open University Press.

Britton, C. (1996) 'Eating their Words: The Consumption of French Caribbean Literature', *Association for the Study of Caribbean and African Literature in French (ASCALF) Yearbook*, 1: 15–23.

Brockway, L. (1979) *Science and Colonial Expansion: The Role of the British Royal Botanic Gardens*, New York and London: Academic Press.

Brown, K. (1991) *Mama Lola: A Vodou Priestess in Brooklyn*, Berkley: University of California Press.

Brown, L. (1993) *Ends of Empire: Women and Ideology in Early Eighteenth-century English Literature*, Ithaca: Cornell University Press.

Browning, B. (1998) *Infectious Rhythm: Metaphors of Contagion and the Spread of African Culture*, New York and London: Routledge.

Burton, A. (1997) 'Who Needs the Nation? Interrogating "British" History', *Journal of Historical Sociology*, 10, 3: 227–48.

Burton, R. (1997) *Afro-Creole: Power, Opposition and Play in the Caribbean*, Ithaca and London: Cornell University Press.

Bush, B. (1990) *Slave Women in Caribbean Society 1650–1838*, London: James Currey; Kingston: Heinnemann; Bloomington: Indiana University Press.

—— (1996) 'Hard Labor: Women, Childbirth, and Resistance in British Caribbean Slave Societies', in B. Gaspar and D. Hine (eds) *More Than Chattel: Black Women and Slavery in the Americas*, Bloomington: Indiana University Press.

Campbell, C. (1987) *The Romantic Ethic and the Spirit of Modern Consumerism*, Oxford: Basil Blackwell.

Cannon, F.M. (1994) 'Botanical Collections', in A. MacGregor (ed.) *Sir Hans Sloane: Collector, Scientist, Antiquary, Founding Father of the British Museum*, London: British Museum Press.

Castles, S. and Miller, M. (1998) *The Age of Migration: International Population Movement in the Modern World*, 2nd edn, Houndsmills and Basingstoke: Macmillan.

Chamberlain, M. (1995) 'Gender and Memory: Oral History and Women's History', in V. Shepherd *et al.* (eds) *Engendering History: Caribbean Women in Historical Perspective*, Kingston: Ian Randle; London: James Currey.

—— (ed.) (1998) *Caribbean Migration: Globalised Identities*, London and New York: Routledge.

Chaney, E. (1987) 'The Context of Caribbean Migration', in C. Sutton and E. Chaney (eds) *Caribbean Life in New York City: Sociocultural Dimensions*, New York: The Center for Migration Studies of New York, Inc.

Clifford, J. (1988) *The Predicament of Culture: Twentieth-Century Ethnography, Literature and Art*, Cambridge, MA: Harvard University Press.

—— (1989) 'Notes on Theory and Travel', in J. Clifford and V. Dhareshwar (eds) *Traveling Theory, Traveling Theorists, Inscriptions*, 5: 177–88.

—— (1992) 'Travelling Cultures', in L. Grossberg, C. Nelson, and P. Treichler (eds) *Cultural Studies*, New York: Routledge.

—— (1997) *Routes: Travel and Translation in the Late Twentieth Century*, Cambridge, MA: Harvard University Press.

Clifford, J. and Dhareshwar, V. (eds) (1989) *Traveling Theory, Traveling Theorists, Inscriptions*, 5, Santa Cruz: Group for the Critical Study of Colonial Discourse and the Center for Cultural Studies.

Clift, S. and Carter, S. (eds) (1999) *Tourism and Sex: Culture, Commerce and Coercion*, London and New York: Pinter.

Collinson, H. (1996) *Green Guerrillas: Environmental Conflicts and Initiatives in Latin America and the Caribbean*, London: LAB.

Cook, I. and Crang, P. (1996) 'The World on a Plate: Culinary Culture, Displacement and Geographical Knowledges', *Journal of Material Culture* 1: 131–54.

Cook, I. and Harrison, M. (2001) 'Not Eating the Other: Jamaican Hot Pepper Sauces as Material Culture', paper presented to the School of Geography, University of Nottingham, 25 October 2001.

Cook, I., Crouch, D., Naylor, S., and Ryan, J. (eds) (2000) *Cultural Turns/Geographical Turns: Perspectives on Cultural Geography*, Harlow: Longman.

Cooper, C. (1993) *Noises in the Blood: Orality, Gender, and the 'Vulgar' Body of Jamaican Popular Culture*, Durham, NC: Duke University Press.

Cooper, F., Holt, T., and Scott, R. (2000) *Beyond Slavery: Explorations of Race, Labor, and Citizenship in Postemancipation Societies*, Chapel Hill and London: University of North Carolina Press.

Cox, C. (1992) *Chocolate Unwrapped: The Politics of Pleasure*, London: Women's Environmental Network.

Craton, M. (1982) *Testing the Chains: Resistance to Slavery in the British West Indies*, Ithaca: Cornell University Press.

Cresswell, T. (2001) 'The Production of Mobilities', in T. Cresswell (ed.) 'Mobilities' issue of *new formations*, 43 (Spring 2001): 11–25.

Cronin, A. (forthcoming) *Advertising Myths: Animating Images, Consuming Addiction, Compulsive Self*, London: Routledge.

Crosby, A. (1972) *The Columbian Exchange: Biological and Cultural Consequences of 1492*, Westport, CT: Greenwood Press.

Curtin, P. (1969) *The Atlantic Slave Trade: A Census*, Madison: University of Wisconsin Press.

—— (1989) *Death by Migration: Europe's Encounter with the Tropical World in the Nineteenth Century*, Cambridge: Cambridge University Press.

Dabydeen, D. (1987) *Hogarth's Blacks: Images of Blacks in Eighteenth-Century English Art*, Athens, GA: University of Georgia Press.

Dash, J.M. (ed.) (1989) *Caribbean Discourse: Selected Essays*, Charlottesville: University of Virginia Press.

—— (1997) *Haiti and the United States: National Stereotypes and the Literary Imagination*, 2nd edn, Houndsmills and Basingstoke: Macmillan.

Davies, P. (1990) *Fyffes and the Banana: Musa Sapientum. A Centenary History, 1888–1988*, London and Atlantic Highlands, NJ: Athlone Press.

Davis, C. and Gates, H.L. (eds) (1985) *The Slave's Narrative*, New York: Oxford University Press.

Davis, D.B. (1975) *The Problem of Slavery in the Age of Revolution, 1770–1823*, Ithaca: Cornell University Press.

Davis, W. (1986) *The Serpent and the Rainbow*, London: Collins.

—— (1988) *Passage of Darkness: The Ethnobiology of the Haitian Zombie*, Chapel Hill: University of North Carolina Press.

Day, M. (1994) 'Humana: Anatomical, Pathological and Curious Human Specimens in Sloane's Museum', in A. MacGregor (ed.) *Sir Hans Sloane: Collector, Scientist, Antiquary, Founding Father of the British Museum*, London: British Museum Press.

Dayan, J. (1998) *Haiti, History and the Gods*, Berkeley and London: University of California Press.

Deere, C.D. *et al.* (eds) (1990) *In the Shadows of the Sun: Caribbean Development Alternatives and United States Policy*, Boulder: Westview Press.

Deerr, N. (1950) *The History of Sugar*, 2 vols, London: Chapman & Hall Ltd.

DeGraff, M. (2001) 'Morphology in Creole Genesis: Linguistics and Ideology', in M. Kenstowicz (ed.) *Ken Hale: A Life in Language*, Cambridge, MA: Massachusetts Institute of Technology.

Deleuze, G. and Guattari, F. (1992) *A Thousand Plateaus: Capitalism and Schizophrenia*, trans. B. Massumi, London: Athlone Press.

Dhareshwar, V. (1989) 'Toward a Narrative Epistemology of the Postcolonial Predicament', in J. Clifford and V. Dhareshwar (eds) *Traveling Theory, Traveling Theorists*, *Inscriptions*, 5, Santa Cruz: Group for the Critical Study of Colonial Discourse and the Center for Cultural Studies.

Drescher, S. (1977) *Econocide: British Slavery in the Era of Abolition*, Pittsburgh: Pittsburgh University Press.

—— (1982) 'Public Opinion and the Destruction of British Colonial Slavery', in J. Walvin (ed.) *Slavery and British Society, 1776–1846*, Baton Rouge: Louisiana State University Press, pp. 22–48.

—— (1987) *Capitalism and Antislavery: British Mobilization in Comparative Perspective*, New York: Oxford University Press.

—— (1994) 'The Long Goodbye: Dutch Capitalism and Antislavery in Comparative Perspective', *American Historical Review*, 99, 1: 44–69.

Dresser, M. (2000) 'Squares of Distinction, Webs of Interest: Gentility, Urban Development and the Slave Trade in Bristol, *c.* 1673–1820', *Slavery and Abolition*, 21, 3: 21–47.

Dresser, M., Jordan, C., and Taylor, D. (1998) 'Slave Trade Trail around Central Bristol', pamphlet published by Bristol Museums and Art Gallery, and Bristol City Council.

Duncan, J. (1999) 'Dis-orientation: On the Shock of the Familiar in a Far-away Place', in J. Duncan and D. Gregory (eds) (1999) *Writes of Passage: Reading Travel Writing*, London and New York: Routledge.

Duncan, J. and Gregory, D. (eds) (1999) *Writes of Passage: Reading Travel Writing*, London and New York: Routledge.

Dunn, R. (1972) *Sugar and Slaves: The Rise of the Planter Class in the English West Indies, 1624–1713*, Chapel Hill: University of North Carolina Press.

Dyer, R. (1997) *White*, London and New York: Routledge.

Elder, M. (1992) *The Slave Trade and the Economic Development of Eighteenth-Century Lancaster*, Krumlin, Halifax: Ryburn Publishers.

—— (1996) 'Lancaster and the African Slave Trade', *Local Studies*, 14, Lancaster City Museums.

Eltis, D. (1987) *Economic Growth and the Ending of the Transatlantic Slave Trade*, New York and Oxford: Oxford University Press.

Emirbayer, M. and Sheller, M. (1999) 'Publics in History', *Theory and Society*, 28: 145–97.

Enloe, C. (1989) *Bananas, Beaches, and Bases: Making Feminist Sense of International Politics*, London and Sydney: Pandora.

Fanon, F. (1968) *Black Skin, White Masks*, New York: Grove Weidenfeld [Paris: Editions du Seuil, 1952].

Farmer, P. (1992) *AIDS and Accusation: Haiti and the Geography of Blame*, Berkeley: University of California Press.

—— (1994) *The Uses of Haiti*, Monroe, ME: Common Courage Press.

—— (1999) *Infections and Inequalities: The Modern Plagues*, Berkeley: University of California Press.

Featherstone, M. (1995) *Undoing Culture: Globalization, Postmodernism and Identity*, London: Newbury Park and New Delhi: Sage Publications.

Felsenstein, F. (ed.) (1999) *English Trader, Indian Maid: Representing Gender, Race, and Slavery in the New World, An Inkle and Yarico Reader*, Baltimore and London: Johns Hopkins University Press.

Ferguson, M. (1991) 'Juggling the Categories of Race, Class and Gender: Aphra Behn's *Oroonoko*', *Women's Studies*, 19.

Fick, C. (1990) *The Making of Haiti: The Saint Domingue Revolution from Below*, Knoxville: University of Tennessee Press.

Fine, B. (1995) 'From Political Economy to Consumption', in D. Miller (ed.) *Acknowledging Consumption: A Review of New Studies*, London and New York: Routledge.

Fine, B., Heasman, M., and Wright, J. (1996) *Consumption in the Age of Affluence: The World of Food*, London and New York: Routledge.

Fisch, A. (2000) *American Slaves in Victorian England: Abolitionist Politics in Popular Literature and Culture*, Cambridge: Cambridge University Press.

Forbes, J. (1992) *Columbus and Other Cannibals: The Wetiko Disease of Exploitation, Imperialism, and Terrorism*, New York: Autonomedia.

Fortier, A. (2000) *Migrant Belongings*, Oxford and New York: Berg.

Frankenberg, R. (1993) *White Women, Race Matters*, Minneapolis: University of Minnesota Press.

Franklin, S., Lury, C., and Stacey, J. (2000) *Global Nature, Global Culture*, London: Sage.

Fraser, N. (1992) 'Rethinking the Public Sphere', in C. Calhoun (ed.) *Habermas and the Public Sphere*, Cambridge and London: MIT Press, pp. 109–42.

Freeman, C. (2000) *High Tech and High Heels in the Global Economy*, Durham, NC and London: Duke University Press.

Fryer, P. (1984) *Staying Power: Black People in Britain Since 1504*, Atlantic Highlands, NJ: Humanities Press.

—— (1998) 'The "Discovery" and Appropriation of African Music and Dance', *Race and Class*, 39, 3: 1–20.

Gates, H.L. (ed.) (1987) *The Classic Slave Narratives*, New York: Mentor.

Genovese, E. (1979) *From Rebellion to Revolution: Afro-American Slave Revolts in the Making of the New World*, New York: Vintage [1981].

Georges, E. (1990) *The Making of a Transnational Community: Migration, Development and Cultural Change in the Dominican Republic*, New York: Columbia University Press.

Gerzina, G. (1995) *Black London: Life Before Emancipation*, New Brunswick: Rutgers University Press.

Giddens, A. (1990) *The Consequences of Modernity*, Cambridge: Polity Press.

—— (1991) *Modernity and Self-Identity: Self and Society in the Late Modern Age*, Cambridge: Polity Press.

Gilroy, P. (1991) *'There Ain't No Black in the Union Jack': The Cultural Politics of Race and Nation*, Chicago: University of Chicago Press.

—— (1993) *The Black Atlantic: Modernity and Double Consciousness*, London and New York: Verso.

—— (2000) *Between Camps: Nations, Cultures and the Allure of Race*, London and New York: Penguin.

Glennie, P. (1995) 'Consumption Within Historical Studies', in D. Miller (ed.) *Acknowledging Consumption: A Review of New Studies*, London and New York: Routledge.

Glissant, E. (1981) *Le Discours Antillais*, Paris: Editions du Seuil.

Goodman, D. and Redclift, M. (1991) *Refashioning Nature: Food, Ecology, Culture*, London and New York: Routledge.

Goodman, D. and Watts, M. (eds) (1997) *Globalising Food: Agrarian Questions and Global Restructuring*, London and New York: Routledge.

Goodrich, J. and Gayle, D. (1993) *Tourism Marketing and Management in the Caribbean*, London: Routledge.

Graham, S. and Marvin, S. (2001) *Splintering Urbanism: Networked Infrastructures, Technological Mobilities and the Urban Condition*, London and New York: Routledge.

Greenblatt, S. (1991) *Marvelous Possessions: The Wonder of the New World*, Oxford: Clarendon.

Greene, G. (1966) *The Comedians*, New York: Viking Press; London: Bodley Head.

Greene, R. (2000) *Unrequited Conquest: Love and Empire in the Colonial Americas*, Chicago: University of Chicago Press.

Gregory, D. (1999) 'Scripting Egypt: Orientalism and the Cultures of Travel', in J. Duncan and D. Gregory (eds) *Writes of Passage: Reading Travel Writing*, London and New York: Routledge.

Grossman, L. (1998) *The Political Ecology of Bananas: Contract Farming, Peasants and Agrarian Change in the Eastern Caribbean*, Chapel Hill and London: University of North Carolina Press.

Grove, R. (1995) *Green Imperialism: Colonial Expansion, Tropical Island Edens and the Origins of Environmentalism, 1600–1860*, Cambridge: Cambridge University Press.

Gunst, L. (1995) *Born fi' Dead: A Journey Through the Jamaican Posse Underworld*, Edinburgh: Payback Press.

Habermas, J. (1989) *The Structural Transformation of the Public Sphere*, Cambridge, MA: MIT Press.

Haggis, A.W. (1941) 'Fundamental Errors in the Early History of Cinchona', *The Bulletin of the History of Medicine*, 10, 3/4 (Oct./Nov.).

Hall, C. (1992) *White, Male, and Middle Class: Explorations in Feminism and History*, Cambridge: Polity Press.

Hall, D. (ed.) (1989) *In Miserable Slavery: Thomas Thistlewood in Jamaica, 1750–1786*, London: Macmillan.

Hall, I.V. (1925) 'A History of the Sugar Trade in England, with Special Attention to the Sugar Trade of Bristol', unpublished MA thesis, University of Bristol.

Hall, K. (1996) 'Culinary Spaces, Colonial Spaces: the Gendering of Sugar in the Seventeenth Century', in V. Traub, M.L. Kaplan, and D. Callaghan (eds) *Feminist Readings of Modern Culture*, Cambridge: Cambridge University Press, pp. 168–90.

Hall, R.L. (1991) 'Savoring Africa in the New World', in H. Viola and C. Margolis (eds) *Seeds of Change: Five Hundred Years Since Columbus*, Washington and London: Smithsonian Institution Press.

Hall, S. (1990) 'Cultural Identity and Diaspora', in J. Rutherford (ed.) *Identity: Community, Culture Difference*, London: Lawrence & Wishart.

—— (1991) 'Old and New Identities, Old and New Ethnicities', in A. King (ed.) *Culture, Globalisation and the World System: Contemporary Conditions for the Representation of Identity*, London: Macmillan.

—— (1996) 'When was "The Post-Colonial"? Thinking at the Limit', in I. Chambers and L. Curti (eds) *The Post-Colonial Question*, London: Routledge.

Hannerz, U. (1987) 'The World in Creolisation', *Africa* 57, 5: 546–59.

—— (1989) 'Culture between Center and Periphery: Toward a Macroanthropology', *Ethnos*, 54, 3/4: 200–16.

—— (1996) *Transnational Connections*, London: Routledge.

—— (2000) 'Flows, Boundaries and Hybrids: Keywords in Transnational Anthropology', in A. Rogers (ed.) *Transnational Communities Programme*, Working Paper Series, WPTC-2K-02.

Harvey, D. (1989) *The Condition of Postmodernity*, Oxford: Blackwell.

Hattox, R. (1985) *Coffee and Coffeehouses: The Origins of a Social Beverage in the Medieval Near East*, London: University of Washington Press.

Helg, A. (1995) *Our Rightful Share: The Afro-Cuban Struggle for Equality, 1886–1912*, Chapel Hill and London: University of North Carolina Press.

Henige, D. (1978) 'On the Contact Population of Hispaniola: History as Higher Mathematics', *Hispanic American Historical Review* 58, 2: 217–37.

Herskovits, M. (1964) *The Myth of the Negro Past*, New York: Octagon Books.

Heuman, G. (ed.) (1986) *Out of the House of Bondage: Runaways, Resistance and Marronage in Africa and the New World*, London: Frank Cass.

—— (1994) *'The Killing Time': The Morant Bay Rebellion in Jamaica*, London and Basingstoke: Macmillan Caribbean.

Hewitt, R. (1986) *White Talk, Black Talk: Inter-racial Friendship and Communication amongst Adolescents*, London: Cambridge University Press.

Higman, B.W. (1999) *Writing West Indian Histories*, London and Basingstoke: Macmillan.

Hobhouse, H. (1986) *Seeds of Change: Five Plants that Transformed Mankind*, New York: Harper & Row.

Hoetink, H. (1973) *Slavery and Race Relations in the Americas: An Inquiry into Their Nature and Nexus*, New York: Harper & Row.

—— (1985) '"Race" and Color in the Caribbean', in S. Mintz and S. Price (eds) *Caribbean Contours*, Baltimore and London: Johns Hopkins University Press, pp. 55–84.

Holt, T. (1992) *The Problem of Freedom: Race, Labor, and Politics in Jamaica and Britain, 1832–1938*, Baltimore and London: Johns Hopkins University Press.

hooks, b. (1992) 'Eating the Other', in *Black Looks: Race and Representation*, London: Turnaround, pp. 21–40.

Howard, D. (2001) *Coloring the Nation: Race and Ethnicity in the Dominican Republic*, Oxford: Signal Books.

Howes, D. (ed.) (1996) *Cross-cultural Consumption: Global Markets, Local Realities*, London and New York: Routledge.

Hulme, P. (1986) *Colonial Encounters: Europe and the Native Caribbean, 1492–1797*, London: Methuen.

—— (2000) *Remnants of Conquest: The Island Carib and their Visitors, 1877–1998*, Oxford and New York: Oxford University Press.

Hulme, P. and Sherman, W. (eds) (2000) *'The Tempest' and Its Travels*, London: Reaktion Books.

Hulme, P. and Whitehead, N. (eds) (1992) *Wild Majesty: Europe and the Native Caribbean, 1492–1797*, Oxford and New York: Oxford University Press.

Hurbon, L. (1995) *Voodoo: Truth and Fantasy*, London: Thames and Hudson.

Hurston, Z.N. (1990 [1938]) *Tell my Horse: Voodoo and Life in Haiti and Jamaica*, New York: Harper & Row.

Inikori, J.E. (1992) 'Slavery and the Revolution in Cotton Textile Production in England', in J.E. Inikori and S. Engerman (eds) *The Atlantic Slave Trade: Effects on Economies, Societies, and Peoples in Africa, the Americas, and Europe*, Durham, NC: Duke University Press.

Jackson, P. and Thrift, N. (1995) 'Geographies of Consumption', in D. Miller (ed.) *Acknowledging Consumption: A Review of New Studies*, London and New York: Routledge.

Jacobson, M.F. (1998) *Whiteness of a Different Color: European Immigrants and the Alchemy of Race*, Cambridge and London: Harvard University Press.

James, C.L.R. ([1938] 1989) *The Black Jacobins: Toussaint L'Ouverture and the San Domingo Revolution*, New York: Vintage Books.

James, P. (1998) 'Rethinking Representations: Photographic Archives and Exhibitions in Birmingham Central Library', in S. Wright (ed.) *Cultural Diversity and Citizenship: Report of a Joint UNESCO/University of Birmingham Seminar*.

Jones, D. (1996) *Bristol's Sugar Trade and Refining Industry*, Bristol: Local History Pamphlets.

Joseph, M. (1999) *Nomadic Identities: The Performance of Citizenship*, Minneapolis and London: University of Minnesota Press.

Kaplan, C. (1996) *Questions of Travel: Postmodern Discourses of Displacement*, Durham, NC and London: Duke University Press.

Kaplan, C., Alarcon, N., and Moallem, M. (eds) (1999) *Between Woman and Nation: Nationalisms, Transnational Feminism and the State*, Durham, NC: Duke University Press.

Kempadoo, K. (ed.) (1999) *Sun, Sex, and Gold: Tourism and Sex Work in the Caribbean*, Lanham, MD and Oxford: Rowman and Littlefield.

Kiple, K. (1984) *The Caribbean Slave: A Biological History*, Cambridge: Cambridge University Press.

Klak, T. (ed.) (1998) *Globalization and Neoliberalism: The Caribbean Context*, Lanham, MD and Oxford: Rowman and Littlefield.

Klak, T. and Myers, G. (1998) 'How States Sell Their Countries and Their People', in T. Klak (ed.) *Globalization and Neoliberalism*, Lanham, MD and Oxford: Rowman and Littlefield.

Klein, N. (2000) *No Logo*, London: Flamingo.

Knight, D. (1978) *Gentlemen of Fortune: The Men who made their Fortunes in Britain's Slave Trade*, London: Frederick Muller Ltd.

Knight, F. (1990) *The Caribbean: Genesis of a Fragmented Nationalism*, 2nd edn, New York and Oxford: Oxford University Press [1st edn, 1978].

Kurlansky, M. (1997) *Cod: A Biography of the Fish that Changed the World*, London: Jonathan Cape.

Lamming, G. (1960) *The Pleasures of Exile*, London: Michael Joseph.

Landes, J. (1988) *Women and the Public Sphere in the Age of the French Revolution*, Ithaca and London: Cornell University Press.

Lane, K. (1999) *Blood and Silver: A History of Piracy in the Caribbean and Central America*, Oxford: Signal Books.

Lash, S. and Urry J. (1994) *Economies of Signs and Space*, London: Sage.

Latin America Bureau (1987) 'Green Gold: Bananas and Dependency in the Eastern Caribbean'; ' "Whose Gold?" Geest and the Banana Trade', London: LAB.

Latour, B. (1987) *Science in Action: How to Follow Scientists and Engineers Through Society*, Milton Keynes: Open University Press.

Lavie, S. and Swedenburg, T. (1996) *Displacement, Diasporas, and Geographies of Identity*, Durham, NC: Duke University Press.

Lawson, P. (1997) *A Taste for Empire and Glory: Studies in British Overseas Expansion, 1660–1800*, Aldershot: Variorum.

Lechthaler, E. *et al.* (1997) *Rum Drinks and Havanas: Cuba Classics*, New York: Abbeville Press.

Lee, R.G. (1999) *Orientals: Asian Americans in Popular Culture*, Philadelphia: Temple University Press.

Lemoine, M. (1985) *Bitter Sugar: Slaves Today in the Caribbean*, London: Banner Press.

Le Page, R. and Tabouret-Keller, A. (1985) *Acts of Identity: Creole-Based Approaches to Language and Ethnicity*, Cambridge: Cambridge University Press.

Levine, P. (2000) 'Orientalist Sociology and the Creation of Colonial Sexualities', *Feminist Review*, 65: 5–21.

Lévi-Strauss, C. (1976 [1955]) *Tristes Tropiques*, trans. John and Doreen Weightman, Harmondsworth: Penguin.

Lewis, G.K. (1987) *Main Currents in Caribbean Thought: The Historical Evolution of Caribbean Society in its Ideological Aspects, 1492–1900*, Baltimore: Johns Hopkins University Press.

Lipsitz, G. (1994) *Dangerous Crossroads: Popular Music, Postmodernism and the Poetics of Place*, New York: Verso.

Lowe, L. (1991) *Critical Terrains: French and British Orientalisms*, Ithaca: Cornell University Press.

Lury, C. (1996) *Consumer Culture*, Cambridge: Polity Press.

—— (1997) 'The Objects of Travel', in C. Rojek and J. Urry (eds) *Touring Cultures: Transformations of Travel and Theory*, London and New York: Routledge.

McAfee, K. (1991) *Storm Signals: Structural Adjustment and Development Alternatives in the Caribbean*, London: Zed Books with Oxfam America.

McClintock, A. (1995) *Imperial Leather: Race, Gender and Sexuality in the Colonial Context*, New York and London: Routledge.

McCook, S. (2002) *States of Nature: Science, Agriculture, and Environment in the Spanish Caribbean, 1760–1940*, Austin: University of Texas Press.

McCracken, G. (1990) *Culture and Consumption: New Approaches to the Symbolic Character of Consumer Goods and Activities*, Bloomington and Indianapolis: Indiana University Press.

McFarlane, A. (1994) *The British in the Americas, 1480–1815*, London and New York: Longman.

MacGregor, A. (1994) 'The Life, Character and Career of Sir Hans Sloane', in A. MacGregor (ed.) *Sir Hans Sloane: Collector, Scientist, Antiquary, Founding Father of the British Museum*, London: British Museum Press.

MacInnes, C.M. (1939) *A Gateway of Empire*, Bristol: J.W. Arrowsmith Ltd.

McKendrick, N., Brewer J., and Plumb, J.H. (eds) (1992) *The Birth of a Consumer Society: the Commercialization of Eighteenth-Century England*, London: Europa.

Macnaghten, P. and Urry, J. (1998) *Contested Natures*, London: Sage.

McWhorter, J. (1998) 'Identifying the Creole Prototype: Vindicating a Typological Class', *Language*, 74: 788–818.

Manthorne, K. (1989) *Tropical Renaissance: North American Artists Exploring Latin America, 1839–1879*, Washington, DC: Smithsonian Institution Press.

Manuel, P. (1995) *Caribbean Currents: Caribbean Music from Rumba to Reggae*, Philadelphia: Temple University Press.

Marsden, T. (1997) 'Creating Space for Food: The Distinctiveness of Recent Agrarian Development', in D. Goodman and M. Watts (eds) *Globalising Food: Agrarian Questions and Global Restructuring*, London and New York: Routledge.

Marsden, T. and Little, J. (1990) *Political, Social and Economic Perspectives on the International Food System*, Aldershot: Avebury.

Martin, S.I. (1999) *Britain's Slave Trade*, Basingstoke: Macmillan.

Martinez-Alier, V. (1989) *Marriage, Class and Colour in Nineteenth-Century Cuba: A Study of Racial and Sexual Values in a Slave Society*, Ann Arbor: University of Michigan Press.

Massey, D. (1999) 'Imagining Globalization: Power-geometrics of Time-Space', in A. Brah *et al.* (eds) *Global Futures*, Basingstoke and London: Macmillan.

Maurer, B. (1997) 'Fractions of Blood on Fragments of Soil: Capitalism, The Commons, and Kinship in the Caribbean', *Plantation Society in the Americas*, 4: 2/3 (Fall): 159–71.

Mercer, K. (1988) 'Diaspora Culture and the Dialogic Imagination: The Aesthetics of Black Independent Film in Britain', in M.B. Cham and C. Andrade-Watkins (eds) *Blackframes: Critical Perspectives on Black Independent Cinema*, Cambridge, MA: MIT Press.

—— (1994) *Welcome to the Jungle: New Positions in Black Cultural Studies*, New York: Routledge.

Midgley, C. (1992) *Women Against Slavery: The British Campaigns, 1780–1870*, London and New York: Routledge.

Miller, C. (1985) *Blank Darkness: Africanist Discourse in French*, Chicago: University of Chicago Press.

Miller, D. (1994) *Modernity: An Ethnographic Approach, Dualism and Mass Consumption in Trinidad*, Oxford and London: Berg.

—— (1995) 'Consumption as the Vanguard of History: A Polemic by Way of Introduction', in D. Miller (ed.) *Acknowledging Consumption: A Review of New Studies*, London and New York: Routledge.

—— (1997) *Modernity: An Ethnographic Approach*, Oxford and New York: Berg.

Miller, D. and Slater, D. (2000) *The Internet: An Ethnographic Approach*, Oxford and New York: Berg.

Minter, S. (1998) 'Garden of World Medicine', pamphlet printed by the Chelsea Physic Garden Company, London.

—— (2000) *The Apothecaries' Garden: A History of the Chelsea Physic Garden*, Stroud: Sutton Publishing Ltd.

Mintz, S. (1960) *Worker in the Cane: A Puerto Rican Life History*, New Haven: Yale University Press [New York and London: W.W. Norton & Co. (1974)].

—— (1985) *Sweetness and Power: The Place of Sugar in Modern History*, New York: Viking.

—— (1993) 'The Changing Roles of Food in the Study of Consumption', in J. Brewer and R. Porter (eds), *Consumption and the World of Goods*, London and New York: Routledge.

—— (1996) *Tasting Food, Tasting Freedom: Excursions into Eating, Culture and the Past*, Boston: Beacon Press.

Mintz, S. and Price, R. (1992 [1976]) *The Birth of African-American Culture: An Anthropological Perspective*, Boston: Beacon Press.

Mohammed, P. (1998) 'Towards Indigenous Feminist Theorizing in the Caribbean', in 'Rethinking Caribbean Difference' issue, *Feminist Review*, 59: 6–33.

Mohanty, C. (1991) 'Under Western Eyes: Feminist Scholarship and Colonial Discourses', in C. Mohanty, A. Russo, and L. Torres (eds) *Third World Women and the Politics of Feminism*, Bloomington: Indiana University Press.

Momsen, J.H. (ed.) (1993) *Women and Change in the Caribbean*, Kingston: Ian Randle; Bloomington: Indiana University Press; London: James Currey.

—— (1998) 'Caribbean Tourism and Agriculture: New Linkages in the Global Era', in T. Klak (ed.) *Globalization and Neoliberalism in the Caribbean Context*, Lanham, MD and Oxford: Rowman and Littlefield.

Morgan, K. (1993) *Bristol and the Atlantic Trade in the Eighteenth Century*, Cambridge: Cambridge University Press.

Morrison, T. (1992) *Playing in the Dark: Whiteness and the Literary Imagination*, Cambridge, MA and London: Harvard University Press.

Morrissey, M. (1989) *Slave Women in the New World: Gender Stratification in the Caribbean*, Lawrence, KS: University of Kansas Press.

Morton, T. (2000a) *The Poetics of Spice: Romantic Consumerism and the Exotic*, Cambridge and New York: Cambridge University Press.

—— (ed.) (2000b) *Radical Food: The Culture and Politics of Eating and Drinking, 1790–1820*, Vol. 1: *Ethics and Politics*, London: Routledge.

Mudimbe, V.Y. (1988) *The Invention of Africa: Gnosis, Philosophy, and the Order of Knowledge*, Bloomington: Indiana University Press.

Mukerji, C. (1983) *From Graven Images: Patterns of Modern Materialism*, New York: Columbia University Press.

—— (1994) 'Reading and Writing with Nature: A Materialist Approach to French Formal Gardens', in J. Brewer and R. Porter (eds) *Consumption and the World of Goods*, London and New York: Routledge.

Nettleford, R.M. (1978) *Caribbean Cultural Identity: The Case of Jamaica, An Essay in Cultural Dynamics*, Kingston: Institute of Jamaica.

North American Congress on Latin America, (NACLA) (1995) *Haiti: Dangerous Crossroads*, Boston, MA: South End Press.

Nuermberger, R. (1942) *The Free Produce Movement: A Quaker Protest Against Slavery*, Durham, NC: University of North Carolina Press.

Okihiro, G. (ed.) (1986) *In Resistance: Studies in African, Caribbean, and Afro-American History*, Amherst: University of Massachussetts Press.

Oldfield, J.R. (1995) *Popular Politics and British Anti-Slavery: The Mobilisation of Public Opinion against the Slave Trade, 1787–1807*, Manchester and New York: Manchester University Press.

O'Leary, B. (1989) *The Asiatic Mode of Production*, London: Basil Blackwell.

Oostindie, G. (ed.) (2001) *Facing up to the Past: Perspectives on the Commemoration of Slavery from Africa, the Americas and Europe*, Kingston, Jamaica: Ian Randle.

Ortiz, F. (1940) *Contrapunto Cubano del tabaco y el azucar*, La Habana: J. Montero [*Cuban Counterpoint: Tobacco and Sugar*, trans. Harriet de Onis, New York: A.A. Knopf, 1947].

Pack, A.J. (1982) *Nelson's Blood: The Story of Naval Rum*, Homewell, Hampshire: Kenneth Mason.

Parker, A. (1991) *Nationalism and Sexuality*, New York: Routledge.

Patterson, O. (1982) *Slavery and Social Death: A Comparative Study*, Cambridge, MA: Harvard University Press.

—— (1991) *Freedom in the Making of Western Culture*, Cambridge, MA: Harvard University Press.

Pattullo, P. (1996) *Last Resorts: The Cost of Tourism in the Caribbean*, London: Cassell/Latin America Bureau.

Paulson, R. (1987) *Representations of Revolution*, New Haven: Yale University Press.

Phillips, W.D., Jr (1991) 'The Old World Background of Slavery in the Americas', in B. Solow (ed.) *Slavery and the Rise of the Atlantic System*, Cambridge: Cambridge University Press.

Pieterse, J. (1992 [1990]) *White on Black: Images of Africa and Blacks in Western Popular Culture*, London and New Haven: Yale University Press.

Pleij, H. (2001) *Dreaming of Cockaigne: Medieval Fantasies of the Perfect Life*, trans. Diane Webb, New York: Columbia University Press [Amsterdam: Prometheus 1997].

Plummer, B.G. (1988) *Haiti and the Great Powers, 1902–1915*, Baton Rouge and London: Louisiana State University Press.

Poole, D. (1998) 'Landscape and the Imperial Subject: U.S. Images of the Andes, 1859–1930', in G. Joseph, C. Legrand, and R. Salvatore (eds) *Close Encounters of Empire: Writing the Cultural History of U.S.–Latin American Relations*, Durham, NC and London: Duke University Press, pp. 107–38.

Porter, R. (1994) 'Consumption: Disease of the Consumer Society?', in J. Brewer and R. Porter (eds) *Consumption and the World of Goods*, London and New York: Routledge.

Poupeye, V. (1998) *Caribbean Art*, London: Thames & Hudson.

Pratt, M.L. (1992) *Imperial Eyes: Travel Writing and Transculturation*, London: Routledge.

Prest, J. (1981) *The Garden of Eden: The Botanic Garden and the Recreation of Paradise*, New Haven and London: Yale University Press.

Price, R. (ed.) (1973) *Maroon Societies*, New York: Anchor.

—— (1983) *First Time: The Historical Vision of an Afro-American People*, Baltimore: Johns Hopkins University Press.

Probyn, E. (2000) *Carnal Appetites: Foodsexidentities*, London and New York: Routledge.

Puri, S. (2003) *The Caribbean Postcolonial: Post/Nationalism, Social Equality, and Cultural Hybridity*, New York: St. Martin's.

—— (ed.) (forthcoming) *Marginal Migrations: The Circulation of Cultures within the Caribbean*, London and Oxford: Macmillan.

Richards, G. (2001) 'Kamau Brathwaite and the Creolization of History in the Anglophone Caribbean', unpublished paper.

Richards, G. and Shepherd, V. (eds), (forthcoming) *Caribbean Intellectual Traditions*, 6 vols, Mona, Jamaica: University of the West Indies Press.

Richards, T. (1993) *The Imperial Archive: Knowledge and the Fantasy of Empire*, London: Verso.

Robertson, R. (1992) *Globalization: Social Theory and Global Culture*, London: Sage.

Root, D. (1998) *Cannibal Culture: Art, Appropriation, and the Commodification of Difference*, Boulder and Oxford: Westview Press.

Ryan, M. (1990) *Women in Public*, Baltimore: Johns Hopkins University Press.

—— (1992) 'Gender and Public Access', in C. Calhoun (ed.) *Habermas and the Public Sphere*, Cambridge and London: MIT Press, pp. 259–88.

—— (1997) *Civic Wars: Democracy and Public Life in the American City During the Nineteenth Century*, Berkeley and Los Angeles: University of California Press.

Said, E. (1989) 'Representing the Colonized: Anthropology's Interlocutors', *Critical Inquiry* 15, 2: 205–25.

—— (1991 [1978]) *Orientalism*, Harmondsworth: Penguin.

—— (1993) *Culture and Imperialism*, London: Chatto & Windus.

Salewicz, C. (2000) *Rude Boy: Once Upon a Time in Jamaica*, London: Victor Gollancz.

—— (2001) 'The Legend Lives On', *BWIA Caribbean Beat*, May/June): 44–9.

Salvatore, R. (1996) 'North American Travel Narratives and the Ordering/Othering of South America (*c.* 1810–1860)', *Journal of Historical Sociology*, 9: 1 (March): 85–110.

—— (1998) 'The Enterprise of Knowledge: Representational Machines of Informal Empire', in G. Joseph, C. Legrand, and R. Salvatore (eds) *Close Encounters of Empire: Writing the Cultural History of U.S.–Latin American Relations*, Durham, NC and London: Duke University Press.

Sánchez Taylor, J. (1999) 'Tourism and "Embodied" Commodities: Sex Tourism in the Caribbean', in S. Clift and S. Carter (eds) *Tourism and Sex*, London and New York: Pinter.

Schama, S. (1987) *The Embarrassment of Riches*, London: Fontana.

—— (1994) 'Perishable Commodities: Dutch Still-life Paintings and the "Empire of Things"', in J. Brewer and R. Porter (eds) *Consumption and the World of Goods*, London and New York: Routledge.

—— (1995) *Landscape and Memory*, New York: A.A. Knopf.

Schiller, N.G., Basch, L., and Blanc-Szanton, C. (eds) (1992) *Towards a Transnational Perspective on Migration: Race, Class, Ethnicity and Nationalism Reconsidered*, New York: New York Academy of Sciences, Annals, 645.

Schivelbusch, W. (1992) *Tastes of Paradise: A Social History of Spices, Stimulants, and Intoxicants*, trans. David Jacobson, New York: Pantheon [1980].

Schwarz, B. (ed.) (1996) *The Expansion of England: Race, Ethnicity and Cultural History*, New York and London: Routledge.

Sebba, M. (1997) *Contact Languages: Pidgins and Creoles*, London: Macmillan.

Segal, R. (1995) *The Black Diaspora*, London and Boston: Faber & Faber.

Sekora, J. (1977) *Luxury: The Concept in Western Thought, Eden to Smollett*, Baltimore: Johns Hopkins University Press.

Selvon, S. (1956) *The Lonely Londoners*, New York: St. Martin's Press.

Shammas, C. (1990) *The Pre-Industrial Consumer in England and America*, Oxford: Oxford University Press.

Sharpley-Whiting, T.D. (1999) *Black Venus: Sexualized Savages, Primal Fears and Primitive Narratives in French*, Durham, NC and London: Duke University Press.

Sheller, M. (1999) 'The Haytian Fear: Racial Projects and Competing Reactions to the First Black Republic', *Research in Politics and Society*, Vol. 6, P. Batur-Vanderlippe and J. Feagan (eds), Greenwich, CT: JAI Press.

—— (2000) *Democracy After Slavery: Black Publics and Peasant Radicalism in Haiti and Jamaica*, Oxford and London: Macmillan Caribbean.

—— (forthcoming) 'Haiti, 1492–1992', in *The Literature of Travel and Exploration*, London: Fitzroy Dearborn.

Sheller, M. and Urry, J. (2002) 'Mobile Transformations of Public and Private Life', *Theory, Culture, and Society*, 19, 5.

Shepherd, V. and Beckles, H. (eds) (2000) *Caribbean Slavery in the Atlantic World*, Kingston: Ian Randle; Oxford: James Currey; Princeton: Marcus Weiner.

Shepherd, V., Brereton, B., and Bailey, B. (eds) (1995) *Engendering History: Caribbean Women in Historical Perspective*, Kingston: Ian Randle; London: James Currey.

Sheridan, R. (1985) *Doctors and Slaves: A Medical and Demographic History of Slavery in the British West Indies, 1680–1834*, Cambridge: Cambridge University Press.

Shohat, E. and Stam, R. (2000 [1994]) *Unthinking Eurocentrism: Multiculturalism and the Media*, London and New York: Routledge.

Sistren with H. Ford-Smith (1986) *Lionheart Gal: Life Stories of Jamaican Women*, London: Women's Press.

Skinner, E. (1998) 'The Caribbean Data Processors', in G. Sussman and J. Lent (eds) *Global Productions: Labor in the Making of the 'Information Society'*, Cresskill, NJ: Hampton Press.

Smith, M.G. (1965) *The Plural Society in the British West Indies*, Berkeley: University of California Press.

Soja, E. (1996) *Thirdspace: Journeys to Los Angeles and Other Real-and-Imagined Places*, Oxford: Basil Blackwell.

Solow, B. (ed.) (1991) *Slavery and the Rise of the Atlantic System*, Cambridge: Cambridge University Press.

Solow, B. and Engerman, S. (eds) (1987) *British Capitalism and Caribbean Slavery: the Legacy of Eric Williams*, Cambridge: Cambridge University Press.

Sombart, W. (1967 [1913]) *Luxury and Capitalism*, Ann Arbor: University of Michigan Press.

Spalding, M., Ravilious, C., and Green, E. (2001) *The World Atlas of Coral Reefs*, Berkeley and London: University of California Press.

Spitta, S. (1997) 'Transculturation, the Caribbean, and the Cuban-American Imaginary', in F. Aparicio and S. Chavez-Silverman (eds) (1997) *Tropicalizations: Transcultural Representations of Latinidad*, Hanover and London: University Press of New England.

Spivak, G.C. (1999) *A Critique of Postcolonial Reason: Toward a History of the Vanishing Present*, Cambridge and London: Harvard University Press.

Stacey, J. (2000) 'The Global Within: Consuming Nature, Embodying Health', in S. Franklin, C. Lury, and J. Stacey (eds) *Global Nature, Global Culture*, London: Sage.

Stevens, A.M. (1995) '*Manjé* in Haitian Culture: The Symbolic Significance of *Manjé* in Haitian Culture', *Journal of Haitian Studies*, 1, 1: 75–89.

Stinchcombe, A. (1996) *Sugar Island Slavery in the Age of Enlightenment: The Political Economy of the Caribbean World*, Princeton: Princeton University Press.

Stoler, A. (1991) 'Carnal Knowledge and Imperial Power: Gender, Race, and Morality in Colonial Asia', in M. di Leonardo (ed.) *Gender and the Crossroads of Knowledge: Feminist Anthropology in the Postmodern Era*, Berkeley: University of California Press, pp. 51–100.

Styles, J. (1994) 'Manufacturing, Consumption and Design in Eighteenth-century England', in J. Brewer and R. Porter (eds) *Consumption and the World of Goods*, London and New York: Routledge.

Sunshine, C.A. (1988) *The Caribbean: Survival, Struggle and Sovereignty*, Washington, DC: EPICA.

Sussman, C. (2000) *Consuming Anxieties: Consumer Protest, Gender and British Slavery, 1713–1833*, Palo Alto: Stanford University Press.

Sutton, C. (1987) 'The Caribbeanization of New York City and the Emergence of a Transnational Socio-cultural System', in C. Sutton and E. Chaney (eds) *Caribbean Life in New York City: Sociocultural Dimensions*, New York: The Center for Migration Studies of New York, Inc.

Sutton, C. and Chaney, E. (eds) (1987) *Caribbean Life in New York City: Sociocultural Dimensions*, New York: The Center for Migration Studies of New York, Inc.

Taylor, F. (1993) *To Hell With Paradise: A History of the Jamaican Tourist Industry*, Pittsburgh: University of Pittsburgh Press.

Tchen, J. K.W. (1998) 'Colonized Tastes and the Port of New York: Prelude to the "Coolie" Trade', paper presented to The Society for Caribbean Studies Annual Conference, University of Warwick.

—— (1999) *New York Before Chinatown: Orientalism and the Shaping of American Culture, 1776–1882*, Baltimore: Johns Hopkins University Press.

Temperley, H. (1972) *British Anti-Slavery, 1833–1870*, London: Longman.

Thomas, H. (2000) *Romanticism and Slave Narratives: Transnational Testimonies*, Cambridge and New York: Cambridge University Press.

Thomas, K. (1983) *Man and the Natural World: Changing Attitudes in England, 1500–1800*, London: Allen Lane.

Tinker, H. (1993) *A New System of Slavery: The Export of Indian Labour Overseas, 1830–1920*, 2nd edn, London: Hansib Publishing.

Titley, G. (2000) 'Global Theory and Touristic Encounters', *Irish Communications Review*, 8, Dublin: DIT/RTE.

Trouillot, M. (1977) *Ti difé boulé sou Istoua Ayiti*, New York: Koléksion Lakansièl.

—— (1988) *Peasants and Capital: Dominica in the World Economy*, Baltimore and London: Johns Hopkins University Press.

—— (1995) *Silencing the Past: Power and the Production of History*, Boston, MA: Beacon Press.

Tullis, F. and Hollist, W. (eds) (1986) *Food, the State, and International Political Economy: Dilemmas of Developing Countries*, Lincoln: University of Nebraska Press.

Turner, B. (1994) *Orientalism, Postmodernism and Globalism*, London and New York: Routledge.

Urry, J. (1991) *The Tourist Gaze: Leisure and Travel in Contemporary Societies*, London: Sage Publications.

—— (1995) *Consuming Places*, London and New York: Routledge.

—— (2000) *Sociology Beyond Societies: Mobilities for the Twenty-first Century*, London and New York: Routledge.

Walcott, D. (2000) 'A Frowsty Fragrance', *New York Review*, 15 June 2000.

Walvin, J. (1994) *Black Ivory: A History of British Slavery*, Washington, DC: Howard University Press.

—— (1997) *Fruits of Empire: Exotic Produce and British Taste, 1660–1800*, London: Macmillan.

Watts, D. (1990) *The West Indies: Patterns of Development, Culture, and Environmental Change Since 1492*, Cambridge and New York: Cambridge University Press.

Whatmore, S. and Thorne, L. (1997) 'Nourishing Networks: Alternative Geographies of Food', in D. Goodman and M. Watts (eds) (1997) *Globalising Food: Agrarian Questions and Global Restructuring*, London and New York: Routledge.

Wheeler, R. (1999) 'Limited Visions of Africa: Geographies of Savagery and Civility in Early Eighteenth-century Narratives', in J. Duncan and D. Gregory (eds) *Writes of Passage: Reading Travel Writing*, London and New York: Routledge.

White, T. (1983) *Catch a Fire: The Life of Bob Marley*, New York: Henry Holt & Co. [Newly revised and enlarged edition, 2000].

Wilentz, A. (1989) *The Rainy Season: Haiti Since Duvalier*, New York: Simon & Schuster.

Wiley, J. (1998) 'Dominica's Economic Diversification: Microstates in a Neoliberal Era?', in T. Klak (ed.) *Globalization and Neoliberalism: The Caribbean Context*, Lanham, MD and Oxford: Rowman and Littlefield.

Williams, E. (1944) *Capitalism and Slavery*, Chapel Hill: University of North Carolina.

Wolf, E. (1982) *Europe and the People Without History*, Berkeley and London: University of California Press.

Wood, M. (2000) *Blind Memory: Visual Representations of Slavery in England and America, 1780–1865*, Manchester and New York: Manchester University Press.

Wrigley, R. and Revill, G. (eds) (2000) *Pathologies of Travel*, Amsterdam and Atlanta, GA: Rodopi.

Yelvington, K. (forthcoming) 'The Invention of Africa in Latin America and the Caribbean: Political Discourse and Anthropological Praxis, 1920–1940', in K. Yelvington (ed.) *Afro-Atlantic Dialogues: Anthropology in the Diaspora*, Santa Fe, NM: School of American Research Press.

Young, L. (1986) *Fear of the Dark: Race, Gender and Sexuality in the Cinema*, London and New York: Routledge.

Young, R. (1995), *Colonial Desire: Hybridity in Theory, Culture and Race*, New York and London: Routledge.

Index

Note: Illustrations are indicated in **bold**. Book and article titles are found under the author's name.